Complime

MW01104145

I can't tell you how impresse
expressed in your writings. I think that it's so very apt; what have you been doing all your life that you haven't produced this sort of thing before? Or was it all always in your head and you have only just started putting pen to paper? Your work never ceases to amaze me; it's a pity there aren't more like you. Your 'Prayer for the world and Facts' demand a much wider audience. You are quite an amazing man; so few people have such depth of feeling and understanding; it leaves me almost speechless. Very few people have such talent; I am almost lost for words.

—Honor Kay, England, UK

"It's not often in life when one gets the opportunity to cross paths with a person who says, with all sincerity and honesty, "I want you to be better than me!" Rev. Joe Brown is such a person. As one of his many students, I have benefited greatly from his teaching, his patience, his compassion, and most of all, his constant encouragement.

It is my wish that Rev. Joe's book not only inspires you, but leads you successfully in exploring and expanding your knowledge of your own inner self. May the Universe bless you in finding what you seek. I know Rev. Joe does."

—Mrs. Linda Anderson, Oshawa, Ontario, Canada

As a past and present student under your tutelage, it will be good to get an introduction to other aspects of spiritual practice in the sequel of your first book.... reading about what others do is not enough. I want to understand how it's done, talk about how I can implement it into my personal development; and to also learn the exercises that one can do to increase one's abilities. Also, I'd like to try a few of others techniques even if it seems like 'playing parlor games' just to understand what is out there to help me in my own growth.

—Diane Douglas, Toronto, ON, Canada

Dear brother: I'm very proud of you for having the courage to follow your heart. Always use your gift wisely and I'm sure it will only bring you and others much good.

—Edith Dicks, Canada

Congratulations Reverend Joe... I just wanted to take a moment and thank you for Saturday's workshop. I truly enjoyed it and your explanation and examples were truly enlightening! I am very cautious when it comes to teachers and from the few courses and workshops that I've attended with you, I must say I truly admire you as a teacher. That was the first time I did psychic symbology and psychic channeling...My partner said that I was "right on" with the information that I was receiving and relaying. On that note, I'd also like to thank you as I think you are great for my friend in your class! I see his self-confidence growing and him refining and trusting to reveal more of his "Christ-like" self...that which I feel privileged to see so often. Thank you for continuing to encourage him and to refine his beautiful gifts. Thank you for continuing to offer courses that help us to see what we already have inside of us! I look forward to attending your next workshop.

—Kathern Bly, Oshawa, ON, Canada

Rev. Joe: Along life's journey we meet people that have a profound effect on us. In the last 5 months I have met 3 such people, you are one of them. Your Thursday night open classes are excellent, well run and very professional. I have really enjoyed them. I have grown spiritually, far beyond anything I could ever have imagined, and, for that I thank you. I also thank you for your compassion and understanding for what has been for me a very difficult 5 months. Your council has kept me focused and with your guidance I have leant to listen to that inner voice. I thank you again for your kindness, and wish you all the best for the future. I'm sure I'll be able to attend church and, some of those wonderful workshops that are coming up. You're a wonderful Reverend. All my love:

—Annette Miller, Bancroft, ON, Canada

I have just finished reading Rev. Joe Brown's book "Psychic Ability, Clairvoyant Powers" for the second time and wish this information had been available when I was turning to Spiritualism. Rev. Joe's book is the most comprehensive, informative and understandable I have read on the subject. It is truly inspirational, encourages introspective thought and takes the student to a new level of intellect in modern spiritualism. I feel this book will be revered for many years to come and I anxiously await the publication of his second book. I sincerely wish Rev. Joe all the best in his future endeavors. I can't think of anyone in the Spiritual community that deserves to be called Rev. as much as you do. You always know the right things to do and say. You are so compassionate, loving and connected to spirit. I am seeing more and more why people just think the world of you. You give very good, down to earth, loving advice. You are extremely generous with your time and talents. Everyone loved your presentation at the workshop and as you know, no one wanted to leave. Also many thanks for all the material you so generously give and for a truly great day. This is due to the fact that I was with a truly kind and spiritual gentleman.

—Rev. Barbara Ann Hamspson, Scarborough, ON, Canada

"Not all want to develop mediumship although it was a wonderful experience. The highlight of my classes with-you was when Judy and I actually allowed the energy to come through us to move that table 'for real' without touching it."

—Douglas Marshall, Whitby, ON, Canada

"I've watched Reverend Joe Brown's spirituality grow by leaps and bounds. First he was a fellow student and then a teacher. He has generously encouraged me to fine tune my abilities as a medium and slowly and gently shed my anxiety of public speaking. I wish the best for him as his spirituality continues to grow in the white light of God."

—Joanne Wheatley, Scarborough, ON, Canada

"I experienced Rev. Joe Brown's patient teaching style that permitted me to believe that the subtle pictures I was seeing in my mind were in fact messages from Spirit. At first I thought it was my imagination; however his knowledge and gentle prodding allowed me to speak freely about what I saw and felt. I was soon able to get confirmation from the message receiver that the "pictures" were in fact accurate depictions of information conveyed by my Spirit Guides. It was exciting to finally break through the proverbial veil and have a look at life on the other side. I'm so grateful to Rev. Joe for giving me the opportunity to experience this very personal and wonderful revelation."

—Judy Shulga, Whitby, ON, Canada

Thanks for guiding us, helping us and supporting us all in our efforts to become a sharper crisper instrument for God's love and light. I love your classes. God bless.

—Gus Racette, Trenton, ON, Canada

Rev. Joe's first book is a very personal guide to understanding Mediumship and Spiritualism. It takes the fear out of the unknown. It's an honest and straight forward approach to development. The exercises are simple and it's very effective at teaching us how to connect to the God source when learning how to develop. I can't wait for his second and third! We need more books, which would include teaching children, on this sort of subject. I'm really proud to have him as a teacher. I recommend his books and guidance to anyone who's trying to enhance their psychic abilities.

—Nicole Brake. Whitby, Ontario, Canada

Rev Joe: I want to personally thank you for the accurate reading I received on November 30, 2007. It was very intense and left me feeling inspired.

I have had readings in the past that certainly did not provide the insight you were able to provide for me. The spirits that came through you, I believe, needed to communicate with me. The moment I stepped into the building, forces guided me to you and, I believe, I was put there for a reason. Your accuracy was amazing and to know names specifically is truly remarkable.

I'm not an individual to give praise unless I feel it's well deserved and earned, and I think you have more than earned any praise I could give. I tend to be very professional most times and I certainly did not reveal much emotion during the reading—except when my Dad was holding me. I could actually feel his presence—it was truly a remarkable moment. The love, affection and concern that came clearly through from my parents is something I will cherish for years to come.

The reading has been a wonderful blessing. You truly are a gifted individual and I look forward to my next reading with you.

—Rachel Banks, Peterborough, Ontario, Canada

Psychic Powers, Mediumship Enhancement

Spiritualism's secrets unfolding

Rev. Joe Brown

PublishAmerica
Baltimore

© 2008 by Rev. Joe Brown.
All rights reserved. No part of this book may be reproduced, stored in a retrieval system or transmitted in any form or by any means without the prior written permission of the publishers, except by a reviewer who may quote brief passages in a review to be printed in a newspaper, magazine or journal.

First printing

PublishAmerica has allowed this work to remain exactly as the author intended, verbatim, without editorial input.

ISBN: 1-60563-657-6 (softcover)
ISBN: 978-1-4489-6907-4 (hardcover)
PUBLISHED BY PUBLISHAMERICA, LLLP
www.publishamerica.com
Baltimore

Printed in the United States of America

This book is dedicated to Rev. Dr. Alva Folkes

Editor's Note:

As stated in his first book, *Psychic Ability, Clairvoyant Powers,* which I had the privilege of reading, Rev. Joe says that there's no coincidence. That statement holds a lot of truth. I was introduced to him in such a way that it was meant to be as now I'm helping, as much as possible, in proofreading this particular book, that you're about to read.

Upon the purchase of his first book I had very little knowledge of his way of life in dealing with Spiritualism and the phenomena of it. Like I had said to him, *"I didn't understand Spiritualism but after reading your first book, and now this one, I come to understand and appreciate your views on the subject that it contains."* He certainly has aroused my interest with his forthright private writings.

As a senior citizen, for a few years now, our age differences didn't seem to matter as we're both on the same path of spirituality, but of a different religion. Does it matter? Not in the least, as our hearts joined in a bond of friendship since our first meeting at a mall where his book is for sale at the bookstore.

Being the personal editor, of this book, has brought me insight into his chosen religion and to understand the spiritual man that he portrays as an ordained minister. I'm particularly impressed with his honesty and in chapter two as tears came to my eyes when reading certain material. As for the other chapters, except for chapter six, I hold interest but at my age I choose not to get to involved. Chapter six tells a lot about where he has been and he wishes for others to follow in his path of love and light.

I honestly believe he's a man you can trust with your innermost thoughts and the contents in his writings has a way of making you aware that he cares.

I've known Rev. Joe for only a short while and we became close friends. His kind hearted and expressed love gives you a feeling that in his medical career his loving care of his patients was expressed with a secure image. They knew, right from the start when concerning their care that they were in very good hands.

Mr. Joseph Anderson

Table of Contents

Preface

This book is the advanced edition of my first book called *Psychic Ability, Clairvoyant Powers*. It's an explanation of what Spiritualism is all about and as you read through each chapter you'll come to terms of how certain phenomena occur. Although each explanation goes somewhat into detail you'll find the examples that follow rewarding, providing you take the lessons seriously. Included are other forms of spirit communication that does not belong in Spiritualism but some use it just the same; more often then not for fun but a somewhat effective means of spirit-contact.

Although some beginners may learn a tremendous amount from this book; what you read and learn from here is directed towards the advanced student. If you're not aware of where to obtain my first book it can be purchased from many on-line bookstores.

Be serious in your thoughts as well as that of your intentions. This is not some form of black magic to be tamper with but reconciliation with your departed loves ones. Those loved ones that are more then willing to make that extra contact to let you know that they're still with you. Their concern and attempts to contact you is to make you aware that they are happy where they currently reside. It's known that both sides cry upon physical death of the body. Those left behind cry from the lost of a loved one. Those that had died (crossed the veil) are also crying because they cannot make that connection with those left behind. It saddens them as they are not strong enough to make those that mourn them aware that they are not dead, but living-on in spirit.

What Spiritualism is and what really happens behind its doors are quite different then what the uneducated person suspects. Some see it as a cult. Others see it as a place to receive messages from their loved ones; and some others take it very seriously and learn all that they can. As there are many good teachers out there, there are those that are not. One should teach by example and if your teacher is unable then you've found the wrong one.

Using this as a teaching guide a teacher should not introduce all that it offers in a Beginner's class; mental phenomena with some light trance is more then enough. As students grow and reach the Intermediate level more may be introduced as one loses enthusiasm with repetitive classes. Therefore in Intermediate go a little deeper in to the courses you wish to bring forth. Don't boggle their mind with to much as much will overwhelm them and they may lose confidence. When students reach the Advanced level all that this book holds should be offered. In addition, encourage them to perfect their growth by writing lectures and frequent platform demonstrations. As each new introduction is given always make room at the end for mental phenomena; meaning giving spirit messages.

As a beginner one is unable to determine a good Medium, or teacher, and who has nothing to offer. As one grows spiritually and gains as much knowledge as they possibly can one will detect a good one within moments. Furthermore, an uneducated teacher won't have the proper answers to your questions, and more often then not, the answer won't be to your satisfaction. How does a new member of Spiritualism spot this? One may not but as you encounter and experience different church workers you'll soon make comparisons. This form of enlightenment will gently sail you towards your spiritual destination. Don't rush forward, be patient in your quest to find the true light. That true light dwells within you, as well as the light given through an authentic spiritual leader. Moreover, self education is a must as many don't teach proper Spiritualism; and from personal experiences many are unable to teach proper mediumship.

When you get the initiative to get started, do so after you have completed reading this book. Then go back to chapter three which gives you 14 weeks of attunement exercises. Follow them diligently and gather all that you're able from its contents. Right from the beginning tell yourself that from this time forward you'll be working along side of those from the spirit world, your guides and past loved ones.

Some topics covered or mentioned in here has nothing to do with Spiritualism as a religion, philosophy or a science. Some of it is being practiced by some individuals in certain churches as a fun event to help raise money to cover financial costs. Keeping the doors open in some churches has proven to be somewhat difficult. One wonders why it had floundered when at one point in time it thrived. Leaders, you're intuitive enough to know the reason why, meditate on it. Changes are often needed to attract members. Gut-feeling, intuition, plays a major role in being successful; this goes for all development students as well as those that have past the class-development-period and now teaching.

Some means of doing readings, which one doesn't have to be a medium, such as—now get ready for this—'Shoe Reading' 'Lip Reading' 'Sand Reading' Dust Reading, Wood-chip Reading and 'Flower sentience', and the list goes on, can be done by any psychic. One doesn't need clairvoyant powers to do symbolic messages or look at a shoe and say what they feel and think; neither for lip, sand or wood-chip readings. Does this belong in Spiritualism? Yes and no may apply, as one craves somewhat of a change or variety along the path of their spiritual growth. These types of readings are never done in a Divine Service but as a fund raiser or at psychic fares. Shoe and lip reading is letting your mind race to gather up some form of message but the message itself in usually very vague. Sand and wood-chip readings are symbolic, somewhat as that of tea-leaf. Flower sentience may be just a little different as all are attracted to different kinds and this may inform the reader somewhat of a personality and that of self-confidence and self-esteem, making it appear like the reader knows what he/she is talking about. As one develops one comes to realize that a psychic will predict future events; mediums will foresee it or will be given this information by their guides or a past loved one.

Are you clairaudient? Here's your first eye-opener; have you even been doing something so intently and your mind is completely focused, and all else put aside? For instance; have you been ironing clothes with your mind totally blank other then concentrating on what you're doing? But there's things going through it that's not related to anything you're doing or what you had previously done or have concerns about? If those words are uplifting and of love or concern for someone else; or you were given a solution to a problem then consider yourself as clairaudient and that you heard words from the spirit world.

Mediumship comes with practice. The most successful mediums have studied all that they're able to get their hands on, plus had attended as many workshops as possible. This is something that should be encouraged as many teachers give different aspects of knowledge. Furthermore, one teacher can't possibly have all the answers.

As you begin your journey of enhanced mediumship, focus on its entirety and not just that of mental phenomena. If nothing else you'll encounter and get a shot at first-hand-experience on what some have actually been able to accomplish through practice. One has to practice and work towards accomplishments to gain perfection; with this attitude you'll most definitely progress beyond your own expectations and imagination.

One of my students was inspired a day after I taught spirit photography in class. While she was looking through her photos and seeing many orbs and an actual head profile as if in a frame, this though entered her mind. *"Start with your beliefs until they come your truths, experience your truths until they become your knowingness."* Linda Anderson 02/02/07. Linda is one of my advanced student-mediums. She did well and will move forward with confidence as praise matters and is given to those that accomplish their goals. As for my truths, they are shared with you in this book.

Another student had also brought something to my attention

while we were chatting over coffee after class one evening. She said, *"One cannot remove Jesus and his teaching completely out of Spiritualism".* Ms. Diane Jenkins. I agreed with her and said, *"as long as one doesn't consider that someone died for their sins and realize they have to be accountable and responsible for their own mistakes."* I went on to say that Jesus and his teachings should not be removed any more then all other past great prophets such as Mohammed, Gandhi, Krishna, Buddha, and the Hindu Gods and so on. All play their part in relation and guidance, through their prophet-hood, to the Divine and their teachings of love. Some Spiritualism leaders, not all, are accepting of all beliefs. Although it's not practiced in some churches their holidays, celebrations and yearly worship events are often recognized and mentioned at the time. My Temple does especially if one of our members remains in touch with it. Furthermore, as one respects your way of life, respect theirs.

When the time comes where you've gained confidence enough to demonstrate your mediumistic powers through spirit messages in public, those that had gained spiritual knowledge and had been born with the 'gift of gab' will be the best performers. Reason for this being that you already have lots to share and you're more then willing to do so as spirit uses what's already in your own brain database.

As you read keep an open mind and prepare yourself to learn all that you can about the whole make-up of Spiritualism and what it entrails. Some material will be thought-provoking and may appear as being 'unbelievable'. Let your inner-self, gut-feeling and intuition guide any personal decisions made. In addition, not only those of Spiritualism speaks with the dead, many people from all walks of life and denominations do, some keeping it to themselves due to ridicule and the like. Be concise and be yourself.

Rev. Joe Brown, author.
www.divinelighttemple.ca
www.dlt.weebly.com

Acknowledgments

I like to thank Rev. Dr. Alva Folkes for being the wonderful woman/leader/teacher that you are in my life. I feel that, without you, things would not have sailed along as smoothly over the choppy water we both faced together. God did well with you and God is portrayed through you continuously. What an inspiration you are; not only to me but too many others that are guided to you, through a Divine source.

Thank you Rev. Jane Suprynowicz from Pennsylvania, USA for your contribution towards my learning skills on Séance and Trance. Rev. Jane is a very gifted medium who has enhanced my knowledge on those subjects. Although there's really no set guidelines on how a séance should be held there's always something to learn from various teachers that delve into the cult of Spiritualisms' acts. Rev. Jane; some of your insight enhanced my growth and I had implemented parts of it into my teachings. I also like to thank you for giving me permission to include it, with your name, in this book.

I like to thank one of Ontario's best Mediums, Mr. Norman Galka. With your quick intuitiveness you become aware of my dilemmas, as you had with many others, and came to my rescue several times with your loving and caring fatherly arms. You not only tucked me under your wing but gave me food to survive. This food is your personal 'educational' material you so fondly entrusted to me to help achieve and accomplish set goals. The books you gave me as gifts and those you recommended has given me the greatest insight into what life, and loving another human being, is all about.

You words of inspiration and guidance has been felt by many others, especially those that are in need of your expertise, knowledge and gentle direction that you give from the heart. Words said by you that will always be remembered is; *"Keep an open mind."* And that I try my utmost to do. Mr. Norman Galka, if any man could be signaled out, is, 'My Father of Spiritualism.'

I also like to thank Mrs. Bonnie Galka, Norman's wife, for also being a major asset to how I dealt with emotional stress in a loving, caring and a positive way. Words said by you that expressed all that we do in Spiritualism, regarding private readings and in how they are done is: *"It all comes from the same source."* God bless you both as He has blessed me, through both of you.

I like to thank all of my students for being a part of my spiritual growth as much as I'm a part of yours. Thanks for the respect shown to me and to each other under my teaching; I'm very proud of your progress. You continue to grow and show more interest each time we're together as a group and that encourages me to want to continue with helping others that wish to develop their mediumship.

I wish to thank my daughter Nadine and grand-daughter Naomi for being a part of my life and for all of the support over the years.

I like to thank T.C. Kendal for singing and playing at my ordination. Your beautiful soft voice brought back many fond memories of my childhood and youth. Each time I listen to you sing, and watch you skillfully play your guitar, I get taken back 'in time' to when my mom did the same, and sang to her children.

Thank you Mrs. Carolyn Matthews of Lunenburg, Nova Scotia, Canada for suggesting the book title.

Most of all, I wish to thank Mr. Joseph Anderson, Scarborough, Ontario, Canada for putting much time in personally editing this book. You are a God send.

Chapter One
Spiritualism

Consider the religions of the world: why so many, why so different, why so many similar and why so much hate and prejudice when it comes to believing in and worshiping a god of choice? Is it not but one god and creator? Then again, who is this creator? Should we believe all that we read in the different bibles of our world or should we listen to our own hearts when what comes from it is of love that God has meant to flow through the arteries and veins of the blood stream?

Sometimes we ask ourselves what is it all about and what is it that we so wish to achieve in our short life here in the material world. I can't answer that for you, only for myself. Spiritual growth and development; and whether this is to accomplish its maximum before I return to the spirit world, I do not know. One can only try their best when one is aware of their calling, even if late in life.

For one to have psychic ability and clairvoyant powers one does not need to be into Spiritualism. Many great mediums of our past were not necessarily Spiritualist and you don't have to be either. Oh yes, it's good to be among like minded people to discuss your growth without being looked down on as being mentally impaired, which some religions think, and also think that you're dealing with evil. How can this be when a medium is speaking to your past loved one? Are they of the devil now that they are communicating from the spirit world? Of course not. Is this particular medium making any sense who says he or she is able to receive and make that contact? You have to decide if it's authentic or not as there are many frauds among us.

Does one survive physical death? Look at all the ghost stories that have been spoken of and witnessed for centuries. Many believe in ghosts especially when they personally encounter them.

By the way, what do you think they said about Jesus the Christ when he was also communicating with the spirit world and speaking to God personally? Did they condemn him? Sure they did, and look what they did to him; also to many great mediums, for instance, burned at the stake.

My point of view about Spiritualism, and I speak only of my own experiences, is that there's a tremendous amount of jealousy between the small churches that I had been associated with. When questioned about this it was brought to my attention (and this is not my words) that many of today's Spiritualisms ministers are dominant and controlling women. It was also said that it's a woman's world and most men are not promoted the same as a woman. Does women's lib have anything to do with this or is this an acquired attribute to control the few members and students that walk through the doors to try and learn the secrets of how to contact the spirit world? As long as jealousy and envy remain among the leaders of Spiritualism there will be no unity as a whole. At the moment, I see unity existing only within friends of individual churches and not as a group. Many are apt to put another down and criticize their teachings and what have you, although they preach of love, respect and forgiveness from the pulpit. If only they practiced what they preach unity would blissfully flow and Spiritualism would prosper; but as long as one tries to outdo the other there'll be nothing but downfall. Why can't they see this? After all they're all supposed to be psychic and clairvoyant.

If you have not read my first book called, *'Psychic Ability, Clairvoyant Powers'* then I recommend that you do before proceeding with the exercises in this book. It will give you a better understanding and will highlight some darker areas of misunderstanding.

First of all, you need to recognize that your psychic being is your intuitive self. We're all psychic but not all are clairvoyant. The secrets of contacting the spirit world are unraveled in this book and it's not as complicated as you have been made to believe or think.

After the Hydesville incident of 1848 Spiritualism began, or should I say surfaced as many have ghostly encounters since life began on this planet. But at that point in time the 'bill of rights' allowed for freedom of worship. Then spiritualist churches began to pop up in the more populated areas for the exponents of mediumship.

But mediumship is a gift one is born with, right? Some say yes, some say no depending on religious upbringing, beliefs and personal past experiences. Sometimes one needs some formal training to enhance different terminology and the quality of a message; in retrospect of the nuances of mediumship. With such understandings and with self education one is apt to be more aware of their gift and what is being sent forth from the spirit, or what is meant to be said by what is given symbolically. We'll get to that later.

Some members of certain churches got offended and still do because God had been personalized as a 'father figure,' as in ***The Fatherhood of God***; Brotherhood as in ***The Brotherhood of man.*** They say it's somewhat outmoded; also their words not mine. This is usually a woman's point of view and I have heard it from young female adults as well as newly female ordained ministers. Fatherhood and Brotherhood includes women as well as men. Think back to when man was created; did it not include woman? It takes both to make another so why all of a sudden do certain individuals want to change the big picture. Father Sky, Mother Earth, it takes both for their children to survive and it takes both to care and to provide; the children being all that is of this world and not just the human child, man.

Then we get the question, why should only the human soul get to enjoy a continuous existence? I'm sure my views and some of yours are somewhat the same. All that lives have a soul and all that has a soul gets to have an eternal existence as many have pets that died and came back—through some mediums.

We are made to believe that the policy in the Spiritualist churches welcomes all cultures and faith. This is not totally true.

When one becomes a member and expresses their points of view on certain religious teachings that they're not ready to give up, the spiritualist point of view is quickly pointed out by certain church leaders, not all. Of course the Christian Spiritualist and Interfaith Spiritualist churches are more tolerant. At first the so-called pure Spiritualism church leaders ask no one to put aside their own religion to come to the church but it's expressed in sermons, lectures and spirit messages. This is a sense of brainwashing as many churches do the same, and then one comes to realize that their beliefs are not so much respected as they were previously led to believe. The spiritualist believes that the main stay of their way of life is the philosophy of unconditional love, but in my opinion, some leaders don't practise it.

Part of being spiritually inclined is to search out and visit a few churches to find out where you fit in and are more comfortable. My suggestion to you is don't judge a church by one service. Leave yourself open and be one of the congregation when the Reverend is chairing, lecturing and/or the medium for that service. I'd suggest that you attend when the Reverend does all three and chances are all three won't be in the same given service. That's a lot of work to accomplish in one service so do attend again before making your final decision. If what you're looking for is not found after a month or two and the Minister or Pastor is not what you expect as a clergy, then move on to better vibrations.

When I heard the name Maurice Barbanell I asked myself, ***"Now who would that be?"*** I found out and now for those of you who still don't know, he was an accomplished writer and erudite speaker, ***er-u-dite*** meaning learning or scholarship; the same as Arthur Findlay.

Maurice Barbanell was a Jewish man living in Britain. He became a medium once he was discovered by a medium by the name of Mrs. Bauerstein, another Jewish person. He spoke for the highly evolved spirit being, known to the spiritualist world as 'Silver Birch.' Silver Birch was Maurice Barbanell's spirit guide and he said, ***"It is through simplicity that you learn."***

Now, let's consider reincarnation. Some spiritualists believe and some don't, and let's not forget karma. Some people have been regressed and have witnessed past lives, me included. Theory considers that the existence of one earthly lifetime isn't enough for one person to learn their spiritual lessons. You have freedom of choice so believe what you will.

Consider the aura, spiritual healing, chakras, spirit drawing, automatic writing and trance just to name a few of Spiritualisms' teachings and beliefs.

Spiritualist churches are known for their mediumship demonstrations. Albert Batten said in his book called *Love and Progress "The spiritualist churches have become an adult church, where are the children?"*

Spiritualism is a new religion; so to speak, it's based on old truths that still stand with certain leaders. Platform demonstrations give Spiritualism religion a continued evidential proof of life-after-death together with continued revelation from spirit, providing the medium is authentic. Some mediums need validation and wish to know that they have the correct recipient and will ask simple questions such as, 'Do you understand' or something such as, 'Is your mother in spirit because I have such a loving motherly vibration here?' Such questions may be acceptable (which I don't agree with) but if one continues to ask, 'Can you take a so-and-so who passed with such-and-such'; and if the answer is No the next questions will be similar until the message bearer finally says Yes. What is this? Is this high quality mediumship? Personally I say he or she is fishing; although these individuals may be very well educated and of high standards in public speaking, they obviously hadn't had proper training. An authentic medium will not ask any of the congregation questions when relaying words from the spirit world. If this happens the medium could be fraudulent or working only from the psyche or is lacking in self confidence. This is not carved in stone, it's only a personal opinion and we're entitled to that. Although it's good to have clarity, a highly evolved medium will not ask questions and will bring proof of survival, as proof of survival is what draws people to this kind of church.

Spiritualism has no one day embarked as holy or labelled as the Sabbath or a specific day of rest but March 31 is somewhat recognized as Spiritualism Day. This is due to the fact that it's the day Mr. Rosna made contact with the Fox family from the spirit world and it was made public. Services are held on any day or days throughout the week, making it convenient for the members.

Some churches offer workshops, meditation classes and spiritual development classes. If a leader tells you that you only need one teacher then that may be so if you're new. But if that teacher continues to hold you back and you're not advancing as you should, then that teacher has brought you to their level and taught you what they know. Then again if you don't get exposure to different workshops and different teachers how are you going to advance in your spiritual education? I personally believe that we are all teachers and that we learn from each other. Don't be controlled as control is what it is. Be assertive in your growth and don't be bullied to believe that God herself is speaking from the platform. One teacher can't teach you everything so move on to another and learn all there is for your spiritual growth. Find the perfect leader/teacher that will encourage you and will get you working with the church services when you're ready.

Spiritualism teaches that God is everywhere and in everyone. As you get to know the best of yourself, your soul and spirit, which is a part of the Great Spirit, will come to know God.

Spiritualism believes that although this life is temporary, soul and spirit lives forever. Don't many other religions believe the same? Why be persecuted? Here's an eye-opener: Spiritualism became the fastest growing religion in the nation during the 1850s, and one of the principal responses to the widespread perception that American society was descending into atomistic particularity. What the heck happened? Maybe this will shed a little light.

Spiritualism emphasis on inspiration from spirit—it has no dogma or creed associated with it and has the essential ingredients that are the basis of every other religion. This has been preached over and over again but get acquainted with certain Ministers and Pastors and you'll soon see that this is not so. There are many dogmas and creeds associated with, and we must not forget, the political side among the controllers, which somehow weeded itself into the movement and in most of the churches. This was witnessed personally. For instance, I recently received a letter stating that since I haven't done such-and-such then I will not be granted ________ when a certain time comes; and you probably can guess the rest. What does threatening another prove other then showing lack of confidents and showing who you truly are; egotistical? It's very difficult to please everybody. Furthermore, I attended a meeting a couple years ago and one of the speakers, who is well known to the spiritualist movement in Ontario and I won't mention his name here, he said, *"For a bunch of spiritualist you're a most miserable bunch."* I was impressed with his honesty and privately complimented him on his observation after his talk. I meditated on the above threat and heard a little song that I remember only hearing as a child. It was, "This little light of mine, I'm going to let it shine, let it shine, let shine, let it shine." Therefore, regardless the threats and the consequences I shall press onwards and upwards shining at every opportunity.

Spiritualism believes that humankind is one family in spiritual union and we're all connected to the One Source. Let's put it this way: it depends on how much you're liked and how well you fit in with certain favourites. We know that humans get "cliquish" and oftentimes have a problem accepting a new individual or change. Do as I did, continue to search until you find your spiritual leader and place in life where your advancement will be encouraged instead of being controlled. Once accomplished you'll live in a positive state of goodness; with responsibility for your own thoughts, actions and the effects that your life will have on the world; therefore enlightening your physical awareness.

Once you learn to improve your spiritual awareness you're on the right path of bringing your innermost soul nearer to God. God is love, and Spiritualism in its true form represents love; for example, when a passed family member comes through—it's usually with love.

We all belong to two worlds; it's in conjunction of our two body forms, that of spirit and material. Our etheric body is a duplicate of our selves and once crossed over we remain the same and that can be a bit scary for some, as not all are spiritually inclined upon physical death. This explains many haunting and horrific ghostly stories.

You may have heard that Spiritualism represents this or Spiritualism represents that. Well, nobody is wrong when it's related to love and of a loving God. Spiritualism has its quirks, and lately it appears more so, as well as any other religion.

A medium is a sensitive being. He or she is the link between this world and the spirit world. A medium has to have a good psychic ability but someone with a good psychic ability isn't necessarily a medium. Some are born with this awareness and for those that don't recognize it, it can be taught. Mediumship is able to differentiate between gut responses or psychic intuition, and a high quality medium can determine what is and what isn't. When a positive link is made a spirit connection has been accomplished. This works in unison with the higher quality medium.

Immortality is the basis for Spiritualism and is demonstrated time and time again proving that love is the force that binds all.

Definitions of what a beginner needs to know that consist of mental mediumship are:

Clairvoyant—able to see spirit

Clairaudient—able to hear spirit

Clairsentient—able to feel spirit

Inspiration—become inspired by spirit

Knowingness—to be impressed by spirit

And the list goes on. You'll read in another chapter.

Some mediums have all of these qualities. Some have one or the other or a couple.

Mediumship for the intermediate and advanced student is explained and guided further on in this book.

With the above gifts, and everyone having different potential, the main requirement for mediumship is patience and, I'd personally like to add 'practice' to that.

The Christian Bible makes some reference to a medium as being a witch. Are there still witches about and among us; is witchcraft still being practised? If you wish my opinion and I've been around for awhile, I would have to say, yes, there is and yes it's still being practised. Many spell books are readily available and for sale on many bookshelves. But putting aside all occult exercises, how perfect can one be and how close to God can one get when one communicates to those of love in the world of spirit through mediumship? This spirit is working its way to the highest level possible, back to the god source. When the bible was written they say that organized religions began; people were made to have a fear of the unknown and speaking with the spirit world was forbidden and condemned, although many prophets and saviours did since time began. The Holy Bible is full of mediums and their great works, but the medium is not favoured anywhere and is referred to as being a witch. Why is that so?

I feel I need to ask, why does The Holy Bible frighten Spiritualisms' leaders and some of their followers? I write lectures and have presented many. I presented one called, 'In search of God', and had presented it in a church outside my district in the summer of 2006. While I was speaking the president of the church was continuously glancing from me to the pastor who just happened to have recently opened this church in the vicinity. Was she also in fear of my lecture or in fear that I would get kicked out because I was using the bible as a reference? Then again, as a student I wrote a lecture and asked my teacher, who happened to be the pastor of this church, to read it and edit if needed, as this is a good way of understanding Spiritualism and their teachings. She had, and once read she summoned me to her office when I attended the church again. She said, "I'm very disappointed in this lecture". Once asked, she pointed out a few things, things I took for granted as many teachings remain with us from childhood teachings and learning. That's o.k. I said and I'll make the necessary corrections as I would like to have the opportunity to express and share with the congregation. Then she said, "Too many bible quotes, too."

Why do most of the Spiritualist leaders react in this manner? The bible is full of Spiritualism; isn't that not what a clairvoyant experiences continuously when in contact with the spirit world? The so-called Christian Spiritualist uses the bible continuously and why not as it's a book, a book of faith. This book of faith should not threaten in any way as well as the many other bible books readily available, which many do not have the word 'bible' in their titles.

Freewill and freedom of speech should be open to all as long as it's about love. Hatred, bias, bigotry and evil do not belong in god's creation, especially when love is expressed to the congregation continuously. So why do we seldom experience it within this small group of spiritualist people? Because, they don't practice what they preach; sound familiar?

There's always someone that will fear you being better than them selves. Especially, I found, in Spiritualism. I have experienced this many times over the past few years. Some are former teachers and fellow students who appeared to have feared me right from the beginning. Although some has enhanced my ability tremendously, I sensed that some didn't appreciate my advancement to the highest level as it became at par to their own, if not better. Some will fear you enough to find a way to rid you of their church. Enough words of untruth were spread around to make others not welcome me as well. It didn't work with the entire congregation though. One such person that was told was a respected friend who would defend my honor, in my absence. There were those that knew the real me and did not make a judgment by another's opinion and premeditated malevolence. Furthermore, there was a newly ordained minister that wanted in at a particular church, whom I considered a friend but I got stabbed in the back nonetheless. My name was slandered as often as possible, which continues, and people believed and also spread this gossip to other members; maybe in hopes that I should lower myself and think myself incompetent. Others had felt the sting of the same venom by the same people. My friend and a personal of-and-on editor who I dearly admire said' *"I hate to say this but they are women and women sometimes tend to do things such as this."* Some do and so do some men, but we're not always prepared for such bigotry and malicious behavior from those we trust and respect, especially those that pretend to represent God. Maybe 'only in Canada' but favoritism and this sort of behavior are not spiritualist traits and do not belong in Spiritualism, as they do not belong in most religions. Moreover, *"It's not very Christian"*, said a friend. I answered, *"It's not very spiritual."*

Many have said over time that ego means 'Edging God Out'. This I find to be the perfect meaning as many had ego-ed in Spiritualism in Canada. Let me express it this way; many I know who represent Spiritualism in Canada have ego-ed; 'Edged God Out.'

If it appears that your teacher may be harassing you and all of a sudden finds fault in your progression, or spiritual abilities in any way, or is a little impatient when it comes to your time-speaking, then beware. Once your popularity increases with the other students and the congregation you may very well be 'out the door.' Then again one door closes and another opens and what an enlightenment when it finally happens. Now as I look back I often wish it had been a year earlier. Listen to your higher self, don't be stubborn. They say 'the devil you know' is better then the one you don't know'. Well, I'm not in favor of this as I experienced the opposite many time over the years.

"The more we get hurt the more critical and judgmental we become, and the less willing we are to forgive," A.J. Mallett in 'Spread the Fire' magazine, Toronto Airport Christian Fellowship, issue 2—2004 in a section called 'Forgiveness'.

Here's an article I wrote; I used it as a lecture and submitted it to the National Spiritualist Summit in the USA a while ago. It's called, "A Spiritual Quest."

Many times in our lives we hear about the realities of one's life or the beginnings of a new one. Some time ago Spiritualism wasn't heard of in certain parts of the world and believe it or not, it still isn't. I feel reasons for this have to do with the promoting of it and the lack of integrity to do so, or lack of knowledge or means. Maybe one doesn't care if it gets to all parts of the globe as long as his or her congregation is up to par, with enough memberships to keep the doors of their sanctuary open. Unfortunately, this is the outlook for certain individuals responsible for the promotion of this fun-religion that I found only ten short years ago.

Questions upon questions entered my mind about what it's all about and what it consists of and how to get a grip on the totality of it all. Questions were asked and many were unanswered. The many that were unanswered were the ones of importance to me in my new spiritual beginning. Did I let this hinder my development or falter the road to progress? Absolutely not; I reverted to books and the subjects of those books were about 'life after death' and books on the supernatural, of which I had many encounters from childhood.

How does one fit into such a category when one is ignorant and remains so, due to lack of responses/education from those were asked? Good question when put forth to those that wish to remain silent about a gift that one doesn't quite know how to control. This gift is what that individual possessed and chose not to elaborate on, for fear of giving a simple explanation to a brother or sister, or a student.

During a time of introduction to Spiritualism one has many questions, especially when one had experienced the supernatural and the phenomena of spiritual apparitions throughout life.

As we all know, this can be a frightening experience when experienced later on in life for the first time. I was fortunate as I always believed in "Ghost" so to speak and had encountered a few in my early childhood. Moreover, making the adult experiences more acceptable when encountered after shutting out or turning off this ability we call a gift for many years due to the expectations of others. In addition, one usually ends up being told that one is crazy and or *"You're ready for the mental hospital,"* where others have been taken after experiencing the same. Other members of my family have this gift but they say they don't wish to have it because it scares them.

For two years I sat, practically in silence, in a Spiritualist Church. I should say I actually zigzagged between two, not knowing which one I'd gain the most spiritually or get the most information from. I approached the pastors and then some of the Mediums and asked questions. Often times my questions were diverted in a way that reason was expected to be understood from the answers given. Not good enough I thought; there has to be more.

My point of view in retrospect to all of this is that while leaders or church Pastors/ Reverends continue to remain somewhat secretive about how to enhance this wonderful gift from spirit, a beginner lacks in knowledge and takes a longer time progressing spiritually towards development to a higher level of consciousness. This individual may just give up and not bother, for some have been known to do so.

When one grasps the wonderment of it all one should express gratitude to those who reached out and offered the utmost best. They should also express themselves to those who took the time and effort to explain, to a certain degree, enough to hold them within their spiritual frame of mind and thought.

I personally gained enough knowledge to be encouraged to buy as many books on the subject as possible, and that wasn't an easy task. Books on what I was looking for were not easily accessible and I never heard of Lily Dale until about five years ago, where there were many books on the subject. Without some individuals' encouragement, understanding, and help I wouldn't have developed or progressed to where I am today; and without their guidance and help my spirit guides would still remain anonymous.

To those of you who may be approached and questioned concerning spiritual development, please take the time to give your best, this promotes the spread of Spiritualism, for who knows what part of the world this message will be taken to next.

Spiritualism is a part of my life and it could very well be a part of yours if you're reading this. It plays a major part for without it I'd find myself lost in a material world without value or means. With it I find myself very rewarded and spiritually blessed as I have many friends of the same nature.

Infinite Spirit works in many wonderful ways; make that way your way as you reach out to help those inquiring about their spiritual quest.

Spiritualism say's that it's a science, philosophy as well as a religion. The explanation they give and as much as I perceive it to be is as follows:

Science: Tested operations of general laws that are concerned with the physical world and phenomena that are sometimes unexplainable. It's knowing or having proof or knowledge of something as in scientific experimentation. It's also a study or a learned proven effect dealing with a systemized technique uncovering general truths.

To know and can be demonstrated.

Philosophy: The total learning of technical precepts and practical arts not including theology, medicine and law. It's discipline metaphysics in pursuit of wisdom and the understanding of values rather than observations. It expresses fundamental beliefs as a theatrical judgment.

Theory is the basis of philosophy.

Religion: The state of service and worship of God. Committed devotion to a particular faith that I feel is an inner faith of observance. A personal belief in attitude directed towards a God of choice and the set laws and regulations of that organization.

Through science and philosophy, Spiritualism had established the basis of their teachings.

The true mission of Spiritualism as from a few designated churches is to teach people how to live, not how to die. My present tutor, educator and leader said, *"The true mission is also to help you understand how to take the simple passage into death without fear".* Rev. Dr. Alva Folkes. My personal opinion is to teach the human race that death is not the end and therefore one does not die. One does not die because the soul lives on after death of the material body. The true mission is to prove, beyond a doubt, that this is 'fact'; and it's often validated through genuine clairvoyance.

D.D. Home (Daniel Douglas) 1833-1886, is one of the world's

greatest physical mediums. He considered himself to be a Christian Spiritualist originated from the Orthodox faith. He says in his book called 'Incidents in My Life' first published in 1864, *"If it be true that the spirits of the dead can commune with us, then it must be, that they can reveal to us what is the state of existence into which they were ushered on dying, and what is the mode of life they are leading there. This they profess to do, and this seems to me to be the primary and main object of this whole movement."* Throughout his life he continued to be a believer in Jesus the Christ, and those he associated with went along with it. He proved over and over again the wonders of the world-of-spirits. Many well-known and respected individuals witnessed his continued levitations plus materializations of spirit hands; plus the movement of heavy objects that couldn't be lifted by men and the playing of an accordion by spirit. According to his book he apparently married and had a son that had the same gift. Since reading his biography I wondered what became of his son and if he too demonstrated this marvelous phenomena.

Mentioning this, one gives thanks to Spiritualism as lost loved ones were no longer lost. The material or physical world is able to communicate with and contact loved ones in the spirit world as if they were still here on the earth plane. This is done through a medium as quite often those recently passed to spirit will remain in the astral plane for a period of time until spiritual development had been gained prior to moving on to the next level. Moving on to the next level does not stop them from descending but one has to earn ascension. In addition, one does not ascend until they pass the first grade of spiritual development; this applies to the material as well as the spiritual world. Moreover, the more you grow and learn spiritually the more you advance on earth; therefore, the higher your plane upon physical death.

Spiritualism manages to fill a huge void for the everyday person, who now has something to cling to and a belief that their friends and family members had gone on to a better place. The raps from the Hydesville house experienced by the Fox family between 1843 and

1844 started a whole new concept. The Fox family just happen to be the occupants to make this known as the Bell family, prior to this, had also experienced the same type of rappings in the same house. They chose not to stay there because they didn't like the so-called haunting and moved on making the house readily available. The owner of the property was informed of reasons for moving out but chose to keep it secret. The Foxes moved in and after a short while Mr. Charles B. Rosna was active in this house and was determined to make his murder known. Fortunately for Spiritualism this was documented as proof by many known scholars and writers of that day. At that point in time this was the best news the world could have imagined to believe. This led to many years of research, making Spiritualism a science, philosophy, and a religion.

I ask: Is Spiritualism the work of the devil? Well let's question ourselves, wasn't the devil 'Satan' created? Spiritualism is not of the devil or of evil but Satan comes in many disguises and all religions have their share of devils in a physical form. It appears more so in Spiritualism because it's a struggling religion and has been since it lost its luster when television was invented. Get-togethers were a form of entertainment prior to this and many phenomena happened that gave Spiritualism its popularity.

Putting aside what you've been taught and read in certain books take a good look at yourself; what is it that you believe, what is your gut feeling about Religion, God and Satan? If you bless yourself prior to giving spiritual healing then by all means continue to do so. If you believe Krishna, Buddha, Allah or Gandhi is your god then that is your soul right, as God is known by many names. If you believe Jesus Christ is your Saviour then He is and let no one change your mind if that is what you truly believe. But refrain from judgment of another's choice and respect it as they will yours. Isn't it but not one god?

You're an individual with a mind and soul all your very own. Value your own opinion as well as that of others and especially value what you receive from intuition, psychic awareness and from God. My God is a loving, merciful and forgiving God. It says this in The Holy

Bible and many other bible books that are not called bibles but is one nonetheless. Yet then again it also contradicts itself several times by saying that God is revengeful and will punish severely for different reasons mentioned.

Who wrote the many books and bibles of our world? Think about it. We all make mistakes and falter in language translations; and things get lost or misinterpreted along the way.

I believe that your God and my God will not punish in any way.

It may appear to some that I'm not a fan of Spiritualism, which would be hearsay. I'm very much a part of the movement but a part of the movement that only a pure spiritualist would understand. Not all in Spiritualism are spiritual and there are many spiritual people not associated with Spiritualism. Once again you don't need to be a part of Spiritualism to be a spiritual person for Spiritualism has many that are not; unfortunately some of those non-spiritualists are in authority and have a controlling nature where ego tends to get in the way. No matter what religion you're familiar with or associated with you'll find this in most. Judge not another but constantly judge yourself and your spiritual path; moreover, you'll travel smoothly to a higher level of advancement to those opposite. I'm not opposed to Spiritualism for it is my choice in life. However, a few that stand at the front to represent it are not held very high on my list of spiritual people; and their unruly and egotistical behavior was personally witnessed.

When you speak to God you pray, when you want to hear God's answers "meditate" and listen.

Below is a prayer I sent out into the world through cyber some time ago. It covers basic religions and their God. Please say this prayer now and let your heart open to an acceptance of all.

Great Divine Spirit, Lord Jesus Christ, Blessed Mother Mary,
Buddha, Krishna, Allah and all other names referred to as God.
Dear Heavenly Spirit, hold all life and all innocent people in your loving hands.
Protect them all.

Bless those who commit selfless acts who felt it was the right thing to do to protect us and our world.
Guide them to inner awareness of Your divine source of love and make them recognize innocent people.
Grant peace within and between the countries of our planet
Let there be quick and peaceful solutions of conflicts between our different cultures and religions.
Make our world a safe and happy place to live.
Omit all hatred and wars.
Watch over all the many wonderful rainbow-colored people in Your universe.
I ask this in 'Your' name.
"Amen."

Stillness, quietness and inner peace are received through meditation and prayer. Once in your meditation listen to God within; ask questions through the thought process and listen for the answers. Answers will be sketched in your mind on your inner slate: images and scenes will be presented on your inner computer screen. Seek the God within and once there you'll most likely find what you're looking for through awareness. You don't need man's interpretation as long as you listen to Gods voice within, with love and compassion.

Here's an affirmation to meditate on. Say it slowly and aloud a few times then close your eyes and listen to the god within your own consciousness. Cast out any negative thoughts if and when they enter, don't focus or dwell on them. Politely say, *"I recognize this; now take it away"*. Then immediately discard it.

A Spiritual Affirmation

I am a child of God
God is my creator and master
I have free will and will follow my intuition
My free will consists of understanding and following the loving teachings of Jesus. (In place of Jesus you may put any prophet's

name or another loving spirit of God, or God.)
I have my own beliefs and wish a greater understanding of others
I will recognize all life as one
I will respect the beliefs of others
I will not be persuaded about my own as I choose to use free will
I will succeed in my spiritual growth
I am a good person and will become better with my spiritual advancement
Thank you
Amen

Chapter Two
Self-Definition (Expressed Through Prayers, Poems and Affirmations)

Who are you and what is your purpose in life? Many have come and gone from this world without knowing the answer. Bonnie Galka.

Let's begin with a simple but powerful word: Love.

Love can and is expressed in a variety of ways; we have but to recognize it when it presents itself. I'm not only speaking of intimate love, but also the love of another human being, animal, and/or plant.

Due to a disabling illness, which some of you already know about, I was unable to continue working at my regular job. At this point in my life, as previously, I began to wonder about a spiritual path. With extra time on my hands I devoted it to examining my personal soul; searching for that missing link that most of us are unaware of, until we're struck down with an illness that stops us from carrying out our daily lives, which we've become accustomed to. Fortunately, soul searching started previously to this, and as I began to explore my inner self, a greater understanding of what lies beyond our material world was discovered. My first book explains a lot about my awareness, knowledge and the development towards expressing through prayer, poetry, and affirmations. If at least one thing in this book touches a special place in your heart then I will feel that I've completed a small task from God, through a divine assistance. Much of my thoughts come from a source far beyond most people's reach, but once tapped into it I write, or record in some form, what is given. Later on I'll put it into a text such as what you're about to read.

From past experience with the spirit world, I realized that there's an existence after what we call death. I have had many contacts with spirits from across the veil, most were very loving and uplifting but there were a couple I didn't appreciate.

One evening I got a message from a spirit and it said, *"When you come in contact with a dog it will check you out each and every time so, therefore, learn from this."* When you make that contact with any spirit remember your pet, make sure you use all your senses and always check them out thoroughly, right from the beginning. If the feeling is negative refuse contact and tell them to go away; if the feeling comes forth with love then it's worth granting connection. Therefore, you'll bring forth words of encouragement, wisdom, and love.

Prayer is a request for God's assistance and quite often a cry of a sudden supplication; this can be through spoken words or through the thought process. A supplication has an order of requesting words and the prayer itself is an earnest request coming directly from the heart. The practice of prayer and praying, to the God of your choice, is a religious favour asked on several occasions, especially during illness or in any state of the many emergencies we see in our daily lives. Prayers are said by a single person and by any number or group of people in a gathering that's focused on one particular request, or on an ailing person. This act of communicating with God is a natural result of a person's belief. A formal or spontaneous prayer spoken in silence comes from within through the centre of your heart; for instance, 'My daily prayer.'

Prayer beads, that are used in many denominations, give a person the ability to keep track of how many prayers said at a given time, and the number a person has in their mind to say to meet the quota expected by their religion; devoting a total commitment. Roman Catholics pray to the Blessed Mother Mary, which supposedly relays the request to our brother Jesus and then finally reaches God the Father. In some Christian religions, prayer consists of forgiveness through confession, a prayer of thanks, appeals, or petitions and words of praise aimed at their God. Spiritual communion is done several times a day by those who have had the fear of God put in them by certain clergies of various religions. As it brings one into a closer relation with the ultimate divine it brings a sense of inner peace and ceremonial praise. A total commitment to God is shared in prayer gatherings when groups by the millions flock to certain places of worship from all over the world, depending on religious upbringing. For example, notice how many Jewish men gather at the "wall" to worship. Many Muslims, Persians, Hindus, and Roman Catholics attend their houses of worship faithfully to pray, for this is a part of their sacrifice, to their God.

Rules and regulations have evolved through the centuries, and as time continues some prayers have been removed from certain faiths, some have been added and some haven't changed much at all. No matter what has been added or deleted faithful followers will go along with the changes made by clergy and board members, and never question whether God had any say in the decision.

A Daily Prayer

God, Great Divine, Our creator
Descend upon my heart, here on earth and make my energy flow
Help me with my weakness; give me inner peace and strength
Direct me to give love, as your will desires
Give me comfort from the Angels; you so lovingly gave to watch over me
Cleanse my soul and make it pure
Let my heart beat with love for my fellow man
Strengthen my Mind, Body and Spirit so that I may be a better person
I will passionately love you as Your Angels do
The Dove, descended from Your Eternal Light, will set my heart aflame
You have entered into my soul and I feel your blessings.
Thank You.
Amen

Poems express a composition in each verse and as they express they tell a story. A poem can also be a prayer, with rhythm, and a focused theme that differs from a lyric poem of love said from a pure heart having a pleasurable experience. A poet who produces such metrical writings formulates an awareness of the imagination that concentrates on past experiences, or creates such beautiful words from within the loving soul and has put in on paper. When a text of words has been chosen and arranged then an emotional response helps to create a specific meaning through rhythm. Once the work of art has been created the poet usually expresses quality in the beautiful expressions of well-formed words. Poetry has been around for centuries and has touched the hearts of many through the receiving of cards on special occasions, or by a book of poems received as a gift.

Shakespeare's work will never die. His plays will continue on and on. Yearly they're acted out over and over again because of the beautiful poetry and the heart-felt messages that it brought forth.

Here is a poem that touched many hearts when I read it New Years Day at a dinner party I held in my home.

Love and Devotion

Cycling down the street one day
Passing by you along the way
I stopped, dismounted to talk to you
Only to find you've noticed me too
We slowly walked toward each other
As we got close I felt a shudder
For what I felt from the start
Came from deep within my heart
We chatted awhile, made plans to meet
I wanted to sweep you off your feet
As days passed, it felt a long time
It finally came and you were mine
A new door opened we entered in

Like a gentle kiss, feelings began
I held you close, as I longed to do
I felt in your embrace you did too
Your love for me as you felt mine
Love at first sight began to shine
Much time has passed, I would not trade
None other than what we had made
You're a special gift within my heart
Let's keep it that way and never part.
All love for you.

Affirmations are declarations said in a positive way and a solemn oath taken conscientiously that creates a direct quotation to the God source. This is affirmed in the mind of the one saying it, given directly as an understanding that God will, and has, granted this favour or protection immediately.

We have incredible minds; we have so much control over our bodies, our destinies and our successes. Our minds can alter and control through affirmative thoughts expressed from deep within. Our brain's ability is limited to a small percentage of its use, leaving the major portion unused and atrophied. There's no greater power than that of the mind, as anything created was first a thought—and that of the mind. Positive strong affirmations are expectations of the life script and its reality is confirming protections granted by God. The ultimate frontier, your mind, your brain, has a great potential that you don't realize but it's easy to make a claim on it once you start your prayers of affirmation. Once you repeatedly demonstrate its effectiveness you'll have the ability to facilitate your inner mind and brainpower. This can be put to the test on a daily basis until you feel the tremendous power of affirming. You are actually telling yourself and convincing your brain, confirming that a loving God will grant anything good that is uplifting and loving, which is directed to the self or to others.

An example affirmation goes something like this:

Affirming God's Care

Great Infinite Spirit:
I am safe with you
You have covered me with your heavenly protection
You send me love and peace as you guide me on my way
I'm shielded by your ultimate power
Your presence is felt
Acceptance of my soul is among your children
You are God divine
You're protecting me daily.
Amen

We all need love in our daily lives. We need to feel it and express it to those we care about. Sometimes we tend to forget about those closest to us as we spend more time together. Sometimes we take another person for granted and assume they know that our love and affection continues without any expression of it for them. This is unacceptable and needs to be taken into consideration at all times. Take a look at the smile on someone's face when you give them a compliment of appraisal and approval. Loved ones at home also would like to hear this on a regular basis as well as 'you' would like to hear it from them or someone else who is important in your life. People in a management situation have the best-composed staff if he/she compliments them on their successes and their job performance. Words of praise in a caring and loving way gets better performance out of anyone who is concerned, especially those you're intimate with, such as a partner of your choice.

Below is a poem that created a stir in my inner self as I reflected back on when I was an adolescent and already had a wee sorrowful heartache behind me.

A Yearning for Love

I long to be held in your loving arms—For a love that's past has done some harm
To a kindred soul such as I—Although they say love should

never die
But take my heart and hold it tight—Safely compassionately forever bright
Cause once it's gone from your embrace
We'll remain together by Gods grace.

When we're younger we seem to go through different relationships, one after the other, but some of us get burned along the way. We have to realize that we've met this person for some reason or another, whether we stay together for a long or short period of time. We meet people and usually learn from those experiences; sometimes it's a hard lesson learned but learned nonetheless. We move on with a little gained knowledge and awareness, a little wiser with a greater knowledge from our past sorrows and hurts. Being young and adventurous, one can cope much better with a hard lesson, but as we grow older we tend to blame ourselves when something goes sour. You're not to blame personally, nobody is. Is it fate, or destiny? Whatever you wish to call it, it was meant to make us wiser for when we're in another similar situation. The poem below is about a love once lived then parted due to a slight misunderstanding and both moved on, but not forgotten. Fond memories remained in the mind of one of the couple and are expressed with endearing affection for someone else but still hold a place in the heart for a past lost love.

Romance Remembered

The time we spent was short and sweet
If not for fate how would we meet
You touched a place within my heart
It went so deep it tore apart
A door that's been closed to someone like you
But now it's ajar what will we do
These feelings have surfaced what can I say
But wish you happiness on this day
Would celebrate this event with you

Situations stop me as they usually do
I'll visit again to hold you tight
Hug you so close with all my might
I may never let go for what have you done
Cause in my eyes you're a part of the sun

From the time I understood what Spiritualism was all about I've felt that I'm a spiritualist more then any other religion I've been in contact with. Since then I recognized several religions that recognize, respect and worship God in very similar ways, but without the clairvoyance offered in their divine services. We're all different and we're all unique. God didn't make two people the same, DNA testing has proven this. So, what would be your views on cloning, keeping in mind the thought of God's creation being tampered with by man, a creation of His divine making?

I've had contact with passed on loved ones and felt their love and caring beyond the grave. Below is a poem that was given to me by such a contact.

Spirit Message from a Loved One

When time has passed and you're all alone
Think of me in our beautiful home
For once we pass through the veil
Death is sweet but who could tell
Of the transformation that has taken place
By God's sweet hands and his saving grace
I've travelled to a distant far off shore
Where loved ones meet and part no more.
So come to me in our beautiful home
When you're ready to be, yet not alone

We as humans tend to be very free with our thoughts and actions. Small children speak the truth without any thought of hiding or concealing what an adult would consider twice before venturing their feelings. What would our world be like if adults acted like children? Granted, a lot of adults act child-like and haven't matured beyond that due to some problem or a difficult upbringing. Nevertheless, we have to over look minor flaws that are not harmful due to an illness of some kind or another. As a mature adult, consider the human side of yourself then consider your spiritual side, the spirit within the soul, the soul within the human body and what part it plays in your daily thoughts and activities. How often do you sit and ponder about something and jump to a conclusion without connecting to the God source that lies within you? Connect with your inner, higher self, the God source, and seek out such awareness, then you'll feel a total change towards any given situation and your outlook will be directed in a more positive and loving way. Below is a poem I wrote when I reflected back on my loving 'American' grandmother; her words of praise and compliments of love when I was a child have never been forgotten. I'll carry those endearing times to my grave, and across to the other side where I know she'll be waiting for me. I often joked with her and with her loving and understanding way she went along with most with an accepting heart for one of her many grandchildren. As you read you'll see the wonderful grandmother this loving woman had been.

A while back I attended a spiritualist church and a young medium gave me a message from my grandmother's spirit. It verified that she's aware of the tribute that I wrote for her. She got in touch with me, beyond the grave via another source other than through me, and it was such a loving feeling to get this message from someone who knew completely nothing about what I had written. Yet again, proof beyond the grave; I didn't need the proof but it felt good to hear from her through someone else.

A Special Tribute

Embedded deep within my mind
Childhood memories till this time
At each togetherness you would say
Remember what happened on that day

You said to me to close my eyes
Open my hands to find a prize
You trusted me with all your heart
No hesitation from the start
As you obeyed my command
I placed a frog within your hand
You dropped it quickly, let out a scream
To see such excitement was but a dream
The trick I played was very real
Many years later a fond memory still
A cherished event of your beautiful heart
Although you've passed we're not apart
I'd love to see you walk through my door
Yet you're with me now and evermore
You're remembered much more than another
Compassionate loving like a mother
Each year we'd make a plan to meet
My visits to you were short but sweet
Remember the butterflies, bees, and birds
I'd bring them to you as in a herd
I knew I impressed you with my caring touch
Your smiles and actions meant so much
For the joy you've brought me with loving words
Were very pleasant, best I've heard
Your loving soul has gone to rest
For in God's presence he has the best
A wonderful woman as you have been
A life of worship away from sin
You often reached out to help many others
Not all can say this about grandmothers
A blessing to me when you were here
But now more so that you are there
You've come to me in my dreams
Life-like events as once I've seen
Many precious moments that we've shared
Over a short time we call years

I speak to you each and every day
In my heart and soul you'll never go away.
"I love you Grandma Gosling."

Have you ever been doing something and then realized that there's a small voice inside your head speaking to you telling you to do it differently and it's better than what you're actually doing? It appears as if you're deeply thinking that you're telling or teaching someone when it's actually spirit, from the God source, telling you how it should be done the right way. Some people may refer to this kind of alertness as hearing from their doorkeeper. It may take a while to grasp this meaning, but until you become aware of a divine presence being a part of your inner higher self you may remain oblivious. Once recognized though, you'll always be aware of its connection. Never reject a communication in this way as it assures you of a heightened spiritual awareness. God, our infinite spirit, hears our prayers and affirmations, He accepts us as we are with an everlasting unconditional love that we should also express and feel for our fellow sisters and brothers.

Each and every religion has a set of guidelines to follow, whether it is the Ten Commandments, Seven Principles or a part of The Holy Koran or Buddhists' teachings. Practising religious people of various religions try to follow the teachings the best they can. But there's the odd one or two who refuse to accept its loving meanings and try to corrupt others to do the same. Unfortunately when a highly recognized member in society tends to do this they'll get as much support as they seek. Unfortunately in those situations we have freedom of choice as well as in all other situations. I feel that there's a need for God's intervention towards a more loving perspective when there's corruption towards another race or country; when all are as one in God's eyes. We're all God's children, what would life be like if we were all the same with no different separateness? Life would be boring with nothing to learn and nothing to gain; it would be quite dull, wouldn't it? Below is a poem with affirmations that were created for mediumship awareness when calling on spirit and connecting with God and the spirit world. Grasp its meaning and gain knowledge from its words. When said regularly belief comes quickly that God, our loving creator, will always be there for you. You need only to call on his assistance, believe that you'll get what you ask for and it will be given; maybe in a different way than you'd like but you'll accomplish it nonetheless.

God's Listening

In earnest prayer the holy stream flows
Where warm devotions dwell the theme sweetly glows
Blessings desired grasps upward gaze
Celestial love eloquence of praise
Voices of sweetness heard by my ears
God's heart rejoiced then dried bitter tears
Spirit ascends utterance from out there
God lovingly accepts the comprehensive prayer

God doesn't judge. Do you? Do you judge others? If so; why? What makes you this way? What makes many people this way?

Being different in someone's eyes is an opportunity to learn from that individual. In big cities it's difficult when approaching another person due to the high volume of crime that goes alongside so many people in a highly compacted environment. Living in small towns and being a little different than most, people sometimes create gossip to hurt the feelings or humiliate someone known by everyone, who lives there. Why would we do this? When it comes to a man being interested in a woman we have no problem with that, do we? When a woman becomes interested in a man we tend to think a little more about that sort of approach and question whether she's a loose woman or not. In frustration, due to society's expectations of women after her approach of a man, she may wonder why a man didn't take interest in her and approach her first. Why should this be? A man interested in another man, a woman interested in another woman is looked at and scorned by a high percentage of our society. Why this when most of us have someone in our family or know of someone's loved one who does? God's love is unconditional for all, whether our sexual preferences are the same or different. 'Judge not for you may also be judged,' and probably not in the way you would like to be.

Hurting someone has no gain for your soul's progression here on earth or when you die and pass through the veil. Oh yes, there's an afterlife and the sooner you become aware of it the sooner you'll be non-judgmental towards your human counterparts, companions, and yourself.

Today it seems that the younger generation don't have this problem, depending on home location and up-bringing, but it can get a little out of control in their teens and adolescent years. One failure at love after another; who says this needs to be addressed when the two people involved had learned its lessons and moved on? After all we're all a part of the animal world, granted we're supposed to be more civilized than any other, yet we're at the top of the line and can be the most destructive of all.

Below is a poem written about God's unfailing love for all his children; not just for a chosen few.

God's Unfailing Love

Another year gone and love remains
Months from now will be the same
Another year older and wiser too
A committed love remains loyal and true
Devoted together two as one
In God's eyes they're never shun
Lovers of same, lost in time
Cause if it's love God doesn't mind
His blessings are sent from above
For two souls—so much in love

Some time ago my brother and I were driving in our home town. As I was coming upon a crosswalk a woman pressed the light to cross the street. I stopped and as I usually do I watch the person or persons crossing until they reach the other side. We both looked at her and we were probably thinking along a similar line when I spoke up and said, *"My goodness, look at how hard her face is".* My brother didn't make a comment, maybe because I didn't give him enough time. I proceeded to say that beauty and a person's appearance are only skin deep and she's probably happier than him or I.

This dear woman was about 35-40 years of age and not well dressed but casually dressed in clean clothes. Then I said to my brother that she probably looks in the mirror and also feels that she's not an attractive woman but knows deep inside that her beauty is within her heart.

My psychic senses kicked in and as my mind raced I was impressed to think that she may have had a history of verbal abuse and her childhood may very well have been one of the worst. Children and adults alike probably made many negative comments about her and she's probably hardened from all the past verbal abuse.

My heart went out to her but who knows what sort of life she's had up to now, and who's to say that any of this has ever occurred. One can only speculate on appearances; and being judgmental is something we all do whether we express it or not. We know people can be very hard on another human being and at times even to those they love.

Constructive criticism is one thing, but critical insults are another. Sometimes small children don't know the difference but they can be the worst when it comes to cruelty towards another. For what reason, who knows; maybe from a learned hurt, angry parent or pressured and bullied by their peer? Whatever the reason for my judgment and words expressed this woman was born with a pure soul just like you and I.

Sometimes as we mature and get older we're not always aware of our soul's progression or that we even have one. As children if we're not enlightened by a parent or another mature adult about our inner selves that we're from God and were born of this purity then there's no room made for improvement.

Life is hard enough, so any negative comments should be kept to ourselves but sometimes we don't. It's spoken and we're not always aware that it has been said until it's out and the damage done.

A friend of mind and I had a little discussion about a couple of years ago when she came to visit. She was a bit on the heavy side when she was a young girl and she said that she was teased quite a bit and had been brought to tears on many occasions. All her life, due to heredity, she has had a weight problem as do a lot of men and women alike. Today she looks magnificent, in her 40's and beautiful with just enough weight to make her sex appeal very noticeable. During my friend's stay an old school colleague of hers found out, through some means, that she was here and got in touch. They made arrangements and met for lunch at a local restaurant. The soul purpose of this meeting was for her childhood friend to apologize for all the slander and all the hurt feelings she caused my friend. This was very important for her to do and it was also a beautiful gesture of seeking forgiveness on her part and to feel accepted by my friend.

Guilt can be difficult when you know that you're not that little mischievous child you used to be; but then again one may look back and wonder why he/she was ever this way. Many of us can relate to this and many understand the reasons for needed corrections when as adults we look at life in a different perspective and know 'God loves us as we are.' God doesn't just love a beautiful face, He also loves the hard looking ones. The soul is of His concern and its progression is what He's interested in, and for us to help make life better for all his coloured children of the world.

Below is a poem I created for this friend, which isn't related to the get together she's had with her school colleague.

Special Friend

Dear friend I miss you more each day
At night I bow my head to pray
For a time we'll be together once more
Awaiting the moment you're at my door
You'll come to me, fall in my arms
Where you're safely held away from harm

It seems forever since that day
You waved goodbye, went on your way
To a distant land far from me
Where life is mellow by the sea
Soon you'll be in my loving embrace
We'll once again meet face to face.
Hurry back.
Love for you D.M.

When I was introduced to the spiritualist religion, I met a Reverend at a church close to where I live. One day, with a little hesitation I ventured to the church door. It seemed as if some other means had taken control of my car and the steering wheel. I found myself in front of the door; I checked to see if it was left open, it wasn't. There was some information in the window concerning the time of the services and a phone number that I could call, if I wished. Eventually I got the courage to phone and spoke to the Reverend. She was friendly enough and gave as much information as required at that time. I asked if I could come by and speak with her at some point and arrangements were made to meet the following day, in the afternoon. We met and spoke of certain books and the authors that I had read, and she wasn't impressed with what I had to say, or it appeared so. This didn't deter me in any way as I was new to this and wanted to learn and experience all that I could about the other side, after we leave the earth plane. I attended a service shortly after and walked in while the spiritual healing was going on, before the divine service. It felt so peaceful with the quietness, soft background music and people sitting in meditation or just in quiet while spiritual healing was being given. Once the service started I listened and observed everything, and all that was being offered. The singing was good even though there wasn't music, the lecture went well, and I took from it what pertained to me. Finally, the time for clairvoyance came. I listened as each individual got a message from spirit or from a passed loved one. I also got a message but don't remember what it consisted of, but I do know it related to something in my life at that time. The service came to an end and there was a social gathering, which I took advantage of just so that I could get to meet people of the congregation and to chat again with the Reverend. I spoke with her and made arrangements for my friend and I to have a private clairvoyant-reading within that week. The price was good and I wanted to hear what the other side had to say to me. I was not totally impressed but there were a couple of things that hit home. My friend was very impressed; her comment was, *"If she knows as much about my future as she did about my past, she's very good."* We left it at that.

I attended the church services for a while and went to an open development circle. I asked if I could be a member of the closed development circle and eventually I was accepted. I developed quickly as I gained great insight and acquired a tremendous amount of knowledge from all the literature I could get my hands on; plus past experiences from childhood happenings from the world of spirit. Eventually I felt that I wasn't progressing. I chose to leave the closed circle but occasionally attended the open, which was for the public.

Further on I grasped the message given to me in this private reading. She could not have been more accurate than if she were the judge overseeing my destiny. Her predictions were accurate and her advice was what I needed, although I didn't see it as clearly as she had.

People come into our lives for a reason, some will stay for what seems like a season and some will remain for a lifetime. Sound familiar? When most people come into our lives it's for a reason and when most welcomed inspirational people do, we hope that they'll stay for many seasons and remain an inspiration for a lifetime of reasons and seasons.

One day I was struck with an inspiration to write a poem about the Reverend at this particular church from what I knew about her, the church, and her teachings. She has a copy but she didn't have a lot to say about it other than that she liked it. A couple of the words differ somewhat to conceal identity.

J's Poem

Love and light was the message sent
I for one knew what it meant
Two words sent by someone like you
Deep in my heart I already knew
The wonderful soul that's there within
Your thoughtful directions let it begin
You know the boundaries of your heart
Send it forth; it's time to start
To be the leader you wish to be
Seek spirit within and set it free
Then let it soar to your congregation
Dedicated members from all nations
Each word of wisdom that you share
Soul searching sought for those that care
About the gift they know God gave
To each individual He has made
Let's all remember the golden rule
Follow its direction; it's a good tool
For what does it mean a proper meditation
To circle members and their dedication
Teach how to meet spirit and how to create
For all of us know that it's more than fate
Leadership is expected by a good teacher
Research and give it like a preacher
Teach and tell them all you know
Think peace and harmony and make it grow
Pleasant warm smiles make true recognition
To a chosen religion such as Spiritualism

Affirmations are a special way of praying with an expectation of it being answered. Strive to better yourself on a daily basis. Learn to love your companion, your neighbour, your country next door and the list goes on and on. Find in your heart a place for love and send it forth during the day as you make contact with your colleagues and fellow men. Open your hearts to those whom you feel need some encouragement and understanding. Send forth your willingness and eagerness of acceptance so that it will be recognized as a sign from another loving individual from God, while helping out others in your daily life. There are times when we ask ourselves, why did I get myself into this mess? Well, it's because we have a calling from God to get involved in a caring and helpful way. Once we're in there we most often follow it through until satisfactory results are accomplished and self-satisfaction is recognized as a job well done; giving one's self a respectful payment in return. The poem below is a form of an affirmation in respect of God and the individual's self-awareness of God's forgiving power and merciful loving.

An Affirmation to Infinite Spirit

I'll continue to do all that's right
With exquisite delight to my soul
Life's more about than to just exist
When it's right your heart will know
Each passing hour one at a time
Accomplishments and duty done
Days and years will be sublime
Devotion for Spirit has won
I'll make the most of every hour
It comes and goes so swiftly
I will strive with all my power
To learn all about God's gift

A message sent out into the universe will definitely have an impact on what is being asked or what is being sought. Think about what you need and what your desires are, but make it a non-material wish. For some reason God seems not too keen on material things when asked for in prayer. We usually have to work hard for this, making a sacrifice in some form or other. Remember the saying, 'Be careful what you ask for'? Well, always keep it in mind, close to your heart and recognize the things you say in jest. Think always on the spiritual aspect of things, especially in prayer and thought. Thought transference creates commotion and has a direct impact on an individual's well being. Think clearly when your prayers are being said, your affirmations being repeated and especially your thoughts.

Being a spiritual person doesn't mean that you have to spend your life inside the doors of a religious dwelling. Spiritual means: to believe in God and his powerful source of understanding and acceptance, relating to sacred matters but not actually being ecclesiastical. Below are words of prayer and affirmation for those who believe in a divine presence that has the ability of governing our universal laws, making it possible to make that contact beyond our human understanding and belief; moreover, at times when we feel a need to hear from our departed loved ones.

Requesting from Spirit

Come loving spirits from realms of light
Breathe your blessings on me tonight
Let me feel that you are near
Guide me from darkness, away from fear
Your heavenly path alight with love
Bring spiritual insight on wings of a dove
Stay among us until the end
Hands happily open as we begin
I shall not doubt nor be afraid
Of the spirit that nears which you gave
Direct all men to live in peace
True faith grows, through charity released

September 11, 2001; which is known as 9 11 in the USA has had an impact on its neighbours and the whole world. This event will never be forgotten. It will go down in history as one of the worst terrorist acts that ever happened to mankind. It will be talked about and aired on television and its successors for years to come. The loss of innocent peoples' lives, the cruel, harsh cowardly acts of suicide bombing done by God's loving people, who have been taught to sacrifice their lives for certain reasons that they have been raised to believe and respect. Those reasons are of religious beliefs. My personal belief is, when something has been taught from childhood it remains ingrained in the brains all their lives, which is very similar to brain-washing. I know they love their God but their God is also the God I love and worship. The only difference is that I don't follow all their standards of religious laws and the name I have for God differs. Nevertheless, it's the same God we both respect and worship. I have friends of this faith and many others. Sometimes we speak about it and most times we leave religion where it belongs, a personal choice. We've had a few conversations but the ending was always pleasant because true friends respect each other's views, whether it's religion or any other given subject. No one person can change destiny or the world as a whole, but many believing in compassionate love and understanding can and will leave a big indent in the negative thinking, hatred, and bigotry.

Let 'Love and peace' be your motto; it's mine.

Unfortunately, some things are out of our reach when other people decide to hurt, injure and kill others whether it's religious beliefs, political issues or just wanting control. If not for religion, then what else is there to fight over? Man, it seems, will find something to try to gain power. War has never made the people of our world one hundred percent happy, but the winners appear to have gained somewhat for the loss of lives sacrificed in the battles.

A friend of mind wanted to travel to the UK shortly after the planes were flying again after 9 11 but she was a little scared. The threat was still there, but she had a desire to spend time with her loved ones, which had been planned prior to the attack on New York, and Washington. She asked for my opinion and somehow I felt it would be safe for her to travel. I sat for a moment and wrote a prayer for her, to print off and take with her. She did this willingly and used it to and from her destinations. Below is that particular prayer. Please feel free to use it on any of your travels. The words aircraft, flight and runway may be changed to suit the travelling vehicle and its source.

An Air Travel Prayer

Dear God, Our Creator and Divine.
Give all of these passengers and me your wondrous protection as we lift off from this runway.
Guide us safely above the clouds and grant us your divine presence while we're on board this aircraft.
Land us safely at our destination, as we're so anxious to be with our living loved ones.
Cover us and protect us with your infinite white light, always.
Thank you.
Amen

The Holy Bible, the Holy Koran and the Holy Scriptures of different religions of the world were presumably passed down by God to one of his prophets: Moses, Abraham, Mohammed, Noah just to name a few. I have no doubt in my mind that words of this sort were given to those wonderful prophets known through the centuries and will continue to live on forever in our teachings and in our minds. Those Scriptures are written books. Those words were given to people of the world such as you and me to be transcribed. Within the process of being written in layman's terms, those people had the opportunity to change the wording to some degree and were able to omit or add to the text (my opinion only). I had read The Holy Bible, from cover to cover, a couple of times and also The Holy Koran and The Worlds Great Scriptures by Lewis Browne. Funny thing though, Spiritualism wasn't one Browne included. From my association with those standing at the head of the line, such as a president representing it, I need no longer question why. Those scriptures are books made up of words passed down by a superior being, known as God. Men interpreted those words and wrote them down as they felt were necessary to keep peace in the world, or at least within their own region and religion. Having read those Bibles and others I choose not to try and live by all of their rules and expectations. I chose from it what pertained to me and what I felt was of use in my daily living. It's totally impossible to live a life exactly as the scribes say so; the world would be full of saintly people if that were the case. To understand the point I'm trying to make, you would have to read those bible books as well, if you haven't already done so. As a spiritualist person, I don't feel the God that's so often mentioned or referred to in the bibles is the God that loves 'all of us' unconditionally. The God I look up to for guidance, forgiveness and acceptance is a loving and forgiving God, not one that will send you into damnation forever. My God and your God do not punish and or threaten us in any way or form.

As you read the scriptures you'll find that they contradict themselves in many areas, especially when putting the fear of God into their devoted religious followers. This is so unfair to the people of the world to be subjected to this sort of control. Your God is my God; and a spiritualist person such as myself understands that the one God of our universe is the one which is governed by natural laws. This Supreme Being—God—is known to me as Divine Intelligence, Divine Holy Spirit and also known as Infinite Spirit, among other descriptions, and names given by many other religions and beliefs. One has to be open to maintain peace. Should it be so hard to understand that there is but one God? It doesn't matter how one worships or by what means; neither does it matter by what names they have chosen to call Him. Unfortunately organized religions have a tendency to want to control the people of their congregations and this should not be. I'm sure God didn't intend this to have happen. Below is a recognition prayer of the past leading towards an affirmative request.

A Prayer of Thanks and an Affirmation Request

God, Great Divine

The happy lifetime pleasures you give is thanked from my heart

The beautiful treasures of spirit lives deeply within

Lately my mind has been yearning for our distant home above
Love, laughter and tears are brought, when enriched by your touch
The depth of human love is bottomless for a Divine Infinite Spirit
Leap of gladness, a thrilling touch makes my pulse flow free
Many times in my weakness and sadness I call on you
Since birth my days are numbered as time brings me wisdom
As I grow old and my eyes begin to dull my soul yearns upward.
Fulfill my dreary slumbering soul as it works towards heaven.
Thank you and Amen

Having a good friend is something to be very thankful for. Not all of us have one that accepts us unconditionally as we hope they do. I, for one, have had that kind of friend for 30 years and she'll remain a lifetime friend. Yes, I see and observe her mistakes in life, as she does mine, and I also see things I do not totally agree with. Do I judge her or give my opinion? No, I do not and would not even if my life depended on it and that's a heavy statement to make. I accept her mistakes, I'm there for her to rely or depend upon, a shoulder to lean on or cry on, if that were the case. I'll give my opinion when she asks for it, and not before, and it will be a constructive one when given. I'm a dependable friend, there for the good times and/or the bad and she has recognized this a long time ago.

We met as friends in a work environment and have remained that way ever since. Never think that a man and a woman can't be best friends without experimenting in the sexual aspect of things. We can prove that, as we have never ever considered that as a part of our relationship and that's where it stands today. I feel that's what has kept our devoted friendship together for as long as it's been. We were both married when we met and both of us have since divorced, one being there for the other in hardships as well as in celebration of new beginnings. On her last visit I felt a sense of loss when she left. As time went on we chatted via telephone and we both look forward to our next reunion. My friend feels we're soul mates and lately I also feel the same. She respects me in the same manner with an unconditional love that can only be recognized by two devoted individuals such as she and I. Below is one of the many poems I wrote for her at some point or another.

Friendship

My friendship with you will never die
Times spent apart can make me cry
My feelings for you seem way beyond friends
I'm sure you agree as each day begins
Those words are meant especially for you
A devoted friend remains loyal and true.
God bless you my friend.

Isn't it amazing how one person can have such an impact on another? I've attended many churches in my lifetime but I have never seen a clerical leader as popular as the Reverend of a small Spiritualist church here in Toronto, Ontario, Canada, until recently.

With my soul progressing as it should I started to search for the missing link in my spirituality. I seemed to be at a loss and reverted to books for world knowledge; and those books were much different than any other I had read prior to looking for that spiritual connection, which I so dearly desired. Within the written text of a few of those books I was given ideas of where I could look for the extra information I was seeking. Those suggestions were directed to a spiritualist church as if they were the spiritualist books that I craved. Up to this point in my life I had never heard about this name for a religion and I had attended many denominations along the way. Eventually, I got bold enough to explore my boundaries but being as I am I didn't want to walk in a new place alone; I desired to have a companion. I was waiting for my newly acquired friend, one who shared books with me, and I her, to have an evening free so that we could attend and explore together but it was quite some time before she was able. Days went into weeks and weeks into months. As I was talking via telephone to another friend, a dear friend of over twenty years, I mentioned this to her. She politely said, *"Do you mind if I go with you, seems that your other friend can't find the time?"* I was embarrassed in a sense for not even considering her as a companion for this excursion. I quickly told her that I loved the idea and that I would love for her to come along with me. We then made arrangements to attend a 'Spiritualist Church' the following Sunday. Sunday came and we finally walked through a door that started a new beginning for both of us. I was impressed by the lecture and the messages given from spirit by a Medium. I continued going periodically and started to realize from the different lectures that I had been experiencing things of this nature all my life, which confirmed my gifted abilities. I met the Reverend and chatted for a short time. I tried chatting with her on several occasions, but it appeared impossible without standing and waiting in line after the service. I tried going to the service early but there were always people ahead of me already speaking, and she was always busy until it was time for service to start. Eventually I got to speak to a couple of her advanced students and was given positive feedback about her teachings and mediumship. I tried to get into one of her classes but they had already started and were full, or this was the reason she gave. I had to wait along with a few others. I attended the open classes and learned from them, plus it gave me an extra chance to chat with the teacher, the Reverend. I eventually got into her class and was impressed with her teachings. It also gave me a chance to put forward and use what I have already learned through research. The Reverend knew I had this ability from attending the open development circle for the public. Once acceptance was in order she said that she could enhance my clairvoyance and spirit connection; and through her open class and her close class she most definitely did. I became one of her students and like the rest of her congregation, I respected the leader that she was and looked up to her for advice, extra spiritual knowledge and leadership. Here is a poem I wrote and presented to her in a frame. She seemed to be pleased with it. A couple of the words had been changed to conceal identity.

D's Poem

Words of praise I've got to share
For this person I know that cares
Compassionate feelings that you show
Makes your true light a brighter glow
Attention given to your congregation
Come one and all from all nations
Some early teachings I did miss
Now as your student I feel blessed
To get where I am I had to fight
I struggled alone for better insight
I knew of spirit and had to research
Restless as a Robin on its perch
Once I got proper information
I felt so good, found my salvation
Soul searching began, I came to you
Your good advice, direct and true
Enhanced my ability you once said
From knowledgeable advice that you give
Opens a new door for someone like me
I found my soul and set it free
It's soaring upward to higher realms
As one would read in the book of Psalms
This dedication is just for you
Your great teaching, well understood, too
Hands-on practice you teach so well
Explained and given clear as a bell
Years of practice made you aware
Willing to teach and anxious to share
Enlightened my soul like none before
The moment I stepped through your door
More development needed now's the time
I waited long for this but now it's mine
Once the circle began, I was in awe
Taught by the best, you gave your all

The friend that was supposed to have gone with me finally got a chance to go. She met and spoke with the reverend on a few occasions and attended open classes with me. Because she knew this person, I sent her this poem via email to get her opinion and this is what she said, *"This is one of the most beautiful things that you have ever written thus far."*

Unfortunately as I reflect back over the years I have come to realize that I was very gullible and pretty closed off to reality as many personalities and true selves are in hidden portrayal.

Be patriotic and also love the God of your understanding. Revise your priorities if you must, with you on top of the list because how can you be of service to others without love of yourself? When a person or a family expatriates and or relocates to another part of the world, propriety plays a big factor in how one adapts and adjusts to their new surroundings. Once you understand the reprisal of a certain country keep in mind that English independents of congregationalism are not all nondenominational.

Fond Memories

Introduced to you by a mutual friend we chatted for some time
Invitation offered to your home hospitality of England's kind
Your mom became known as nanny to me, face sparkled during my stay
Up in years, well able to go on weekend excursions we're on our way
North to the cottage we went four of us together
Travelled the distance one and all hoping for decent weather
Finally arrived, unpacked the car, placed it all in the boat
Nanny was next with little effort, we managed to stay afloat
Arrived at the dock safe and sound, secured the boat alongside
Nanny is unsteady, she may slip, in my arms we went for the ride
Up she goes, a little laugh, arms around my neck
I held her tight as can be, love, trust and respect, what the heck
A steep grade threatened our destination, nanny was my concern

Slowly but surely advancement was made, I held her strongly and firmly
Finally arrived at the door, no steps to get inside
Once again dear nanny is up in my arms again for the ride
I raised her about four feet in the air as I held her for awhile
Accepting my assistance willingly, once up, she gave a smile
Nanny Dines, I adored you so, your daughter's a devoted friend
On the other side now, in a new home, I think of you now and then
Fond memories stay within my heart; you know that now you're there
I feel your presence many times, great moments we did share
I see your smile, I feel your touch, you come to say hello
You're happy again not far away I knew you had to go
The man you loved had gone before; he patiently waited for you
When leaving this material world, somehow we all knew
He'd be there with open arms to hold you close to his heart
Gently, passionately as he had, now together, never to part
Love to you Nanny Dines

Nanny Dines had two beautiful daughters; one that became known as an 'eternal friend' once said by the older sister; we had shared many happy and spiritual times together. 'Eternal Friend'; How this came about had to be from a source she is not aware of, or wish not to share, as one has their own beliefs and thoughts of a spirit world and an afterlife. Whatever the case, and although she's 20 years my senior, I feel she hit the mark dead on. I feel eternity is exactly where we came from and where we're heading together. Anyone that has been as encouraging as she and continues to be comes from and surpasses, man's perception and the scientific lab.

My friend's sister who remains in the UK and used to visit occasionally became an acquaintance and we have remained in touch, although periodically, for several years. For some reason her birthday was special this year, and I sent an email with a poem. To my delight my poem was answered with one of her own. Personally I feel she outdid mine.

H's birthday, March 5th, 2003

Roses for a lady—A beautiful one indeed
Reflect back today a memory—To a time when you were in need
Of a special love to mould you
Another to hold you tight
For the past is but fond memories
Still remember that first kiss? Good night?
Happy Birthday

H's Reply

Oh, thank you for the flowers,
And for the poem too;
Your greeting quite made tears well up,
You old romantic, you!
The days of beauty long have gone
And ne'er will come again
But as you say, in later years
The memories still remain
(Most good, some rather naughty
Of wonder days gone by…)
But I still have the present
And days go flying by
With love of family and friends
And interests anew
I think that I am very blessed
In everything I do.
('PRICELESS')

Our songbooks of the world are full of knowledgeable information, chants, prayers, affirmations as well as poems. The next time you pick up a hymnbook take a good look at the words that make up the hymn or a spiritual song. A student of mine who has become a friend gave me an old hymnbook to take a look at, one that she found in an old house. I was thrilled with it because I saw things that I had not taken notice of in others. I began to read the songs and for the first time I began to take into account the messages that the writer or composer meant to get across to the people singing them. After having read most of the hymnbook I began to write down the messages that I felt were meant to be grasped. It covers much in that particular book as to what I felt is a personal message to me. I try to leave myself open to spiritual education and its interpretation as much as possible, as we all should leave room for everything in our lives. Having written this I began to read it. It has a message that's very understandable to most people, but it may take reading certain ones a few times before the message is grasped or what is meant for you. As you read please keep in mind that there's an afterlife in the spirit world, where each and everyone of us will go. What you haven't finished here on earth you'll take up right where you left off once you've crossed over. The earth plane is a school; we're here to learn; from our mistakes and errors we'll gain knowledge within ourselves so that we may direct our learning onto others. Each time I read this I feel a connection with God and get a sense of all his wonderful loving energy being sent forth, towards his entire "rainbow coloured" people of earth.

Songbook Prayers, Poems and Affirmations

Great Infinite Spirit: Abide with me till we meet again For truly death is a holy air all around us All is God's will for that of all common things	Bless all as one for all men are brothers Nature and all people are now seeing God as all things beautiful and all things bright.
What though angels descend again Angels from high and angels our brothers Arise O man as pants the heart Assembled at the author of good Awaken my soul to a beautiful home Be firm	If you believe not, bless ye the Lord The happy is blessed with love Blest are the poor and the scared Blest be the tie and blest are the spirits Blow ye the trumpet to break new-born year And breathe on me
Brethren awake to days brightly shining Brothers, will you, by each saving grace catch the sunshine? Cherish faith and the children's voices for they are in the city of God	When cold and cheerless, come gentle spirits Come to the father and come all loving courageous brothers For death is but a fading down the dark future
Each tiny leaf that earth is making Eternal father by whose hand But only from your eternal father, who art good He's our Great eternal God, eternal source, eternal spirit, God supreme	O thou who driest – the mourners tears Whose perfect goodness as truth thou art Worship the king ye who dare not O'er the truth of thy love
I'm floating on the breath of all blessings forever with the Lord He brings us beauty as we wait for the green spring and for those we love We go forth in thy name, forward press to conquer Forward as the day from the fountain of	Realms supernal sent from the Holy Land. From Thee all skill gentle twilight, go bury thy sorrows Go forth among the poor go forth ye heralds Go when the mornings come and God be with you till then

living waters Friends above hold firm and friends on earth never leave us For you are friends of truth For God moves within a mysterious plane	God is in each native fold for God is Spirit God is love with great mercy As God is love, let heaven shine
God of our fathers hear. God of our fathers in spirit God of the granite. God of the living God of the universe. The God that speaks to us The God that made us all We thank thee gracious source	Gracious spirit dwell, for as we sing you guide us truth Hail, all hail. Hail great creator Hail nature's source for we believe in you. Hand in hand, hark from grove
My soul angelic, a soul of thy fathers Hark my heart the angel voices For the songs of angels what do they mean? Hath not thy heart he liveth long For he who seeks Heaven, it's already here. Heavenly Father: Here at thy grave	Ye exemplars as holy ministers of light, Holy Spirit kindly bless us, Holy Spirit truth divine You're the rainbow of hope, how blessed are the sacred How pure in heart as you sweetly hush the tones Hushed was the evening hymn I ask not.
Life is the hour as light after darkness Light emits from the spirit world as we listen to the angels' message For it be words of kindness Live for something good For lo in the golden sky becomes a day of rest Look up O man	Kind words of knowledge in its empire Lead kindly light Let monumental pillars rise, let superstition fade Then let the still air brighten Let all that have a gladsome voice be life's dearest gift For life is onward
For you are a Lord of beauty, A Lord of the everlasting A Lord of the wide Thus Lord, as in eternal, your loved ones live. Loving Father:	Lord dismiss us Lord dismiss us now Lord God of morning Lord, keep us safe Our Lord of all being

Our father, God eternal Father God who art the light Our father we entrust Our God is love and all in peace Peace eternity.	As your pleasant peace Lay on this beautiful country O brothers, sisters, O call on this O come with us on our day of God Of everlasting lif
The heavens declare the leaves of autumn The Lord will stay amongst us For he has built an eternal force As real as the Lords my shepherd	Not on this day? Cause now in the tranquil of this wedded pair For now Lord you doth not part.
Our eternal Spirit source of all eternal wisdom Everlasting changing never far from mortal Father and friend Father, fill our souls and hear our prayers Lead me and let thy kingdom shine Father of all and lover of my soul Creator of earth oh hear my voice Proof of thy wonders as we look up to thee, Fill thou my life.	I cannot always see and cannot always find thee Yet I hear the angels As we hear your sweet voice We hear the kind words of Immortal love In darker days of nature's opening In the sacred books in the sky Love is there in this place for it came upon the midnight It is a truth for us and remains with us forever Joy and pain with joy bells ringing. Kind Father
Make channels and may the grace of your mighty spirit bring millions within Mourn amid God, my Father, for my heart was sad Nay speaks no ill Nearer my God Nearer my God with adoration Make new every morning with new wonders of you. No other creed Where no power can die	Oh Father bless us Oh Father great eternal. We give thanks To a God who is a God of love God our helper of all our light Whose will is of a gracious heart The God that holds our hearts most sacred Let me strive towards a God of heaven. O Lord of life a love that wilt Praise to God as a radiant sun

Sacred presence a source divine Spirit freed from evil as it sweetly sinks O thou, our father, God O thou the great unknown To whom as thou true life gave O thou who art the source We forever praise thee.	Purer yet and purer still Put thou thy trust in Infinite Spirit Rejoicing through storms Be reverent and listen Ring out the old Say not they die for loved ones remain To shine on our lives
Oft when of God The one and universal father: Onward comrades One by one as like the sands Open my eyes Our day of peace on our earth so green Make new every morning with new wonders of you. No other creed Where no power can die Silently the shades are drawn Sing to the Lord Sing ye your fathers slowly by God's hand Soft and low song of gladness Souls of men sow in the morn Spirit Divine, attend.	Peace, a welcome sound and praise the glorious Praise God, praise to the Lord Praise to thee ye the Lord Prayer is the soul's strength So press on pure souls To this wondrous world, The world hath felt, The world hath much. There's a sacred book in the land mines eye Step forward dear friends. Remain still and silently bow Still, still with thee O God. Summer suns as sweet are the ties Sweet is the prayer that binds
Sweet spirits hear us a star of hope Tell me not in mournful cry Tell me not my life be o'er Ten thousand beauteous days thou gave The dead are like a friend so dear The God of harvest we praise.	The morning light the outward world The purest bright records of time The spacious firmament the spirit world The true voice and turf on mind The voice of an angel The wise may bring
Spirits bright are ever nigh Spirits come stay with us Stand for the night As a star of progress	This land of pure beyond the veil Where there's no death, tell out For there's no death among the stars But a pathway towards a better land

There's good in everything Not a bird without it Not a tint that doesn't glow As everything bright that shines These things and all shall be blessed As they are winging and come at morn They come, they come they whose course The child that's dedicated a gladsome life This is your day of light.	Thou art O God a grace divine Thou great creative mind Thou great first cause who art enthroned Whose almighty words were born Brought the changings all about Throughout the night of doubt God Bless and Amen.

Prayer is everything, as I've heard many people say, but how many of us do actually pray? Well, I'll ask it this way; how many actually pray on a daily basis? When things go wrong and we need divine intervention we all speak words of prayer. Some will kneel down and give an outward cry for help while some others will sit in silence and send out thoughts of prayer to the God source. No one should be expected to pray daily but if you feel it's the right thing to do then by all means do it. God listens to your mumbled words, thoughts, and spoken prayers. He doesn't condemn you for which way you pray or in the manner that you give thanks. Keep in mind that he hears all and sees all because that part of God is connected directly to you as well as within you.

When our hearts become hurt they become hardened, that's a time to learn humility, but at that stage it's probably the biggest task one would have to conquer. Try intercession, prayer or meditation? Or if you have a good friend or know of a spiritual group you could ask them to be an intercessor for you as well as self-inner focus on forgiveness and acceptance.

Here are prayers and poems that give a sense of direction on what it means to send a prayer out into the universe.

<u>God's Listening</u> In earnest prayer the holy stream flows Where warn devotions dwell the theme sweetly glows Blessings desired grasps upward gaze Celestial love eloquence of praise Voices of sweetness heard by your ears God's heart rejoiced then dried bitter tears Spirit ascends utterance from out there God lovingly accepts the comprehended prayer	<u>A Prayer Recognizing God's Loving Power</u> Holy Spirit Divine: You've guided me on a path of understanding your law The powers that be are within your grasp Protect and lead me in your path of righteousness Wrap your loving arms around me as I envision the light of my loved ones Bring our souls together although we're in two different worlds Bind our love in your heavenly embrace For eternity. Amen
<u>A Prayer, a Song, an Affirmation</u> God, our creator. Within your eyes we're all brothers and sisters Let there be peace in our world Make each step a personal goal Take each moment so we may live in loving harmony Great Spirit, make peace on Mother Earth Peace eternity. Amen	<u>Angel Guidance Prayer/Affirmation</u> My Angels: As I've walked hand in hand with you, my eyes finally opened Your tender voices cheer me as we're heavenward bound You're leading me in the path of God's White light While your soft hands cover my mortal grasp You firmly hold my soul while walking to a higher source The chains that held me to earthly sorrows have been lifted Doubt binds my soul no more We're journeying to the loftiest Spirit, in higher realms above. Amen

Divine Intelligence—God—sent down the revelations. He also spoke of the hereafter and this has been scrutinized down through the ages. Most religions teach you to fear God and to be aware of the punishments due you for sins committed while here on earth. I went through that route, but I felt there had to be something else, something for the better. After giving this some thought in my later years, I still remember the words I heard my father repeat so often when I was a child, he would say that Jesus said, *"Those without sin cast the first stone".* Then he went on to say that not one stone was thrown. I guess we all have sinned in some form or another. So, if we're all going to be judged and punishment's going to be handed down then we'll have lots of company, won't we?

Let's teach our selves diligently because deception brings no justice to anyone. Try relaxation to a state of tranquility; most of us are actually omniscient. Below is an affirmation that you may speak aloud prior to a peaceful meditation. Following this are prayers of protection that you may want to use after the affirmation. I do recommend a prayer of protection when connecting with spirit through meditation. There are a few ending prayers you may use after you have finished your meditation and that you may use at any given time when you have finished your reparations.

A Meditation Affirmation Spirit, flow and release all my fears Use me to channel your love and peace Fill me with your power and make me strong Make me a receptor of your divine intelligence Heal me and let myself be renewed Express my perfection, as I remain loyal to you Fill me with your love, so I may also give love in return Fill me with devotion, so I may live for thee. (Some words used are of inspiration from a spiritualist song)	A Trance Prayer Heavenly Spirit of the universe: Surround me with your bright white light of protection Guide me inward as I search for you within my higher self Connect and present me with my spirit guide I'll rely on his guidance Enlighten my soul with your wonderful knowledge of existence Give me peace within Show me the way to project it onto others. Amen
God of love and light Protect me with your Infinite White Light Guide me as I go within to communicate with spirit Keep all evil entities away Give me your protection Safely lead me on my spiritual journey of meditation. Amen	Infinite Spirit Thank you for your protection Thank you for the contacts I've been given May your protection remain with me Make me more knowledgeable each day Lead me safely on my spiritual journey. Amen

Prayers of Protection and Thanks

Great Divine Spirit, I'm aware of your wonderful powers and abilities, Thank you for being with me at this time. Please make me aware while I sit in your presence. Bring spirit through to be by my side while I go within. Give me understanding of your presence so that I may gain knowledge from you when the time comes for me to do so Protect me with your white light and lead me to my higher self so I'll be in silence with your infinite spirit. Amen	Dear God, our universal light of love and peace Thank you for giving me a special guardian to watch over and care for me throughout my lifetime. Bring my personal angel into my sight so we may finally meet face to face for a better understanding of each other Bring my guardian with love and I will greet him or her also with love and endearment of appreciation. Amen
Our heavenly father of divine intelligence Guide me on my spiritual journey Keep me safe with the protection of your white light Surround me as I go within my higher self Guide me onward to meet a long awaited Spirit Make the meeting pleasant and peaceful Make it a loving contact as we meet. Amen	Divine light of the world: As I sit in your presence guide me to a heightened awareness of your wondrous powers Commune with me through a source of a divine intelligence so that I may comprehend all that's being brought forth. As you bring words of love and wisdom my faith looks up to Thee. Thank you and Amen

Who has the most authority and who has brought about prophethood? Some of us are unacquainted with who this may be. Take posterity for instance. Depending on the religion one has grown up with, some could actually be recognized, once reflected back through time, feel that they are actual descendants of Abraham, or

Isaac for instance. The inheritors of this bloodline are probably the same religion today as that which was chosen by those prophets. A chosen religion is like every other chosen belief and once one has taken to heart all the facts that are important to them, then they have gathered their harvest. We sometimes create our own destruction and do things that are prohibited by the laws of God, or the universe. Being self-sufficient in assiduous studies we're most certainly capable of being who God has meant for us to be and should be able to live in harmony with our fellow-men and women.

What is sin? Webster's dictionary says it's an offence against God; a weakened state of human nature in which the self is estranged from God; and it goes on to say that it's a fault.

We've all sinned at some point in our lives if that were the case. I refer again to the Christian Bible and The Ten Commandments. Breaking any one of those is considered a sin. As long as you stay away from the big one I feel that there's forgiveness in God's heart for all the others once it's been recognized by you and you've learned the lesson from the inner punishments given to yourself. In 1 Corinthians chapter 15 verse 34 it says, *"Awaken to righteousness, and sin not; for some have not the knowledge of God: I speak this to your shame."* There you have it, once recognized and you're delivered to your natural god-given state, live on and put the past behind you. Yet, then again in 1 John chapter 3 verse 9 it says, *"Whosoever is born of God doth not commit sin; for his seed remaineth in him: and he cannot sin, because he is born of God"*.

All well said-and-quoted; but does that make a person who has taken a grape to taste at a supermarket before buying, and then not buying them a thief and a sinner? How about taking a flower from someone's garden to give to a loved one or the 25-cent piece you pinched from your parents as a child? No, that's not really considered a sin in itself, it's similar to telling a little white lie to keep the peace and that doesn't make you a sinner. I could go on and on with examples, but I'm sure you see the big picture. Most of us are born of God but according to the commandments we do falter on occasions and God still loves us nonetheless. Below is a prayer asking for God's forgiveness for past minor sins that still lurk in the back of our minds only to resurface from time to time; first here's a poem to offset it.

Descendants from Afar

Children of Abraham come what may descendants of Noah's son's
Certain religious beliefs are strong we read of the chosen ones
We're all God's children one and all scattered across the nations
Being here on earth, individual souls, all of God's creations
Life on earth, a beautiful gift, given to us all
Follow God's rules, His loving thoughts; be aware of his natural laws
We are the ones, descendants of old, sent from heaven above
A beautiful soul, a human body, immortal, entrusted with love

Dear God of the Universe

We as children are born pure in heart
It's not easy for some of us to grow up as your will desires
We make our small errors in life
Yet life continues on and we continue to make more
My past errors and my so-called sins were of minor nature
I have learned from them and am now a better person because of it
Having you, Great Divine Spirit, by my side, has helped me tremendously
Your love and understanding has been my light of peace
Please forgive me for past sins and errors
I'll strive to continue to follow in your messenger, (Jesus') footsteps.
Amen

You may place the name Jesus with Moses, Isaac, Mohammed or any other prophet that you hold great respect for.

About nine years ago when I bought the house I'm presently in I decided that after all those years of wanting a little dog I was going to have one. Memories of childhood wishes caused me to search for my dream puppy. I investigated a few breeders and chose one that was close by. Distance was a factor as working full-time at a 12-hour shift job and a part time job on the side made it difficult.

I made a phone call and was told that there were two litters on the way. I waited in anticipation. Then finally I got a call saying that I could go and view them and choose my puppy. I chose a black one with four white paws and a white spot under her chin as there were no white puppies available. I was told that she was a 'teacup' Chihuahua. Cricket was born December 27, 1997.

I made a second visit to see her with a down payment as the cost was $800 and I was told this was cheap for a "teacup." When she was a little over five weeks old I was told that I could have her permanently. Excited to have her at last I went to a bank machine to get the last $100.00 to cover the cost. I happily took her and brought her home. To my surprise, at feeding time she couldn't chew her food as the dog food samples the breeder gave me were hard and her little teeth didn't seem to have developed enough. I did what any parent would do for a small child; it just so happened that I had chicken for dinner that day so I chewed some for her. Once placed by her nose she opened her little mouth and accepted it, only to want more. And, of course, she got as much as she desired.

I was impressed to take her back as I felt she was much too young. With more thought, which didn't take long, I came to the conclusion that she stays. She proved that she would eat chewed food so that's what I gave her, chewed human food, until she was able to do so, on her own. She was very small and wasn't able to walk well but within a week she was well on her way.

Unfortunately she grew a much larger size than a teacup and I felt cheated out of my money. Was I about to take her back after she's six months old and ask for my money back? Definitely not; by this time I loved her as one would love a child and was as protective as a mother with a new offspring.

She became center attention as a bond between human and animal is of such magnetic energy. Anyone that shares this bond could very well understand that this bonded love was meant to be, and may very well have been directed by an unseen force.

She grew quickly and brought much joy to my life. She alerted me on many occasions when I wasn't aware of someone about the grounds outside. She chased away many squirrels from destroying plants in my garden and alerted me to the racoons that came to eat the grapes at night. Needles to say, I still have yet to taste them, as the racoons always win in the end.

Cricket didn't turn out to be a teacup Chihuahua as her weight hovers around the six pound mark but she's very intelligent and easily trained to do tricks. She also learned to use a kitty litter box while in the house.

It's been ten short years now and although I have other animals she's as precious as the rest.

From past experiences I've received personal proof that there is a supreme being, there is a God. I've had prayers answered and didn't always have to wait long either. I didn't request material things, unless you feel that asking for a puppy is considered material.

After finding a beautiful little dog why would I ask for a puppy in prayer? Well, because I have two small dogs, one female, completely black, and the other is a black-and-tan male. I permitted the female to have two litters. The first litter of four was three black and one black-and-tan. Three were like the mother and one was like the father. Due to a car accident, a head-on collision, the driver, the owner of one of the puppies, was badly hurt and in critical condition.

(Here's how I summed Cricket up when I wrote poetry. I could add a lot more by now but choose to leave it as it is.)

Cricket	**Life and Light**
My gift to me was long overdue Wanted a friend that's loyal and true Looked for that one to hold close to my heart Searched Ad after Ad, didn't know where to start Finally I managed to fill that gap When we first met was like ball and bat To see such a beauty, held out my hands I held her so gently and felt real grand A precious little love right from the start She's meant to be mine, and never part Several years of joy she's brought to me Each time we meet I'm welcomed with glee I pray to spend many years with my friend With unconditional love until the end As time goes by she's brighter than gold For love of a puppy never grows old.	Time seemed so slow when I was young A child in a swing those songs I sung Pleasant courses of hymns oh how I knew Sang them with gusto as I grew Towards that light I knew was there Not far beyond but always aware The potential power it held within Confronted its meaning again and again Finally a new door opened my mind Knowingness was there but held in time Now that I'm older time travels so fast Subconscious awake, light recognized at last.

His wife and the black-and-tan puppy that were in the car with him were killed. While he was in hospital in an intensive care unit in a coma I told a mutual friend to whisper in his ear that if he decides to stay in our material world he'd get a replacement puppy. He decided to stay, and that's the only reason I let 'my small dog Cricket' have a second litter.

By this time I had been diagnosed with an illness that has no treatment and no immediate cure, and I wasn't permitted to carry on working. I was declared disabled which took a huge blow to my ego because I had never been without a job. Two weeks prior to the delivery of the second litter I had been home and unemployed, without any financial support for about three months. Needless to say, I was depressed beyond thinking properly and had to deal with this emotional aspect of my life without any emotional support. It was hard. I thought another little puppy would help. I didn't want just any little puppy, I wanted one that was almost impossible from my pair of dogs.

One day while I was sitting in the sunroom looking outside at the weather I was rubbing Cricket's tummy, which she loved. She was much bigger with this litter. I had to actually carry her about because it was very difficult for her to walk. This particular day, as I was rubbing her tummy, I closed my eyes and asked God, in prayer, for a big favour that one could consider as an impossible request. This prayer went like this:

Dear God
I know you can do anything you want to do.
You can do anything that is considered impossible.
May I please have a little white puppy, for me, and another black and tan puppy for my friend to replace his loss?
Amen

I continued to rub her tummy while visualizing God hearing my prayer. What will He do? I let it go at that and continued to want my prayer answered, but didn't dwell on it for it had been already asked?

Two weeks later she went in labour. I was well aware of what was happening as she spent most of her time in my arms. I was alone with the two dogs in the sunroom. I was rubbing her tummy and felt each contraction which alerted me when they were getting closer. I had her wrapped in a blanket with only her head sticking out; my hand was underneath still rubbing her firm little tummy. I was humming and singing softly to make her more relaxed and at peace when I felt a hard push. I said, *"Well Cricket, something just happened."* I lifted the blanket to take a look and 'lo-and-behold' there was my little white puppy, all of about four inches long, wiggling about struggling to break the sack from around her little nose so that she could breathe on her own. I was deliriously happy, I broke the little sack, watched her take her first breath, cleansed her little nose of fluid and then wrapper the blanket around them both and jumped up with joy saying, *"Thank you God, thank you God, thank you so much for my little white puppy. Thank you for answering my prayer."* I carried them downstairs to their room and continued to take charge.

Cricket had been a little reluctant to take care of her puppies, at the beginning with the first litter, and was doing the same now. For some reason it took 12 hours for her to complete the birth of her litter, both times. The puppies were anywhere from two to four hours apart. Thank God for a medical career as working in a case-room many years ago with human delivery I had gotten experience. I cut the cords and sealed them, cleansed the puppies as much as possible and kept them warm until she was ready to care for them herself. Two hours later I received the second portion of my prayer, the second puppy was granted. It was a black-and-tan male, an exact duplicate of the first that was killed. Once again I thanked God but with less enthusiasm because it was like the sire dog, and that's a 50% possibility of happening anyway. To make it an exception and more realistic as a part of the prayer; the second request in the prayer was granted in sequence of asking as the second puppy was identical to the one killed, making my prayer completely answered.

The rhythm (Song) below is something I felt came from an unknown source, the source that only comes from a Divine, God.

Beautiful G.G.

Loneliness has no tomorrows
Sadness no light in sight
When my life was filled with sorrows
I asked a favour from the light
There's a special little baby
Sent to lighten up my way
Since I met my little baby

She has brighten up my day
I used to dream about my baby
Its reality came with love
She was sent down from heaven
By the angels up above
Beautiful little G.G
Beautiful as can be
I do love my little G.G
Oh how she means the world to me.

I was impressed to move on with my spiritual advancement and it was not coincidental that I was introduced to another teacher just prior to my decision. They say, when one door closes another opens. This I agree with but, oftentimes one door is ajar and is known to be there before the other door closes as it had happened to me on a few occasions.

Once I met this wonderful woman I had the feeling that she would enhance my development to its maximum and now I'm very pleased to say that I'm glad I listened to my intuition. She gave me full attention when required and gave me the opportunity to catch up on what the last teacher did not wish for me to receive or learn. I was accepted unconditionally as she does with all that go to her for advice, help, assistance and the like. She's well known as a woman of talent and has mastered many gifts along the way with certification and diplomas to prove their authenticity. From the time she first accepted to read my first manuscript she became, not only someone capable of proof-reading written material but someone that I could reach out to at any time for support. Since that time I've grasped a greater understanding of my present endeavours and my future spiritual education and progression. A woman as giving as this deserves more than a poem and oftentimes I make sure that she gets it. She gave me the chance to grow and encouraged me to speak more in public and gave me the means to do so within her own church. She is not only the pastor and leader of my chosen church but we became friends. When I met Rev. Alva Folkes I was writing some poetry and I felt an impulse to write one for her. But as with others, and with time past, I could add a lot more but choose to leave it as it is, as this is the copy she has.

A's Poem

Polarity consultant, says sign on the lawn
Easy to see even before dawn
Contact is made with the spirit realm
Opposite of a psychic that reads a palm
A technique so different from everyday life
A lady so witty, sharp as a knife
A sweet disposition introduced to you
No falseness, no games, just honest and true
Once you've been in her aura's vibration
Awareness, togetherness, a loving sensation
She'll reach out to spirit to bring forth love
From loved ones past that views from above
Her wonderful talent she's so willing to share
For the believer, who's willing to dare
To venture beyond this material world
To grasp the messages sent in a twirl
Her understanding of spirit is so well advanced
Do not hesitate when taking a chance
You'll be more than pleased of what comes through
Great Spirit knows—it was meant for you.

Mothers:

Such a wonderful word as we call on her thousands of times during our lifetime. I feel so lucky and grateful to have had such wonderful parents and not a day went by that they didn't kiss and hug each other in front of their children. What a marvellous example to set. Although my father was an engineer they were never rich, nor poor, but there was always enough food on the table. Having eight children one couldn't be spoiled with material things, but we sure were spoiled with love and compassion. That was plentiful and we, the children, never hesitated to accept it. Not only did they have hungry mouths to feed; there were those in the neighbourhood that required help and it was gladly given. Plus, they were always there to lend a helping hand when things needed fixing. There were many people in the town of similar manner but I know my parents better; therefore, I'll speak only of my experiences because things look differently in the eyes of a child than that of an adult.

My father passed to spirit eight years ago and my mom has since met an old acquaintance, which the whole family approves of.

A couple of years ago on Mother's Day, which is still recognized and respected in Canada, I decided to write a poem for my mother as she knew I had written for others.

I could go on and on as to how good both of my parents were, but the poem itself expresses a considerable amount of affection towards someone that has given me birth and stood by me for over half a century.

A Childs Reflection

So many children to attend with love
We both know help came from above
I remember the hard times and also the good
Those times you heated our house with wood
You cared, you shared everything you owned
All eight children came from a happy home
Day trips by water how did we keep afloat
Cause once all in the Flat was a bloat
Family picnics were many up the bay
Fresh lobsters, some mussels along the way
As I reflect back couldn't ask for better
My friends were welcomed it didn't matter
Happy times remembered berry picking and all
Blue berries by the gallons close to the Fall
You worried at times way beyond belief
Now we've all grown you feel great relief
But a mother's concern will never falter

Her caring continues for her sons and daughters
Family expansions, have grown a lot more
Those grandchildren of all she now adores
A new life has started since my dad passed away
She has my blessings each and every day
I know deep down she's my dear mother
Though a little change some way or another
My heart still cares for this wonderful mom
Cause when we were kids life wasn't a song
Oh how she managed to raise us all
Not one has faltered but some a slight fall
I know you know this and still remain true
Your child number three—loves and adores you.
(Love to Verna and Albert Brown, my parents. February 14, 2003)

The vitality of ancient enunciated words inscribed so long ago continues to change people's lives. What has been written tends to keep faith with those who have been taught with sentiments. Even today incantations are used by those who have lost that little bit of faith or hope and have reverted to such use. What they've accomplish only the affected person truly knows. Life, as we live it, has been set for us all; some believe in karma and some believe that our selves have prepared our destiny in life, prior to birth.

Although this may be a possibility, I personally believe we have the ability to change our so-called predestined futures by free-will and freedom of choice. Most of us believe in a God, some do not. Spiritualist believes in natural law and a divine spirit with a major practice in meditation. People of the Buddhist faith also hold meditation, as a major practice, but without the belief in communication with the Divine/God or the spirit world. A few years ago I worked with a Buddhist. She went to many retreats for meditation and was one of their best participants. She had encouraged me to attend but I declined continuously because I practised meditation at home and within a spiritualist group. I didn't need to spend big bucks to receive what I could accomplish right in my own home. I once asked if she believed in a God, and we had quite a long talk without giving me a complete answer. I also asked if she heard voices and or spirit people chatting to her when she was in a deep meditation. She said she did. I asked if she spoke to them and she said "no I do not, I just tell it to go away because I don't believe they're there." I said "well, I assume you don't believe in the spirit world and continuous life after the body dies." She said "no she did not;" and also added that "when you die you die, nothing more." Okay, all very well said, I thought. The reasoning behind the chatting in her head, she said that it's your own thoughts and chatting to yourself. I would personally dispute this as I know better from self experience and that of many others. I didn't confront her as we were in the work place, and if I did, what would it prove?

Previous experience holds a deep appreciation for prayer prior to meditation, which brings the mind into silence. Therefore, creating a path to God and providing a window through your mind. Below is a poem that all can relate to, considering the way life can be at any given time.

Life's Lessons

Creation is divine influenced
Direction given with love
Set free in a material world
Guidance from above
Go make your daily errors
That's a way to learn
Reflecting back like mirrors
You notice you've got burned
A natural law says, "What will be will be"
Yet at times you can be your own worst enemy.
When difficulty is brought, sometimes upon yourselves
Common sense alerts, anyone that delves
Go ahead and be who you're meant to be
Keep your eyes open, so your mind will see

Minds will register information to your brain
Soul will define, and refine it to keep you sane
As we make our mistakes in life
Understanding's a precious dove
Nothing comes to us in strife
God gives unconditional love.

In the beginning of law and order, when the rulers took counsel together, they sat in the seats of leadership to create and govern the rules and regulations of our world. Using God as their idol they delighted in the laws that were passed down by Him. They, as a counsel, had the ability to scrutinize and put forth a man-made version that was given and presented to the congregation of the righteous. Although you may hear a scornful cry from certain individuals or groups, those laws and regulations seem to have had a big impact on their followers; and also a big impact on the people who were not, and tend to differ in opinion. Who documented all those laws and why are they so different from one religion to another? Man's influence? Believe if you may, but you also have free-will and may also choose to disbelieve. Below are words of prayer, poetry and affirmations. Choose from it what you feel reaches that part of your being and what you can also associate yourself with in the hidden aspects of your soul.

Aspects of the Soul

Blessed are those that trust
When in distress you'll be enlarged
Hear my prayer I create no fuss
Have mercy and don't disparage
My sepulcher, be it a grave
You have not chastened me
Change of iniquity before you God
Persecute not and deliver me free
Be mindful, your marvelous works
Destruction is a perpetual end

Everlasting is definite
I'll be the avenger
The heathen will not be rebuked
Hearken thyself to a strong reprimand
Do not deny your God
Memorial won't perish but endure
Triumph will prevail, search and reach out
Do not persecute, especially the poor and the unwise
Be a humblest
Vanity has its faults and creates mischief
Adversity will cease, be proud and love God.

My daughter forwarded me an email, which said 'A friend's test.' I didn't send the same one back as it requested to show that I loved her as a daughter and a friend. I sent a personal reply called:

Friend's Test Echo

I know you're not asking—But maybe it's so.
A daughter like you—Sets my heart aglow
So when it comes to an FW like this—I'm on the boat so don't think I missed
An opportunity to express—What moves to and fro
That I love you very much—And yes, you already know.
For now I expressed my love for you—Think joy, hearts no longer sad
Good Night my angel—God bless you—Love from dear old dad

Affirmations are very helpful; they're positive statements that affirm moral responsibilities bringing an individual happiness through spiritual laws governed by the God source. Hold your thoughts of affirmation; take time to meditate on them while keeping God and spirit close by to awaken your idle mind.

Affirming Gods Leadership

Your wonderful power; Great Spirit of light
I trust in you more each day
Your true laws will grant me communication with those up above
Enter my consciousness and teach me to help mankind
Comfort me so that I'll give through the love of you
Guide me as I pray for strength and courage to gain wisdom
Peace has entered my heart draw it near to those I hold dear
Love is the true meaning of your great spirit
Guide me, lead me and use me as your scepter
Thank you

Many people come and go in our lives. Some leave not only their footprints on our hearts but an in-depth amount of love and joy that will remain with us and will continue so, even up to and when we cross the veil to meet once again.

In my medical profession, as well as with others that deal with the general public and with the same people continuously, we find certain individuals that blend with our aura and are on the same energy level or vibration of our own. Most that touched my inner soul and heart seem to have been the elderly; those that many push aside for various reasons only known to them. The elderly have been, or appeared to be, more of a challenge as they had years of growth and learning and came to a stubbornness, sometimes beyond a breaking point. I am also attracted to young inquisitive children that are at a learning stage where they continue to ask question after question. In the bible it says that you have to be that of a child to enter the kingdom of heaven. To me this would mean that you have to acquire the innocence as that of a child because a child is born in innocence. It's later on in life that they learn not to be.

Various women and men have brought a greater understanding of life and what it had to offer them. They shared it with me willingly once the barrier of communication was broken. For such people to trust another after years of neglect and sometimes abuse is a major step. Friendship never dies when one is apt to allow it to grow and prosper, which I permitted. Even though I met most while they were ill and in my care, we became friends. After their treatments I had many invitations to various occasions but declined most due to the fact of crossing boundary lines of a caregiver and client. But once it was safe and within the guidelines of my contract with the medical college, I didn't hesitate with a few of them as I knew they would further prosper with having a friend, and many did.

One such lady is a woman named Maria. She brought tremendous joy to my soul as I had hers. She would look forward to my visits when opportunity permitted. When I picked her up I would drive her to different places; places she no longer had access to and family were not prepared to take or spend the time with her. What a magnificent woman; truly blessed and adored by the Spirit, and by me. She was a precious gift that shared her wonderful loving self with someone that cared: me. I sent a card to her, via post, with roses on it; and oftentimes I gave her flowers from my garden to plant in her own. Here's the personal verse/poem I included.

Maria's Blessing

There's this lady I know so well
When she phones how I can tell
The excitement to hear that she's at home
Not somewhere ailing and all alone
Her disposition accurate and so true
A woman as you; like roses and dew
Beautiful inside as well as out
Your soul is from God—that there's no doubt
Protection and guidance coming from above
Yellow roses from me, comes with love.
Love to you my dear friend Maria

She now has passed to spirit and visits me occasionally, which I gave permission before her earthly departure. I gladly welcome her beautiful face as it smiles down upon me as it did so often while here on the earth plane.

When our great prophets and messenger's eons ago started to write words of wisdom, love, harmony, peace and words to make you fear a God who loves you, they had the idea and hopes of creating subtlety. When one has a desire to be humble prosperity will succeed and remember, discretion will preserve you as it probably has many times during your lifetime. A 71-year-old woman, who was once a client/patient of mine, and I became friends through a hospital setting. I wasn't able to stay in my career due to a disability that had slowly crept up on me with devastating effects on my personal well-being. One day while I was out I met her at a shopping mall; we had coffee, chatted about her health and her interest in spiritual matters. She was raised a Roman Catholic and remained devoted to her religion all her life. Although she had a very strict religious background she remains open to others' views. This led to a once a week chit chat over coffee and as we socialized we began to enjoy each other's company. There are many days I felt much older then she, due to my illness, although she's twenty years my senior. Never-the-less we cheered each other up and held mutual respect; sometimes I didn't know who was assisting whom in walking although I look and appear much better in health. She often seems to have a more balanced posture and a better gait then I. One day she presented me with a poem/prayer that she received from her church; she was very impressed with it. The words flowed in rhythm and were very nice, but I was also impressed in a different sense. The message in the words was that if you carried a cross in your pocket or on you, God would protect you.

If you feel protected by carrying a small cross on your person then by all means do so. I was raised with a somewhat similar belief and I still have one or two in my home.

Getting back to my friend and the poem she was so proud of. I asked if I could borrow it so that I could, in perspective, answer it. She handed it over but I sensed her fear of me criticizing it beyond her understanding. That I assured her I would not do. Once home in a peaceful environment I sat and meditated for a few moments and then began to write. Below is the answer to her poem/prayer. This is in my first book but it's worthwhile repeating here as you may not have read it. I gave her a copy to place alongside the one she has; and yes she was also very impressed with my written response.

A Reminder of God

You carry a cross in your pocket a Christian you may be
It's not magic, a good luck charm or a means to protect thee
That cross is a reminder of a price he had to pay
But for what reason had he died on that frightful day
You strive to serve him better in everything you do
But God protects from physical harm and takes care of you
The cross simply reminds us to comfort and bring peace
Yet Jesus is our brother and that will never cease
He'll be there when you need him as well as God above
A Christian will go through him reaching for divine love
For God our infinite spirit is the one and only law
No need to have a reminder; he will not let you fall
Jesus Christ is Lord to a person of Christian faith
But as a renowned Spiritualist living by God's grace
Infinite Spirit my master, Jesus Christ my brother
Divine Spirit and Jesus Christ I love you like no other
Connecting God through another source doesn't do any harm
Allah, Buddha, Mother Mary welcomes with open arms
They're all connected to our God and if it satisfies you
Continue on with what you do but respect the other few
That directly goes to the greatest source Infinite Spirit Divine
I do this with my daily prayer, because a true God as this is mine.

My lovely and cherished friend died August 2007.

In our youth we take a lot of things for granted. In our middle age we oftentimes reunite through some means such as a sense of loss or one wishing to reunite for various reasons. Over the past a few old acquaintances had gotten in touch, which I welcomed and a couple that weren't so much, but accepted just the same. While old memories reminisce, old friendships don't always prosper. Making that contact is often important to many and those who wish should be granted as reasons exist for wanting so. Such a person and I got together a few years back and our friendship continued as if we were not apart for that 15 years. She's mentioned earlier but friends cannot be mentioned enough when love binds the bond. Here is a poem that many in my home town can relate to and also those who lived in a small town as a child, such as I.

Distant and Loving Friends

Let's take a moment, go back in time
When we were young and free
This beautiful woman I once knew
Has always been there for me
Young adults not realized that inner bond
Somehow we kept that connection
We held each other at arms length
But embraced our souls through loving reactions
Old cottage hospital was but a dream
For people as you and I
Happy days gone by but not forgotten
Yet it wouldn't, if we tried
To relive those memories once again
Would be a gift from heaven
To witness things from Paton Place
With Nurse V. and Dr. K.
But nothing will mar that wonderful feeling
That once we all did share
Kitchen was off to certain folks
With E. E. Mae who would dare
Although old cottage has been torn down
Memories still remain
Within our hearts we both know
God made us, one and the same

Together as friends but far away
Our hearts still keep in touch
A treasured friend, that friend is you
I love and respect so much.
Happy Birthday; dear friend
March 18, 2003

Faith and trust unlocks doors to the spirit world and gives one connection with God. As we link ourselves to the universal powers we find that the most powerful gift is prayer. One of the world's greatest messengers of all times believed in prayer and spent many hours doing so, this wonderful soul is Jesus Christ. His prayers were very forceful and powerful.

Believe in prayer, ask for protection, trust in a God and live life to its fullest as in this world all things are related, interconnected and interactive with others. Never close the doorway to reformation if it's going to be for the betterment of others and for you. God will never turn his back on those who seek his help. As a renowned Spiritualist I also seek assistance from my guides and spirit helpers; they're always close by to give of themselves as well as the divine source. Set your foundation, grow upwards and give of yourself. Our life journeys and the missions that we accomplish here on earth will bring our progression to a finer understanding with knowledge and expectations about life on the other side. As you assist, give of your learnings and wisdom so that you'll make a contribution to the world. Below is the spirit-call that my students repeat in unison at the beginning of class. They quietly summon the spirit world, with a chosen person continuing on to say the beginning prayer prior to meditation. At the end of the class, just before the students leave, the same person says the closing prayer. They are as follows:

A Song, a Chant, to Spirit

Come to me Great Spirit
You're surrounding me

Bring forth many contacts
Those that come from thee
Enlighten all the power
That I do possess
Use me as your scepter
So I may confess
The message brought from loved ones
From the other side
Enhance my mind Great Spirit
With me you'll abide.

Beginning Prayer
Great Divine Spirit
Thank you for bringing us together
Cover us with your heavenly white light
Protect us as we go within
Send forth our Spirit Guides
Bring us loving contacts from the other side
Heighten our awareness so that we may be a bearer of your divine love.
Amen

Ending Prayer
Thank you for being with us and for your protection
Thank you for the connections from the other side
Guide us safely home to our loved ones
So that we may gather again in your presence
Amen

House Blessing and Protection
Divine Infinite Spirit
I'm calling on you to grant us your blessings

Please bring forth your love and peace
Completely surround our home with your white light of protection
Bless this house with Your Divine Power
Fill our home with love as you carefully watch over us
Keep us happy together under your guided laws of the universe
Open our hearts to a better understanding of your love
Make our home a happy environment as we live in harmony
Keep us healthy and safe so we may continue to provide for our children
Give us your protection as we commute back and forth to work
Keep guard over our souls so we may continue to worship you
Protect us and our property, now and always. Thank you. Amen

A Poem for Peter Ferris

I woke up this morning as every day I do
The sun was brightly shining the sky a perfect blue
I happily walked outside—sunrays fell on my head
My car started as usual but I chose to walk instead
I remembered my assignments; exams had passed them all
I held my head proudly thanked God for such a windfall
God, thank you for your protection as things go my way.
He lovingly said, “My Child, you’re granted this every day.”
You blessed me as usual and always a metaphor
You never seem too busy to grant it more and more
I haven’t had a sickness where I didn’t regain my health
No major financial problems you’re acceptance a part of my wealth
I’m never in need of clothing you direct me to a sale
Food is plenty when I need it you see to that as well
You never ignore me Great Spirit as I go about my day
When I needed something, you gave, in your own way
You’re there when I need you, every day of my life I’m told
When all things are going good I tend to put you God, on hold
You provide me with shelter—sometimes it’s not enough
At times I get selfish when my wants become material stuff
I don’t have to kneel, to show you my gratitude

Understanding God, like you Great Spirit, I sit quietly and converse with you
I will never need to put my God to a test
Cause as I reflect back, many times I have been blessed
I have always realized, what Infinite Divine had to say
For when I sit and meditate; with God my way to pray
Great God will compliment, as we learn to accept and forgive
Remember our true selves each and every day we live
When hardships arise take a good look at the impact
Go within yourself search the answers and then re-enact
Don't hesitate to seek what life has to give
Go for the maximum and don't forget how to live
Fill your daily life with joy; help alleviate a task from a friend
A simple smile, a casual hug, is a great way to begin
Pass this on to everyone, especially Peter Ferris
When someone sees the negative side, hold him or her in dearest
Peter, learn to love your God whoever that may be
Remember,
God loves us unconditionally.
Call on and trust him at your own accord.
Love and Light.
God bless

Above poem relates to this:

ALTHOUGH YOU'RE OFTEN CHALLENGED, GOD DOES NOT TEST YOU.

SOMETIMES IT'S WHAT WE BRING ON OURSELVES.

YET ONE IS ALWAYS ABLE TO LEARN AND BENEFIT FROM ITS TEACHINGS.

This is a statement I sent to my daughter to pass on to her friend who had sent her a poem about The Lord, God, and Jesus Christ. It was a touching poem in a sense, but my daughter decided to send it on to me for some unknown reason, maybe to get my opinion, something she has always valued.

It had to do with how God, Great Spirit, and the Prophets tested us from time to time and I feel that it was presented in a negative manner. It struck me as being wrong and it encouraged me to meditate on it for a while. Then I wrote a response. I hadn't included what she sent as I don't know where it came from, and whether or not there were any copyright laws. This is my response which she passed on to the friend who sent it to her. This friend has given me permission to use his name.

I asked Peter for his views on the poem and also reminded him that God is within us, as well as all around us. He gladly sent a reply. With his permission I chose from it what I felt was appropriate to be included here.

> **His reply:** (with permission).
>
> I feel I need to give a little background concerning my views on religion/God. I was raised Christian, baptized as well as christened and confirmed. When I was in high school, I found an old bible that included the rules a priest had to follow. It was then that I began to really question what "God" was.
>
> I began to get interested in the stories and the meaning or messages that went with them. I began to divert and began to read mythology from other areas. Greek, Roman, African, etc. and there's a huge similarity between the messages. I started to think that we as human beings invented God(s) to make us feel less alone in the world. That was my viewpoint for most of my high school and part of my university life. I started taking Kung Fu and my Sifu (instructor) told us a Koran (story). After that I began to think more and more on the story and realized that it didn't quite fit the stories of other religions, but it still carried a message. Further looking into it I came to Buddhism, the looking into self and growing from within. I liked that aspect of a divine inner self—one

growing through self-knowledge and self-growth.

So taking all of this together, I feel "God" is something that people believe in to keep themselves in balance. I don't see "God" as good or bad but neutral. I don't believe there is a devil or a type of God that the catholic religion believes in. I tend to think that there is a desire in each of us to be balanced—which I came to realize that religions all have equal, God/Devil, inner peace, Mother Earth/ Father Sky, Zeus/Hades, which all have some balancing force, or is centered around being balanced.

Taking this to a larger aspect, I periodically see the world as unbalanced. I feel people are too worried about material things and not about the actual world we have to live in and balance with. I think that is the reason why an underlying principle of wars and diseases are going on today.

My opinion on this poem is that it's understood by most people on a simple level and has a good message in its contents. It gives me the feeling of longing for something.

Life sounds like 'a life of little hardships, no challenges, or ones that do not seem that difficult to overcome.' My life has not been hard. I've been very lucky, and, for the most part, happy.

The grades mentioned tend to be a result of our inner selves and the work done in obtaining those grades resulting in the choices that were made.

I see not the blessing that came from God but the decision to make a positive change in life for the better.

I don't think we should always have to be thanking God—but rewarding ourselves for making the decisions to better either our life, or something—someone else's life.

> I remember one thing distinctively from the Catholic religion—God is everywhere—I see God as inside everyone—letting us make our decisions—Good—Bad—or middle of the road. I tend to believe that good ones eventually balance out bad decisions—and good decisions are a result of learning from past mistakes. **Peter.**

A beautiful answer from a young adult, don't you think?

When all this was taking place I was in perfect health. Who's to say what lies ahead? Make each day a wonderful and loving day as one doesn't know what tomorrow brings.

The portion below was written over eight years ago.

There are many major disasters in our small world at the moment, and many other smaller ones happening all the time which we're not even aware of and will probably never be known to most people. Nevertheless, innocent people suffer and die because of it. I joined a Spiritualist church a couple of years ago, but I still follow the loving teachings of Jesus that was taught to me by my parents. In honour of all the innocent people of the world and the people involved, whether volunteered or involuntarily; I decided to write an article and had presented it to the National Spiritualist Summit. The summit is a monthly magazine published by the National Spiritualist Association of Churches in Glendale, Arizona, USA and distributed to patrons of that faith via private mail or through a church organization. I can't be certain if they published it or not.

Don't take to heart and don't believe everything you read, hear or what you have been taught in the past. Deal with the here and now; concentrate on who you are and what you have become because of it. After all it's an individual or a group of individuals agreeing on the same subject. Take for instance the interpretation of the Bibles of different religions of the world. Read and listen, but take from it only what you feel is important and what pertains to you. You're also an individual with a mind and soul all your very own. Value your own opinion as well as that of others and especially value what you receive from intuition, psychic awareness, and from God. The God I know and respect is a loving, merciful, and forgiving God. It also says this in The Holy Bible as well as in The Holy Quran/ The Koran. Yet then again it also contradicts itself several times by saying that God is revengeful and will punish severely for different reasons mentioned. Human beings have interpreted those Bibles. From articles that I have read I realize that there's a lot left out and or added because of control. I believe that your God and my God will not punish in any way. God will bring on awareness and let us be the judge of our own faults and sins, giving us the opportunity of decision-making to sentence and punish ourselves. Judging ourselves beyond the veil takes on a totally different aspect. Judgement will be severely given by none other than by our selves. As a spiritual being we become more aware of the saying,"What we sow so shall we reap;" therefore, giving each individual soul the ability to sentence themselves accordingly. Moreover, granting us the ability and providing us with the decision-making, taking in account of past ire, and to give ourselves the most effective punishment for lessons that need to be learned.

Stillness, quietness, and inner peace is received through meditation. Once there, listen to the God within, ask questions through the thought process, and listen for the answers. Answers will be sketched in your mind on your inner slate: images and scenes will be presented on your inner television screen. Seek the God within and once there you'll most likely find the correct answers through awareness.

When we were children most of us had spiritual inner peace but as we approached adolescence some of us tended to lose it and lean towards an indispensable thinking. Some of us felt indestructible: beyond harm; creating a number of deaths at an early age through accidents and self-neglect. Many are more fortunate in adolescence, getting through it with minor cuts and bruises. Some experience little difficulty because they have never lost the awareness given to them at birth or lost that contact with the God source throughout their lifetime. Once living through the difficult adolescent stage we tend to change as we mature and take a closer look at our spiritual selves as we again begin to start our search for God. We remember our childhood and the peacefulness we once had that stayed buried deep within our subconscious mind. We recognize and resurface once again as we're now ready to accept, focus, and press onward to meet that spiritual individual that has always been there.

We all know the same prayer said by many, whether together as a group or as many individuals, has a major effect. The power of thought put together as a prayer, then sent out into the universe as thought energy, can create a balance where needed getting attention from God, our Divine Intelligence. It may take a while for an answer or to get a desired effect, but it will eventually get the recognition and attention that's required or desired, if love and peace are involved.

This time in our world there are many disasters, new viruses to contend with and incurable illnesses popping up from who knows where. Also, there seems to be unending wars.

Below is a prayer. Please say it with me and feel free to share it.

World Peace Prayer

Great Divine Spirit, Lord Jesus Christ, Blessed Mother Mary,
Buddha, Krishna, Allah
and all other names referred to as God.
Dear Heavenly Spirit, hold all innocent people in your loving hands.
Protect them all.
Bless our care-takers for the selfless acts they feel
they have to commit to protect our world.
Guide them with as little harm as possible as they protect the
innocent.
Grant peace within and between the countries of our planet
Let there be a quick solution to all problems
Make our world a safe and happy place to live.
Omit all hatred and wars.
Watch over all of your many wonderful different-colored people
of the universe.
I ask this in your name.
"Amen."

To be spiritually-minded is to live life in harmony and peace. Peace is found within, or you won't find it at all. It doesn't lie in the external world; it lies within your soul.

It's through your own soul that the voice of God speaks, which is the light of every one. This is the conscious, the intuition, the voice of your higher self, the voice of the soul, the voice of God.

When you realize the great fact of oneness of all life and that we all partake from one infinite source, we recognize that the life of one individual is the same as another. Once prejudice and hatred cease we'll then recognize God within our fellow man (which includes women); love grows and reigns supreme.

In the Christian Bible it says, "Enter into thine inner chamber and shut the door." To me this is understood as going into the silence through meditation as we're guided by our own soul communicating with the higher self and with God.

Buddha said to his disciples, *"All that we are is the result of what we have thought: it is founded on our thoughts: it is made up of our thoughts."*

Natural law indicates that God is no respecter of persons, races or nations. God didn't create the many leaders as such; God created all men and women as well as everything else in the world. Take for instance, people in biblical times, they expected to see angels and they did; many people see them today. Universal laws haven't changed; why shouldn't we see them today as well as back then.

But that's like everything isn't it? If we keep doors closed to our angels or we don't invite them they don't come; unless, of course, we need them immediately and they hear our cries. When you open yourselves to the highest inspirations they'll never ignore you. The power source of the universe will continue to work and manifest through you. All you have to do is open yourself, recognize it and follow its divine guidance.

I received a document in the mail a while ago. I anxiously opened it only to be shocked by its contents. This document came from someone I respected and looked up to. After reading it I thought to myself, I don't deserve this and no, I didn't. Maybe I read it differently than it was intended or maybe I was in a down frame of mind to begin with. Whatever the case, I felt as if I had been degraded and was discouraged by someone I always felt was the most spiritualist person I had ever met. Ten years ago something such as this would have left my mind like water off a duck's back. It wouldn't have bothered me in the least.

Being in Spiritualism for a number of years has changed me to a spiritual level that I have come to realize that some comments do hurt. Even though I'm a man, and sometimes people think that being a man one can take more abuse just because of that. Well, a spiritual man and a spiritual woman are very sensitive to others' feelings and are in total awareness of their own, especially when negativity comes from another supposedly spiritual person. Hence, "A Medium is a sensitive."

Mr. Douglas Marshall, president of the board of my current spiritual location said, *"Something like this can't hurt you, only if you let it."*

You know, no matter what we do in life someone will complain, someone will criticize, someone will make a snide remark, someone will give a look of disapproval and someone will be downright rude and verbally put you down continuously and intentionally while spreading gossip of untruths.

Is this love and spiritually minded? Indeed not.

The world has many lessons, but, if we but realize the law of retribution will never change and will always be in effect; we all reap what we sow, oftentimes ten fold. But, here's something that you may not realize: there'll always be someone there to help pick you up and assist you through your hardships if you but only reach out. A kind word, a good deed, a smile of appreciation or a nod of recognition and approval is what makes members of any chosen religion 'a spiritual person.'

From many books written concerning Spiritualism by our pioneers, and I read many, it states over and over again, serve your fellow man and serve him and her with love and compassion. Basically, it tells us to do what Jesus taught to his disciples.

While I was having my down-and-out, I had a strong desire to phone someone whom I looked up to, respected and appreciated. She gave me the best advice one could give to another. I listened, she expressed her hurt and feelings regarding how I felt. Plus she took a lot of 'my hurt and anguish' on her own shoulders. Needless to say, I felt a lot better and put such trivial matters behind me.

It's wonderful to have such a friend as this; this friend is the Minister of my current spiritual location. She has said on many occasions, "*I'd do it for all my members and for anyone in need.*"

God works in ways that we sometimes find hard to comprehend, but one comes to realize its wonders and recognizes the amazing aspects of it the longer one remains a spiritual person. By saying that, that very same day I received an email, from a church member that contained something God wanted to bring to my attention, or that's how I perceived it. I'm going to share this with you. It's called, 'Daily Guru,' taken from Elder's Meditation of the day. "*The ego wants to elevate itself in any way it can. It will happily set off on the spiritual path because it enjoys the feeling that is becoming more spiritual. It loves spiritual knowledge and power.*"

Immediately I questioned myself; did my ego get in the way? Well, I didn't think so, and I sure hope not.

It went on to say:

"It will continue on the path as long as it continues to accumulate more spiritual knowledge or power. In other words, the ego is becoming spiritualized, which is most unhelpful for one who is truly committed to full awakening. The illusion that we need to awaken from is the world of the thinking mind, which includes all our spiritual knowledge and concepts. Just focus on what is here now. If you can see it, hear it, feel it, taste it, or smell it, you can focus on it. This focus will bring you to the truth of life. All you have to do is bring yourself into that which is present."

Lelia Fisher said, *"Wisdom comes only when you stop looking for it."*

When I was about to stop writing for the day I received another email from a church member. In it were a couple of short paragraphs that I would also like to share with you. It said, *(1) We are here to ensure the movement into the "new earth" reality. We have had visions of living in complete harmony with nature, others and the earth consciousness itself. Now is the time to stand in the power of our own "knowing" and to trust the wisdom of our authentic self. (2) The storm of fear which surrounds so many may get stronger; be the light, the beacon for others who are not yet awakened to themselves.* (Author unknown to me.)

We can learn much from others and those that come from the source of 'Love and Light.'

Whatever we do in life there's a purpose behind it, whether we're aware of it or not. We gain knowledge and we try to fulfill our life's missions. As we grow and learn spiritually we come to understand that love is one of the best expressions we can give. It's one of the most sought after in every human being, animal, and or bird. Humans need validation and love is taken very seriously.

Love is the power of life. God loves us all equally, He has no favourites, we're loved just the way we are. His Divine love is what moves the universe, for love is the reason we're here and it's the most important thing in life.

Someone you don't know can't hurt you like someone you love or feel a close kinship towards; a little sneer, an unkind word or something as simple as a look of disapproval can alter an innerness of discontentment and sadness. That's intimidation.

Just try some random acts of kindness for someone that you feel could use it and you'll be amazed what you'll receive in return. Show consideration, treat people with compassion, help and care, understand, forgive, and serve one another; the poor as well as the rich, as love reigns supreme. Helping others should be our primary purpose in life with goals of important accomplishments in mind. We need not pretend perfection; the person that often sits next to you isn't perfect either when it comes to actually being what the word means in our dictionaries.

Don't search too hard for that perfect man or woman to be in your life; that special someone may not be found, but yet, it may very well be as close as living next door or a working colleague.

We may be perfect in our thoughts and actions but sometimes we falter badly with ourselves, and with others. Reality strikes when we realize we're not as perfect as we thought we were. We need not hide or bear shame. Let's take responsibility for our mistakes and then life becomes more realistic.

Perfection is a matter of what one perceives it to be. There are times when you find fault in yourself so chances are you'll definitely find fault with everyone else about you, given the right amount of time and circumstances. Whether you voice that opinion or not it's there nonetheless, and oftentimes expressed through body language. Acceptance of another brings happiness and love. We're all born in perfection but we all become imperfect at some time or another.

Life's mission has a guiding principle to seek perfection in everyone. Like I said, we're born in perfection, not in sin (my personal opinion) although the Christian Bible differs from mine. Why would it be considered a sin when conception is an act of love? Usually. A friend happened to notice what I had written and he said, *"That's not a Christian belief."* I said, *"I was raised as such and hold much Christian wisdom and knowledge but I am not Christian in this sense, I'm Spiritualism."*

Being in love changes an outlook from charcoal to gold when a new love appears in your life; you feel the gift of God all around you. Fall out of love or be rejected by a lover and the world loses its luster. Heavenly dimensions are filled with love.

Did you ever hear the loud sound of drums and/or the bass vibrations beating in the music of today's teenagers? I guess we all have, especially when we're driving by a car with it unbearably high and all you hear is thump, thump, thump. May I suggest to you to put your ear on someone's chest, preferably someone that you feel comfortable with or have affection for. The sound of the heartbeat is exactly the same, thump, thump, thump. If you don't have someone that you're comfortable doing this with, then fill your bathtub with water, lie down on your back and let your ears submerge. Listen to the sound of your own heart beating. Oh, you can hear it. It's thump, thump, thump. The thumping of the drums represents heartbeats to our teenagers and young adults searching for love. They may not even realize that this sound is equal to a heartbeat, but it attracts them to turn the music higher to get a fuller effect of the sound, hoping that someone's heart is beating in love and admiration for them. A beating heart is the sign of life, the sign of affection, the sign of admiration, and the sign of acceptance and once again, the sign of love.

Your heart is a muscle, love radiates from it.

How do we show love? How do we know it comes with love? How can we be certain that it's genuine? Whether showing, giving, receiving and/or feeling; it's all in the approach and the perception of it. So, do it with tenderness and a caring attitude. We often hear that someone needs a little TLC. Well, we all do, stronger at times than others but it should be included in our daily lives. Show kindness.

Here's a poem I wrote quite some time ago. Brother mentioned, is also referred to as a sister and is also referred to as the man across the street or the woman on the other side of the planet.

Kindness

Show some kindness—do your best
Kind words put aching hearts to rest
Enlighten a soul—do a kind deed
Care for a brother—when he's in need
Don't wait for tomorrow—do it now
Don't borrow a promised future vow
Words spoken of peace—nighttimes shall rest
Stars brightly shine—on God's people blessed
Fulfill your vow—my dear brother
No time to dream—help another

What's so difficult about giving someone a smile or a glance of recognition? What's so difficult about loving and accepting another person of a different skin colour, religion and or creed? It depends on who it is, doesn't it? We, as loving human beings amidst our own race, or, our own kind of people as I heard some people say, have no problem doing this. We're all the same really, some people look and appear a little different but the structure of the body is that of ourselves and they say we, the human race, are made in God's image. They'll bleed if their skin is cut; they grieve and also have to be of accepting when a loved one has passed. They hurt, they're sad and they cry when a companion has left them for another.

Let's promote our soul and recognize how to love and respect all the people of our world. We have to try to accept the unchangeable past and leave the past where it belongs: behind us.

Let's practice how to love and respect others, putting aside all that we have read, taught to us by other adults and the bad feelings that we may have had once felt for some individual or another. Let's express the love that we know is in our hearts through the expression of ourselves. Some people may find this a difficult thing to do, but why should it be. Accept past faults and move forward, living in harmony with the rest of God's people who you're associated with and living with in the same world.

From the time I understood what world religions were all about, I felt that I was a spiritualist person and belonged in Spiritualism more so than any other religion I've been in contact with. Since my greater understanding I know that what's preached isn't always practiced whether in Spiritualism or any other. Considering we're all different and we're all unique, God didn't make two people the same: DNA testing proves that.

I created a poem while I was waiting for my mother, who I took to see a medium for a reading at her home. As I was sitting there waiting, I quieted my mind and began to write. For those of you who know of the seven principles of Spiritualism, below is a poem that holds a message, even for those who do not.

Vespers Message

Welcome each new day with grace
Togetherness as one need be your base

A soul's enlightenment—like grains of sand
Principle number two—brotherhood (or sisterhood) of man
For what do we mean
Such a statement as this
It's a message—a loving dream
Carries forth—a heavenly bliss
As you arise—from sleep each day
Remember this principle—on your way
Live up to those words
Greet people with love
Don't think it absurd
Cause it's granted—from above

We all need love in our daily lives. We need to feel it and we should express it. Sometimes we tend to forget about those closest to us as we spend more time together. Sometimes we take another person for granted and assume they know that our love and affection continues without any expression of it for them. This is unacceptable and needs to be taken into consideration at all times. Take a look at the smile on someone's face when you give them a compliment of appraisal and approval. Loved ones at home would also like to hear this on a regular basis, as well as you would like to hear it from them or someone else that's important in your life.

For instance, people in a management situation have the best composed staff if he or she compliments them on their successes and their job performance. Words of praise in a caring and loving way get a better assurance and a better feed back out of anyone that's concerned, especially those you're intimate with, such as a partner of your choice.

There are numerous love songs out there and they sell well because we all yearn for love and to be loved, but love comes to those that give. I read in The Christian Bible, *"Give and ye shall receive*," that also pertains to love.

John Lennon composed a song called—"Imagine." I was quite young the first time I heard it and was alone in my room preparing for bed. I sat down and listened to the words. The impact of the meaning he was sending out into the world with his musical lyrics touched a teenager's heart.

Here are some of the words:

Imagine there's no heaven, it's easy if you try
No hell below us, above us only sky
Imagine all the people, living for today…
Imagine there's no countries, It isn't hard to do.
Imagine all the people, Living life in peace!…
You may say I'm a dreamer, but, I'm not the only one.
I hope some day you'll join us, and the world will live as one…
(John Lennon)

I remember it so well; I was alone, with tears in my eyes.

I needed some unconditional love in my life a few years ago. So, as you know I got myself a puppy. I never knew that I could love something so much. It's a different kind of love than that of my child but it's a wonderful feeling none the less. All those that have such a pet experience a relationship that's shared between human and animal as it, too, is love unconditional. Story previously set.

Why is it that sometimes the bad appears to overrule the good in first reactions or impressions? Is it because evil will show itself in threatened-felt circumstances, or is it a form of self-defense?

Nevertheless it has to be ridden so that one is able to recognize the good and loving aspect.

When young, we seem to go through many relationships of some sort, one after the other, but some of us get burned and hurt along the way. We have to realize that we've met this person for some reason or another, whether we stay friends for a long or short period of time.

We meet people and usually learn from those experiences. Sometimes it's a hard lesson learned but learned nonetheless.

We move on with a little gained knowingness and awareness, a little wiser with a greater knowledge from past sorrows and hurts. Being young, and adventurous, we can cope much better with a hard lesson but as we grow older we tend to blame ourselves when something goes sour. We're not to blame personally, nobody is. Fate, destiny, natural law, or harassment; whatever we wish to call it, it was meant to make us wiser for when we're in another similar situation. When we move on with a loving heart we're much wiser once we grasp the knowledge or the lesson that was meant.

It nullifies me when one is trying very hard to advance spiritually but continues to hear gossip and lies by those that are supposed to be spiritual loving people with an advanced knowledge of Spiritualism. As mentioned previously, is it not true that we reap what we sow? But knowing this to be fact doesn't lighten the heart of hurt, pain and betrayal when the dirty deed has been done by someone you respected and thought to be a friend. Infidelity doesn't belong in Spiritualism or in any other religion. One may ask; where is Spirit in all of this, where is the Love and where is the Light?

Some may think that controlling is a form of love but it isn't, it's none other than what it is, **control**. To control is selfish, love is not controlled it's letting another be whom he/she really is. Moreover, self-love is of the greatest importance to every human being; never forget to love yourself, always, but don't overdo it or you'll spend your time looking in the mirror.

Without love there'd be nothing that could stand in the universe. We must realize that love is supreme and we need to show consideration for all things. As we fulfill life's missions and grow spiritually, we come to recognize and show love through humanity; it's usually the answer to many things.

Freddie Mercury composed a song titled; *"One year of love is better than a lifetime alone."* Sometimes we ask ourselves, was it worth it? Most definitely!

All life has meaning and purpose. Love is something that was placed in your hearts and soul by none other than Infinite Spirit, God. Once you bring that forward you will start to recognize the wondrous being that had placed it there.

What is Spiritualism?

Put in to practice the theme of what you have just read—because what you read is a major part of what Spiritualism represents.

If you wish to have something to meditate on from this chapter, which I highly suggest, choose one of the poems included.

Author's Note:

The next chapter consists of several weeks working with mental phenomena through meditation.

Further on you'll have a few weeks working with physical phenomena.

Just in case you haven't bought my first book and gained from its contents, which I suggest you do if you're new at this, it is most important that you ready yourself for visualizing through meditation. Visualization is how you open your psychic to clairvoyance. With much practice using this meditation and you feel confident please move forward with the next chapter. You need to be able to fully grasp the scenario and the concept of how it works before starting the following weeks of mediumship.

Visualization-Meditation from *Psychic Ability, Clairvoyant Powers*

Rest your lower arms and hands on your upper legs, with the palms facing up.

Close your eyes and listen carefully.

(Prayer)

Great Divine Spirit, protect us with your Infinite White Light. Guide us as we go within to communicate with spirit. Keep all evil entities away; give us your protection while we're on our spiritual journey of meditation. Amen.

Visualize a white beam of light coming through the ceiling. It's descending upon you. It touches and covers your head and you feel a sense of peace and love from God.

Feel the blissful comfort emitting from it.

It's slowly moving down around your shoulders. It's now covering your arms, your chest and back, tummy and down over your hands. It's moving down your hips, upper legs, your knees, your lower legs and slowly moving down around your feet. It's now covering your feet. Now, visualize it going through the floor underneath you and going deep into mother earth.

You're now grounded and also connected to God.

Don't be afraid, relax: you're safe.

Take in a deep breath. Let it out slowly and breathe normally

Feel your feet relaxing.

Lower legs—Upper legs—Hips—Tummy—Chest—Shoulders—Arms—Hands—Mouth—Face, and Head relaxing. Clear your mind. Listen to the silence.

Breathe normally and continue to listen.

Imagine yourself walking on an old cobblestone road in a beautiful tropical environment. The air is pleasantly warm and you feel a slight breeze coming from the ocean. Look in the distance, to your right and see a path with tall evergreen trees on both sides. Walk towards it. Enter the path through the trees and smell how sweet and fresh the air is. Look ahead a short distance and you'll see the sun breaking through them. There's a ray of sunlight filtering through and shimmering on the green branches. You'll gradually feel the warmth touch your face as you come from the shade.

There's a low stonewall just in front of you, it's about knee-high, turn around and sit down on it. Swing your legs in over and stand on the other side.

Lift your head and look in front of you. There's a beautiful meadow surrounded with rose bushes that are all in bloom. You'll notice as you look around that there's a few large rocks scattered about with many varieties of shades of green grasses.

There are several patches of daylilies of different colors as if they have grown wild with the wild flowers. Take a moment to notice the bright orange, yellows, and reds and smell the aroma that's all around you.

Turn your head slowly to the right and see the rose bushes lining that side of the meadow, as a hedge. Walk over to the first pink rose, bend down and smell how beautiful it is. You'll feel the scent travel deep into your lungs and you know that it's a gift from God. The rose bush next to it is a deep red.

Now, take a look down that side of the meadow, across the back hedge and look back up the other side.

Take notice of all the different colors of roses that God has created and presented to us.

Go and sit comfortably on one of the big stones in the meadow or sit back on the wall to begin your journey of spiritual contact.

Imagine a white dome covering this meadow and protecting you. This whole meadow is surrounded with roses and covered with God's protection of White Light. Here is a place where we're all safe from any harm. God, love, and light is all around you now.

Your Spirit Guide just came and sat down by your side to guide you along the way. Rely on him or her and ask for assistance when you feel you need help.

Now, within your peaceful mind become aware of all your senses and recognize any contact that may come to you. When it presents itself, your awareness will stimulate your mind so that you may start to have a conversation with this spirit.

Sit in silence, let telepathic communication commence between you and your spiritual contact. Be at peace and communicate. I'll speak with you again in five minutes.

Give up to five minutes' silence and then speak softly saying:

Five minutes are up now but stay within and remain calm and peaceful. Let your mind be taken by your guide to a person meditating with you. Direct your energy to them and feel it in their vibration. Feel yourself as one with him or her.

Remember, in this meditation you need to visualize in your mind a spirit entity and with much practice you'll see the spirit clairvoyantly without meditating.

When you feel you have a complete message, ask who gave it to you. Listen for a description and ask how this spirit is related to your message bearer. Once you've gotten all the answers direct your vibration to another. Go through the same procedure. Try not to forget your first message. Stack your messages for now as you're a new beginner but eventually you won't need to.

Telepathically ask the spirit for a message. Notice any images, pictures and scenery.

Visualize what spirit is sending forth and etching on your mind. Listen to what is being said: look at what's being presented. Speak with and ask your guide questions. Use your imagination, sense as well as visualize. If you see a color, a flower, any object or a symbol, hold on to it. Create from what you see, feel, and sense. Imagine what it all means to you. The meaning you create in your mind is the message meant for the person you focused on?

Listen to your inner self and your inner thoughts; it's there within that you'll get your answers. Those thoughts and answers are coming from the God source.

Stick with your first impressions.

Go ahead—create. I'll bring you back in five minutes.

Your time is now up.

Prayer

Great Divine Spirit, thank you for your protection. Thank you for the contacts we've been given and may your protection remain with us. Make us more knowledgeable each day and lead us safely on our spiritual journey. Amen.

Wiggle your feet back and forth. Come back to reality.

Please note: Make your meditations as repetitive as possible; this way you'll gain easy access and enter 'within' to connect with your higher self and guides. Moreover, you'll be able to attune and connect on your own without a taped voice or by a leader's guidance.

Chapter Three
Mental Mediumship

There's a brief explanation on mediumship and what it holds for you at this point in your development, considering that you bought my first book and used it as recommended. In this chapter there are '14 weeks' of working with mental phenomena, with meditations. Tape each meditation; preferably have a friend do it for you other than yourself as you'll only listen to yourself speak and not follow the meditation. As I said before, taping your own with today's modern technology is easy as a small fountain with water running may be used as background noise, which is very soothing. When at break time, when the speaker stops speaking, let the fountain continue running in the silence. At the allotted time the speaker should speak softly to gently arouse your state of consciousness as abrupt noise, whatever it may be, can cause alarm.

"Week" means that you may use one meditation once a day or every day of the week but stay focused on one lesson per week.

After teaching classes for the past three year I have come to realize that not all students participating in mediumship development hold an interest in Spiritualism as a religion. Although their learning are gained through the teachings of Spiritualism, some remain loyal and faithful to their previous given and taught religion.

From my experience as a former student I like to ask: "does it matter what a student's inner belief and feelings are?" When one takes any class today one has to pay; quite often up-front. Moreover, if you pay for something then the teacher should not expect you to put aside your beliefs as long as you don't express or push them in the class being taught.

Nevertheless, this is insignificant to the lessons and growth of your abilities towards your mediumship enhancement.

Mental phenomena which is usually taught to students today, is a combination of clairvoyance, clairaudience, clairsentience, inspiration, knowing, and intuition as in gut feelings, visualization, imagination and creation and so on. Physical mediumship has sort of disappeared since the giving of spirit messages became popular as many wanted to hear from their beloved departed. I teach both to my students as my previous teachers taught me. In retrospect, I educated myself to a higher level which also includes séances. In the past I had conducted such in my home as well as in private homes, plus open séances in a spiritualist church so that others could learn the technique. I gained a greater understanding about séance from Rev. Jane Suprynowicz while in Lily Dale, New York, USA. Rev. Jane is a very gifted medium living in the state of Pennsylvania USA. I strongly recommend her workshops as they are very informative.

In order for a student to make a contact with the world of spirits he or she has to discipline his/her self to meditate. You may say to yourself, *oh that's easy; all I have to do is to sit in silence*. Then try it for 10 to 15 minutes and you'll soon find out that it's more difficult than you had thought as your mind will be bombarded with things left undone; daily activities, what you should have for dinner or you may even wonder when the one you love is going to call you again. There are many distractions that you have to condition your brain to avoid when you decide to take this seriously. Self discipline is a must to prepare yourself for the experiences you so desire.

Here are eleven senses of Mental Mediumship:

Clairvoyance is a direct response to a physical object or event given through a past loved one. This is quite often without any sensory contact and precognition, or a non-inferential response to a future event. To see clairvoyantly is to see a spirit-being within your own mind, that has presented it self to you. To see an entity standing in a cloud form is called manifestation and is known to be ghostly.

Clairaudience (hearing/listening) is the power or faculty of hearing something not present to the ear but regarded as having objective reality. Sometimes when you're in contact with spirit you'll hear different sounds like music, chimes, the sound of birds singing, the sound of a train, waterfalls and so on. Oftentimes a medium is more clairaudient than clairvoyant. They hear words as if having a conversation with them selves as the words are placed in their inner ear and not heard audibly; making it clairaudient, which means to hear clearly.

Clairsentience (feeling/touching) is the sensing you feel from spirit. You can actually sense a problem that this contact once had while alive or an actual illness causing his or her death. This is a way that this particular spirit can make itself known; by giving verification of something that only the receiver would know. To sense something, as in to pass on a message via this means, for example, is to feel happiness and sensing that the person you're drawn to is feeling much joy or will experience it in the near future. In clairsentience you oftentimes will try to interpret what you sense, and that may not be a good thing as it may be the opposite and in the past. Nevertheless give what you get until your interpreting has gotten better. That's what class is for; to be able to err and decipher what is right or wrong.

Clairalience (smelling) is a form of extra-sensory perception wherein a person acquires psychic knowledge primarily by means of smelling.

Clairgustance (tasting). This is an awareness of an entity by the sense of taste experienced in the mouth. It could be a favorite food associated with a deceased entity, or in many instances the way a deceased person prepared the food to taste. It allegedly allows one to taste a substance without putting anything in the mouth. It is claimed that those who possess this ability are able to perceive the essence of a substance from the spiritual or ethereal realms through taste.

Claircognizance—Knowingness (knowing) is having an absolute feeling or sensing from spirit entities or from your guides. This will indicate to you that, without a doubt, what you have for the sitter is coming through so strong that you know it has to be genuine. What I recommend upon knowing is that it's of your higher self and not that of something you knew prior. Knowing about something you don't know will be strongly received and without a doubt you'll know it's from a source outside the physical world. It's known as intrinsic knowledge; the ability to know something without knowing how or why you know it. Giving a message from a visible form of knowing is fraudulent; therefore not very wise.

Inspiration is something that you had being inspired to give as in a related message that had been inspired from the spirit world or something you may have thought of in your own consciousness, as in your higher self. If this happens it means that those impressions were placed there by your guides or a spirit entity; so never underestimate your perception. Being inspired is usually inspirational, and inspiration is of a loving nature. Being inspired in a negative sense is connecting with the wrong entity and should be filtered within your own state of consciousness before relating any of the messages. Never give what you wouldn't wish to receive yourself. In addition, never give anything that would upset a sitter or cause him/her to worry. You can and may also be inspired leading to an event and not know who the entity belongs to as many are anxious to get through. Sometimes a medium will leave an open door and not realize they have.

Intuition, as in gut feelings, is exactly what it means. We all have intuition whether working with spirit or not. Intuition is sensing, knowing, and realizing what is and isn't, such as whether you should do something when your gut feelings say no. That is intuition, and it will also commune to your psyche when working with the spirit world. You need to be intuitive, and to accomplish this you may try intuitive exercises such as closing your eyes and listening to your inner thoughts on how to work out or solve daily problems.

Here's an example of a personal intuition: I love garage sales and find the most amazing things such as books for my spiritual education advancement, and other things of interest. A couple of weeks ago I felt the need for at least five nice classic cups and saucers for class events on fun nights. Usually I'll have about ten students and five cups and saucers will be sufficient. Last week I found a very small set of six, never used and in their original packaging. I bought them at a bargain price. When I brought them home, my brother being a collector, said he'd like to keep them. Of course, I gave them to him. He then proceeded to go to his collection and brought out four small cups and saucers in exchange. I need at least five and he said that he had two more of the cups to match the other two extra saucers, making a total of six. These were sturdier and might possibly do but the other two cups never showed up. The following Saturday I left home to go to a part of the city on business. It was morning time and it was garage-sale day. It was also September 2nd and in hurricane season. The weather was cool with an overcast sky. It felt like rain was on the way as the cool air drifted from the hurricane that recently hit Mexico. After my finished business I wanted breakfast and thought of looking for a restaurant in the area, but chose not to. I decided to drive to a place I frequent. All the way across town I didn't see any signs for garage sales. Close to the restaurant I came across one. I felt a calling to go but the hungry urge was intense so I drove by thinking I'd go after I had eaten. Immediately I had an inclination that I did the wrong thing. The sky was darker now and was about to rain. Before the next side street, which was about 60 feet away, if that,

I was made aware that I should go now and not later. I immediately turned the car around and drove back. There were many people as people tend to do as I do; look for Saturday morning sales. I walked in and immediately went to the books; nothing for me there. I walked a little further in the driveway and lo-and-behold, on the table at the back were seven beautiful cups and saucers. Six matching with blue leaves and flowers, gold trim edges and made in England; the other had pink roses. The seven cups and six saucers were of the finest china made in England with an un-matching saucer, but can be used as a set that was made in China. I asked the price. The woman looked at me and said: "*You can have all of them for $2.00 and you're getting a good deal.*" I said sold, and that I knew I was getting a good deal. I gave her the money and as she was busy with the others I asked her adolescent son for a bag to put them in. He had to go inside the house to fetch it and as he returned to the driveway he saw his mother with her hand over my ear, speaking quietly to me, up close. I wasn't sure what he thought, but his approach was with caution and wonderment. When this lady came back to assist me with the wrapping of the cups I let her know of my lack of hearing and she immediately reached out. As she placed her right hand over my left ear I felt a surge of healing energy. She looked directly into my eyes as I looked at her lips to understand what she was saying; she spoke lovingly and with kindness. She spoke of how it will get better in time. I asked if she was a spiritualist; she said, "No I'm a Christian, I believe in Jesus." I told her that by her placing her hand over my ear I felt healing taking place. She smiled and left, walked back down the driveway where there were some magazines which I had passed and didn't see. She brought back nine and placed them in my hand. She said these are free and that I should read them and in the contents I would find comfort and help for my continuous ear problems. I gladly accepted, left and went for breakfast. As soon as I sat down in the restaurant it began to rain.

I took a closer look at my odd purchase on my return home. The first magazine has a picture of an eagle with its wings spread from opposite corner to corner and is called, 'Spread the Fire' published by the Toronto Airport Christian Fellowship. On the back is her name and address. Only a trusting individual such as this would leave it, as in a big city we have our share of crime. Intuition told her it would be safe to leave it there, as well as my intuition, or was it my heavenly guides, that led me to her? Nevertheless I found the cups and saucers and was also given magazines of words of a loving God from a God-loving woman. God bless people such as this, and now I can honestly say that she was very Christian in her acts, and I may add that her acts were very spiritual.

Visualization always helps when you receive symbolic signs and when you need to bring proof of an entity that's with you. Bringing proof can be somewhat challenging as spirit will work with what you have in your memory banks. Bringing proof of a spirit entity can go something like this: you feel a vibration, it feels a bit rough or masculine; you now know it's male. Then you may sense an elderly person, which indicates that he died in old age. As for true visualization of this entity your guides may place one of your own loved ones in your consciousness such as an uncle, father, or a grandfather or just a male acquaintance. Then while seeing and visualizing this male entity in your mind you describe the appearance. The appearance may change somewhat and you may also be impressed to distort or refine their features. Always listen to your guides and go with the flow when it happens.

Imagination holds a specific place in mediumship for without it you won't be able to get into visualization meditation; hence you won't become a medium as all mental mediums use it. Imagination is most important with psychic symbolic messages, which I recommend that you should start with, as well as psychometry. Imagination is a gift we have and used from childhood; and one uses it throughout life or life would be quite dull. Everything has to enter your imagination before any creating can be done; it all works in unity and in conjunction with each other. Remember, there's nothing more powerful than that of the mind.

Creation covers all of the above for if one cannot create in their mind, one cannot relate to another. To begin your mediumship all of this should be done in discipline meditation. If you don't and you continue to do psychic readings, then you'll find yourself among fraudulent psychics that call themselves clairvoyants, which they are not. Don't follow this route as it will eventually backfire...

A friend of mine made a deck of cards. Not sure how many altogether but there are several, maybe 50. Those cards are ideal for psychic symbolic messages as when one works symbolically one has to see or visualize a symbol in their mind. Interpreting that symbol may be tricky but in class those cards were ideal for beginners as with beginners one's brain is apt to freeze up due to pressure or nervousness speaking in public; or what have you. Eventually those cards will be for sale and if interested you may ask about them at www.alvafolkes.com.

During a platform presentation the medium will give a better demonstration if he/she possesses all of the above qualities. Many mediums have trained themselves to recognize all, with advanced education and practice. Correct and authentic messages once validated make for confidence where it has been lacking.

People brag about being clairvoyant and are proud of it. We're not infallible so don't let your ego get out of control. Always maintain a professional poise and realize that you're not the only person with mediumship qualities. A large ego makes an unwelcome presence and will eventually be your downfall. It was brought to my attention that EGO means, Edging God Out; perfect sense I thought

This is how it works and it's what I've often said to my private students and many others used it before me. You are spirit, receiving a message from spirit, to give to spirit, meaning that you don't have to die to become spirit, you already are a spirit in a human body. Another point I try to make clear is that being a Medium in a physical body is being the vehicle or receptor for a spirit whether in a light or deep trance or channeling.

Medium: what would it represent when you take a look at it standing alone? Most don't think of a spirit contact, most would think of it as being a size. I tell the novice to put it this way: small, medium, large; where does the medium belong? It rests between the two; dead centre, making the large the spirit world and the small the physical body of the receiver. Therefore, one can say that the Medium is the gateway to both worlds joining the two.

To verify this, look in the Christian Holy Bible, in the book of John, chapter 4 verse 24. Jesus said: *"God is spirit: and they that worship Him must worship Him in spirit and truth."*

You have to learn attunement which means that you need to know how to channel universal life force energy. It's a spiritual awakening and a time of transformation when the two aspects of the greater person, the personal self and the higher self, come together as one. It's the blending of those two aspects of self into one expression of Infinite Spirit. Attunement is done with a general and a spiritual attitude through meditation; as one adjusts with respect, one connects the resonance at a particular frequency bringing in harmony. With a peaceful frame of mind, in meditation, one makes aware the responsive changing trends. Once attuning begins you feel your soul grounding in your body and it reconnects in an organic way. Attunement is the major factor in connecting with the spirit world and you do this by meditation.

Attunement is a simple but yet a powerful process that enables you to immediately connect with your inner spirit; attuning and resonating with the Divine. It's a spiritual blessing feeling. Make your perspective on attunement by relaxing your mind and body by hearing and responding to the call of awakening and believing in the possibility while turning your consciousness inward. Shift your vibration of the lower self using imagination and center a wandering mind. Call forth the presence of your higher self and accept the work of your soul while in a passive/receptive state. When you surrender to the wisdom listen for direction and trust in your intuition. Henceforth, when you attune you must clear your mind of daily activities and stress, go within your higher self (this can be done through a fast meditative state, close your eyes if necessary) and think only of a spiritual nature. Direct your energy out into the universe, ask for enlightenment and be aware and affirm that you will receive it. Then you must open your consciousness in order to receive from the spirit world. Be alert and recognize any words, images and/or feelings experienced that have been given to you.

You'll find that you'll converse with spirit through frequency and the connection is usually telepathic; unless your spirit guides use some form of telekinesis to move objects or manifest objects to reinforce their connection with you. Spirit guides are higher; it's like when I have my hearing aid out and then put it back in. I hear more clearly. It's like fine tuning the sound and reception. As the spirit world works with you, in time it will become clearer, unfortunately it may not be as easy as putting in a hearing device but it will come with practice and patience.

Practice makes perfect, the more you use it the better it will be; it's like any other gift. I'd suggest that a beginner medium—in the early stages—give what you get when trying to relate a message. Chances are the receiver or the sitter will know its meaning and will know the message behind it. At one point I was shown a bow and arrow for a particular woman. I immediately knew it was a symbolic message but then on second thoughts I questioned my higher self that she may have been a Native American. One sense out-ruled the other and then I heard *"no it's cupid."* A beautiful message was obtained and given from this symbolic image. She was quite pleased.

On another occasion I was shown a bad automobile accident. I thought that this person was going to be in an accident. I stopped in my tracks, so to speak, but then I was shown a man who had passed via an accident and this was his way of letting the receiver know who he was. Needless to say, even today I question and sometimes have to analyze what spirit is presenting. A good medium will question their inner or higher self and believe me they can do this very quickly. It's undetected by the congregation or a sitter as a medium has to condition their speed and vibrations to a faster rate to receive the quick responses from spirit, as that of spirits are much faster than their own. Both parties have to compromise and adjust, such as the medium speeding up the vibration, and the entity making contact from the spirit world will slow it down. Because spirit guides are entities, physical and non-physical, they come to realize that this is essential for proper communication.

Acquiring mental phenomena is the easiest to accomplish in Mediumship. You may be led to believe that it's difficult and may sit in a development class for years before you finally realize that what you were sensing, seeing and hearing (in your mind) is all that it takes to begin your journey. So begin your journey believing that what you sense, see and feel is the door opening for you, and never fear to present what you receive as once you start to express, more will come forward. Furthermore, one will benefit if one is blessed with the 'gift of gab'; I say blessed here as the gift-of-gab isn't always appreciated as many can't join a conversation. Spirit knows and uses gift-of-gab receptors. Don't fear being the shy, quiet and silent type. With practice spirit will open your consciousness if you're open to developing it. Like everything else it can be learned with persistence. I speak of this because I was one of the silent types but now watch out. Once I let spirit take control away I go, sometimes non stop. Hence, one must know when to stop as there are others from the spirit world that would like and need to get through to their loved ones.

Some development classes don't hold a meditation, not even for beginners. As a beginner you'll need to accomplish the feat of meditation so that you'll be able to go quickly within without it. Meditation prepares the way and clears the path to the spirit world.

The perfect way to begin is to attune by meditation followed by psychometry. Webster's dictionary defines psychometry as '*divination of facts concerning an object or its owner through contact with or proximity to the object.*' That's what it's all about. I recommend that you have more than yourself present as the more who work together, in unison, the better the results. Have those in your group or the person sitting with you remove an object from their person or bring along something the other can hold. Once you hold something from another let your mind go blank and then let it wander or drift to where it wants. Remember, spirit can only work with what's in your memory banks. While holding the object you may see something that you had experienced in your past, then by all means share it as this may very well pertain to the person who owns the object. Once shared, focus on the object again and let your mind drift. Continue to express what you sense, see or hear. You may continue this route until you feel that you're not picking up anything else.

A psychic, which we all are, has an inherent sensitivity that is sensitive to non-physical or supernatural forces and influences marked by extraordinary or mysterious sensitivity, perception or understanding in varying degrees relating to the psyche with heightened awareness of ESP. Physic perception is lying outside the sphere of physical science or knowledge of immaterial, moral or spiritual in origin or force, without mediumistic abilities. When undeveloped it cannot always be controlled and can link with the spirit world without realizing it. Psychics are known for their prophecies of future events and known worldwide for telling an individual's future.

A medium, who is able to do all of the above, is one that acts as a mediator. He/she is one with special faculties and is held to be a channel of communication between the physical world and the spirit world. In addition, they are much further advanced beyond 'a psychic' and hold a greater psychic ability. A medium is naturally sensitive to mental influence from the spirit world; and through the proper training is able to control and recognize the level of spirit communication. Further on in development, a medium is able to become more selective because their vibrations increase. A medium serves many functions other than Mental Phenomena; they are able to provide 'Spiritual Healing,' 'Trance lectures or writings' as well as 'Automatic and/or Inspired Writings.'

Very important! A new medium may want to press past their

given time and their psychic force of vital energy. This energy has a limit and may have been used up, draining them. Therefore, nervousness will become recognizable. Don't push yourself beyond your limit; you'll get there eventually with persistent and diligent practice. Be aware, a skeptic and a critical audience oftentimes collapse a beginner's confidence making them nervous and may get what is called 'a freeze' causing them to discontinue.

One word of advice, never go with facial expressions of those from whom you're relaying a message, many have come forward to validate it as 'authentic' after the medium thought that the message was all wrong and not meant for them. Maintain your confidence.

Psychometry, as my students are taught, is the holding of an object and while using all your senses it's possible to pick up the past, present and future events; personal things and matters, places of interest to the owner and also that of the objects' previous owners. Be careful in what you relate about each object as sometimes all that is held in it is not known by the owner. If you have something that you feel will upset, do not relate it in public but tell them that you'll speak to them after the class or service.

Once you hold an object, let your mind race and go to wherever it wills. Look within to see, feel and sense with eyes opened or closed. Closed is best when you're a beginner. Try interpreting some of what you get but this isn't necessary for what you get is what you should relay; except what you feel will upset, hurt or cause grief.

Be reminded; don't be frightened if you see your dead grandmother or grandfather. When you see either of them it means that the object you're holding relates to a grandmother or a grandfather; possibly theirs and not your own. This is how spirit works sometimes and you'll come to recognize how spirit or your guides work with you. I can only teach you how my guides work with me and I teach this to my students.

"One can't take you beyond themselves," Rev. Alva Folkes.

Take guidance and learn and then become aware of how they

work with you and follow that route. Strive for perfection. This is an affirmation that I had used many times over the years in whatever field I challenged, ***"I'll be better than most and as good as the best."*** Use this in your thoughts prior to a class sitting or meditation and believe that this is what you'll accomplish.

In an open meditation and development class for the public at my chosen place of enlightenment, The Fellowship of Spiritualists' Church in Oshawa, Ontario, Canada, where I'm currently the Associate Minister; a gentleman I'd never seen before attended one evening. The usual explanation of mediumship was given and then a guided meditation. Within this guided meditation I usually speak to the group about three-quarters of the way through to try to get them to see a spirit entity through visualization. When I asked this gentleman about his experience he had little to share. If I know someone is interested and wishes to learn I will guide them along the way. I asked him if he would close his eyes again and go back to his comfortable place where he was in the meditation. He did as I asked. I then spoke gently to him, I told him to move his vibration or energy to the lady across from him. I called her by name which he knew then I told him that to the side of him was an object for the woman he'd focused on. Then I said: "when you see this object in your mind and have it open your eyes." Well, he was there for some time and then I called him back. I asked if he saw anything; he said "no." I asked if he could visualize anything in his mind; he said "no." Then I told him to look at something in the church, which he did, and then I asked him to close his eyes and see it through visualization. He did as I asked with no results. Then I said: "close your eyes; which he did again, I then said: 'can you visualize your mother's beautiful face right now?' he nodded his head yes. I told him to open his eyes. When he did I explained that when he saw his mother's face he was visualizing and that's how visualization from spirit also works.

Imagination, visualization and creating are all it takes to start to work with spirit in presenting a message. This will be psychic-symbolic-messages and it's a great way to start and gain confidence. The rest will follow more easily after you've accomplished this. In addition, to meditate is opening yourself to channel from the spirit world, simple as that, as long as you clear and rid your mind of daily activities and stresses. Moreover, when you use your computer and click on Internet Explorer you're opening a window to the cyber world. For instance, your brain is your individual personalized computer so, therefore, when you open to channel; make sure your browser is operative and has 'Spirit World' as your home page.

Once again I recommend that you have a friend tape any meditations that you choose to listen to and practice with. Have this friend sit where he or she won't be disturbed and have a small electric home fountain running as background sound. Music is not required although I often use it for my students; silence is better. As you listen to the silence within, not music, you'll quickly adjust and connect well with the spirit world; when you use a small fountain the sound of flowing water connects you with nature and it's to nature we belong.

Here's a list I go over with all new students and it seems that I continue to add to it as I too obtain a greater understanding of spirit and the teaching of it to others.

Rules to follow with you being the medium, the worker, and/or the message bearer:

YOU—the instrument of the Divine.

REMEMBER

1. You represent Spiritualism—Infinite Intelligence—God, your leader and your church—so be polite and act accordingly.

2. Trust in a divine intelligence, Infinite Spirit or whatever name you call God.

3. Prepare yourself to serve the Divine prior to each time you do serve.

4. Attune by meditation, whether it's 3 minutes or 20.

5. Start with a silent prayer and ask for your highest guides; they change as you develop.

6. Ask for protection before each meditation and before giving proof of survival.

7. Relax and put yourself at ease, in that way so will the message bearer and the group.

8. Be respectful and polite and speak at a comfortable level so that everyone will hear you.

9. Your message should be uplifting and of love because—it's from Spirit.

10. Give proof of survival from the world of spirit when it's presented to you, if it's not easily seen or recognized, ask and it shall be given,—but you have to be able to recognize it when it is. Give it with love and compassion.

11. Be enthusiastic and positive and always give thanks to your guides and Infinite Spirit when you've completed your clairvoyance and or a reading.

12. Laughter uplifts the spirit, both here as well as in the spirit world, so don't be afraid to laugh—but don't be silly.

13. A teacher may interpreter a message for you but it's not necessarily the correct interpretation. Take from it as you see fit; yours is the correct approach, which may need refining, and sometimes the receiver may be the best interpreter.

14. Remember, you are the controller of your guides and spirit entities and you, only you will determine when they make contact, not them. Never leave an open door as to be bombarded. It this should happen be firm in your decision and demand that they leave and come when you give them permission, not before.

15. The palms of your hands holds an amazing strong Chakras and is directly connected to the seat of your soul

16. Dress accordingly and comfortably, not provocatively; we're only human.

17. Don't let your **ego** get in the way of your spiritual progression. As your ego grows your progression will quietly cease and evaporate. Always think before your ego has time to react so that the real loving-you is continuously portrayed.

18. Any circle group, whether home, church or public should be totally committed to spiritual growth and mediumship development. All students should refrain from daily activities and "quote on quote", gossip, when time comes to begin class.

19. Keep the length of a developing group to about one and one half hours and not to exceed two. 1 and ½ is more then enough

20. ALWAYS BELIEVE IN YOURSELF AND BE KIND TO ONE ANOTHER

21. If you're serious in your mediumship development, affirm "I'm going to be better than most and as good as the best." Rev. Joe Browns quote

22. Never think negatively as you have to be a spiritual person to attract spirit guides and to make a divine connection. Always present yourself in a positive spiritual manner to set a good example of the church you represent.

23. The people attending as well as you 'the Medium' create the energy.

24. Never assume you're better then others as we all connect differently with spirit.

25. It's best to keep your opinions to yourself and let the teacher or leaders do any necessary corrections—unless that individual asks for it.

26. Questions are not necessary when giving spirit messages as a good Medium will give what they get. Good clairvoyance is done without questioning the sitter. Asking questions is not a part of messages from spirit. It's what it is, questioning to give psychic messages (meaning it's not good mediumship).

27. Some mediums need clarity and sometimes will ask 'Do you understand' or 'Do you know what I mean.' which is acceptable.

28. Never ever give a spirit message as in diagnoses of an illness; never inform a sitter of a pending illness, hospitalization or suggest certain drugs they should take. That's diagnostic and only allowed by doctors. This is illegal and in a court of law one is liable for lawsuit. We are Mediums, not doctors. Never leave a sitter with concerns or with a fear of their health as in potential chronic prognoses.

29. Do not give a message that relates to 'personal appearance', appearances are quite often wrong.

30. Always recognize a negative spirit and never give a negative message. Be firm and send the negative spirit away and remain quiet about it.

31. Never wear heavy colognes or aftershave at a circle gathering or when working the rostrum; many have allergies and some fragrances are appalling to others.

32. Never, **never,** touch another person while they're in a deep meditation or trance

33. Never assume you're infallible as spirit communication comes from a divine source and you are the instrument, we're all capable of error.

34. Try your utmost best to get along with each other; we're 'all' a spark of the Divine. Furthermore, don't talk down about someone until you take a closer look at yourself and your own personal faults, which we often don't see. Then, if that should be perfect feel free to express your opinion. If not, keep it to yourself. Always remember 'Natural Laws' concerning 'Cause and Effect'. For instance, eventually, what you put out will rebound **back** on yourself.

35. If you're pregnant or think that you may be never consent to trance or give your guide, or any other entity, permission to use your body.

36. If you're a young woman about to enter puberty, or have recently entered it, never use the Ouija board or give a spirit entity permission to enter or use your body.

37. A demonstrator, you the medium, should never feel that you had not gotten enough from spirit when you do get something, no matter how small it may be. You're putting yourself down when you do.

38. ALWAYS THINK SPIRITUALLY, BE YOUR OWN WORST CRETIC, & PRACTISE MAKES PERECT.

39. DO NOT bring your personal problems to the class

40. One last thing—Never give a message you wouldn't want to receive yourself. Rev. Doreen Baulds quote

REMEMBER; you DO NOT touch anyone while in meditation or abruptly disturb them in any way. This applies to all, especially Trance. If the leader or teacher has a problem bringing someone back let that person be and they'll come back when ready. Continue to converse with others in the group. If an entity has taken possession of someone then listen to what it has to say. If it's of a negative attitude tell it to leave and, if necessary, shout at it to leave but never shake an individual to rid them of this. This could be detrimental to their health. If it's of a positive and loving manner then you just witnessed trance. Therefore a tape recorder is encouraged to have running.

Week 1:

The first week's week lesson consists of psychometry.

As previously mentioned, it's important for all to have an object for someone else to hold. If you have a group, I suggest you do as I do in my class. Have a cardboard box and have everyone place their object inside concealing it from all. The leader holds, or is in control of, the box until the time comes for each to try their psychic sense. After this is done the leader takes full control and begins, or use your previously taped meditation and join in.

Always: Protect, Ground & Connect. Start with a Prayer, cover all with God's white light, and ground to mother earth via visualizing roots coming out of your feet and going deep in the ground. Then feel and sense a connection with your guides and the spirit world.

General Relaxation Meditation

Sit comfortably. (Prayer) Great Divine Spirit, protect us with your Infinite White Light. Guide us as we go within. Grant us the ability to connect with our guides. Keep all evil entities away while we're on our spiritual journey. Amen.

Visualize a white beam of light coming through the ceiling.

It's descending upon you. It touches and covers your head; you feel a sense of peace and love from God. It's slowly moving down around your shoulders. It's now covering your upper arms, your chest and back, lower arms, stomach, hips and down over your hands. It's moving down your upper legs, your knees, your lower legs and slowly moving down around your feet. It's now covering your feet. Now, visualize it going through the floor underneath you and going deep into mother earth. You're now grounded and also connected to God. Don't be afraid: relax, you're safe. (Pause momentarily.)

Bring your attention to your feet. Relax.

Focus on your lower legs and knees. Relax.

Focus on your upper legs. Relax.

Focus on your hips, pelvis and buttocks. Relax.

Focus on your stomach and lower back

Relax: let your intuition or gut feelings prepare for spirit contact. Ask your guide or doorkeeper to bring on this awareness. If you don't know them just telepathically ask your higher self and recognize that it had been granted.

Now bring your attention to your chest, upper back and shoulders. Relax.

Focus on your upper arms, lower arms, hands and fingers. Relax.

Bring your attention to your throat and neck. Relax.

Continue on; focus on your chin, mouth and nose. Relax.

Focus on your eyes, ears and forehead. Relax.

Focus on the crown of your head. Relax.

Now, bring your attention to your third eye, that's located in the center forehead—between both eyes.

Prepare yourself and attune to the spirit world.

Meditation begins.............(Recommended time allotted here is 15 minutes with music, the fountain running, or in silence.)

After 15 minutes, or allotted time is up, call all back in a soft spoken voice and raise your voice a little higher as you speak. Saying: Your time is up now, bring yourself back. Come back to reality. Come back to the room. Continue to speak until all have their eyes open.

When all are back pass the box to one person and let him or her take an object without looking in the box. Then listen to what they get and express. Continue until all have had a chance at psychometry. Once all are finished you may ask if anyone has anything to add. If not, then close with a prayer thanking God and guides for assistance.

(Prayer)

Divine Spirit; we thank you for being with us and for your light of protection. We also thank our guides for assisting us. As we depart from here we ask that you continue to protect us in our daily lives. Until we meet again we're under your care and guidance. Amen.

Having gone through all of the above there's a way to make a 'somewhat spirit connection' as in psychic symbolic messages through meditation. This is a way to work with your psychic power, which we all have, to enhance your clairvoyant ability. These exercises are a lot of fun and it will get you started at speaking to another person, as in interpreting a message. Use the meditation above for attunement, which is of the greatest importance. The real spirit connection will come, in time, once you gain confidence and have faith in yourself. Each time you sit in a meditation group most teachers will give you this time, in silence, or in privacy of your own home with background music. As soon as the teacher stops talking and you're within, focus on someone in the group, someone you don't know or know little about. Then let your mind wander keeping that person in mind. Moreover, take that someone on a journey with you in your meditation and notice all that occurs on the way. When the teacher calls you back from your meditation, you then will have something to share with one person. Start out as you had been taught and proceed to tell your receiver the journey, but be certain that it won't be upsetting. If so, do not give it. In addition: if you did see something that upset you, or that would possibly upset the receiver, don't give it but speak to your teacher afterwards and out of earshot of everyone else present. The teacher will clarify as best as possible. Let's say for instance you focused on a person sitting in the group and you took them on a voyage. The voyage consisted of a ship sailing on smooth waters, and all aboard were having a good time. Then when your turn comes to speak you may say, "*I see smooth sailing ahead for you.*" Or let's put it another way: the voyage consisted of a ship sailing on smooth waters and all aboard were having a good time but encounter a bit of heavy current and some choppy waters and then sailed away unharmed. Then when your turn comes to speak you may say, "*I see smooth sailing ahead for you but there will be some choppy waters, but you're more than capable of dealing with it.*" No need to say anything else. Or start with psychic symbolic messages. E.q. Use your time in silence to work with your higher self and try to bring something back for someone meditating with you. For instance, search your mind for an object of some form, or something as simple as a flower, but be aware of the kind of flower, the color and general appearance, etc. If you can't find anything this way then think of what gift you would give to this person if you had to give one on a certain occasion. When you're called upon to share tell this person what you have and tell them what you see with this object or flower (or what have you,) and what it means to you. You're a student and more will come with practice and dedication so be patient and give yourself time to attune so that you will receive easily.

Week 2— Chakra Meditations:

If you're experienced in dealing with Chakras then you may go through opening, cleansing and alignment in one meditation, which is Chakra Meditation number 4. If you have not dealt with them before and don't know what they're for and their purpose, please do one meditation after the other. 'After the other' means one per day or one every 24 hours as your body will need to adjust to the change that is taking place.

Use a "Flame pot" for cleansing the room of any negativity; explanation below.

Psychic Ability, Clairvoyant powers has a chapter on auras and chakras and I try not repeating it here. The meditations will appear so but it has to be repeated somewhat for a fuller coverage. If you're able to get a video tape or DVD of Shirley McClain's chakra exercise by all means do so. I highly recommend it.

Once you're aware of your higher self, start visualizing while listening to your taped meditations below. The meditations are completely safe to do alone. Do remember that no matter where you are and who is in charge of a chakra meditation, always close them at the end as a lot of mediation leaders don't go through this procedure with you.

Your chakra colours are projected through your aura. If one of your chakras is off balance or need cleaning you'll be sensitive enough to become aware of it as it will show through your inner self.

Chakras consist of seven major spiritual energy points of different coloured wheels, referred to by some as spiritual points. Your whole body is covered with chakras, some smaller than others. The seven here are considered the main ones. Once you open up you can use them as a single energy focus point or use them in totality, working together. When you put them to use your psychic forces and bodily functions will merge and interact. The three main Chakras are: Number 7: Crown, top of your head; Number 4: Heart, centre chest; and Number 1: Base, end of the spine; but they all hold significance to each other.

An individual with a good knowledge of the chakras and its energies will easily go within through meditation. Your visualization of colors will enable you to gain full control of the powers they possess. Buy yourself a scrap book that has sheets of all colors included. Place a round object on the color papers that are closest to the charkas and draw a circle with a pencil. Cut it out and place it on a white sheet of paper where the chakra is located on the human body. Once set and glued in place hang it on a wall where you or the group can easily see it. If there's a group you'll need about three or four copies.

Here's a simple explanation of all chakras:

Number 1 is the Base, end of the spine. This is your grounding point. This one deals in relation with your fear, restlessness, prosperity, trust, health and physical dimension. Its color is Red.

Number 2 is the Sacral, over the genitals. This one deals in relation with your sexuality, emotions, desire, pleasure and creativity. Its color is Orange.

Number 3 is Solar Plexus, over your abdomen. This one deals in relation with willpower, strength, self-esteem, vitality, sensitivity and personal power. Its color is Yellow.

Number 4 is Heart, over your centre chest. This one deals in relation with self-acceptance, compassion, balance, relationships and love. Its color is Green.

Number 5 is Throat, over your larynx. This one deals in relation with communication, expression, creativity, resonance, judgment, and speech. Its color is Blue.

Number 6 is Brow, centre forehead, directly between your eyebrows and connected with the pineal gland; its considered your third eye. This one deals in relation with your psychic, intuition, imagination, interpretation, spiritual nature, and perception. Its color is Indigo, a mix of blue and red.

Number 7 is Crown, top of your head. This one deals with the God Source, spiritual, intellectual, consciousness, awareness, knowledge, and wisdom. Sometimes it is seen as the color violet or a combination of colors; its color is White.

> **Chakra**: (chä-kr) according to Webster's dictionary, is any one of several points of physical or spiritual energy in the human body, according to yoga philosophy. Sanskrit chakra, literally wheel: a circular diagram of spectrum used to show the relationship between the colours.

In most of my teaching meditations I have a metal pot that has a handle and a lid which sits on a cork coaster center table or on a stand in the middle of the room or circle. Inside this pot is a partial paper towel roll, rubbing alcohol, a small amount of Epsom salts and two drops of lavender oil. First, you need a metal pot. Be certain that you only use it for this purpose and use it safely. Use a pot with a handle and always have the cover close by.

Get an unused roll of paper towel and be certain the first towel is stuck to the second so it won't unravel. Use a very sharp knife or a carpenter's cutting blade for cutting. About 1 to 2 inches in, cut the complete roll in a circle. Do not remove the cardboard centre once finished as this holds it in place.

Place this part into the pot. Pour a large amount of 90% rubbing alcohol into the pot soaking the paper towel circle. Add a very small amount of Epsom salts, (not to much as it clings in the air and will interfere with your breathing,) and two drops of lavender oil in the centre of the roll. This may be used over and over again, but add to it as needed. If you see that the paper is sagging too much for your liking, you can turn it over instead of using a new roll. Be certain that there's always enough rubbing alcohol so that the paper doesn't burn. While there's enough rubbing alcohol the paper remains as a wick.

This combination of ingredients rids the room of any negative vibrations and guards the person or group of any evil or negative interference. To activate: take the cover off and place it along side of the pot; strike a match and toss the burning match in the center of the roll, touching the fluid. It does not burst into a quick flame; it's a gentle beginning, making it safe and relatively harmless if properly controlled.

Chakra #1 Meditation: (Opening and traveling up to your higher-self)

Watch the flame for about a minute. Then the leader should place the cover back on to extinguish it and then close your eyes and listen to the meditation, which should be taped or the leader will read from here.

Say your own protection prayer, or one that's included in chapter 2.

Protect, ground and connect, and you may use my way:

Visualize a white beam of light coming through the ceiling.

It's descending down upon you.

It touches and covers your head.

It's slowly moving down around your shoulders.

It's now covering your arms, your chest and back, stomach and down over your hands.

It's moving down over your hips, upper legs, your knees, your lower legs.

And slowly moving down around your feet.

It's now covering your feet.

Now, visualize or sense it going through the floor underneath you and going deep into mother earth.

You're now grounded and also connected to God.

Focus on your total body and relax as in previous relaxations, Such as:

Feel your feet relaxing. (Proceed slowly here to give time for relaxation)

Lower legs—Upper legs—Hips—Stomach—Chest—Shoulders—Arms—Hands—Mouth—Face. Relax your Head.

Clear your mind.

Focus on Chakra # 1, the Base, end of the spine; open it gently.

Visualize the color RED flowing out of it. Fill the room with the color Red.

Now breathe the color Red deep in to your lungs.

Chakra # 2—the Sacral, over the genitals; open it gently.

Visualize the color ORANGE flowing out of it. Fill the room with the color ORANGE.

Now breathe the color ORANGE deep into your lungs.

Chakra # 3—the Solar Plexus, over your abdomen; open it gently.

Visualize the color YELLOW flowing out of it. Fill the room with the color YELLOW.

Now breathe the color YELLOW deep into your lungs.

Chakra # 4—the Heart, over your centre chest; open it gently.

Visualize the color GREEN flowing out of it. Fill the room with the color GREEN.

Now breathe the color GREEN deep into your lungs.

Chakra # 5, the Throat, over the larynx; open it gently.

Visualize the color BLUE flowing out of it. Fill the room with the color BLUE.

Now breathe the color BLUE deep into your lungs.

Chakra # 6, the Brow, center forehead,—the third eye-; open it gently.

Visualize the color INDIGO flowing out of it. Fill the room with the color INDIGO.

Now breathe the color INDIGO deep into your lungs.

Chakra # 7, the Crown, top of the head; open it gently.

Visualize the color BRIGHT WHITE flowing out of it. Fill the room with BRIGHT WHITE.

Now breathe it deep into your lungs.

Remain concentrating on Chakra # 7, top of your head. Open it as wide as you can. Look up through the opening. Visualize the BRIGHT WHITE BEAM OF LIGHT going towards the sky.

Picture yourself stepping inside of a balloon. Don't move until you have permission, then you'll move upwards very slowly.

You're now inside the balloon; let the balloon take you slowly upwards as if you're hoisting a flag.

Go slowly upward now.

Stop, look around: this is level ONE above your conscious. You're now in a form of 'Astral Travel'.

Move slowly upward again, go upward.

Stop, look around: this is level TWO

Move slowly upward again, go upward.

Stop, look around: this is level THREE

Move slowly upward again, go upward.

Stop, look around: this is level FOUR; see the beautiful fairy tale scene and step out.

I'm going to leave you here for a short while so that you can commune with your angels and spirit guides. As you sit and chat ask for a message for a person or two sitting by you.

If you don't get messages, ask for an object or a symbol such as in week 1 meditation.

You're time is now up.

Step back into the balloon.

Start to come down, slowly.

You're at level #3

Level #2

Level #1

Now enter inside Chakra # 7, top of your head.
Close the opening to its normal size.
Step out of the balloon.
Start to feel and become aware of your body.
Focus on your chakras again.
Chakra # 7—Crown—Close it tightly.
Chakra # 6—Brow—Close it tightly.
Chakra # 5—Throat—Close it tightly.
Chakra # 4—Heart—Close it tightly.
Chakra # 3—Solar plexus—Close it tightly.
Chakra # 2—Sacral—Close it tightly.
Chakra # 1—Base, end of spine—Close it tightly.
Bring yourself back to reality.

Chakra #2 Meditation, Unblocking:

Watch the flame until it burns out, then close your eyes and listen to my voice.

Protect, ground and connect as used previously

Breathe normally.

In your mind visualize Chakra # 1—the Base; end of the spine. See it as being closed with a twist on cover. Now visualize your hand moving towards it. Gently hold the cover and turn it anti-clockwise; remove it. Put the cover to one side. Now, visualize your own hand or the hand of a spirit being gently massaging the area with an herbal remedy, such as Lavender Oil or something that is of a spiritual nature. Whatever you create will work for you.

Massage it open, remove any debris and discard it.

Visualize Chakra # 2—the Sacral, over the genitals. See it as being closed and covered. Now visualize your hand moving towards it. Gently hold the cover and twist it off; anti-clockwise. Put the cover aside. Visualize the area being gently massaged by you or a spirit being.

Massage it open, remove any debris and discard it.

Visualize Chakra # 3—the Solar Plexus, over your abdomen;

See it as being closed and covered. Visualize your hand moving towards it. Gently hold the cover and twist it off. Put the cover aside. Visualize the area being gently massaged. Massage it open, remove any debris and discard it.

Chakra # 4—the Heart, over your centre chest;

See it as being closed and covered. Visualize your hand moving towards it. Gently hold the cover and twist it off. Put the cover aside. Visualize the area being gently massaged.

Massage it open, remove any debris and discard it.

Chakra # 5—the Throat, over the larynx;

See it as being closed and covered. Visualize your hand moving towards it. Gently hold the cover and twist it off. Put the cover aside. Visualize the area being gently massaged.

Massage it open, remove any debris and discard it.

Chakra # 6, the Brow, center forehead, the third eye;

See it as being closed and covered. Visualize your hand moving towards it. Gently hold the cover and twist it off. Put the cover aside. Visualize the area being gently massaged.

Massage it open, remove any debris and discard it.

Chakra # 7, the Crown, top of the head;

See it as being closed and covered. Visualize your hand moving towards it. Gently hold the cover and twist it off. Put the cover aside. Visualize the area being gently massaged. Massage it open, remove any debris and discard it.

Now that your chakras are unblocked let's go on a little adventure.

I want you to take yourself to a beautiful tropical environment or to a sandy beach that holds a beautiful memory for you. Sit in the shade and feel the warmth of the sun as it's filtered through the trees.

You're safe here, don't have any fear.

Sit in this quietness with your guides and bring back a message for 1 or 2 people in the group. Try to focus on someone you don't know well. If you don't get any messages bring back an object.

I'll leave you here for___________minutes.

Your time is now up.

Listen to my voice.

Remain within; start to become aware of your body.

Focus on Chakra # 7—the Crown

Pick the cover up, place it over the chakra. Turn it clockwise and close it tightly

Chakra # 6—Brow

Pick up the cover, put it in place and close it tightly.

Chakra # 5—Throat

Pick up the cover, put it in place and close it tightly.

Chakra # 4—Heart

Pick up the cover, put it in place and close it tightly.

Chakra # 3—Solar plexus

Pick up the cover, put it in place and close it tightly.

Chakra # 2—Sacral

Pick up the cover, put it in place and close it tightly.

Chakra # 1—The Base

Pick up the cover, put it in place and close it tightly.

And—Bring yourself back to reality.

Chakra #3 Meditation, Alignment:

All stand, hold hands with thumbs pointing to the left. This gives way to an easier energized flow in a group setting which increases vibration frequencies from the spirit world.

The leader, the teacher, or the control person removes the cover from the pot, strikes a match and drops it in the pot.

The flame may be slow to start, don't be impatient; give it time.

Once you're satisfied with the flame go back to your position and hold hands with the two next to you.

You, as a leader, should speak or recite a prayer or an affirmation.

I suggest that you follow my approach until you come up with what you feel is right for you and/or your group, which is:

I speak to the group as they stand and then I ask them to close their eyes as I say a prayer.

My approach:

Watch the flame, become one with the flame and blink only when absolutely necessarily.

Stare at the flame and feel the flame enter your total being. Feel the inner cleansing deep into your soul. Now, visualize the whole room being cleansed. Imagine all negativity leaving the room and being filled with God's loving 'bright white light' of protection.

(Give a moment and then continue with a prayer, such as):

Divine Spirit,

Mother/Father God.

Cleanse our souls and make them pure.

Cover us and protect us with your loving light.

Guide us on the path of righteousness as we work with our chakras.

Heal and cleanse where needed and use us as your scepter.

The time spent here is time spent under Your divine love.

(Remain standing for a moment. When you feel enough time has elapsed then say **Thank you; Amen** and tell all to sit in their chosen seats. Put the lid on the pot so the flame goes out. Go back to your seat before continuing).

Protect ground and connect. Always use a similar one as in time it will come quickly and automatically when doing platform or rostrum work.

Such as:

Visualize a white beam of light coming through the ceiling.

(Don't let it travel further than my command.)

It's descending upon you.

It touches and covers your head.

It's slowly moving down around your shoulders.

It's now covering your arms, your chest and back, stomach and down over your hands.

It's moving down over your hips, upper legs, your knees, your lower legs

And slowly moving down around your feet

It's now covering your feet.

Now, visualize or sense it going through the floor underneath you and going deep into mother earth.

You're now grounded and also connected to God.

Focus on your total body and relax as in previous relaxations,

Such as:

Feel your feet relaxing. (Proceed slowly here to give time for relaxation)

Lower legs—Upper legs—Hips—Stomach—Chest—Shoulders—Arms—Hands—Mouth—Face

And relax your Head.

Clear your mind.

Now;

Focus on Chakra # 1, the Base; end of the spine

Visualize the color RED circling around inside of it.

Make sure that it's closed. Take a deep breath in; shift this chakra slightly to its original place and seal it in its place, do not seal over the entrance. What you use to seal it is entirely up to you, but I suggest a paste made of natural herbs. Whatever you create in your mind will work for you. Then breathe normally.

Chakra # 2—the Sacral, over the genitals;

Visualize the color ORANGE circling around inside it.

Make sure that it's closed. Take a deep breath in; shift this chakra slightly to its original place and seal it there. Breathe normally

Chakra # 3—the Solar Plexus, over your abdomen;

Visualize the color YELLOW circling around inside of it.

Make sure that it's closed; Take a deep breath in, shift this chakra slightly to its original place and seal it there. Breathe normally.

Chakra # 4—the Heart, over your centre chest;

Visualize the color GREEN circling around inside it.

Make sure that it's closed. Take a deep breath in, shift this chakra slightly to its original place and seal it there. Breathe normally.

Chakra # 5, the Throat, over the larynx;

Visualize the color BLUE circling around inside it.

Make sure that it's closed. Take a deep breath in, shift this chakra slightly to its original place and seal it there. Breathe normally.

Chakra # 6, the Brow, center forehead,—the third eye-;

Visualize the color INDIGO circling around inside it.

Make sure that it's closed. Take a deep breath in, shift this chakra slightly to its original place and seal it there. Breathe normally.

Chakra # 7, the Crown, top of the head;

Visualize the color VIOLET or BRIGHT WHITE, whichever is suitable to you, see that color circling around inside it. Make sure that it's closed. Take a deep breath in, shift this chakra slightly to its original place and seal it there. Breathe normally.

Now, in your mind visualize yourself holding a yardstick and hold it in front of you. Bring that yardstick close to your body, holding it upright from chakra # 1—the base—and align it with Chakra # 7—the crown. Take a good look and be certain that they're all aligned. If any need adjusting then adjust them; the paste hasn't totally dried yet. Arrange them in a straight line.

Now your chakras are perfectly aligned—feel the energy in Chakra # 1.

(Move this energy only upon my guidance please).

OK, let that energy travel upwards to Chakra # 2. Sense any feelings you experience.

From chakra # 2 let this combined energy travel upwards to Chakra # 3. Sense the feeling.

From chakra # 3 let this combined energy travel upwards to Chakra # 4. Sense the feeling.

From chakra # 4 let this combined energy travel upwards to Chakra # 5. Sense the feeling.

From chakra # 5 let this combined energy travel upwards to Chakra # 6. Sense the feeling.

Right now—gently open Chakra # 7.

From chakra # 6 let this combined energy travel upwards to Chakra # 7. Sense any feelings.

Now you're ready.

You're safe, don't have any fear.

Open chakra # 7. (You can do this by visualizing unscrewing a bottle top cover).

Now, let this combined energy out into the universe and direct it to where you want it to go. This may be your own personal quiet place or a place that you wish to explore. Go along with this energy.

Once there, sit in quiet with your guides and bring back a message for 1 or 2 people in the group. Try to focus on someone you don't know. If you don't get any messages bring back an object.

I'll leave you here for___________minutes.

(You choose the time you think will be needed).

(When time is up softly speak saying):

You're time is now up.

Listen to my voice.

Remain within,

From above visualize your head and your crown chakra. Go back inside and bring your chakra energies with you.

Now, gently close chakra # 7.

Imagine a cover being placed over the opening.

Twist it and seal it tight.

Start to feel and become aware of your body.

Let the combined chakra energy dissipate through your body.

Let it freely flow within as you balance the energies.

On my direction distribute the energies back to their original place.

Focus on your chakras again.

Chakra # 7—Crown; Leave the equivalent amount of energy and move down to

Chakra # 6—Brow; Leave the equivalent amount of energy and move down to

Chakra # 5—Throat; Leave the equivalent amount of energy and move down to

Chakra # 4—Heart; Leave the equivalent amount of energy and move down to

Chakra # 3—Solar plexus; Leave the equivalent amount of energy and move down to

Chakra # 2—Sacral; Leave the equivalent amount of energy and move down to

Chakra # 1—Base, end of spine; Leave the remainder of energy.

Once more, make sure all your chakras are closed and the energy is balanced out.

Again visualize your chakras in a perfectly straight line.

And—bring yourself back to reality.

Chakra #4 Meditation, Opening, Cleansing and Alignment:

Use the flame, stand and watch it intently for a full minute or a little longer while holding hands with thumbs pointing to the left. Blink your eyes only when necessary and let yourself become one with the flame. Once you become as one, feel and sense that your body, mind and soul are being cleansed; and then visualize the whole room being white-washed with pure white light.

(While students watch, the leader may say a protection prayer or, if alone, say one for yourself, with eyes open. After the prayer, have them close their eyes, (or close your own if alone) and call their guides and or your guides forward. Pause a moment and then all sit down.

(Cover the flame by putting the lid back on the pot).

(Sit comfortably in a meditative state).

(Do a quick 'protect ground and connect,' or your usual style).

(Use the relaxation procedure, as used above or your own and continue.)

(Leader speaks or tape starts).

In your mind visualize: Chakra # 1—Base, end of spine. See it as being closed with a twist on cover. Visualize the color RED circling around inside it.

Now visualize your hand moving towards it. Gently hold the cover and turn it anti-clockwise; remove it. In your mind see a small table and put the cover on it and each cover in sequence. Now, visualize your own hand on the hand of a spirit being gently massaging the area with an herbal remedy, such as Lavender Oil or something that is of a spiritual nature. Whatever you create will work. No abrasive cleansers please as it will do more harm than good.

Massage it open. Remove any debris and discard it and let the color RED fill the room.

Take a deep breath in and hold it and align this 'Chakra'; now shift this chakra slightly to its original place and seal it in its place, do not seal over the entrance. Then breathe normally. What you use to seal it is entirely up to you, but I suggest a paste made of natural herbs. Whatever you create or choose will work but don't use toxic chemicals.

Visualize Chakra # 2—the sacral, over the genitals. See it as being closed. Visualize the color ORANGE circling around inside.

Now visualize your hand moving towards it. Gently hold the cover and twist it off, anti-clockwise. Put the cover aside. Visualize the area being gently massaged by you or a spirit being.

Massage it open. Remove any debris and discard it and let the color Orange fill the room.

Take a deep breath in and hold it and align this chakra. Now, shift it slightly to its original place and seal it 'in its place,' do not seal over the entrance. Breathe normally.

Visualize Chakra # 3—the solar plexus, over the abdomen. See it as being closed. Visualize the color YELLOW circling around inside.

Now visualize your hand moving towards it. Gently hold the cover and twist it off; anti-clockwise. Put the cover aside. Visualize the area being gently massaged by you or a spirit being.

Massage it open. Remove any debris and discard it and let the color Yellow fill the room.

Take a deep breath in and hold it and align this chakra. Now, shift it slightly to its original place and seal it 'in its place', do not seal over the entrance. Breathe normally.

Visualize Chakra # 4—the heart, over your centre chest. See it as being closed. Visualize the color GREEN circling around inside.

Now visualize your hand moving towards it. Gently hold the cover and twist it off, anti-clockwise. Put the cover aside. Visualize the area being gently massaged by you or a spirit being.

Massage it open. Remove any debris and discard it and let the color Green fill the room.

Take a deep breath in and hold it and align this chakra. Now, shift it slightly to its original place and seal it 'in its place,' do not seal over the entrance. Breathe normally.

Visualize Chakra # 5—the throat, over the larynx. See it as being closed. Visualize the color BLUE circling around inside.

Now visualize your hand moving towards it. Gently hold the cover and twist it off; anti-clockwise. Put the cover aside. Visualize the area being gently massaged by you or a spirit being.

Massage it open. Remove any debris and discard it and let the color Blue fill the room.

Take a deep breath in and hold it and align this chakra. Now, shift it slightly to its original place and seal it 'in its place,' do not seal over the entrance. Breathe normally.

Visualize Chakra # 6—the brow, center forehead, the third eye. See it as being closed. Visualize the color INDIGO circling around inside.

Now visualize your hand moving towards it. Gently hold the cover and twist it off; anti-clockwise. Put the cover aside. Visualize the area being gently massaged by you or a spirit being.

Massage it open. Remove any debris and discard it and let the color Indigo fill the room.

Take a deep breath in and hold it and align this chakra. Now, shift it slightly to its original place and seal it 'in its place,' do not seal over the entrance. Breathe normally.

Visualize Chakra # 7, the crown, top of your head. See it as being closed. Visualize the color VIOLET or WHITE circling around inside.

Now visualize your hand moving towards it. Gently hold the cover and twist it off; anti-clockwise. Put the cover aside. Visualize the area being gently massaged by you or a spirit being.

Massage it open. Remove any debris and discard it and let the color Violet or White fill the room.

Take a deep breath in and hold it and align this chakra. Now, shift it slightly to its original place and seal it 'in its place,' do not seal over the entrance. Breathe normally.

Now, take a couple of moments to recheck them to be certain they're cleansed well and aligned properly. (Pause for one or two minutes).

(Then speak softly saying): Your chakra's are now unblocked, aligned and sealed in their proper places. Remain within and become aware of your body.

Now focus on Chakra # 7—The crown.

Pick up a cover and place it over the chakra. Turn it clockwise and close it tightly.

Focus on Chakra # 6—The Brow.

Pick up a cover and place it over the chakra. Turn it clockwise and close it tightly.

Focus on Chakra # 5—The Throat.

Pick up a cover and place it over the chakra. Turn it clockwise and close it tightly.

Focus on Chakra # 4—The Heart.

Pick up a cover and place it over the chakra. Turn it clockwise and close it tightly.

Focus on Chakra # 3—The Solar Plexus.

Pick up a cover and place it over the chakra. Turn it clockwise and close it tightly.

Focus on Chakra # 2—The Sacral.

Pick up a cover and place it over the chakra. Turn it clockwise and close it tightly.

Focus on Chakra # 1—The Base.

Pick up a cover and place it over the chakra. Turn it clockwise and close it tightly.

Now, bring yourself back to the room.

Bring yourself back.

Come back to reality.

Week 3:

White light meditation deals with God's protection. White light is what your soul possess and you need to let it radiate through your total being at all times. This meditation magnifies its effect. As you visualize your body being filled, a small portion at a time, it'll lighten up your total self as you feel yourself connecting with the Divine.

White Light Meditation

Relax and sit comfortably.

Protect, ground and connect (Your usual style or as previously).

Close your eyes. Say a protection prayer.

Breathe normally and listen to my voice.

Block out any noises or sounds other than what's from spirit.

Bring your attention to your feet. Relax them. Now fill them with white light.

Focus on your lower legs and knees. Relax. Fill that space with white light.

Focus on your upper legs. Relax. Fill that space with white light.

Focus on your hips, pelvis and buttocks. Relax. Fill that space with white light.

Focus on your stomach and lower back. Relax. Fill that space with white light.

Right now, let your intuition or gut feelings prepare for spirit contact. Ask your guide or doorkeeper to bring on this awareness. If you don't know them just telepathically ask your higher-self and recognize that it has been granted.

Now bring your attention to your chest, upper back and shoulders.

Relax.

Fill that space with white light.

Focus on your upper arms, lower arms, hands and fingers.

Relax.

Fill that space with white light.

Bring your attention to your throat and neck.

Relax.

Fill that space with white light.

Focus on your chin, mouth and nose.

Relax.

Fill that space with white light.

Focus on your eyes, ears and forehead.

Relax. Fill that space with white light.

Focus on the crown of your head.
Relax.
Totally fill your head with white light.
Now, bring your attention to your third eye, that's located in the center forehead—between both eyes. Prepare your self for spirit contact.
Right now open your third eye and let if be filled with pure white light, pure light from God. Soak it in; soak in as much as you possibly can.
Be totally relaxed and release any tension that you may feel.
Your guides are now with you.
Open all your senses to the spirit world.
Focus on one or more people who are with you in the group.
Feel and let your vibration intermingle with theirs.
Remain focused on them and chat with your guides and bring back messages. Use your imagination and create.
I'll call you back in a short while (Choose an appropriate time frame).
Your time is now up; bring yourself back.
(Say a prayer of thanks).

Week 4:

Mantra meditation conditions your mind to keep a focused point and not that of a wandering mind. This meditation is good to use in any stressful situation or difficult circumstance when you have a few 'alone' moments and need to unwind. You may use another focus point other than 'Love and Peace' but what you use should be of good and not bad.

Mantra Meditation

Relax and sit comfortably.
Protect ground and connect (Your usual style or as previously).
Say a protection prayer.
Close your eyes. Breathe normally and listen to my voice.

Block out any noises or sounds other than what's from spirit.

Bring your attention to your feet.

Relax them.

Say in your mind, "Love and Peace."

Focus on your lower legs and knees.

Relax. Say in your mind, "Love and Peace."

Focus on your upper legs.

Relax. Say in your mind, "Love and Peace."

Focus on your hips, pelvis and buttocks.

Relax. Say in your mind, "Love and Peace."

Focus on your stomach and lower back.

Relax. Say in your mind, "Love and Peace."

Right now, let your intuition or gut feelings prepare for spirit contact. Ask your guide or doorkeeper to bring on this awareness. If you don't know them just telepathically ask your higher self and recognize that it had been granted.

Now bring your attention to your chest, upper back and shoulders.

Relax. Say in your mind, "Love and Peace."

Focus on your upper arms, lower arms, hands and fingers.

Relax. Say in your mind, "Love and Peace."

Bring your attention to your throat and neck.

Relax. Say in your mind, "Love and Peace."

Focus on your chin, mouth and nose.

Relax. Say in your mind, "Love and Peace."

Focus on your eyes, ears and forehead.

Relax. Say in your mind, "Love and Peace."

Focus on the crown of your head.

Relax. Say in your mind, "Love and Peace."

Now, bring your attention to your third eye, that's located in the center forehead—between both eyes. Prepare your self for spirit contact.

Right now open your third eye and let if be filled with pure white light; pure light from God. Soak it in; soak in as much as you can and totally fill your body.

Be totally relaxed and release any tension that you may feel.

You are at peace and you are loved.

Your guides are now with you.

Now, open your Crown Chakra. Let this pure white light go out into the universe

Open all your senses to the spirit world. Say, Love and Peace.

Focus on one or more people who are with you in the group. Feel and let your vibration intermingle with theirs. Remain focused on them and chat with your guides and bring back messages. Use your imagination and create. I'll call you back in a short while. (Choose an appropriate time frame).

Your time is now up;

Stay focused;

Bring the white light back inside your crown Chakra.

Now close your Crown Chakra.

Say, 'thank you, Love and Peace'.

Bring your awareness back in to the room; bring yourself back.

(Say a prayer of thanks).

Week 5:

A mindfulness meditation also keeps you within a one-mind focused point. But with this one you should use an object, a flower or a person. You may also use anything that's appealing to you but make it something you love and respect even if it's of your own nature for self-healing.

Mindfulness Meditation

Protect ground and connect (Your usual style).

Say a protection prayer and then open your eyes for a moment.

Relax and sit comfortably.

(This time is used to look at a picture of what you have chosen so that all will see it in their mind with eyes closed).

Keep your eyes opened and focus on: (such as, a Butterfly, a Rose, a Deer or anything that appeals to you).

Breathe normally and focus on each breath while looking at

I'll let you focus for one minute then I'll speak to you again.

(Time 1 minute; 60 seconds).

One minute is now up: listen to my voice.

Bring your attention to your feet. Relax.

Focus on your lower legs and knees. Relax.

Focus on your upper legs. Relax.

Focus on your hips, pelvis and buttocks. Relax.

Focus on your stomach and lower back

Relax; let your intuition or gut feelings prepare for spirit contact. Ask your guide or doorkeeper to bring on this awareness. If you don't know them just telepathically ask your higher self and recognize that it has been granted.

Now bring your attention to your chest, upper back and shoulders. Relax.

Focus on your upper arms, lower arms, hands and fingers. Relax.

Bring your attention to your throat and neck. Relax.

Continue on; focus on your chin, mouth and nose. Relax.

Focus on your eyes, ears and forehead. Relax.

Focus on the crown of your head. Relax.

Now, bring your attention to your third eye, that's located in the centre forehead—between both eyes. Prepare yourself for spirit contact.

Bring your awareness back to ____________________. Keep that vision in your mind. Be totally relaxed and release any tension that you may feel.

Right now open all your senses to the spirit world. Your mind may leave ________________ occasionally. Let it go when you focus and receive spirit messages but always bring your self back to the__________

Your guides are with you.

Now—focus on one or more people who are with us in this group. Choose those whom you don't know well. Feel and let your vibration intermingle with theirs. Remain focused on them and chat with your guides and bring back messages. Always bring your mind back to __________________ when not conversing with your guides. Use your imagination and create.

I'll call you back in a short while. (Choose an appropriate time frame).

Your time is now up; bring yourself back.

Week 6:

The two healing meditations are directed at you (the one who is meditating) but it can be used for someone you know who needs healing. It's perfect to use at any time whether it's for you or another whom you wish to send distant-healing to. All you have to do is visualize the other person instead of yourself when listening to your taped meditations or visualizing your own when you've advanced enough to create your own, in your mind. Personally, although I feel advanced, I prefer to follow someone else's voice. By this time you should be able to easily go within and relax much sooner.

Healing Meditation #1

Sit comfortably.

(Prayer)

Great Divine Spirit, protect us with your Infinite White Light. Guide us as we go within to receive a total body healing. Grant this healing to take place immediately with your wondrous power. Grant healing guides that know where healing is needed; grant only the highest and the best. Keep all evil entities away. It's now left in your divine care. Amen.

(Protect, ground and connect).

Visualize a white beam of light coming through the ceiling. It's descending upon you. It touches and covers your head and you feel a sense of peace and love from God.

Feel the blissful comfort emitting from it.

It's slowly moving down around your shoulders. It's now covering your arms, your chest and back, stomach and down over your hands. It's moving down over your hips, upper legs, your knees, lower legs and slowly moving down around your feet. It's now covering your feet. Now, visualize it going through the floor underneath you and going deep into mother earth.

You're now grounded and also connected to God.

Don't be afraid, relax, you're safe.

Take in a deep breath. Let it out slowly and breathe normally.

Feel your feet relaxing.

Lower legs—Upper legs—Hips—Stomach—Chest—Shoulders—Arms—Hands—Mouth—Face and Head relaxing. Clear your mind. Listen only to my voice. Block out any other noises. Breathe normally.

Imagine yourself walking in a tropical park. The park is a beautiful unspoiled forest covered with palm and citrus fruit trees. Take a look around and see the various cacti growing alongside the pathway. The air is warm and you feel a slightly cool, pleasant breeze. Look straight ahead and see the ocean in the distance; walk towards it. Now, step out from the shade; step on the sandy beach and walk down towards the water. Smell the salty aroma and smell how sweet and fresh the air is.

You have a swim suit underneath your casual clothes; now prepare yourself as if you were going swimming.

Step into the water and feel it invigorating you. As the water covers your feet you begin to feel a sense of gratitude from the refreshing feeling. Now walk out to knee level. The water is touching your knees now, bring your awareness to the ocean floor and feel the sand beneath your feet and between your toes. This feeling is uplifting and very pleasant. The water is calm; the air is peaceful; the birds are happily singing nearby and you hear the call of the forest animals in the distance.

Don't be afraid; you're totally safe. The lifeguards are watching and all is well. There's a sand barrier further out and the water is too shallow for any unexpected danger.

Now, lower your body and sit down in the shallow water. Right now feel the water totally covering your body—up to your chin. Keep your head above the water and sit in the quietness. Feel the comfort from the coolness and relax in the healing environment.

Feel the sun touch your face. It brings on awareness.

Take a handful of sand from the ocean floor and rub it on your feet.

Feel the fine grains caress your toes and feet and feel the healing effect.

Take another handful of sand and rub it on your lower legs and knees. Feel the healing effect. Take another handful of sand and rub it on your upper legs. Feel the healing effect.

Take more sand and rub it on your stomach and chest. Feel the healing taking place.

Take some more sand and rub it on your neck. Feel the healing take place and feel it soothing your throat and lungs.

Take more sand and cover both shoulders, upper arms, elbows, lower arms, hands and fingers. Feel healing taking place.

Now, slowly stand up and walk back to the shore, but stay in the water.

OK, now lie down with your head on the beach and your body in the water. There are no waves, the water is calm.

Take some more sand and rub it on your head and in your hair. Feel the healing effect.

As you're lying on the sand, feel the fine grains on your back and feel it as if there were thousands of acupuncture points lightly piercing your flesh. Feel the healing envelop your total body.

Sit up now and remain in the water. With both hands scoop up some water and let it fall over your head, it's clearing the sand out of your hair. As the sand falls from your head it passes over your face and upper body. Feel the healing taking place.

Continue to do this for a while and feel your total body healing as you become energized.

Now step out of the water. Walk back to the shade and sit down on the old fallen tree.

Right now with your healing energy I want you to focus on one or two people in the circle, preferably someone you don't know well. Mix your vibration with theirs. Speak with your guides and bring back messages. If you don't get messages bring back symbols.

Use your imagination: sense, as well as visualize. Create from what you see, feel, and sense.

I'll call you back in _____________

Your time is now up.

(Prayer)

Great Divine Spirit, thank you for your protection; thank you for the contacts we've been given and may your protection remain with us. Thank you for the healing—given with your divine love. Make us more knowledgeable each day and lead us safely on our spiritual journey. Amen.

Bring yourself back.

Wiggle your feet back and forth.

Come back to reality.

HEALING MEDITATION #2

Sit comfortably

(Prayer, as above).

(Protect, ground, and connect).

Visualize a white beam of light coming through the ceiling.

As it's descending over your body let your body relax as well.

It touches and covers your head and you feel a sense of peace and love from God.

It's slowly moving down around your shoulders. It's now covering your arms, your chest and back, stomach, and down over your hands. It's moving down over your hips, upper legs, your knees, lower legs and slowly moving down around your feet. It's now covering your feet. Now, visualize it going through the floor underneath you and going deep into mother earth.

You're now grounded, and also connected to God.

You're body is totally relaxed.

Breathe normally.

Imagine it's morning and you're in a beautiful park with lots of people around. You just got out of your sleeping bag and you exit the tent or trailer. The briskness of the morning atmosphere invigorates you to go for a walk. You feel slightly unenergized from the night's activity of partying with friends and going to sleep late.

Yes, you'll go for a walk. A walk by yourself is just what you need to start your day off right. You take a look at a big Oak tree and start to walk down the pathway to the river. The flow of the water is gentle and smooth. You walk with a carefree attitude and a sense of bonding with nature. The running water in a river has always been important to you; you know of the healing powers that purified water holds. Walk further upstream; you come to a waterfall. This waterfall is a natural shower and is frequently used by the park's guests. At this time of the morning most people are still asleep and you feel in need of a healing.

This reminds you of the way people did this in biblical times and a dejavu feeling overpowers you. You have a memory of this but can't quite place it. Nevertheless you walk slowly to the falls as if being drawn there by an unseen force. You reach it and touch the falling water with your hand and the temperature feels perfect. The feeling of past experiences continues to beckon you underneath the water. You slowly walk under and keep your nose out just far enough so that you can breath.

Feel it cascade down over your body. You're standing there almost motionless and the water runs down over your head, feel the healing effect take place. Focus on your chest and back and let the water run smoothly over; recognize and bring your vital organs to the healing attention and feel the healing take place.

Let the water flow down over your shoulders, upper arms, elbows, lower arms, hands and fingers; visualize the healing take place.

Discard any aches and pains.

Feel the water flowing down over you hips, buttocks, and stomach and feel the cleansing effect. Let it cleanse your bowels of any chemicals that you may have consumed in recent food. Now, let the water descend over your upper legs, knees, lower legs, feet, and toes; feel the healing effect and discard any aches and pains. Let the water take it downstream.

Now let the water flow from the top of your head to the tips of your toes and feel your total body healing. As it continues to flow visualize it as pure as the whiteness of angel dust. Let it take away any discomfort, aches and pains and imagine the healing taking place.

You feel invigorated and refreshed; the stream from the waterfalls has healed you. Now, step out from under the water and sit on one of the big rocks in the sun. Let the sun dry you and as it does I want you to converse with the spirit world. Bring your attention to one or two people in the circle and bring back a message. If you don't get a message then bring back an object.

I'll call you back in __________.

Your time is now up, stay within and listen to my voice.

The sun has dried you very nicely.

Now stand up and make your way back down the pathway by the river.

Continue to walk.

Ok, you've reached your starting point. Walk back around the big Oak tree and find yourself back in this room.

(Prayer)

Bring yourself back.

Week 7:

Some people thoroughly believe that healing and other phenomena can and do take place through the use of crystals. If you have an interest in crystals and believe, then what you use them for will work. All one has to do is believe it will happen and it will, with or without the stones. I have a few stones that were given as gifts and appreciate what they're supposed to do. I don't put a lot of emphasis on, or have a lot of faith in them, but I do wear an amethyst hanging from a chain around my neck when I feel I need an extra bit of protection. After saying that one may be led to believe that I rely on one more so than others. Why the amethyst? Maybe it's because it's my birth stone, but I do feel somewhat extra protected when I wear it, but that's not often.

Crystal Room Meditation

Sit comfortably.

(Prayer)

Great Divine Spirit, protect us with your Infinite White Light.

Guide us as we enter the Crystal Room. From each crystal grant immediate energy, and direct it to where it's needed with your wondrous power. We ask that you keep all evil entities away. It's now under the guidance of your divine care. Amen.

(Protect, ground and, connect the usual way).

Imagine yourself at the entrance of an elaborate castle. On the door in front of you is a big round iron handle that's used as a doorbell. Lift it up let it drop loudly to make your presence known. The door is opening and you're greeted. Look at who's inviting you in.

Enter the castle; the door closes behind you. Look around and see how beautiful it is. It makes you feel like you've entered a palace. This place is yours to discover. You may follow my guidance or travel off on your own. There's a door in the far right-hand corner, walk towards it. Open it; the room is dark. The light switch is on your left, at shoulder height. Turn it on and go inside. You now find yourself in the corridor leading to the crystal room.

Look in front of you and see the row of display tables lining the corridor.

Look at the table on your right. On this table is a **GARNET.**

This is a stone of health, commitment, devotion, and passion. It stimulates Kundalini and assists in the flow of energy.

Move close and touch it. Now let it do its job. Feel the healing, feel the energy and let it enter your total being.

Walk to the next table, it's on your left. On this table is an **EMERALD.**

This is a stone of loyalty, sensitivity, success, and domestic bliss. It enhances memory and mental capacity, eliminates negativity and allows you to focus. It brings harmony to all aspects of life.

Move close, touch it, and soak up its blessings.

Walk to the next table, on your right. On this table you'll find a **TOPAZ.**

This is a stone of love and success. It promotes individuality, expression, and creativity; stores energy, thoughts, and love.

Step close and place both hands on it. Soak up as much energy as you are able to.

Walk to the next table, on your left. On this table is a **RUBY.**

This is a stone of love, purity, spiritual wisdom, knowledge, and wealth. It amplifies energy and it's a protector.

Move close, touch it, and soak up all that it has to offer.

Walk to the next table, on your right. On this table you'll find a **ROSE QUARTZ.**

This is a stone of positive love energy to relationships, compassion and forgiveness. It has a calming effect. It helps clear stored anger, resentment, jealousy and fears. It replaces negativity with harmony, eases emotional imbalances and enhances self-confidence and creativity.

Move close, touch it, and feel all that it has to offer; and accept it.

Walk to the next table, on your left. On this table is a **QUARTZ CRYSTAL.**

This is the universal stone. It corresponds to all zodiac signs. It has a pure and powerful energy source. It receives, activates, stores, transmits, and amplifies energy. It stimulates your brain functions and activates all levels of consciousness.

Move close; wrap your arms around it. Take in as much of this as you possibly can and let it bring harmony to your soul.

Walk to the next table, on your right. On this table you'll find a **SAPPHIRE.**

This stone comes in a variety of colors: blue, white, black, purple, yellow or green; it's your decision. This is a stone of joy, peace, beauty, intuition and known as the stone of prosperity. It supports the fulfillment of dreams and the desires of the consciousness.

Move close, touch it and sap up as much of this as you're able.

Walk to the next table, on your left. On this table you'll find an **AMETHYST.**

This is a stone of peace and strength. It's a physical representation of the violet ray that cuts through illusion. It enhances psychic abilities and it assists in channelling. It sedates, protects, enhances feelings of contentment and connects you to your spirituality.

Move close and wrap your arms around it, soak up as much as possible and let it activate your crown chakra.

Walk to the next table, on your right. This is the last one.

On this table you'll find a large **HERKIMER DIAMOND.**

This is a stone of attunement. It alleviates tension, provides harmony and spontaneous awareness. It stimulates clairvoyance and telepathic communication.

Move close, reach out and pick it up. Hold it with both hands and place it next to your third eye. Let it fine-tune your emotions, ESP, psychic ability, and clairvoyant powers.

Now, place the diamond back on the table.

You have now been granted spirit connection and communication.

In front of you is one step down. Go down that step; you're now in the crystal room.

Go and sit in the lounge chair by the fireplace. Your spirit guide is there waiting for you. Converse and bring back messages for some people in the circle, preferably those you don't know well.

I'll call you back in _____________.

Your time is now up.

Now, rise up from your chair and turn around; there's a door behind you. Go through it and you'll find yourself back in this room.

(Prayer)

Great Divine Spirit, thank you for your protection; thank you for the contacts we've been given and may your protection remain with us. Thank you for the crystal healing and wisdom and also for experiencing the Crystal Room. Make us more knowledgeable each day and lead us safely on our spiritual journey. Amen.

Bring yourself back.

Week 8:

The sanctuary is a place of refuge; a place that's totally yours and yours alone. Think of a place where you felt great peace, love and joy, or a place that you had visited and that you often reflect on. This place is, and should always be, your place for self-refreshment when you need time to feel good about yourself and those around you. All you need to do is sit for a moment, before your meditation, and visualize this place. For instance, let this serene place return to you so that you can return to it when the time comes within your meditation. Once you've visited or created this place again, hold on to it in your mind so that you'll have easy access when you're ready to experience it. This meditation deals with the colors of the chakras.

SANCTUARY MEDITATION

Prayer

Protect, ground and connect as previous.

Visualize the color RED filling the room.

Take a deep breath and breathe it deep into your lungs.

Visualize the color ORANGE filling the room.

Take a deep breath and breathe it deep into your lungs.

Visualize the color YELLOW filling the room.

Take a deep breath and breathe it deep into your lungs.

Visualize the color GREEN filling the room.

Take a deep breath and breathe it deep into your lungs.

Visualize the color BLUE filling the room.

Take a deep breath and breathe it deep into your lungs.

Visualize the color INDIGO filling the room.

Take a deep breath and breathe it deep into your lungs.

Visualize the color VIOLET or PURPLE filling the room.

Take a deep breath and breathe it deep into your lungs.

Visualize BRIGHT WHITE filling the room.

Take a deep breath and breathe it deep into your lungs.

Concentrate on those colors, shift your mind back and forth and see each one, or just focus on all that comes to your mind.

Those are the colors of the rainbow, gods colors to all.

Now prepare yourself to travel.

You're safe, don't have any fear.

Let those combined colors energize your awareness.

Start to feel their intensity; now take yourself to a Sanctuary where the windows are of stained glass and the room is bathed in mixed colors of crystal.

Now sit in quiet with your guides and bring back a message for one or two people in the group. Try to focus on someone you don't know well. If you don't get any messages bring back an object.

I'll leave you here for___________minutes.

Your time is now up.

Remain within.

Listen to my voice.

Focus on the color RED and send it out into the universe.

Focus on the color ORANGE; send it out into the universe.

Focus on the color YELLOW; send it out into the universe.

Focus on the color GREEN; send it out into the universe.

Focus on the color BLUE: send it out into the universe.

Focus on the color INDIGO: send it out into the universe.

Focus on the color VIOLET/PURPLE; send it out into the universe.

Focus on the color of WHITE LIGHT and let it totally cover you.

And, bring yourself back to reality.

(Prayer of thanks).

Week 9:

I believe in power animals. Maybe it's because I grew up in the country where one has access to the wild life more so than those who live in the city. I use animals and birds in a few meditations. I feel that my personal power animals are 'the wolf, the eagle and the dove.' When I see one or any of these in my meditation I feel great comfort and joy. Moreover, I feel an extra protection and guidance. Each animal holds a meaning. I'm fairly certain that the Internet will provide you with those meanings if you type "Power Animal" in the search and press enter, or what have you.

Power-Animal Meditation

Sit comfortably.

(Connect, ground, and protect).

(Prayer)

This is very important.

What is your favorite season? What is your favorite sport? What is your favorite hobby? Where is your favorite place in the world other than your place of residence or your place of birth? Where have you always wanted to travel but haven't? Or where did you travel that made a dream come true?

Consider the Mountains, the Desert. Consider tropical places that hold an abundance of wildlife. Consider South America, Peru, Cost Rica, the Rain Forest, Egypt, and any other place that draws your attention. Most of all consider Africa.

Imagine yourself standing inside a circle. There are four open doors, (DON"T GO THROUGH ANY OF THEM UNTIL YOU HAVE PERMISSION). One door is to the East, one to the South, one to the West, and the other to the North. Find yourself dressed to enter the door you choose. You'll be protected from the heat, the rain, the snow, and the cold. Be assured that protection is given from any predators that you may encounter or experience. Remember, your power animal totem could include birds, reptiles and the wildlife that lives in water, as well as all that live on land. They won't harm you in any way. Your totem or power animal is your guardian and protector.

One door looks more inviting than the other.

Now, choose a door and walk towards it.

Start to walk, feel safe. Go through the door and look at all the beauty it has to offer.

Continue walking, you'll find that it's very pleasant and uplifting. You begin to feel elated from the atmosphere.

Look ahead and see a clearing, whether it's a snow clearing, a patch of grass, or a sandy beach: walk towards it. Continue walking; just ahead of you are a few trees and some rock boulders that surround it. You now find yourself at the entrance. Walk slowly forward; now look in and around—to your left—and look in the far corner. Use you imagination and visualize. What animal do you see? This will be your power animal, your totem. If you don't see one, keep looking. Your power animal welcomes you; and you both walk slowly towards each other.

Meet your power animal, your animal protector, and your totem.

I'm going to leave you here to get acquainted and while sitting together your power animal will protect you. If, up to this time, you haven't met your power animal please continue to search.

For those who have, connect your vibration with up to four people in the group and bring back a message. If you don't get a message then bring back a symbol.

I'll leave you here for ________________.

Time is now up.

Stay within and listen to my voice.

Now, stand up and walk towards the door you entered, bring your power animal with you.

Come back through the door—and when you do—you'll find yourself back in this room.

Your totem, your power animal is with you, feel its presence.

Bring yourself back.

Week 10:

Angels, angels, angels. Most believe and many have witnessed them. In near death and out-of-body experiences angels have been encountered by many. My best friend passed to spirit about seven years ago and on his deathbed he spoke of the many angels that were with him in his final hours. I felt their presence also, as the room was very peaceful. One could hear the sound of silence with the stillness as friends chatted quietly. All of a sudden he asked, *"Don't you see them, there are so many?"*

This particular evening his guardians went out when I arrived as they had been with him all day. In his last couple of hours, he lay quietly. I sat on his bed and picked up a prayer book that was on his night table. I held his hand with a feeling of sadness, because he was so young. I spoke his prayers aloud while he was preparing for his transition.

When his guardians returned I was amazed that I hadn't heard their entrance as my hearing was very acute at that time. I was still speaking his prayers when I was made aware of someone else's presence. As I turned around both were peering through the doorway listening as I spoke. Then I realized that I had sat and prayed with him for about two hours. On my departure, one of them said, *"I'll never forget the moment when I returned and looked through the door and saw you sitting there in reverence and praying."* I had just reached home when the phone rang saying that he had finally passed and was asked if I wished to return before any further arrangements were made. I said no as we had said our good-byes before I left. He comes to visit me often in spirit and has come to me through a few mediums giving verification that he hasn't forgotten me.

Meditation—Archangels

Sit comfortably.

(Prayer)

Great Divine Spirit, protect us with your Infinite White Light. Guide us as we go within. Grant us the ability to get in touch with the Archangels. Keep all evil entities away while we're on our spiritual journey. Amen.

Visualize a white beam of light coming through the ceiling. It's descending upon you. Now let it slowly travel down over you, totally covering your body, way down, down to your feet. Now send it deep into mother earth. You're now grounded and connected with the God source.

Right now, feel your feet relaxing. Relax your lower legs. Relax your upper legs, Hips. Stomach, Chest, Back, Shoulders, Arms, Hands, let all tension go. Relax your Mouth and Face. Clear your mind. Take a moment and listen to the silence.

(Give a moment).

Now focus on your third eye that's in your centre forehead, directly between both eyes. Look into it and see all that is good and of God.

Now, focus on the top of your head. Open your Crown Chakra as wide as possible. The light of God that covers you, as your protection, appears to be a white tube from inside. Look up inside this tube right now.

Focus on sending telepathic messages up through this tube.

The first Archangel you're going to contact is **Zadkiel**. In your mind say his name "Zadkiel." Now invite him to come to you. Visualize and see him in your mind. He deals with the mystic and the diplomat. His qualities are: ordered service, culture, refinement, diplomacy, and invocation. His master is St. Germaine. (Give a moment).

The next Archangel is **Uriel**. In your mind say his name, "Uriel." Invite him to come to you. Visualize and see him in your mind. He deals with priesthood, ministry and healing. His qualities are: devotional worship, ministering and peace. His master is Jesus. (Give a moment).

The next Archangel is **Raphael**. In your mind say, "Raphael." Invite him to come to you. Visualize and see him. He deals with invention and doctoring. His qualities are: scientific, truth and development. His master is Hilarion. (Give a moment).

The next Archangel is **Gabriel**. In your mind say, "Gabriel." Invite him to come to you. Visualize and see him. He deals with musicians and artists. His qualities are: artistic development, resurrection, and purity. His master is Serapis Bay. (Give a moment).

The next Archangel is **Chamuel**. In your mind say, "Chamuel." Invite him. Visualize and see him in your mind. He deals with arbiter and peace making. His qualities are: tolerance, gratitude and love. His master is Paul the Venetian. (Give a moment).

The next Archangel is **Jophiel**. In your mind say, "Jophiel." Invite him. Visualize and see him. He deals with students and teaches. His qualities are: illumination, perception and wisdom. His master is Kuthumi. (Give a moment).

The next Archangel is **Michael**. In your mind say, "Michael." Invite him to come to you. Visualize and see him in your mind. He deals with executive and rulers. His qualities are: initiative, power, and protection. His master is El Morya. (Give a moment).

Sit for a while and commune; ask one or any of them for a message for a couple of people in the circle.

I'll call you back in ________________.

Time is now up, focus on your crown chakra again and close it tightly.

Come back to reality.

PRAYER of thanks.

Week 11:

The aura consists of all the colors of the rainbow. Most of those colors are pastel but will shine much brighter when someone is feeling exceptionally well. It will also show signs of dark grey to black when a person is extremely depleted of energy or is terminally ill. Both your chakras and aura interact and oftentimes will work in consistency with each other as one reflects the other.

We all have an aura, some much bigger than others as it depends on your environment, health, emotions, and personal well being. Mediums with clairvoyant powers are able to see them with the naked eye and give character readings.

Peace and love usually emit from your aura, but let something sadden or upset you and your aura will be noticed by many, even those that can't see them; they will feel and sense the change in energy. Auras are very real. They have been photographed in laboratories; they're not illusions. You'll learn how to see an aura if you look in my first book.

As you work with each meditation you will continue to open your clairvoyance ability. Furthermore, each meditation gives you the option of connecting with spirit and receiving spirit messages. Keep with it and grow spiritually.

Extended Aura Field Meditation

Sit comfortably, close your eyes.

(Connect, ground, and protect your usual way).

(Prayer)

Go quickly over the colors of the chakras.

Focus on your:

Base Chakra, **Red,** Etheric layer of the Aura;
Sacral **Orange,** Emotional layer of the Aura;
Solar Plexus **Yellow,** Mental, Intellectual layer of the Aura;
Heart **Green**, Astral layer of the Aura;
Throat **Light Blue/Indigo**, Etheric Template layer of the Aura;
Brow **Indigo /Purple**, Third Eye, Celestial layer of the Aura;
Crown, **Violet or White**, Ketheric layer of the Aura.

Now concentrate and look at the aura outside of your body.

The first segment is **The Etheric Aura**: it extends about two inches out from your physical body and is a shade of blue. This relates to your physical condition and health. In this section you feel all sensations, both pain and pleasure. Take notice of what you feel, sense, and see.

(Pause momentarily between each)

The next portion is **The Emotional Aura**: it extends about two to four inches from your body and appears as light-rainbow-colored-clouds. It's associated with your feelings. Positive feelings create bright colors; negative feelings create dark colors. Problems in this aura segment will eventually lead to problems in the first and third auras. Take notice of what you feel, sense, and see.

Next outer field is **The Mental Aura**: it extends about four to eight inches from your body and is a bright shade of yellow. Your thoughts and mental processes are within this. The more active your thinking, the brighter it becomes. Within this section thought forms can be found. Take notice of what you feel, sense, and see.

Next is **The Astral Aura**: it extends about eight to twelve inches from your body and is brightly-colored-rainbow-clouds. This is the bridge between the physical world and the spiritual realm. Take notice of what you feel, sense, and see.

Next is **The Etheric Template Aura**: it extends about 12 to 24 inches from your body and it's a blue-print form. There is an empty groove in the etheric aura into which the etheric aura fits; similar to a ring around Saturn or a halo over an angel's head. This section holds the etheric aura in place. It's the template for the etheric dimension. Take notice of what you feel, sense, and see.

Next is **The Celestial Aura**: it extends about 24 inches from your body and it's a brighter shimmering light of light pastel colors. This is the level of feelings within the world of your spirit. Here is where you communicate with all the beings of the spiritual world. Take notice of what you feel, sense, and see.

Next is **The Ketheric Template Aura**: it extends about 36 to 48 inches from the physical body. It's an extremely bright-golden-light that is pulsating rapidly. This aura segment surrounds and protects everything within its boundaries; it's protecting you. Take notice of what you feel, sense, and see.

Sit quietly for a while and bring back a message for a couple people in the circle.

I'll call you back in __________.

(Choose an appropriate time frame and from now on lessen it as you continue to advance).

Time is now up.

Bring yourself back to reality.

(Say a prayer of thanks).

Week 12:

Your personal haven is a place similar to that above but with a different concept in mind. This place should be uplifting and bring a magnitude of bliss to your total being. This meditation may be used to bring about a tranquil atonement when you need peace of mind or just want to treat yourself to something special. Without putting yourself first and taking proper care of yourself how will you be able to assist and care for another with full attention? Therefore, you need to love yourself first to give that which you wish to receive. Make your night class special which also includes a bonding of Love-and-Light as we're all connected as one with the universe. Do remember: when you're in your quiet time of meditation ask for messages to relate to others in the group and don't forget to ask who's giving them. Furthermore, make each meditation time shorter and try to make a contact with an entity after the fact. It should be getting easier by now as you have had a few weeks' practice. Don't hesitate to give it a try even if you feel that you're guessing. Hence, what is a class all about but to learn by trial and error? Be patient, be enthusiastic and above all be persistent to reach your goal.

Personal Haven—Meditation

Sit comfortably.

Connect, ground and protect.

You're in a large parking lot and have just found a parking space.

Get out of the car.

Look at the beautiful green houses and the magnificent gardens surrounding them.

This place looks familiar and you feel an encasement of sunshine covering you. You speak telepathically to your higher self and say: "what a beautiful day." Your guides answer to affirm that they're with you. You feel elated with a sense of nostalgia.

Choose a path; start to walk towards the greenhouse directly in front of you.

The lilies are in bloom; admire them. Look at the large white one to your left.

There's a small blue one to your right, very tall, slender and elegant.

Touch it gently and feel its softness.

A cluster of pink lilies are a little further ahead. You feel yourself being drawn to them like a magnet. You reach them and the aroma is much like a mix of hybrid tea roses. Take a deep breath in through your nostrils and enjoy the pleasant scent.

You're at the door of the greenhouse now. Open it. Smell the earthly acid aroma.

It's a little overpowering at first, but you enter and close the door behind you.

You hear birds singing and water falling.

Walk the cobblestone path towards the falling water.

Look at all the different plants and take in their beauty. Feel peaceful and at ease.

You reach the falling water. There's a three-tier shell-shape fountain. The water is slowly cascading out of the top and gently falling from one tier to the other and falling in the pond beneath.

Move closer and look in the pond. Look at the fish: white, blue and silver Koi, large fan-tail goldfish; golden and brown minnows darting back and forth as if they're afraid. The minnows are slender about 1 to 2 inches long and swim very fast. This behavior is normal; watch them for a moment.

(Give a moment here).

Walk a little further now. You come to another door. Open it. Go in, close it behind you. You're now in your 'Personal Haven.'

Now go and sit down on the bench beside the pretty young girl in the white dress. She's there in the shade admiring the swans in the pond. Go ahead, she was invited and she's waiting for you.

Sit close and feel her presence. The feeling is angelic and the attraction is mutual.

Talk with her; ask her questions and listen to what she has to say. She has messages for you to bring back to a few people in the circle; people that you don't know well.

Chat with her for a while and I'll bring you back in_______________.

Your time is up.

Give the pretty young girl a hug and thank her, bid her farewell with God's blessings. Stand up now and walk to the last door. Open it, go inside and you'll find yourself back in this room.

Bring yourself back.

(Say a prayer of gratitude).

Week 13:

This meditation is similar to Chakra # 1 Meditation: (Opening and traveling up to your higher-self) but without using your chakras. You should only open your chakras under the guidance of a teacher or the use of a taped meditation with more than yourself present. Chakras are not to be tampered with and should not be taken lightly. They should be respected as they hold a tremendous power and once open and not closed you're leaving yourself open to just about any entity. Entities that are closest to the earth plane are those not contented in their crossing or troubled entities looking for a human host. This type of invitation, which is known as leaving-an-open-door, encourages possession. Never forget to close your chakras once opened as a few teachers forget to guide you at the end of class or a meditation.

Higher Self at Level 4—Meditation

Sit comfortably.

(Prayer)

Great Divine Spirit, protect us with your Infinite White Light. Guide us as we go within. Grant us the ability to ascend above our consciousness to communicate with spirit. Keep all evil entities away while we're on our spiritual journey. Amen.

Visualize a white beam of light coming through the ceiling. It's descending upon you. It touches and covers your head; you feel a sense of peace and love from God.

It's slowly moving down around your shoulders. It's now covering your upper arms, your chest and back, lower arms, stomach, hips and down over your hands. It's moving down your upper legs, your knees, your lower legs and slowly moving down around your feet. It's now covering your feet. Now visualize it going through the floor underneath you and going deep into mother earth. You're now grounded and also connected to God.

Don't be afraid; relax, you're safe.

Take in a deep breath. Let it out slowly and breathe normally.

Feel your feet relaxing. Let them become very light.

Relax your lower legs, feel them becoming very light. Relax your upper legs, feel them becoming very light. Hips feel the lightness. Stomach, Chest and Back, feel the lightness. Shoulders, Arms, Hands, let all tension go and feel yourself as light as a feather. Relax your Mouth and Face. Clear your mind. Take a moment and listen to the silence.

(Give a moment).

Now focus on your third eye, that's in the center forehead directly between both eyes. Look into it and see all that is good and Godly.

Now, focus on the top of your head. Open your Crown Chakra as wide as possible. The light of God that covers you as your protection appears to be a white tube from inside. You're inside this tube right now.

Now I want you to think about leaving your body for a short while. Don't move any faster than what I say, follow my guidance. Slowly start to ascend in this tube. You're safe, don't be afraid.

Begin to travel; go up, up, and up. Now stop. This is level 1 above your consciousness. Take a look around, what do you see?

Start to go upward again: go up, up, and up. Stop. This is Level 2 above your consciousness. Take a look around.

Up you go again: go up, up, and up. Stop. This is Level 3 above your consciousness. Take in its surroundings.

Continue upward again now; go up, up, and up. Stop. This is Level 4 above your consciousness.

Look around and see the beautiful scenery. It's like a scene from Cinderella Land. You're now very close to the spirit world.

Leave the tube of white light and go out and explore. Be comfortable in this magical land and communicate with spirit. While there pick up a message for a couple of people in the circle, preferably someone you don't know well.

I'll bring you back in ___________________.

Time is up now.

Come back from the fairytale land.

Get ready to descend.

Enter the tube of white light.

Start to come down slowly, down, down; you're now at level 3

Once again, come a little further down, down, down and you're now at level 2

Continue downward, down, "down you come"; you're now at level 1

A little further down now, come down slowly and come down.

Now go back inside your Crown Chakra.

Focus once again and look up into the white light tube. Thank the world of spirits and then tightly close your chakra.

Become aware of your third eye again; never let it wander too far from your consciousness.

Now bring your awareness back to the room.

Come back.

(Prayer)

Divine Spirit; We thank you for your protection and guidance while we ascended above our consciousness to communicate with the spirit world. Thank you for keeping all evil entities away while we were on our spiritual journey. Amen.

Week 14:

From the meditations I've used I'd consider the 'Interplanetary travel' the best. Even if you haven't studied the universe I feel that you'll enjoy this as much as I do. We often look at the sky several times a day or night. What we see above sends our thoughts into wonderment of what lies beyond our small planet. What's out there can be reached through this meditation but, like many have said, *"You need a great imagination to do this."* When I'm out there, and I astral travel often, I no longer feel it's my imagination as it feels very real. The scenery is so spectacular that it has to be more than my imagination. You decide for yourself but, looking at a photo of the universe and where the planets are located is a must so that you'll always know your exact location. This is a long meditation so don't rush it, go along for the adventure and enjoy the experience.

INTERPLANETARY TRAVEL—MEDITATION

Sit comfortably.

(Prayer)

Great Divine Spirit, protect us with your Infinite White Light. Guide us as we go within. Grant us the ability to ascend our planet and project interplanetary travel in our universe. Keep all evil entities away while we're on our spiritual journey. Amen.

Visualize a white beam of light coming through the ceiling. Let it travel down—totally—over your body. Now, visualize it going through the floor underneath you and going deep into mother earth. You're now grounded and also connected to God. Take in a deep breath. Let it out slowly and breathe normally. Feel your feet relaxing. Let them become very light. Relax your lower legs, feel them becoming very light. Relax your upper legs, feel them becoming very light. Hips feel the lightness. Stomach, Chest and Back, feel the lightness. Shoulders, Arms, Hands, let all tension go and feel yourself as light as a feather. Relax your Mouth and Face. Clear your mind. Now focus on your third eye, that's in the centre forehead directly between both eyes. Look into it and see all that is good and Godly. Now, focus on the top of your head. Open your Crown Chakra as wide as possible. Now, get prepared to guide your soul's consciousness to travel beyond Earth. Don't be afraid, you're safe: you'll be traveling with God.

Go out into the universe. Feel yourself out there.

You're now free from your physical body; start to move towards the sun.

Go ahead, start to fly. Let your soul travel. See the **Sun**, the stars and distant planets.

You're traveling over **Venus,** continue on towards **Mercury.** You're now above **Mercury**, take a look at how close you are to the Sun, feel its rays and observe it. Now go ahead, land on **Mercury.**

Sit quietly and realize that this planet deals with past lives and reincarnation. Take a look at your past life's mistakes, look at the positive and negative, and take appropriate action. Focus on and receive wisdom, and, while you're there, do a little self-healing.

(Pause a moment).

Tell yourself that you're in a more positive spiritual frame of mind and get ready to travel to the next planet.

OK start to travel once again. Up you go; start to move away from **Mercury** and the **Sun** and travel towards **Venus**. See Venus and move towards it. You're above **Venus** now; this is the soft planet. Go ahead, land on **Venus**. Sit quietly and feel the comfort emitting from this planet. Experience the feeling of perfect love; feel the perfect love of God, of brothers and sisters. Confirm and focus on giving unconditional love. (Pause a moment).

Tell yourself that you're in a more positive spiritual frame of mind and get ready to travel to the next planet.

OK start to travel once again. Up you go; start to move away from **Venus** and travel towards **Earth**. You're above **Earth** now, quietly and quickly pass over it and continue towards **Mars.**

Go ahead, go to **Mars.** You're above **Mars** now; land on it. Sit for a moment, focus on your dislikes and learn how to deal with them. Tell yourself that you're going to be more tolerant of things that bother you and you'll always control your temper. Tell yourself that you'll remain calm and even-minded; cleanse your soul of any harsh qualities of anger. (Pause a moment).

Tell yourself that you're in a more positive spiritual frame of mind and get ready to travel to the next planet.

OK start to travel once again. Up you go; start to move away from **Mars** and travel towards **Jupiter.** You're now above **Jupiter;** land on it. Feel the pleasant feeling from this planet. Become introspective, examine your thoughts and feelings, and assess your shortcomings. Sit for a while; focus on achieving spiritual mastery. (Pause a moment).

Tell yourself that you're in a more positive spiritual frame of mind and get ready to travel to the next planet.

OK start to travel once again. Up you go; start to move away from **Jupiter** and travel towards **Saturn**. You're now above **Saturn**, land on it. This planet has a blissful atmosphere and is adored by God; feel and sense this adoration. Sit for a moment and take a good look at yourself. If need be, refine your consciousness and rid yourself of any egotistic behavior.

(Pause a moment).

Tell yourself that you're in a more positive spiritual frame of mind and get ready to travel to the next planet.

OK start to travel once again. Up you go; start to move away from **Saturn** and travel towards **Uranus**. Go ahead, fly quietly along. You're now above **Uranus**; go ahead, land on it.

Sit for a moment; think righteously; focus on resentments and indignation; any torments and undone deeds; on any negative feeling and rid them from your spiritual body. While there form a peace treaty with yourself. (Pause a moment).

Tell yourself that you're in a more positive spiritual frame of mind and get ready to travel to the next planet.

OK start to travel once again. Up you go; start to move away from **Uranus** and travel towards **Neptune**. Go ahead, go towards it. You're now over **Neptune**, land on it. Feel its beneficial and tranquil energy. Sit for a moment, lay down any burdens and become totally devoid of any cares; feel and sense nothingness. Maintain a restful state. Feel very peaceful and feel its seduction. (Pause a moment).

Tell yourself that you're in a more positive spiritual frame of mind and get ready to travel to the next planet.

OK start to travel once again. Up you go; start to move away from **Neptune** and travel towards **Pluto**.

Travel to the end of the universe as we know it and go towards **Pluto**. Go ahead, move quickly through the atmosphere. You're now above **Pluto**. Take a good look around and remember what you see here; now, land on **Pluto**. This is the re-evaluation station of your spiritual progression. Sit for a moment; focus on dealing with improving your determination to succeed. Also, become acquainted with your personal union with God. (Pause a moment).

Tell yourself that you're in a more positive spiritual frame of mind and get ready to travel back towards **Earth**.

OK start to travel once again. Up you go; stop for a moment and once again observe your surroundings. Now start to move away from **Pluto** and travel back towards planet **Earth**.

Let yourself go, quickly and smoothly. Travel quietly and feel the spiritual bliss that you've acquired. Continue on, you're now traveling over **Neptune,** now over **Uranus**, over **Saturn,** over the big planet **Jupiter**, you're now over **Mars**. You see **Earth** and you're close to the **moon.**

Go ahead, land on **Earth's moon**. Sit for a moment, realize and sense your unfamiliar self. Recognize your subconscious that's carrying your past, and become aware of your instinct.

(Pause a moment).

Tell yourself that you're in a more positive spiritual frame of mind and get ready to travel home.

OK start to travel once again. Up you go; start to move away from the moon and travel towards **Earth.**

Go ahead; you're now above **Earth**; land on it. Sit for a moment and feel the comfort; feel and sense the difference in yourself from when you left.

Whatever part of **Earth** you may be in right now guide yourself back to this room.

Time is now up...

(Prayer of thanks).

When your turn comes speak about your experiences and with the help of your teacher, your higher self and guides, focus on the spirit world. Call forth those who wish to offer a message such as the groups passed loved ones who are trying to connect. When you've made this connection relate what you're receiving. If you can't see or hear them ask that they show you an object, in your mind, so that you may interpret it.

Chapter Four
Old-Fashioned Séances

The reason séances are located between the mental and physical phenomena chapters is because in séances both are prominent and both rise to the surface, as the medium or mediums involved use all their sensory perceptions. The cabinet may be used in an open-to-the-public or a closed on-going séance for the purpose of physical phenomena. Séances that are open to the public draws many curious people, skeptics as well as believers. With open séances the skeptics decrease the energy as they come with a negative attitude, but in hope of something phenomena happening. As for the closed and on-going séance all that attend are believers and the energy increases each time they get together. The cabinet and its use are explained in the next chapter.

Séance Example #1:

Many people are drawn to study more about life after death and try to develop their own psychic ability, which opens their mind to the spiritual laws that govern life. With this approach it helps many people to turn their lives around by helping to find their own connection with God. These exercises will assist you to recognize and hear your own inner voice (The small voice you often neglect and pay little attention to.) and provide you with the tools to advance you towards your own spiritual fulfillment without fear.

Spiritualistic séances were held frequently back in the late 1800s and are still being preformed in certain individuals' homes today. This has always been of interest, and with greater understanding and practice I now teach how it's properly done.

Each séance is always a little different as oftentimes there are new attendees. To make a séance work in its entirety one needs to have a devoted and committed group and it should be held at least once a week if not more, although more-often is advisable for best results.

A Dark Séance: Meaning that it's held in darkness with only a dull red light, but some people like a few candles burning. If the moon is bright and the room has a window then moon-light alone is the perfect lighting.

Each séance is unique in its own. As you continue to read this chapter you'll notice that it's a bit repetitive at the beginning of each séance. Reason for this is for the teacher, the leader, to be able to take the book into the classroom, or the séance room, instead of making copies and searching the contents of the chapter for information.

Of course, each séance is as unique as the reason for it being held. You'll eventually come to terms of how each is to be 'personally' held. Follow the guidelines in this book but your own personal approach will eventually be best for you.

Things that I use and feel is required for most séances are:

Chairs to accommodate all that attend
Incense
Alcohol
Lavender oil
Burning pot
Lantern, red
Tape recorder
Candles
Slate & chalk
Writing tablet
Pen

Bell
Stones
Balls
Trumpet
Paper towels
Waste basket
And whatever you wish to use for your own personal séance.

When at the designated place:

Boil water, put 3 drops of lavender oil in the cleansing bowl then pour the boiled water in with the oil. Let it cool and sit it at entrance.

Be certain that the floor is clean in the room being used.

Make sure it's heated comfortably.

Clean the atmosphere by burning the incense of your choice as you circle the room 3 times. Then put the incense in a safe place to burn out.

Have a round table, if possible, in the centre of the room

Place paper towels, waste basket and a table at door to hold the water bowl

Have a tripod or hang a lantern from the ceiling. If that's not possible then place it on the center of the table.

If you choose to use candles burn them early and put them out prior to the séance to make the room as dark as possible. If there's a full moon and the room appears sufficient then no other light source is needed. A full moon is the perfect time to interact with the spirit world.

Accept money, at the entrance, if this is a paid séance.

A Séance for Beginners—(Student Info Prior to a Séance):

A séance is about connecting with the spirit world through love and compassion.

You as the medium, beginner or advanced in your clairvoyance, is the relay point in which a spirit will make a contact. New attendees, don't feel threatened by those words, be your self.

Prior to attending a séance you may make an appointment with one of your passed loved ones for when you'd like for that communication to happen. Do this daily at the same time for one week prior to the event. Time recommended is the hour the séance will begin. Call on them and tell them a specific hour and day of the week you wish them to come through. Make a commitment with them and to yourself to meet at that specific time and place. Don't cancel after this week of calling on them. They'll make the commitment because you made a promise while you sent out thought waves. Write down what you're going to say to him/her and keep it consistent each time you converse with them. Don't forget: But if something happens so that you can't call on them at that particular time, do it later when you get a moment. But please do it every day before the event.

Prepare yourself in advance and try to be in an altered state of mind prior to arriving. That means that you need to be quiet within yourself and your surroundings. Make your mind and body aware that it will be tapping into another dimension.

Throughout the day of the séance switch your mind to a high intuition, to logic, and to a low periodically. That means take a few moments throughout the day to bring on awareness of the event soon to take place. If you're traveling to a séance with friends be certain that you remain respectful; avoid loud noises and loud music.

Feel spiritual and feel a feeling of lightness prior to your arrival. If you find that you're a little to hyper, due to it being your first séance, than please do a meditation to calm your spirit and let it become one with Spirit.

At the Event:

Have a table, round if possible, with chairs in the centre of the room for as many attending. Have the burning pot in the center (The burning pot that's explained in a previous chapter.) and have certain objects on the table for spirit communication if something should happen; who knows. For instance, writing tablet with pen, chalk board with caulk, semi to round stones that can be easily rolled, a small bell, trumpet if you have your own or if you can borrow one; and anything else you feel spirit could and would use to make a contact. If used, leave a red light on (situated at the back of the chairperson if that person has to read from a text.) If not, a light in the centre ceiling is more suitable. Candles may be used as well but a darker room is more appropriate for a Dark Séance.

Prior the séance the chairperson/leader/teacher should burn incense in the room. (Preferably Mire and Frankincense, Sandalwood and Lavender.) Mire for the soul purpose of purity. Frankincense and Mire can be bought as one blended together, which I use. Frankincense because it expands consciousness and aids in meditation; it's one of the best fragrances to burn for cleansing and clearing. It can clear and refresh even the toughest and worst atmospheres. It's good for clearing a room of other people's left-behind energy. It's particularly good for people who are working on their spiritual progress and want to clearly open up to higher spiritual elements, as it can help communication on a higher plane. Moreover, it has warming and relaxing properties and it's a good choice to relax with, as aromatherapy. Sandalwood as it grounds you and helps you to stay focused. It eases anxiety and its scent is effective in calming even the most agitated feelings. Lavender because it's renowned for its calming energy, helping to rebalance tired and distorted emotions. It's particularly good for easing anxiety and it's also helpful for restoring a connection to the sacred realm.

Say a prayer prior to the start, and then circle the chairs in the room three times with the incense burning in your hand. Then place the incense somewhere in a safe place to burn out.

Have a bowl of cool boiled water (Add extra purity by placing three drops of Lavender Oil) and a stack of off-the-role single paper towels at the outside entrance—of the room—for all to dip their hands before entering. While dipping their hands they should 'Visualize' their total body being cleansed. If they go to the washroom or leave the room for any reason they need to re-do it.

Dry their hands, (Have a waste basket handy for paper towels.) enter the room and sit in the chair that feels right. Bottled drinking water should also be available at the entrance for those that wish to have it.

Education and Séance Procedure:

The leader speaks:

If anyone has any fear and feel that this isn't for you then feel free to leave before it starts. Once it begins you are obligated and committed to be a part of the total energy. If anyone feels hesitant and remain, make sure you DO NOT disturb the group until it's over.

Be reminded:—(Sit in a circle and please don't leave until séance is completed.)

Question to the group—(Does the place you chose to sit feel right for you?)

(Then say)—If you feel an uncomfortable feeling where you are then the energy isn't in harmony, so, you may change your place with someone else, if both agree. (The leader may be the best person to choose the seat for each individual as he/she will sense the best harmonized energy.)

Let this be a joyous and an exciting experience, not one of fear from previous séances or from what you've heard from other people about them.

Know your part and take responsibility for it. We're all in this together.

If at any time you feel a sense of fear, laughter is the best remedy as fear cannot stand up to laughter. Laugh and feel relief but don't be silly. (Please note. Stress the fact that they should let someone know that they're going to laugh, just don't burst out in a loud laughter if all are quiet.)

Now—Feel a sense of peace in the room. (Give a moment)

(Pass around the commitment for all to grant the spirit world to work through them. Make sure they all say it or the energy will be broken and little will happen.)

(After its back in your hands say a prayer.)

Séance Commitment

(The first part is taken from Rev. Jane's séance procedure)

MY NAME IS _______________

I CALL FORTH MY GUIDES (Each person may mention the names of their guides here)

KNOWN AND UNKNOWN TO ME

I ASK FOR—ONLY THE BEST AND THE HIGHEST

LOVE ONES AND FRIENDS IN THE SPIRIT WORLD, PLEASE COME FORWARD

(This part is my own)

DOORKEEPER AND SPIRIT GUIDES;

DURING THE NEXT HOUR I PERMIT YOU TO USE MY ENERGY FOR THE PURPOSE OF MENTAL AND PHYSICAL PHENOMENA.

THANK YOU.

During the Séance

(This portion was enhanced by Rev. Jane's influence as well)

MY NAME IS_______________

I FEEL (And express what you feel, see, hear, smell, taste and so on.)

I SEE

I HEAR

I SMEEL

I TASTE

THANK YOU

(After each time you speak always say Thank-You so that each will know you have finished)

Let us pray.

Divine spirit:

Thank you for this gathering of people whom were chosen. Not by me but by your divine intervention. Lead us towards the enlightenment of your awareness as we make contact with those from the spirit world.

Our week of preparation has conditioned us for what we're about to encounter.

Give us your blessing and your protection.

Amen

(Explain to the group what you have on and under the table and its use. Things should be under as well as on top of the table and the tablecloth should reach to the floor)

Prepare yourself and get in the mood to correspond with a spirit during our time together. Never feel that it's crazy or that other people will think it is. We're all here to experience, so feel free to express, in your turn. Repeat what the spirit has to say to you.

You may only hear one word; you may not get anything. There might be a full sentence or maybe you'll feel a very strong sensation. If that spirit had never spoken English you'll receive it in English. There's a decoder in the spirit realm.

(Take note.) (Red light attracts physical phenomena. No other light is really needed.)

You may see shades of light around another person. Recognize the colour and express what you see, in your turn. You may feel psychic breezes, cold drafts and physical sensations of your solar plexus being pulled. Recognize any occurrences happening that is out of the ordinary, especially chills and coldness in your legs and body. Coldness is an indication that spirit is trying to materialize and is using your energy to do so. ALWAYS express all that you experience while in a séance.

Find the courage within yourself to release unlimited potential. Have an enquiring mind and leave it open to all possibilities. Call on and try to contact those you love. The spirit that presents itself and makes it self known is either for you or for someone in the group. What you'll experience will be real and hopefully it will be validated; if not now it will be by someone that you know. Don't be afraid, we all know that there's no such thing as death. Those that'll come through in a God protected séance are of good and not of evil. You'll receive information and guidance. You may even see an entity appear in front of you. Don't panic and scream, what is a séance about? Speak quietly and converse with that spirit; that spirit had been called upon to converse with you.

This may also be similar to a mental mediumship contact, probably with a much stronger force. There may also be some physical phenomena happening, just recognize and express it, and let it happen. Your guides will come forward to help you communicate, call on them. Link your thoughts with a spirit. Listen, feel, sense and visualize to a point of actually seeing. This spirit may move from person to person if that spirit is in some way connected to those that are present. Listen for a name. Listen for actual words of speech. Look for something that distinguishes that particular spirit from another. If the information that you're getting doesn't make any sense, pass it on anyway. If you feel any heaviness or are left with an emotional sadness let it pass as soon as possible so the event will continue smoothly.

If by any chance you wake up with a headache the next day it'll probably be because of the extra activity in your brain by speeding up your level of conscious connection with that particular entity. Their power of thought is at a much faster pace then any spirit still in a human body. Creating a balance requires your brain waves to quicken to increase your vibrations and the entity's vibrations will slow down to cause a balance to provide communication between both worlds.

If you smell smoke or any other threatening aromas, don't panic, it may mean that the spirit coming through was a smoker or died in a fire. Distinguish the difference. Pay attention to other aromas such as flowers, perfumes, colognes and tobaccos. Pets may come through as well. Pay attention to how you yourself actually feel within this surrounding. (Be alert and be aware of any unusual odors as smoke may also mean that there really is smoke in the house. Be wise, leave the room and check it out.)

Once you let go of holding hands please don't reach out and touch another until all are at ease and back to full reality, unless in an emergency.

(Seal the circle. All hold hands.)

Let your adrenaline start pumping. Collect your wits. Relax your total body.

Take a deep breath and think strong positive thoughts. Don't become anxious or nervous.

Let specific information flood your mind and make the best communication possible.

If you find that your mind is under siege by one strong particular spirit then express it at will.

If you feel that a spirit is negative, send it away immediately.

You may close your eyes of leave them open. Whichever you choose please remain calm and relaxed. (Another Prayer)

Dear God.
Divine Spirit of the universe.
Protect us and surround us with your white light of protection.
With your permission, let our called upon loved ones from the spirit realm, make their presence known to us.
Send only pure, clean and good spirits from you.
Keep all evil forces away.
Amen

Open your eyes.

(Make sure you have lots of rubbing alcohol in the burning pot, Light the flame and go back and sit down.)

Remain holding hands. Now focus on the flame and on the objects on the table. Feel the energy coming in to your left hand and out through your right and going in to the other person.

(Let this energy circle for about one minute and have them all direct this energy at the table.)

Now let go of hands and hold palms towards the table as if you can actually see light shooting out of them. Direct all this energy to the table and as it hits the table visualize it going to the ceiling, up through the roof and out into the spirit world. (Give a moment for this)

Then tell them to hold each others hands again and the two by you hold hands behind your back. You may need to move slightly forward for this. You'll also need to stand up between OM'S. **Leader:** Hold your arms and hands straight out and slightly upwards, with hands facing up and call the spirit world. Make sure the group begins the OM'S on schedule as to maintain a total and complete rhythm, which should be a total of six. This makes for a great chant as chant beckons spirit. You, the leader, may start each Om (Which probably would be the best at your first séance as you're then in control) but keep a count (-on your fingers if you have to-) as six should be the limit.) (It's best to use a trusted student to be in charge of this)

Group: OMMMMMMMMMMMMMMMMMMMMMMMMMMMM
Leader: Spirits of love and light
You are welcome here
Come forward and communicate
(Group starts the Om immediately when the leader says communicate)
Group: OMMMMMMMMMMMMMMMMMMMMMMMMMMMM
Leader: Spirits of love and light
You are welcome here
Come forward and communicate
Group: OMMMMMMMMMMMMMMMMMMMMMMMMMMMM
Leader: Spirits of love and light
You are welcome here
Come forward and communicate
Group: OMMMMMMMMMMMMMMMMMMMMMMMMMMMM
Leader: Spirits of love and light
You are welcome here
Come forward and communicate
Group: OMMMMMMMMMMMMMMMMMMMMMMMMMMMM
Leader: Spirits of love and light
You are welcome here
Come forward and communicate
Group: OMMMMMMMMMMMMMMMMMMMMMMMMMMMM

Leader: Spirits of love and light
You are welcome here
Come forward and communicate

(Leader: Give a moment of silence and release handholding then sit back in your chair.)

Release handholding, remain comfortable and express all that you feel, sense, hear and see.

(This time, which should not proceed one hour, is the time to sit quietly for something phenomenal to happen. Encourage all to express everything.)

(When the time limit is up, announce that it's time to end the séance. Then pass around the ending séance procedure below. The group may need extra light to see so a portable reading light, one that attaches to a clip board, is recommended)

Ending Séance

MY NAME IS ____________________

GUIDES, FRIENDS AND LOVED ONES IN THE SPIRIT WORLD,

I THANK YOU FOR YOUR EFFORTS TO MAKE YOURSELF KNOWN. PLEASE GO NOW AND COME AGAIN WHEN REQUESTED.

DOORKEEPER AND SPIRIT GUIDES;

AS OF NOW I NO LONGER GIVE YOU PERMISSION TO USE MY ENERGY FOR PYSCIAL PHENOMENA UNLESS IT'S OF IMPORTANCE FOR MY SPIRITUAL GROWTH AND DEVELOPMENT.

THANK YOU

Séance Example #2:

Spirit communicating séance with a ghostly entity within a private dwelling

(Give the information below to the people that will be attending—a week prior to the event.)

(As previous séance 'Number 1') Prior to you attending this séance—make an appointment with your spirit guides, guardians and angels. Do this daily at the same time for about a week prior to the event. Time recommended is the hour the séance will begin. Call on them and tell them about this specific evening, including date and the hour you need their protection and assistance. Make a commitment with them, and to yourself, to meet at that specific time and place. Please don't cancel your attendance after this week of calling on them. They will make a commitment and be there because you made a promise to them, when you sent out your thought waves.

Write down what you're going to say to them and keep it consistent each time you converse with them. Don't forget. If something should happen that you can't do this at this particular time daily, do it later when you do get time alone or with your attending partner. But please, do it every day before attending. If you wish, you may bring a picture of a passed love one that you'd like to hear from, from the spirit world.

On the event day prepare yourself in advance and try to be in an altered state of mind prior to arriving at the séance. That means that you need to be quiet within yourself and your surroundings. Make your mind and body aware that it will be tapping into another dimension.

Throughout the day switch your mind to a high intuition, to logic and to a low periodically.

Feel spiritual and feel a feeling of lightness prior to your arrival. If you find that you're a little to hyper then please arrive early enough to do a short meditation to calm your spirit and let it become one with your guides and the spirit that you seek.

At the Event:

Have a table in the centre of the room with chairs for as many people that will attend. Leave a red light on, situated at the back of the chairperson because that person will most likely have to read from a text, plus a red light attracts physical phenomena. No other light is really needed but three scented candles are to be placed about the room. One behind the person sitting across from the chairperson and the other two located at half way between the leader and the candle across from him/her. Those candles should be in a glass container and located directly on the floor, (preferably,) as a darker room is more appropriate for the Séance.

The chairperson burns incense in the room; (preference is Mire and Frankincense but choose what feels right for you,) and prayer said at the time. He or she should walk in a circle, around the complete room, for instance around the table at a wide birth.

Have a bowl of cool boiled water (as described above) and paper towels outside of the room for all to dip their hands in before entering. Bottled drinking water should also be available for those that wish to have it.

Before Entering the Room:

If you have any fear and feel that this isn't for you then please feel free to leave before it starts. Once it begins be a part of the total energy.

There's a bowl of water by the door as you enter, dip your hands in it and dry them off. As you do this visualize that you're total body is being cleansed. When you had dried them and discarded the paper towel, enter the room and go sit at the table. Choose a place that feels right for you, other then where the red light is located, that's my place (the leader) and please—don't leave until it's over.

Sitting at the Table:

A séance is about love and compassion.

This séance is about communicating and directing a lost soul to the God source.

Each attending acts as the sensitive or the medium whether a beginner student or advanced in your spirit connection. You are the relay point in which the world of spirits will try to make contact. New attendees should not feel threatened by those words, just be your self. Let go of any fear you may feel. If you feel an uncomfortable feeling where you're sitting then the energy isn't in harmony, therefore change your place with someone else, if both agree.

Let us pray.

Divine spirit:
Thank you for grouping us together: those of us whom were chosen by your divine intervention. Enlighten our awareness as we make contact with the spirits that are within this dwelling and within the environment of this house. Also grant us the privilege to make a contact with our loved ones from the spirit world. Protect us with your white-light as we begin our time in search of those lingering spirits that remain within our material world. Our week of preparation has conditioned us for that which we're about to encounter.
Once again, protect us and give us your blessing.
Amen

Let this be a joyous and an exciting experience, not one of fear from previous séances or from what you've heard from other people about them.

Know your part and take responsibility for it. We're all in this together.

God is stronger then any other spirit, we have **His** protection. Feel protected and safe.

If at any time you feel a sense of fear, laughter is the best remedy.

Fear cannot stand up to laughter. Laugh and feel relief. Please try to let someone know that you're going to do that first, just don't burst out in a loud laugh if we're in silence.

Right now—listen to the quietness—Feel a sense of peace in the room. (Give a moment)

Prepare yourself and get in the mood to correspond with a spirit during our time together. Never feel that it's crazy or that other people will think it is. We're all here to experience this, so feel free to express, in your turn. Repeat what the spirit has to say to you. You may only hear one word; you may not get anything. There might be a full sentence or maybe you'll feel a very strong sensation. If that spirit had never spoken English you'll receive it in English. There's a decoder in the spirit realm.

You may see a shade of light around a person sitting here. Recognize the colour and express what you see, in your turn. You may feel psychic breezes, cold drafts and physical sensations of your solar plexus being pulled. Recognize any occurrences happening that is out of the ordinary. Find the courage within yourself to release unlimited potential. Have an enquiring mind and leave it open to all possibilities. Call on and try to make contact with the spirit or spirits that's within this atmosphere. Identify it and express what you see. Don't lose the contact. Speak to it as if you were speaking to me or someone else. This spirit was once human and still thinks it is and don't realized that it has left the physical world. Let's find out why it's still hanging around.

I'll stress again, **don't be afraid**, we all know that there's no such thing as death. Those that'll come through in a God-protected-séance are of good and not of evil. If you see entities appear in front of you, don't panic and scream, **why are we here**? Speak quietly and converse with it; that spirit had been called upon to converse with us. You'll receive information and guidance; if you get a freeze just inform me of what's happening.

First of all we'll be doing a deep meditation contact with a much stronger force then what you have done previously; let your-self go. Your guides, guardians and angels will come forward to guide you, protect you and to help you communicate, call on them telepathically with the thought process.

Pay attention to aromas such as flowers, perfumes, colognes and tobaccos. Pets may come through as well. Pay attention to how you yourself actually feel within this surrounding.

Once we let go of holding hands please don't reach out and touch another until all are at ease and back to full reality, unless in an emergency.

Let's now focus and call on those particular spirits.

Seal the Circle:

NOW

Let your adrenaline start pumping and sense a connected feeling deep down in the pit of your stomach.

Collect your wits.

Relax your shoulders.

Take a deep breath; clear your mind of daily activities and think **strong** positive thoughts.

Don't become anxious or nervous.

Let specific spirit-world information flood your mind and at this point make the best telepathic communication possible.

If you find that your mind is under siege by one particular strong spirit, communicate with it and express it at will.

If you feel that a spirit is negative, send it to the light immediately. Tell that spirit that it's physically dead and to look above to see the light of God where his family and loved ones are waiting. If this spirit is stubborn send it away regardless or have me, (the leader) guide you on how to do this.

Place your hands on top of the table.

Hold hands with the one next to you with thumbs pointing to the left. Or place your right hand flat-down on the table and the person to your right will place their left hand on top of yours. Another acceptable way is for all to have hands flat on the table with the little fingers overlapping or just touching. Personally I feel that connecting hands in any manner creates a combined energy. I often had every second student, starting from my left; place their hands on their knees, palms up. Then the person on each side will place their hands on top of theirs. It's ok if knees are touching as well; please don't get to personal, we're working with Spirit, and spirit, and one needs to remain respectful. You would need an even number of people for this to work properly.

If the leader is reading from a text; the two that's next to him/her may hold each other's hand, in front or behind him/her. This may cause tiredness for those two so I recommend that both place a hand on the leader's knee, palms down to complete the circle.

Close your eyes

Remain calm and relaxed.

Now; Link your thoughts with spirit.

Let us pray.

Dear God.
Divine Spirit of the universe.
Protect us and surround us with your white light of protection.
Bring this unrest spirit to communicate with us so that we're able to send it home to you.
Keep all evil forces away.
Amen

Open your eyes.

Please follow the sound I'm (the leader) going to make.

I'll say Om and the person to my left will say it immediately after me, then the next person and so on until it comes back to me. Continue each individual sound until all are out of breath. (As the last person in the group begins the leader should immediately begin again, making it seven in total.)

(The Om sound brings divine intervention. At the end of the chant—please remain silent for a couple of minutes.)

PRACTISE ONE IF YOU WISH

Ommmmmmm Ommmmmmm Ommmmmmm and so on.

(A moment of silence and then start the first set of seven.)

(After the seven give a moment of silence.)

A Spirit Call-Up Meditation:

Feel free to go in and out of this meditation on your own if you sense a spirit presence in the room. If you open your eyes and still see a spirit—please don't be frightened or alarmed. Speak quietly to the spirit immediately so it will remain visible. Gently and quietly the group will call themselves back—or I (the leader) will call them back if some are still within meditation. Continue to speak to the spirit. Use you common sense as if speaking to someone lost and ask it questions. If there's a problem I, (the leader) will guide you with the questions and direct you as to what to say and we will guide this spirit home to their loved ones and to God.

That's the reason we're here.

Don't be afraid; we're all together; we're all safe and protected.

DO NOT RELEASE HAND HOLDING UNTIL I SAY SO. THE ENERGY WILL REMAIN STRONGEST THIS WAY.

You may repeat my words—out loud, quietly—if you wish; it will make a stronger invitation if you do. If we don't ask we won't receive. I'll speak at the beginning of each minute; there are seven in all.

(Leader: HOLD YOU ARMS AND HANDS STRAIGHT OUT, SLIGHTLY UPWARDS, WITH HANDS FACEING UP AND SAY TIMES SEVEN.)

1. FREE SPIRIT—WELCOME AND COME FORWARD.

(Give a moment silence. If the students repeat after you then make sure there's a moment of silence.)

2. FREE SPIRIT—WELCOME AND COME FORWARD.
(Moment of silence)

3. FREE SPIRIT—WELCOME AND COME FORWARD.
(Moment of silence)

4. FREE SPIRIT—WELCOME AND COME FORWARD.
(Moment of silence)

5. FREE SPIRIT—WELCOME AND COME FORWARD.
(Moment of silence)

6. FREE SPIRIT—WELCOME AND COME FORWARD.
(Moment of silence)

7. FREE SPIRIT—WELCOME AND COME FORWARD. (All students should close their eyes and be in silence for up to 5 minutes, if no appearance of a spirit.)

(Remind students to continue to call on this spirit telepathically.)
(After five minutes say) Open your eyes.
(Leader: HOLD YOU ARMS AND HANDS STRAIGHT OUT, SLIGHTLY UPWARDS, WITH HANDS FACE UP AND ONCE AGAIN SAY TIMES SEVEN.)

FREE SPIRIT–COME FORWARD AND COMMUNICATE. (Moment of silence)

FREE SPIRIT–COME FORWARD AND COMMUNICATE. (Moment of silence)

FREE SPIRIT–COME FORWARD AND COMMUNICATE. (Moment of silence)

FREE SPIRIT–COME FORWARD AND COMMUNICATE. (Moment of silence)

FREE SPIRIT–COME FORWARD AND COMMUNICATE. (Moment of silence)
FREE SPIRIT–COME FORWARD AND COMMUNICATE. (Moment of silence)

FREE SPIRIT–COME FORWARD AND COMMUNICATE. (5 minutes silence if no appearance of a spirit and call this spirit forward—telepathy.

Open your eyes.
(Leader: HOLD YOU ARMS AND HANDS STRAIGHT OUT, SLIGHTLY UPWARDS, WITH HANDS FACE UP AND SAY TIMES SEVEN.)

FREE SPIRIT–SHOW YOURSELF AND COMMUNICATE.
(Moment of silence)

FREE SPIRIT–SHOW YOURSELF AND COMMUNICATE.
(Moment of silence)

FREE SPIRIT–SHOW YOURSELF AND COMMUNICATE.
(Moment of silence)

FREE SPIRIT–SHOW YOURSELF AND COMMUNICATE.
(Moment of silence)

FREE SPIRIT–SHOW YOURSELF AND COMMUNICATE.
(Moment of silence)

FREE SPIRIT–SHOW YOURSELF AND COMMUNICATE.
(Moment of silence)

FREE SPIRIT–SHOW YOURSELF AND COMMUNICATE.
(Close your eyes and continue to call on this spirit telepathically for 5 minutes if no appearance of a spirit. Then thank Divine Spirit for His protection and for the spirit that made contact or tried to.

Divine Spirit,
We thank you for your assistance and protection.
Amen

(Bring back those that are not back by saying) Open your eyes. Bring yourself back to reality.

(When you know that all are back tell them to release holding of hands.)

(Have the group express their findings, feelings and or any connection made clairvoyantly.)

Extra Séance, Meditation:

For those who had brought photos—place them face down in the center of the table. Now let's try your mediumship abilities and see if you're able to make a connection with the spirits of those that are in the pictures on the table.

The spirits that presents itself and makes it self known to you is either for you or for someone in the group. What you experience will be real and hopefully it will be validated, if not now it'll be by someone that you know.

Listen, feel, sense and visualize to a point of actually seeing a spirit.

Listen for a name.

Listen for actual words of speech.

Look for something that distinguishes that particular spirit from another.

If the information that you're getting doesn't make any sense to you, pass it on anyway. If you feel any heaviness or are left with an emotional sadness, let it pass as soon as possible so we may continue.

Meditation Time:

Place you hands on your upper legs, face up and both feet flat on the floor.

Close your eyes.

Visualize yourself surrounded with white light.

Visualize the total group surrounded by white light.

Visualize the room totally surrounded by white light.

Visualize and feel roots growing out of your feet and going deep into 'Mother Earth'.

Feel everyone here and yourself safe and protected.

Now visualize the right hand of God over you. We're now grounded to mother earth and in Gods hands.

Ask God for permission for your passed love one to come through.

Call on a spirit now. (Give a moment silence)

In your mind see the spirit of someone that you feel is in one of the pictures on the table; preferably one that you didn't bring. Feel it with such great force as if you can actually reach out and touch them.

Focus on making a contact.

Trust in God. Trust in yourself. Feel the love.

Now; make that contact.

(Pause momentarily)

Right now, feel the beautiful white light that's surrounding you.

Look in front of you and see a big balloon.

Walk towards it and feel your self glide inside the bubble.

The balloon and you are now rising.

Drift into lightness, rising higher and higher.

You're drifting upwards.

Up. Up. Up you go.

Feel yourself drifting up.

Drift up high, higher and higher......................

You're slowing down now. Your speed has slowed.

The balloon has stopped.

Now; look in front of you and see a door of whiteness.

Step out of the balloon.

Go through that door; sit down in a comfortable place and seek a spirit.

I'll speak softly at the beginning of each minute; please don't be alarmed when I do. Remain in silence and meditate.

I'll call you back in a while—if no one else does.

(Give seven minutes for silence and meditation.)

(Leader, speak the words below, very quietly, almost at a whisper, at the beginning of every minute. 7 minutes in all.)

Each time you speak, HOLD YOU ARMS AND HANDS STRAIGHT OUT, SLIGHTLY UPWARDS, WITH HANDS FACEING UP WHILE SPEAKING SOFTLY.

1. SPIRITS OF LOVE AND LIGHT COME FORWARD AND COMMUNICATE. (Give one minute and speak again)

2. SPIRITS OF LOVE AND LIGHT COME FORWARD AND COMMUNICATE

3. SPIRITS OF LOVE AND LIGHT COME FORWARD AND COMMUNICATE

4. SPIRITS OF LOVE AND LIGHT COME FORWARD AND COMMUNICATE

5. SPIRITS OF LOVE AND LIGHT COME FORWARD AND COMMUNICATE

6. SPIRITS OF LOVE AND LIGHT COME FORWARD AND COMMUNICATE

7. SPIRITS OF LOVE AND LIGHT COME FORWARD AND COMMUNICATE

(At the end of the seven minutes say)
Time is up now; Stop conversing with spirits
Feel a feeling of fulfillment.
Now, go back out the door of whiteness.
Step back into the balloon.
Now; feel yourself drifting back down.
Lower and lower
Come back down
Come back.
You're drifting back to reality
You're back down to Mother Earth now...
Step back out of the balloon
And feel yourself coming back to normal consciousness.
Open your eyes.
(Discuss experiences, in turn.)

Extended Séance:

Mix the photos together. Each person may reach forward with eyes closed and pick one up and work with phychometry. To those that are not familiar with this, it means, speak whatever is in your mind concerning the photo of the person that you're holding. In your turn express anything that you may feel, sense or imagine.

Now; feel the energy and vibrations from the photo without looking at it—then speak up and share with the group what spirit gives you.

(After all has had their turn then an 'Ending Prayer')

Divine Spirit.

Thank you for your protection.

Thank you for permitting those spirits to come forward.

We also like to thank the spirits that tried to come through but couldn't.

Thank you for the friendship as we were gathered here.

You're with us now and forever shall be.

Guide us all, and guide us safely home to our loved ones.

Grant us the opportunity to gather again in your presence.

Amen

Séance Example #3:

This séance was held in a church for beginner and intermediate students as a teaching guide. It's short and to the point. The usual procedure, as above, was carried out and explanation was given as per previous séances.

The first ½ half hour was 'get-acquainted-time' as many people did not know each other previously. Therefore the floor was opened to the mediums to give any instant spirit messages that they may receive.

(Actual séance began at 7:30 but a later time is more appropriate such as midnight. Some call midnight 'The witching hour')

Leader: Explain procedure.

Remind them of being skeptic and to be very serious when inviting the spirit world

Heart felt laughter also brings connection but don't be silly

All stand:

Begin the séance with a heart felt song that most people know, such as 'Do Lord'.

Prayer—All hold hands; let go of hand-holding and sit after prayer.

Pass around commitment paper as all need to commit for spirit to use them in any way.

As you sit and with eyes open, all hold hands towards table.

(In this hall there's a large silver ball hanging from the ceiling just above the table. What the group was told to do was to send their combined energy towards the table and let it bounce off the edge of the table and then let it escalate upwards towards the ball.)

When singing 'O Great Spirit' hold hands towards the table and place them on your upper legs and visualize your energy going towards the table, connecting with everyone else's energy. See it bouncing off the end of the table and descending upwards towards the ceiling. When it hits the ceiling it remains open to spirit. Demonstrate with hands

Words to song are: O Great Spirit; Earth; Sun; Ski and Sea, you are inside and all around me.

Light burning pot and let it burn and sing 'O Great Spirit' while burning

(Loud X 4—Low X 1—Lower X 1)

(Then Start with individual Om's. Each person takes a deep breath and Om's loudly until out of breath. Then without breakage the next one follows suit and so on until it has returned to the leader.)

(After finishing the first round the leader may remain sitting or stands to beckon spirit by saying)

Spirit of love and light
We welcome you
Come forward and communicate

(Then the group OM's loudly X 3.)
After each OM, beckon the spirit world by saying:
Spirit of love and light
We welcome you
Come forward and communicate
On the third OM the leader speaks again saying.
Spirit of love and light
We welcome you
Come forward and communicate
(Give a moment then)

Tell the group to release the energy around the table and while doing so sing a group Om. While doing so tell all to raise their hands slowly towards the ceiling. Something on the table may move.

Then feel what spirit brings forth and express in their turn as in previous instructions.

An Actual Séance in a Private Home:

This séance was held in a private home that had a lot of spirit activity. This activity was seen and felt by all that lived there, plus others.

Shortly after arrival the conversation went to the purpose of my sleep-over. Tales were told of the owners ghostly encounters. This entity was addressed in the male category when they both spoke of his misdeeds.

The room I was to sleep in was in the basement just off the den, which was very cozy. As we chatted I was given a complete history of all that had taken place since the purchase of this house, a little over two years ago.

It was also brought to my attention that their son, who had experienced the male ghost in his room, the one I'm to sleep in, had also experienced a female ghost while he was painting in the garage one day. Apparently, so he says; this entity appeared as if in the flesh scaring him enough that he wouldn't go back to the garage that day. As he approached his mother to tell the tale he was ghostly-looking himself.

Events that were brought to my attention are:

(1) Lights in the living room flashed a blue light when the switch was in the off position. 10 people witnessed this.

(2) They were both locked out of the house while stepping outside for a short period of time.

(3) The father of the lady of the house was locked in the basement bathroom while visiting. (The lock is controlled only on the inside but he was unable to open it regardless of how hard he tried.)

(4) Their son exited the same bathroom one morning and he heard the door lock behind him. He checked it and it was.

(5) Their son experienced a male entity/ghost in the guest room in the basement area. The room suddenly became very cold while the rest of the house remained relatively warm. He left the bedroom and went upstairs to sleep on the couch, which is a no-no.

(6) All of them experienced shadows and dull lights, as in orbs, at different times.

(7) Two alarm clocks had been tampered with, which the gentleman of the house got blamed for. Needless to say, he threw them in the garbage, which I asked him to fetch as I wish to use it in the up coming séance, with a few friends.

(8) There was an electronic device in a dresser drawer in the hallway that had been switched to the on position twice, disturbing them while they slept.

It was nearly 10:00 PM when I went to bed with little worry or concern as I had encounter many ghostly spirits throughout my life. I closed the door and turned slightly towards the corner behind the door and I immediately thought the spirit had appeared. Not so, as it was a small statue of an oriental woman on a shelf. Oh well, thought my luck was at its peak.

I set my trumpet on the dresser, placed the tape-recorder close by and had a clip-board and pen at a close distance; on top of the other pillow.

Before the lights were turned off at 11:01, I had noticed a flash of light in the mirror above the dresser. Although it was momentarily

I thanked the spirit. There's no way a light could have come from anywhere else other then the entity as the shade covering the window is very thick and no light what-so-ever can penetrate it.

At 11:06 PM, a shadow passed over the roof of the room. It moved very quickly and dispersed.

At 11:11 PM I turned the main light off and the room was pitch-black. I turned on my book light and started to read.

At 11:20 PM I heard a rap/knock. I thanked the spirit for this and asked it to knock louder; it didn't.

At 11:24 PM another rap/knock was heard. I went through with the same request with no result.

At 11:30 PM all lights were turned off; I was quite sleepy by now.

As I lay in bed I spoke to God and asked that I should be protected throughout the night. I also spoke to the entity and welcomed it to this room to converse with me.

At 4:00 AM I was gently awakened. I thought it was the lady of the house wishing me a good day before she went to work, it wasn't. Then I couldn't get back to sleep for some time. At 5:10 AM I was on the verge of sleep, somewhat like in a deep meditation or trance. A young man appeared to me clairvoyantly; or mentally if you wish. He was a bit heavy-set, as in stocky. He was about 38 years old. His complexion was somewhat yellow as if tanned and faded but I feel it was his natural color. He reminded me of someone from Sweden, Holland or possibly from Poland. His hair was dirty blond, cut short and trimmed as if he kept himself well groomed. He had a round face, full set of natural teeth, clean shaven and smiling very pleasantly. I tried to make a conversation with him but he kept on smiling as if he was happy that I could see him. He impressed my brain with a similar gentleman I knew in my late teens. The name David was also impressed in my mind as I commented to him that he looked like an old friend. He smiled and faded away. I thanked him for coming.

Then I drifted back to sleep.

Other then that, I had a great rest and a wonderful night's sleep; a sleep badly needed.

The following day when the lady of the house returned from work she sent an email which said: "*Hello: Glad you had a good night sleep. I was glad to hear that you experienced something last night. My experience was that at around 2 AM I felt something push down on my bed. I have a waterbed so it made the head of the bed rise up. My husband also says that he too had a male visit him in his sleep, so I guess the night was really eventful. Thanks for spending the night to seek out this entity; it was real nice having you as a guest.*"

Soul Rescue:

Soul rescue, believe it or not, is assisting God in finally getting his loved ones home. As one has personal responsibility one also has personal choice. The decision for personal choice may be somewhat confusing when one doesn't realize they're in spirit form. Souls such as this are lost and in need of rescuing.

As they continue to exist in the subtle planes they're not aware that they had died. Although living their lives, good or bad, they continue to try and make human contact by projecting their awareness. Being here on the earth plane and consciously aware of this can be frightening to an individual that don't accept the fact that life continues after death. They may see or sense this as being an evil ghost.

There are a number of reasons for such entrapment. Some souls are trapped due to sudden death, which is the most likely cause. Others choose not to move on due to emotional ties to their once physical existence, which they refuse to give up.

Soul rescue is reaching out through a normal means of communication. Normal if you believe in higher-self, attunement with spirit via deep meditation or trance, and astral travel. One has to condition them self to be a part of the accepted reality of that of the entity being rescued. The entity may completely deny that you're there but those seeking rescue will welcome with open arms. Expect emotions to flow when you mention what has occurred to them and what your intentions are. Not all will believe what you have to say at first but with encouragement and a profound and forceful but loving attitude they'll come to realize that they can now be freed.

If you sense that a spirit is in need of rescuing follow those guidelines:

Begin with connect, ground and protect as you have done on other occasions if you followed the exercises in this book.

See and sense yourself being protected by the god source, guides and angels. Then sense the guardian and angels of the soul that is in need of rescuing.

You may call on any high-developed-being to assist you. Any spiritual person working with subtle energy will often call on an Archangel such as Raphael, Jophiel, Michael or Gabriel. In addition, you may call on past family members such as a mother and so on.

If you come across a disorientated entity and they become somewhat rude, (and believe me some can be quite nasty) you may need to play their game to gain their confidence. Nonetheless what seems like a very difficult experience will eventually reap its rewards. Once accomplished the chances are you'll feel exhilarated for a couple of days, if not longer. Furthermore, many who have grown with the right belief system and attitude will allow themselves to move on effectively when they die, whether quickly, accidentally or from normal and natural causes.

Here's an exercise to follow when in a group setting such as a séance; or alone for that matter if you wish to have it recorded.

Go within and attune to the spirit world.

Send your vibration out, (or do what I do 'soul-travel).

Search for a lost soul.

When you meet or get in touch with this spirit, speak out loud and mention your name as in a séance. (For example, my name is Joe and I have such and such an entity, and describe them as what you see them as.)

If in a group séance, while one person is speaking all others please refrain from speaking; let one finish first. When you had finished please say thank you. This then gives the signal that you've finished and another may take this opportunity to speak, and so on.

When you make connection with an entity please let them know that they are now dead, lost and confused in the spirit world.

Then tell them they should search for a light within the darkness. If one isn't seen then remind them to look behind, up and or above until one is seen, if only a flicker of light.

Then you, (The Medium) should take control and direct them towards the light.

In a group please speak loud so that all will hear.

There's no wrong way to do this if the loving intent is there.

When you've finished please do not speak up again because you had already guided or given them some sort of solace and guidance. You speaking up again after you say 'thank you' may confuse the entity and the group.

If you feel that you're having a problem or had come across a stubborn entity then the teacher may guide them, through your channeling. Channeling here means that you will have to give the entity permission to speak through you, if not, you may have to relate what it has to say.

Any others that make a contact may go through the same scenario.

Soul Rescue Meditation:

Place your open hands on your upper legs with the palms facing up.

(Prayer) Great Divine Spirit: We're aware of your wonderful powers and abilities. Thank you for being here at this time. Please give us protection: Send forth our guides: Protect us with your white light and guide us safely as we travel outside our bodies to rescue lost souls. Amen

Close your eyes and listen closely to my voice.

Visualize a white beam of light coming through the ceiling. *(Don't let it travel further then my command.)* It's descending down upon you. It touches and covers your head and you feel a sense of peace and love from God.

Feel the blissful comfort emitting from it.

Let it move way down over your body. Down over you feet and deep into mother earth.

Don't be afraid, relax, you're safe.

Take in a deep breath. Let it out slowly and breathe normally

Feel your feet relaxing.

Lower legs—Upper legs—Hips—Tummy—Chest—Shoulders—Arms—Hands—Mouth—Face and Head relaxing. Clear your mind. Listen to the silence.

Breathe normally and continue to listen.

Concentrate on your breathing.

Be-aware of it. In. Out. Clear your mind.

Your mind is quiet. Keep your mind clear.

Be at peace with your higher self. Be at peace with God.

You're safe here. Stay Relaxed.

Feel the presence of Spirit, your guides, your angels and listen within the silence.

You're now within.

Now, slowly open your crown Chakra.

Let yourself travel outside

Let your guide's guide-you to any lost soul that's in need of help.

When you find a lost-soul assist them to the light.

I'll call you back in 15 minutes.

Stay within: Come back inside your crown chakra and then close it tightly.

(Prayer)

Great Divine Spirit, thank you for your protection: We also thank our guides for their assistances. Amen

Bring yourself back.

Become aware of your surroundings.

At the Séance Event Four Days Later:

As you may have gathered by now there's no set guidelines for a séance as a séance consists of a group of people sitting in the dark waiting for physical phenomena to happen.

Different examples gives a person a better understanding and a better judgment of how one would wish to conduct their own.

I chose only the strongest and the-most-advanced students for this evening but a couple could not attend due to other commitments.

Once we've all arrived and introductions made, which most knew each other, it began like this.

The room has been prepared in advance to our arrival. It was set up with a table in the centre, with six chairs around it and a table cloth reaching to the floor. On the table were the two clocks I had asked for and a writing tablet. I set the clocks as they were to be used; set the CD player to start to sing songs to raise vibrations and placed my trumpet and a few other objects on and under the table. I also included a tape-recorder and a chalk board with chalk. Then I lit incense and walked around the table three times requesting the spirits to be in attendance in a short while. I walked out and closed the door behind me.

I then got the group to sit down as they were busy preparing themselves and their cameras.

As we sat I read to the group what I had experienced during my sleep over. A few comments were made and a few questions asked. After this each person walked to the cleansing bowl and then proceeded to enter the room. With the cleansing in place each felt protected and as each entered, the women got to choose to sit where they wished. As for the male energy I felt it needed to be balanced. The gentleman of the house and a student of mine were requested to change places as he should sit directly across from me. With all sitting I explained why I wished to have six attending; to form the 'Star of David', which many so called witches of our past had used. Not that we are witches but some still seem to think so.

It began with me saying a prayer of protection, requesting the spirits to come forward to communicate and making the group feel at ease. With a brief explanation of the procedure to follow, it began.

I ask that each person be co-operative and to believe in getting a contact and to participate with full attention. I started the opening with a long and drawn out 'OMmmmmmmmmmm' then the woman to my left started, within a second of my start, with a long drawn out OOoooooooooooooooooooooo. Then the woman next to her started out, within a second of her start, with a HUMmmmmmmmmmmmmm. Then it comes to the other male in the group, which he starts within a minute of her start with an OMmmmmmmmmmm and the chant repeats itself and so on until it reaches back to me; and I'm still chanting my OM with the same breath. As the rest were still drawing out their chant I called the spirit world. I spoke out-loud and said, *"Spirits in this house, come forward and communicate; you're welcome here".* This went around the table three times and at the end of each I summoned the spirit.

A moment of silence was sought. Nothing seems to have happened other then raise the vibrations and energy of each person.

I turned the CD player on with a CD that consisted of several play-time songs. The first one began; some of us knew it, others didn't, but hummed along with the words and music. At the end of this song a couple got restless and felt it didn't add much to the séance and requested to sing, 'O GREAT SPIRIT' which we did for about up to nine times. The words to this is, O Great Spirit, earth sun sky and sea, you are inside and all around me. With those words each person is giving them selves a greater protection while summoning their guides and those in spirit. I proceeded to call the spirit that occupies the house at each interval while the group sang on.

On the ninth chant it's such an amazing energy in the room and it has gotten almost uncontrollably hot. The heat lasted for quite some time. After a short while the man of the house began to speak as if in a slight trance. When he finished I called each individual to trance and asked them to express what they were receiving.

After this I made certain that Joanne, (who is one of my advanced students) was well back from hers and told her that she was in charge of me while I tried to make a trance-connection. I don't recall all that happened and the tape ran out long before the end. But I'll give it to you as it was written for me.

Here's Joanne's write up, which had been read by the group for any omissions.

Full Trance Control:

(Joanne's write-up of the event.)

It's a Friday night (November 17th) and I've been invited by my teacher, Rev. Joe Brown to partake in a séance at the house of a classmate and his wife in Bowmanville, Ontario, Canada. Linda and Judy, other classmates were there also. We began the evening with trying to bring forth spirits that have been haunting their house. We did several things to raise the vibration in the room, but little was happening. Rev. Joe had us all give what we were getting and then he told me to lead the circle because he would try going into trance. It took a few moments but finally when I asked if anyone was there and if George had joined us (the name of the spirit entity that the young man of the house gave him)....this voice came out of Rev. Joe that was not that of his own. It was very deep and very loud. I asked him if he was George, he said yes and then barked at us that we had it all wrong. I asked him to straighten us out and tell us where he was. He replied, "I'm right here". I asked him how he died. He said that he was shot by his brother. I asked him when, he said 1934. I asked him where, he said in the chest and through the heart. I asked him how he was feeling and he said he was not happy and that he was always in the dark; and then he got kind of whinny... I think he may have been crying. I told him he didn't have to stay here and that he could go to the light. He said he didn't want to go there either. I continued to encourage him to go towards the light. He said "what light?" "I don't see a light." I said there must be a light, keep looking, perhaps it's just a spark….look for a spark and if you go towards it, it will get brighter. I continued to speak and said: That's where your loved ones are, that's where God is. He got sad again and said "no one wants me." I told him that God loved him very much and it didn't matter what he did, God would take him in his arms. He said that he was just going to stay where he was and wasn't going to go any place. I said, "But are you happy?" he said, no, I'm lonely and I'm sad and scared. I told him he wouldn't be sad anymore if he just when to the light. That is where he would find people that loved him and would care for him. I said that there must be people there that he liked and wanted to see again. That's when he said, he liked me and wanted me to go with him. I told him that I couldn't go with him and to keep looking for the light. He insisted over and over again that he could not see any light. I kept speaking to him, telling him that there must be a light and to even look for a spark; and this went on for quite some time. He then said, "I see a spark now." I said "good, now go towards it." He got scared and said too many people….too many people. I asked the spirits if they could all back off except for one. He then said I see my mother. I said, good, now go towards your mother, she has her hand outstretched and can help you. (I don't know if I actually said this, but I could see his mother with her arms outstretched.) He said she was excited to see him and that she hadn't been able to find him all this time, because he was left in a ditch when he was shot. I kept on encouraging him to go towards his mother. He finally took her hand and crossed over. As soon as George's spirit crossed to the other side, Rev. Joe's body slumped in his chair and then he fell to the floor, hitting his head on the edge of a treadmill. Now, I've heard in the past that when you are doing spirit work, you will not get hurt, no matter how hard you fall or what happens to you, but this was the first time I actually witnessed it. I wouldn't let anyone touch him, until he had re-entered his body. When he did, he didn't know what he was doing on the floor. He thought perhaps he had fallen asleep while doing trance. He had no memory of what just occurred.

I'd like to thank Spirit in-writing for allowing me this incredible honor of helping a soul cross over to the light with the help and energy of my friends.

All was quiet in this house for about 3 months. Then their son came back from his job, working on a cruise ship in the Caribbean. Shortly after his arrival activity once again began to occur. After he had been there for about two months this is a conversation I had with him.

J.S: Oh by the way the spirit in the house is still with us.

J.B: I understand that. What happened for you to know he/she is still there?

J.S: lots of things. One is that my room went ice cold and I could see my breath. I asked him to leave but he wouldn't. I went upstairs and slept on the couch.

J.B: Interesting. Is there anything else?

J.S: I didn't feel good energy from it; this occurred a couple of times now.

J.B: Talk to him the next time. Try to make contact even if he knocks for an answer; like one knock for yes two for no. Were you scared or nervous?

J.S: I'm normally not but when I'm sleeping it bothers me.

J.B: I understand as that's when my recent ghost used to bother me the most; when I was sleeping.

J.S: When it goes cold like that I feel bad energy. My dad also felt it last week. Normally I don't mind the ghost.

J.B: When it goes cold that's when he's using your energy to materialize. You attract him and he's trying to show himself to you.

J.S: Well if that's the case he's done that already. I've seen him a few times but at night when it gets cold like that there's something not right about it.

J.B: If you stay in the room you would see him eventually.

J.S: But I've seen him and it never got cold.

J.B: Great, tell me what he looks like?

J.S: He's a little shorter then me. (Which is about 5'10 "). Brown hair, brown eyes, no glasses and a lumber jacket top.

J.B: About how old, approximately?

J.S: About forty-five or fifty.

J.B: Go on

J.B: Wearing black pants.

J.B: Any more?

J.S: And when he looks at me I get the message that he left the earth plane owing money and he doesn't want me to leave owing money.

J.B: Well done.

J.S: I think it's his unfinished business and if he gets his message across to me then he can move on.

J.B: Who does he owe the money to?

J.S: And late at night my mom, dad and I hear talking like the television is on and it isn't. Plus there's noting electronic on at all. Sometimes it's like a group of people having a party.

J.B: Interesting.

J.S: I don't know who but I know he left owing money and he's afraid of another female entity.

J.B: Is that entity his wife?

J.S: I don't know; she doesn't live in this house, she lives across the street. I've only seen her twice.

J.B: That's an interesting story.

J.S: Both times during a bad thunder storm she appeared as florescent green and he's afraid of her.

J.B: That's funny.

J.S: The thunder may wake her or disturb her in some way and gives her enough energy to materialize. Besides she looks deathly and she scares the heck out of me too.

J.B: Wow, why is he afraid of her?

J.S: I don't know but one time I saw her as she past by and as I looked over my shoulder I saw the beads in the basement doorway moving as if somebody ran through them.

J.B: It was probably him.

J.S: Then I saw him run in to the room where mom told me you had the séance.

J.B: That's interesting enough.

J.S: When I saw him he looked straight in to my eyes and he looked scared and frightened.

J.B: I believe it.

J.S: I was scared too because the female entity was crossing the street with her arms strait out as if she were coming to get us.

J.B: Oh My Goodness.

J.S: I didn't like that at all. Mom and dad were out west at that time; I was alone.

J.B: I can imagine how that must have scared you. Bet you didn't sleep well that night.

J.S: Surprisingly enough, I did.

J.B: You're funny, God bless you.

J.S: I went to sleep about 2:30 AM and slept like a dream.

J.B: Thank you for sharing this with me. Please keep me posted as to what happens next.

(Within a week J.S. got a request to go back to work and he's usually at sea for six months.)

Attn: For those that have an interest in their Doorkeeper—Gatekeeper—Control and have not encountered him/her, this exercise should be considered prior to experiencing the physical aspect of mediumship.

The Doorkeeper:

Your Doorkeeper is your main guide. He/she is the one assisting you, practically, if not so, from birth. He/she will protect you to the best of their ability but you have free-will and if you choose you can over-ride their protection, which you receive telepathically.

Until you pass to spirit (die) your doorkeeper remains with you, such as your guardian angels. The two are not one; they are totally different, but work in unison on your behalf.

Your overall protector in life's journey your doorkeeper assists in what you're here to do on earth. He/she watches over and watches out for you. As he/she holds your best interest they forever remain close so that no harm may come to you; please pay heed and listen. Some clairvoyants see them and when they do they'll see them standing behind or in front of their medium. Normally they are seen wearing some form of cape wrapped around themselves with lots of folds, enough to cover their medium, you. Once the doorkeeper wrap's the cape or cloak around the medium it signals that he/she is protected and then it's identified as the doorkeeper-guide. Once you become aware of your doorkeeper you'll recognize that he/she will have similar characteristics to your own. This feeling will trigger a familiarity as though your acquaintances travel back to a past life.

Your doorkeeper, which some refer to as gatekeeper, is your first guide and he/she will continue to guide you through life. Being number one in your group of guides he/she is your most prominent guide. He/she holds much love as they're the one that works closest to you as protector, guardian and angel combined together.

Always listen to your doorkeeper. He/she is the guide who gives his/her approval or disapproval to all decisions made on your part. For instances; being directed to the right teacher, to those of like minds and also when you do private readings they direct the clients that visit. Furthermore, they also direct new guides, teachers and loved ones in spirit.

They will intimately communicate with you, the medium, and as you relay, channel, what they give they'll continue to be of a higher service.

Your doorkeeper, gatekeeper, control, decides which spirit entities are allowed to come through.

As you advance in your mediumship you'll become acquainted with him/her.

Doorkeeper Meditation:

Protect, Ground & Connect the usual way
Bring your attention to your feet. Relax
Focus on your lower legs and knees. Relax
Focus on your upper legs. Relax

Focus on your hips, pelvis and buttocks. Relax

Focus on your stomach and lower back. Relax

Let your intuition or gut feelings prepare for spirit contact. Telepathically ask for this awareness.

Now bring your attention to your chest, upper back and shoulders. Relax

Focus on your upper arms, lower arms, hands and fingers. Relax

Bring your attention to your throat and neck. Relax

Continue on; focus on your chin, mouth and nose. Relax

Focus on your eyes, ears and forehead. Relax

Focus on the crown of your head. Relax

Now, bring your attention to your third eye, that's located in the center forehead—between both eyes.

Look out through that eye.

Prepare yourself now, and attune to the spirit world

Find your soul drifting in space.

See yourself in a void of nothingness other then all the stars brightly shining in the distance.

Let your **soul** journey within itself and go beyond the boundaries of life, you're consciousness and of the universe you're now in.

Let it take you in to the realms of fantasy, into the realms of dreams and it will guide you into the realms of reality.

Look ahead and see a blue star.

Travel towards it.

Continue to journey in fantasy and dreams as you move closer to it.

As you gain in closeness to the blue star this fantasy becomes your reality.

Let this reality of soul lead you to the path on which you are traveling.

You're traveling very quickly now

The blue star has become your destine place of arrival

Now, land on this star, your star, your home

Once landed, you now have transformed into a human being, the one you are today.

You begin to find yourself walking as you do in this life.

Look ahead and see The Golden Road.

Everyone is welcome to walk the golden road.

As you continue to walk your wisdom increases

Let this quest enlighten and uplift your senses.

You come across a beautiful chalice sitting on a marble table and is full of crystal clear water

Put your hands in and scoop up as much as possible and raise it to your lips

Now drink of its knowledge.

You feel cleansed and are now prepared to continue your journey.

Continue to walk the golden road.

Keep walking

Keep walking

Go ahead, walk some more

You begin to feel tired and anxious to arrive home

Now, see and visualize a beautiful castle in front of you

Continue to walk

You're tired and exhausted by now

Finally; you have reached the door

There's a huge metal handle on the wooden door and you lift if and let it drop

It drops with a slight clang

No one answers

You lift it again, a little higher then before, and let it drop

It makes a louder clang

Finally

You hear someone on the other side speaking as though they're talking to themselves

The door slowly opens

You walk inside

As you do a large cloak wraps around your shoulders and covers your total being.

You turn around and come face to face with your doorkeeper.

(Give a moment silence)
You feel totally protected
He/she guides you through this room towards another door
As he/she guides you through it you find yourself back in this room.

Chapter Five
Physical Mediumship

Development circles are a great way to learn providing you have the time and give the effort it takes. The home circle is often a first start and believe it or not you may start with two people; a colleague, a friend or your partner, who are like-minded and wish to advance. Any group gathering should be held in an appropriate location with as little disturbance as possible. The home circle should be held where there are no children or pets, as noise is a factor that will deter spirit contact. This circle may evolve from the gathering of a few friends and after a few episodes some will become influenced with some phase of mediumship.

This type of circle gives those on the earth plane an opportunity for spirit-friends to communicate. Those in spirit are as anxious to make their presence known as the members of the circle are to connect with them. The conditions, such as grouping together in a harmonious way with earnest and devoted members who are in good mental state, should be of a loving source—God.

Many have inquired about circle gatherings, and the home circle was highly recommended for the beginner, granted that there's a capable leader/teacher. Here the members know and have confidence in each other with no disturbing elements of distrust. This environment is of a loving nature where hate or fears seldom ever enter. Accepting and being on the same vibration level is of the greatest importance, as with group harmony spirit welcomes a trust. In such conditions phenomena is readily available for experimentation and for relaying messages across the veil.

Closed and open church development circles, which often consist of several people, may not be an ideal organization for the development of a beginner as there are many wanting the same and time does not permit the teacher to teach successfully in one year. If there's no other option then remember this: an ideal beginner's development group consists of one leader/teacher (a medium) and up to six sitters making seven in the group, but this is not carved in stone. Chances are the leader/teacher will be a medium, as that's the usual in Canada. Some circles use a taping device or have a designated secretary or recorder to record pertinent information and keep track of all that happens. Later, as one reflects back, one is capable of correcting oneself through error. I recommend this only if one wishes to reflect back, as in a small group one recognizes growth. The role of the medium is to maintain communication and co-operation with spirit guides and operators. He/she will lead and advise all regarding physic conditions and help by describing developments concerning them, plus the presence of a medium will induce mediumistic powers.

A good attitude, which should be adopted by all, is very important. They should follow routine and not break it; for instance, sitting in the same seat at each gathering, being committed to the group, and being punctual which is of the utmost importance.

As a circle leader, it's important to be very selective about who sits in your group. Prior to the gathering the leader's duties should be to try to cover and arrange and designate duties to others. Once in effect, any decision-making or changes should be approved by the leader and all should respect this.

The criteria when choosing students is that they be of sound mind, clean, healthy, and spiritual, as in Spiritualism for a while with an understanding of it; educated in Spiritualism and about the spirit world. They should have some experience with meditation as this is how you make first contact. Be respectful, unbiased, loving, and enthusiastic, have self-mastery and be harmonious with all in the group. One needs to have these qualities (or most) to embrace communication with the spirit world and should continuously obey the rules.

The designated location should be in a room that is seldom used for other purposes. The room needs this consistency, with suitable furnishings. Drapery and floor coverings are not recommended, but one needs privacy. I also recommend hardwood floors. The furnishings should be as little as possible and no more than required, such as sufficient chairs for all and a round table. As time continues, and with development and progression, other objects and apparatus may be introduced.

Each gathering should begin by creating the right atmosphere. Start out with a prayer, then a short meditation. Being harmonious in a well ventilated room with the right temperature and the right amount of lighting makes it a certainty that some form of phenomena will occur. Unexpected alarms, such as telephones should be turned off and if a dog should happen to bark he should be out of ear shot. This will confirm that all will remain quiet, which is essential.

All should prepare themselves prior to each get-together. For example: eat lightly and be cleansed as in body, mind and spirit.

At the beginning it's recommended to always say a personal prayer for guidance and protection and personally call your guides forward. Then go briefly within as to do a short personal meditation to calm any excitement and to rid your mind of as much daily activities and personal concerns as possible. The reason for this is to be at ease, comfortable, feel spiritually connected as well as self-attunement to prepare for the events that are about to unfold.

Perception is a total focus on the students when psychic development is enforced. At the beginning of the semester or the year, psychometry is recommended as the first tool to enhance sensitivity. This can be classified as psychic symbolic messages as a new attendant has to begin somewhere, and that somewhere as it begins, should remain the simplest.

Students will react and respond to spirit influences according to the guidance and instruction of the leader. They'll become aware of sensitivity changes and the different levels of consciousness. They'll make a connection with their guides, in their own way, and this should not be rushed. They should be encouraged to obtain the correct information on what it's all about. If an entity should present itself they should be encouraged to find out as much as possible about it. The things they should associate themselves with in regard to a discarnate they feel connected with should be: age, gender, name, profession, relationship and even the cause of physical death so that they may give as much as possible to the one for whom it is coming forward.

As a control procedure the students should maintain a closed door until advised otherwise, and then only attempt to open it under the leader's guidance. They must always use common sense and reason and not be averted to any discarnate that wants to come through. We have to remember that we all go to spirit, the good and the evil. It's important for the student to remain wise and alert at all times until they feel a positive control, which is guided and brought forward. As each one progresses it's possible that trance will eventually occur, but maintain control unless under the teacher's direction and guidance.

When you sense a feeling of numbness, as in a loss of physical sensation, sudden jerks, a slight fluttering in the heart or a feeling of coldness in the lower extremities, this is an indication to react and respond to spirit influences. For example: cold breezes, pulling on the abdomen or solar plexus and tingling in the tips of the fingers. Your personal experiences are yours and yours alone as you may not experience what others do. Some students will give way to fantastic actions and feel out of control but it's not feasible and should be avoided at all times. This is when it's important to have the correct teacher/leader who would know how to handle such flair-ups.

Again, in respect to being devoted to physical phenomena it's usually held in the dark with a red light. A trumpet, a cabinet, a table, a bell and other objects may be required. Precaution, and this I stress, should be taken to avoid sudden exposure to light and to noise and sudden abruptness of awakening from meditation or trance.

The general idea behind the circle is that the students should have experienced the opened and closed development circles and this should have been recognized as having the ability for this development. One should have studied the mechanics of mediumship (to a certain degree) to gain an understanding and acquire as much background knowledge and history of Spiritualism and its wonders. One should be educated about 'The code of ethics' and understand their responsibilities and obligations.

A circle should be brought to a close after a designated time, perhaps one and one-half hours, as energy is used up and the students, or the teacher, need not overly exert themselves. This should be encouraged as a routine practice.

At the end of the gathering the teacher should make sure that all are back to reality. If still in a darkened room ask all to raise their hands, that way the leader will know that all is well. End with a prayer giving thanks to God for protection; also give thanks to your guides and spirit entities for coming forward.

A short discussion may take place after the event and it should pertain only to the events that had taken place; not time wasted on idle chit-chat.

Let's get started!

The account of physical phenomena is most interesting, as some of it defies the 'law of gravity,' or so it seems. It covers a variety of subjects; some that you may never need or use but it's always good to be knowledgeable about it just in case you happen to experience something on that line or have someone needing that information.

Although you may already know, I'm going to bring it to your attention as I can't stress this enough.

(1) If you're pregnant or suspect that you may be, please refrain from Trance, or the use of an Ouija board. Meditation is always good for relaxation and inner wellness, but a deep in-depth meditation that may lead to trance should be avoided until your child is born. Remember, quite often in trance, especially an in-

depth trance, a discarnate takes over your body, partial or total. You're carrying another life within so please protect it from any intrusion whatsoever.

(2) If you're a young woman about to enter puberty or recently have, please stay away from any contact with entities for about a year, as you're susceptible to give control to any discarnate that has attached itself to you. This is the worst time to explore what is beyond the veil, the spirit world. Remember, we all go to spirit, the bad as well as the good.

(3) If you have angina or suspect that you may have a weak heart, or know that you do have some form of heart trouble, please do not try trance or delve into any of the exercises that would cause your guide or an entity to enter your body, whether light or full control. This sort of spiritual activity often causes a rapid heart rate. As a novice or a beginner, often times your heart will race when your guide has your permission to enter and use you as a scepter.

Do not under any circumstances give an entity permission to enter your body if you consider yourself one that would fit-in the above category, or you get a negative feeling from an entity.

Physical phenomena is possible through a physical medium and is the process whereby someone in spirit, usually known as a spirit guide, works through the mental and physical energies of the medium, which causes something physical to happen. This form of mediumship is unusual in its nature but quite astounding when everyone is able to witness it. The implications are quite staggering where the mind is capable of affecting matter, making this the most pertinent implication, lying at the foundation of physical mediumship. Not everyone can become a physical medium unlike mental mediumship, which can be developed within most people to some degree. Physical mediumship requires certain elements to be present within the physical organism of the medium. Some say that you either have them or you don't but ectoplasm, which is the basis for physical mediumship, can be developed with much practice. Ectoplasm is an abundance of etheric substance within the etheric vehicle. This substance is a subtle counterpart of the physical body excreting through the body's orifices.

A person who exhibits paranormal abilities has an abundance of vital energy and has the potential of becoming a physical medium. Spirit works in operating the use of this abundance of etheric matter and energy in order to produce various phenomena, such as manifestations. The medium will be in deep trance when this occurs, (called total control). This helps place the medium's mind on the sideline and he/she is outside of their body at this point. While allowing the intelligence of the spirit guide to work with and manipulate their energy, the medium remains unaware of what is taking place. Spirit assists in attaining this state but only after the permission of the medium. During manifestations the physical medium usually sits within an enclosed area (known as a cabinet) which helps focus the energies and creates a type of battery from which the phenomena can be built and energized. Most physical phenomena take place in a darkened room with the use of a red light, which energizes the phenomena; a white light inhibits it.

Levitation, telekinesis and psychokinesis, which is the demonstration of mind over matter wherein physical objects are moved without the use of any instruments or known physical energy or power. This comes under the mental and physical aspects of physical phenomena. A physical medium produces physical phenomena such as raps and table tipping, moving objects, voice or music, levitation of objects, living persons or animals and materialization of spirit forms and objects.

Physical mediumship is usually held in a darkened room although history informs us that from our pioneers it doesn't necessarily have to be. A trumpet, a cabinet, a table, and other objects may be required. Be cautious; make sure all are informed that sudden exposure to light and loud noise should be avoided, as in a séance.

A beginner, as well as a sitter, may react and respond to spirit influence by the feeling of 'coldness to the skin' 'cold breezes' and 'pulling on the abdomen or solar plexus.' Some experience other feelings such as 'a tingling in the tips of the fingers' and or 'a feeling of cobwebs on the skin.' The novice may also react and respond to spirit influence by a 'feeling of numbness' as in the loss of physical sensation; 'sudden jerks', and 'a slight fluttering in the heart.' Some beginners may appear bewildered as they're experiencing something for the first time but they should try to avoid expressing it during this time.

An open door to your consciousness and physic means leaving a door open for just anyone and any discarnate to enter. This may be dangerous and should be avoided. Education and proper teaching guidance is most valuable here. Because of excitement and wanting to learn or experience, new mediums often present an open door and may experience just about any discarnate who would casually venture in, unexpected or unwelcome. Discarnate's who are (a) closest to the earth plane (b) those recently passed over (c) those not knowing they no longer posses their material body or (d) an evil negative refusing to accept his/her crossing, such as being in denial of physical death are all susceptible. This can be avoided by education and proper training by having a high quality medium as a teacher/leader teaching you how to protect yourself and how to close down properly. You'll come to recognize this as you progress and will learn how to avoid certain energies that are trying to get through. It's not wise to be attracted to a negative spirit and the new medium (or experienced one for that matter) should always question until there is absolute certainty and feel comfortable with their understandings. Working with spirit is absolute and should be approached with caution. The apostle Paul said, *"Test the spirits first."*

To cover all that happens in a continuous and dedicated circle one should be open to what spirit can and will do through physical means.

Although some people believe in 'flower sentiments' and 'shoe readings' one must realize that it all comes from the same source, as it's mental mediumship that's being addressed. Some people have never heard the like and have never witnessed it; they're neither losing nor missing anything. But if one does not witness it then one does not gain from the many ways people give spirit messages through symbolic means. Symbolic interpretation is recommended for the novice as it gives confidence in relaying something that is felt from another source, and it could very well be. Conditioning yourself to speak to another with the intention of bringing something from the world of spirit can feel threatening as at first you'll have self-doubt. Until you gain enough courage or confidence to say, 'this is what I see, this is what I got' and/or 'this is what I feel,' chances are you'll remain quiet and won't share your experiences. When you have the 'nerve' (as it takes nerve to confront some teachers for fear of being dismissed) to address your teacher or those about you in this manner you are on the path of being a confident message bearer. Some teachers will try to interpret a message for you and that's not always the answer, for what you get and what you interpret is what spirit wants to bring forward. Your interpreting may be all wrong but class is to learn. Therefore, speak and make the effort; mistakes are expected as that's how you learn to correct them. Learning from a skilled teacher is very beneficial and a skilled teacher will guide you along the way and let you be the interpreter of such messages.

A good teacher will guide you.

A good teacher will enhance what you have so that you'll progress ahead to betterment.

A good teacher will never make you feel inferior.

A good teacher will patiently and lovingly correct you and not belittle you.

A good teacher will be proud when you appear to succeed and will promote you.

A good teacher will not feel threatened of being defamed or feel inferior to a student.

A good teacher will be proud of the fact that they have brought you to a level where you can now go and teach this wonderful gift to others.

A good teacher will always praise students when they advance.

A good teacher will provide the means for spiritual education, as in hands-on opportunity.

A good teacher will never hold you back but will encourage your soul's progression.

A good teacher will encourage you to follow your heart's desire even if that means taking classes with someone else. A student should follow his/her own path and take classes where they feel it's appropriate.

A good teacher recognizes that one person does not have all the answers as each has their expertise to share. In addition, each student must find where they belong.

A good teacher will be tolerant and patient.

A good teacher will maintain and enforce a mature and professional leadership.

A good teacher will encourage peace and respect between his/her students and will encourage others to do the same.

A good teacher will be there in good and bad times when it relates to and/or involves what he/she is teaching.

A good teacher will stress that ego must not get in the way of spiritual growth as ego means, Edging God Out.

A good teacher will provide a place of practice for the student when she/he is ready as practice makes perfect.

A good teacher will encourage students to participate in other areas outside of their comfort zone when he/she feels that you're ready.

Most importantly: A good teacher will teach by example.

(It's difficult to find such a teacher, and I'm very proud to say that I did. She's a God-send.)

After each class of Physical mediumship some time should be allotted for Mental mediumship and sharing a few messages.

Week 15:

Ectoplasm is the substance from which the spirit forms or materializes, and is able to make physical phenomena occur. That is one of the reasons why it's important to practice safe physical mediumship. As you continue to read you'll realize that its use is most valuable when working with physical phenomena.

During physical séances the spirits use this psychic substance that they extract and build from the medium while in trance, and may also draw smaller quantities from the group attending. This substance may seriously harm the medium if exposed to immediate light, such as someone turning the lights on for the purpose of catching a fraudulent act. With this act of cruelty, when the medium is genuine, the substance will quickly return to its natural place of origin, back into the medium, as mentioned in Helen Duncan's biography. "***Ectoplasm** will disappear quickly when exposed to white light, and a fast dissolving of ectoplasm back into, especially the medium, will cause harm. It is said that this process will burn the medium, and she had burning marks on her stomach from where the ectoplasm appeared and disappeared."*

This substance was given its name in 1894 by a former president of the society for psychical research, a man named Charles Richet. He states that *"Its jelly-like body becomes faintly parceled out into an outer form (ectoplasm) and an inner soft (endoplasm) layer, conversely the inner layer termed as Cytoplasm."*

Ectoplasm should not be touched by anyone taking part in the gathering because it's produced from the medium's body and returns to it immediately afterwards. That's why it's very important for everyone and everything to be clean, especially the floor, as the medium is the bridge between this world and the spirit world. Spirit photography will show apparent shadows or fog around a medium's body. Take note of the stomach, mouth, ears, nose and eyes, as it excretes from all orifices. In some photos the face of the medium appears as if in a cloud.

Students and beginners when first experiencing it will feel a cobweb like substance, mostly around the face and the head area. When experiencing this, the students should be reminded not to touch that area no matter how great the urge. To rub their face will break its growth; therefore, they should refrain from touching until they're back from trance. Once back he/she may rub their hands, from the forehead down over their face until completely down over their chin. If the sensation continues redo it.

Here's an exercise that you may wish to do to know if and when you start to create ectoplasm. This can be done at any time, but it's recommended that you do it in the quiet of your own home or in a development circle. Although being in an excited mood enhances spirit, take this little exercise seriously and don't play around as if it's some sort of joke.

Get an unpainted wooden lead pencil or any other round piece of wood the size of a pencil or a little larger, about four inches or longer. I break a pencil in half and each half is used by a student. If you're right handed place your right hand flat on the table or on any other flat surface. Left-handed people please use your left as you're more in control, connected and familiar with its use. Your upper leg may be used if there's no table close by. Keeping your fingers together, place the pencil between your index and middle fingers with the eraser at the back where the fingers connect to your hand. While your hand rests on the table, or on your upper leg, go within to attune. Once you feel you've attuned, slightly open your eyes to observe your hand in its resting place. Remaining in a sitting position, lift your hand slightly up and then move it out, parallel, not touching your leg when it is moved towards the floor. Keep your body aligned and slowly move your hand, bending at the elbow, down towards the floor and continually repeat in your mind over and over again: attune, attune, attune, as your hand descends. If the pencil falls, and does not stick to your fingers when the tips are pointing straight down, repeat the process. When you're producing ectoplasm the pencil sticks like glue. Do not repeat this more than 5 times as you'll be pressuring yourself and those in spirit when you're both not quite ready.

Practice this exercise to try to move a small table

Be certain that the table is small and short; about 18 inches high and the top close to 18 x 12 give or take a few inches. The smaller the tables the better to work with as you work towards your physical achievements. Be accountable for your actions and take this experiment, like all the others, seriously.

Usually a group of people will gather at the same place and at the same time to build up the energies to create the right atmosphere for this. You are more than welcome to try this at home although this sort of practice was frowned on by my development teacher. There's no reason why you cannot take responsibility and work safely with your physical guides alone. The table may move, who knows, it has for others. Don't get discouraged if it doesn't, as this does not usually happen in a first sitting. It's possible that it may take several and it's more than likely that it should take a year or more.

If you're in class or a group sitting it's best to work as a team. One person sits on a chair with the table directly in front. Place all finger tips, including thumbs, of both hands (very lightly) touching the table. As you momentarily attune and telepathically call on your guide, all others should focus on sending you energy. When you feel a connection, open your eyes, and then try to move the table forward. While in deep concentration focus on what you're doing and send mind power towards the table through your fingers. To further enhance the phenomena the group should sing uplifting songs to help create ectoplasm, thus greatly enhancing the energy.

Remember, if the table moves stand up and move along with it, otherwise it will stop. It needs a force of energy to move. Once you break the connection the table usually stops unless you're a very powerful and experienced physical medium. Work towards that goal.

Some examples of Physical Mediumship and exercises to follow are:

Week 16:

Levitation which is a phenomenon of psychokinesis (psychokinetic, PK) in which objects, people and/or animals are lifted into the air without any visible physical means and float as if by itself. The two methods are: (1) by energies gathered from the circle sitters and (2) by ectoplasm used from the mediums body.

For this to work you'll need a devoted group to participate

regularly, as in a group there'll be a greater energy. What actually happens depends on you and those who attend. Levitation doesn't usually happen at a first gathering, it takes a considerable amount of devoted time to work towards your goal. Over a period of sitting together the leader will become aware of any skepticism held by any members. It will iron itself out as eventually the skeptics will drop out leaving those that believe behind. Like anything else that involves the spirit world it has to be taken seriously and one has to firmly believe that it will occur. Eventually, with great practice, it will. To practice, you should start with a small object such as what I had introduced to my students. I use a small hand-made feathered bird that is suspended in the air by a very thin wire, with its base on the table. First of all, the group needs to attune and this can be done by a short meditation, such as 'protect, ground and connect' and a basic meditation. To attune enough to create ectoplasm takes a considerable amount of devoted and on going time and patience. The deeper you go within, the more attuned to the spirit world you'll become. Moreover, you're giving the spirit world permission to use your body via the means of your own natural etheric substance, ectoplasm.

A basic meditation for attunement may or can go like this:

Start with a prayer such as:

Great Divine Spirit, protect us with your Infinite White Light. Guide us as we go within. Grant us, as a group, the ability to advance towards levitation of a simple object. We ask that you keep all evil entities away while we continue on our spiritual journey. Amen

THEN:

Visualize a white beam of light coming through the ceiling. It's descending upon you. It touches and covers your head; you feel a sense of peace and love from God.

It's slowly moving down around your shoulders.

It's now covering your upper arms, your chest, and back, lower arms, stomach, hips and down over your hands. It's moving down your upper legs, your knees, your lower legs and slowly moving down around your feet.

It's now covering your feet.

Now, visualize it going through the floor underneath you and going deep into mother earth.

You're now grounded and also connected to God.

Don't be afraid; relax; you're safe.

Bring your attention to your feet. Relax.

Focus on your lower legs and knees. Relax.

Focus on your upper legs. Relax.

Focus on your hips, pelvis and buttocks. Relax.

Focus on your stomach and lower back.

Relax. Let your intuition or gut feelings prepare for spirit contact. Ask your guide or doorkeeper to bring on this awareness. If you don't know them, just telepathically ask your higher self and recognize that it has been granted.

Now bring your attention to your chest, upper back and shoulders. Relax. Focus on your upper arms, lower arms, hands and fingers. Relax.

Bring your attention to your throat and neck. Relax.

Continue on; focus on your chin, mouth, and nose. Relax.

Focus on your eyes, ears, and forehead. Relax.

Focus on the crown of your head. Relax.

Now, bring your attention to your third eye that's located in the center forehead—between both eyes.

Then choose the appropriate phrase or phrases below, or use that which is appropriate for you.

(a) Prepare yourself and attune to the spirit world. Or

(b) Prepare yourself for spirit contact. Or

(c) Speak to your guides. Or

(d) Commune with your guides. Or

(e) Speak to your guides and ask for their assistance.

After this has been put into motion have the group to partially come back and ask them to turn their hands slightly inwards and up, while still on their lower legs, as if they were opening them to summon a small child to come to their arms. Then bend the hands back just enough so that the palms are directed towards the object you wish to try to levitate. With group energy tell them to feel the energy leaving their hands and visualize it going directly to the focused object. With that in motion and being a sensitive medium you may see lines of energy or a line of ectoplasm extending out from some members' hands, or other body parts, if not all. Continue with this combined energy for a while, but be certain that all remains comfortable. Don't stay in this position for a long time as it will deplete the energy of those that are doing it properly and they'll feel fatigued. Moreover, chances are that with too much time elapsing and a continued focus, there will be a considerable amount of energy being released and this may cause headaches. The leader should be the judge, keeping in mind the safety and well-being of the students/members.

Once the allotted time has neared for this sitting say a prayer thanking God for protecting the group; thank your guides for assisting and also thank those in the spirit world who tried to assist in any way, even with no noticeable results.

Week 17:

Transfiguration is a change in form or appearance in facial alterations by means of an ectoplasmic mask. The medium is usually in a deep trance when this occurs. As well as facial changes taking place, the voice also changes if the spirit speaks. The onset of transfiguration can feel like cobwebs touching the outer part of the face, which is connected with the gross magnetic activity in the aura field. This usually occurs (around the face) during the presence of oncoming spirit communication due to the fact that spirit friends mould their earth like appearances over the physical features of the medium. Sometimes you may look at someone and see another's face superimposing over theirs and that person may not even be aware of it. This sometimes happens when one visits a medium for a reading, and a loved one is desperately trying to make himself/herself known to them.

My first experience witnessing this was extraordinary as I saw a face that looked very familiar but I couldn't place it. Once the medium had heard all that the people experienced and wished to share he proceeded to channel entities. He brought through a man, and given the description and the full name, I felt he presented himself for me. Once I checked with my mother she informed me that I knew him as a young child. He was the man who drove the oil truck and delivered the oil for our furnace.

When teaching transfiguration you may use a similar meditation as above and let the group stay within for about 5 minutes. The procedure should take place in a darkened room; but be certain that there's enough light for all to see. If you have a student in mind to use, which should be agreed to by the student, the group should be made aware of it. The volunteer should be placed, if possible, in something like a lazy-boy chair with the legs raised off the floor for comfort or on a bed with the head raised to a 30 to 45 degree angle. Within meditation time all the other students should send the chosen, or volunteered, student some of their energy and call on their loved ones to come forward to visit through the volunteer. It's amazing how many will come through, one superimposing themselves after another.

Once 5 minutes of meditation are up, gently call the group back and tell the volunteer to remain within. Then the students should quietly stand and disperse, but remain at a comfortable distance in full view of the volunteer's face.

The leader then moves close to the student, preferably behind the head, and speaks softly and gently to him/her. The leader will remind the student to stay within and to go much deeper within, such as a form of hypnotic suggestion to welcome the spirit world. Wait a short time and the leader should speak again to the volunteer's ears, which should now be the guides. When addressing the guide ask him to move the volunteer's head (call the person by name) very slowly from one side to the other. That is, move (the person's name here) head to the right, very slowly, and then tell the guide to move it in the opposite direction. If you see that the head is moving too fast tell the guide to slow it down and vice versa. Then the head should be moved backwards; that is, raise the chin upwards and then slowly down again until the chin is firmly pressed down on the chest. The leader should remain with the student volunteers at all times to protect them from accidental physical contact with others. This should not go any longer than 10 minutes, five may be sufficient.

Once time has elapsed, thank the guide for coming and have the volunteer thank those from the spirit world telepathically and gently call him/her back. Once he/she is back have the group sit down and have them express what they witnessed, if anything.

End the class with a prayer of thanks to God, the guides and the entities who came through and also to those who tried but couldn't.

Week 18:

Trumpet: A get-together of friends to contact and connect with the spirit world is often called a séance. A trumpet which is made of aluminum in the shape of a cone is used in such a gathering for direct voice phenomena, as explained below in "direct voice." Trumpets are generally placed in the centre of the circle; directly on the floor or in the center of a table. During the séance and while the group remains seated the trumpet will pass all around the circle. This happens in a manner in which it would be quite impossible for the physical medium to do unless he/she got out of his/her seat. The 'spirit voice' will speak through the trumpet to a person seated within the circle. The trumpet will be horizontal and at a convenient height for the person being addressed (at ear level). The sound of the voice may come out of both ends, but normally it's out of the smaller as it needs the larger end to create the voice box from ectoplasm. The trumpet may be used in all séances or closed circles, especially when direct voice is expected. If a cabinet is used and if there's a consistency of group energy it should also be present.

A trumpet séance is a spirit circle consisting of various amounts of people and a medium. The medium should be familiar with channeling for the ability of physical phenomena. Physical phenomena mediums are rare; because it takes an extraordinary amount of psychic energy for theirs to vibrate at such a high frequency. All present provide the battery for the medium and he/she then is able to call in the spirits.

Light will often break up ectoplasm but a black light or a small dark red light may be used for skeptics that may be present. Because most are held in complete darkness the bottom of the trumpet should have some form of 'glow in the dark reflector tape,' which can be bought at some hardware stores. With results the voices that come through will be heard by all of the sitters. A message that's given to one often contains information that is useful to all.

A circle such as this may last for up to 3 hours, depending on the number in the group. Some believe that there's a specific number to use for the right amount but any number is sufficient with the right intent, the right atmosphere and the right energy. Skepticism always deters the spirit world so be choosy with those who participate.

The group will sit in a circle and the medium may designate certain seats to create a balance of energy. The medium will go into a deep trance while the group chants Oms, Ohs, Hums and/or sings uplifting spiritual songs. As this is happening, the group is feeling a natural high. As they continue to sing or chant this acts as a channel for spirit; welcome them with your singing voice and chanting. Those being beckoned will vary depending on the group energy and what is needed by the group or certain individuals for spiritual growth. Once the spirits arrive levitating of the trumpet is achieved; then direct voice phenomena will occur.

With channeling the spirits need to use the vocal cords of the medium, speaking through him/her and using his/her vocal chords. This may happen at a private reading as well as any given séance without the trumpet rising.

The reason for a trumpet séance is for the spirits to use it to relay messages to their awaiting loved ones. Good luck.

Week 19:

Apports; and Other Objects in a Séance: Other objects used in a séance have been explained in 'Séance example #1.' Although this is a personal set-up your personal set up is what's important for your personal séance. Pick and choose what you feel is needed. Don't despair if at first you have some difficulty in choosing, or any of the objects don't move. Choose objects that are easily movable, and when spirit moves them with ease add heavier objects to increase the choice, or selection.

Apports are gifts that are given to the sitters from the spirit world. They are transported from one place to another through the manipulation of energy and a change in the frequency at which they vibrate. Only objects that had been lost or will not be missed by anyone are the gifts given. Spirit will not take anything from one to give to another, therefore, when you receive such a gift it's from spirit and not from someone who will be searching for it in our material world.

I was given such a gift but it didn't fit; my brain received a suggestion that it was to be given to a family member, which it fit perfectly. If you're fortunate enough to experience this phenomenon and receive a gift, don't question its past. Just take it with an open heart and feel blessed that the spirit world recognized you enough to present you with such a treasure.

Week 20:

Direct voice—Independent voice is a voice that comes from another part of the room from an invisible force and not from the mouth of the medium or any of the sitters, such as by physical means. Direct voice is also associated with other phenomena related to spirit deviation. Such voices have been heard in séance rooms in past years and became more public in the wake of modern Spiritualism.

Although the search for direct or independent voice was being held in a darkened room not all were fraudulent. As one became more attuned with the spirit world one was able to add lighting so that all were able to witness it. It's O.K. to start out this way, but in any given group there are those who need proof; if able, give it to them. Furthermore, as a darkened room is required it assists in creating the psychic energy and ectoplasm which is required for this type of phenomenon. Once again, a red light may be used as it attracts those in spirit. Some use a trumpet. It should be noted that more than one ectoplasmic materialization has been known to take place simultaneously. In the past it was taken for granted that trumpets were to be used. Although today a trumpet is normally used, with little activity, it's not necessarily needed as an ectoplasmic voice-box will materialize, outside any instrument, if the energy is strong enough.

They say that a trumpet should be a gift and not bought by the medium intended to use it. I find this to be inaccurate as in the past the trumpet was made out of cardboard by the medium and results were phenomenal.

The trumpet is placed in the centre of the circle, on a table or a clean floor, and when the atmosphere is right for spirit, the trumpet will float in the air. This trumpet is raised by ectoplasm and the voice is that of the spirit communicating from the spirit world. The purpose of the trumpet is that it's directed to the person concerned and the sound is concentrated in that direction. The sound is created from an artificial voice box formed out of ectoplasm and usually comes from the smaller pointed end of the trumpet. The artificial larynx or voice box is built up from ectoplasm drawn from the medium and oftentimes as well as that of the sitters. Trumpets will float around unsupported and will approach a person for whom a message is intended. The trumpet amplifies a faint voice and facilitates the phenomenon. In the wonder of it all many had witnessed those that passed into another world and oftentimes the entity could be seen by many.

On several occasions instances have been recorded; different sounds related to the entity trying to make contact as well as music being heard.

What makes this phenomenon interesting is that the circumstances in which it occurs resembles that of a familiar voice and is said to be recorded independently. With all sorts of sounds being heard the actual voice is validated by the person it was intended for. Moreover, validation is also made as each person in the group has not known or had any access to each other's history.

As an example, use your trumpet in a séance room. Call spirits forward and welcome them and then focus entirely on direct voice. You may need to guide them on what to do so don't hesitate to give them permission to use your energy as well as that of the group. Plus, tell them to use the trumpet to form the voice-box and take it to those to whom it wishes to speak. Please note that the larger end of the trumpet is used to form the voice box. The smaller end is pointing to the ear of the sitter and not the other way around as most believe.

Results should not be expected during your first session as it may take several sessions with a devoted group over a number of gatherings, perhaps years.

Week 21:

Electronic Voice Phenomenon is spirit-voice caused by a (PK) psychokinetic means; it's also known as (TK) or telekinesis. Interest in this began somewhere in the 1920s. It's alleged communication by spirits through tape recorders and other electronic devices such as an answering machine. It's the paranormal ability of your mind to influence matter or energy without the use of any physical means. A taping device is needed; digital defines better but an ordinary tape recorder will do. Spirit uses noises to communicate as they need some means to create words. Have background noises such as slow running water, a fan and/or a radio off station, where only the static is heard. Other sources may be used as long as it's not too loud and has a continuous and even rhythm such as, an electric razor or a hair dryer on low speed. Those objects should be hanging because loud vibration noises are made if they're resting on something.

The voices usually respond directly to the person asking the question and making the recording. Extreme concentration is needed to hear and detect voices as they're not easily heard. Headphones are a must and several playbacks may be required. There may be one word or a short sentence. Nevertheless the word or words may be much slower than your regular speech or at a faster rate.

Spirit voices are not usually heard at the time of recording as they're from another dimension. It's only when the tape is played back that it's heard. Sometimes amplifying, as playing it on your stereo system, and if able, noise filtering may be required to hear them.

After saying this, I dispute this toady as I've been very successful while first hearing audible voices in my own home and then setting up my recorder. However, the atmosphere, and the environment, was right considering my past experiences. The environment was natural; a crackling fire place, a ceiling fan, raining heavily outside and water running down the side of the sunroom wall, over a metal pillar.

A few pieces of commonly found equipment and some patience with the use of simple technology may create the wonders you desire. You'll need repetitive listening to your repetitive questions as a word or short phrase may go undetected.

What one could use at home is a small AC or DC table size fountain. Place an aerial or an extendable metal picker-upper with a magnetic tip that's used by an electrician to pick up screws and nuts off the floor and so on, in the water. Make sure it's secured in some way as not to fall down. I use masking tape; and have a small electrical fan blowing air towards it.

This is a learned gift; be patient. Remember that you'll be hearing the voices of your dearly departed, and recognizing them will confirm and reward you for your laborious work and may also be your guides.

Another example: If you wish to do this at home your bathroom may be the best place. A small enclosed place gives spirit a better means as your energy is also confined. Spirit uses all and any source to communicate. Be certain that you're alone and won't be disturbed. First of all you need to make an appointment with your departed loved ones. This can be affirmed each day for a week prior to the event. Make an appointment with them as you read in one of the séances' examples. Don't break this appointment as you've committed yourself and they'll do their best to comply.

Prepare your questions ahead of time and stay with those questions, don't change them once you set your mind on them.

At the designated time take a comfortable chair in your chosen room (which should be small) so that you'll sit comfortably. Set up your recorder, microphone, close to the noise makers and away from the running water so as not to fall in. A small table is recommended to place your recorder, a radio and/or a fan on, if you use them. Be certain that the radio and the fan, if bumped, won't fall in the water. Place a small bowl or saucer in the sink for the water to fall in but make sure the water drains out. Most bathroom sinks have an overflow-escape located at the top, so, if the water flow is slow this may be used. For safety measures, as electrical devices are used close to water, I recommend a saucer or a small bowl and leaving the drain open. Electricity is created from water. Water is most important as it holds the main ingredient. Have your fan plugged in and turned off; have your radio plugged in, or better still use a battery operated one, and set it off-station hearing only low static. And, an extendable metal picker-upper with a magnetic tip, bottom or larger end in the water, secured as not to fall over. Have your tape recorder set in Rec. mode and on pause. You may not need the radio if you have fans going and set at low speed.

Once all is set up and ready to be activated you need to attune and once again speak to your dearly departed. Go within, via meditation, your usual style and attune. Go as deep as you're able without going into trance. Once you feel a strong connection with the spirit world bring yourself back and proceed. Turn on the water, fan, and radio static and then your recorder. Invite your loved ones to communicate with you. Welcome them, tell them you love them and want to hear from them. Call them by name if you wish and ask a question; you may need to speak loudly to hear yourself on tape above the noise. It's always good to hear the questions to be able to decipher the answers. Ask one question, let the noises run for up to five minutes, no longer then ten, and ask another. Continue in the same manner for about half an hour which should give you a maximum of 6 questions. Don't deplete your energy by pushing spirit if they're not ready. Furthermore, don't feel it was a failure and give up if no results are heard the first time. Practice makes perfect. It's like everything else worthwhile learning and succeeding at in life. In addition, create the right environment and atmosphere and you'll be amazed at the success. Recently, in the middle of the day with water running off the sunroom roof, the ceiling fan on low and the fireplace fan running, there was a lot of activity at the ceiling of the sunroom. One was able to hear faint noises. I set up my recorder with a powerful microphone and taped one half-hour of chanting. As I began to listen with the headphones, a chill ran down my spine as my first impression was that of a small child moaning in pain. As the sound continued I came to realize that it was most likely a guide chanting as it reminded me of old movies where Indians chanted around a fire or the medicine man summoning spirits. Thirty minutes of chanting, as the snow melted from the roof creating water and providing the right atmosphere for electronic voice phenomena, is a treasure to have so easily obtained.

Week 22:

Materialization is an apparition that's linked to a medium capable of doing this. Example, it's something similar to that of a baby's umbilical cord to a mother. This apparition consists of ectoplasm from the medium and is subject to changes with the interactions of the mediums mind or direction. A cabinet is used for this type of phenomenon because energy needs to accumulate to create the life-like form. This smaller space provides the atmosphere for the formation to take place (using a 'dark red light' as the only light source in the room). Not only is it possible for a spirit to show its face at the time of physical death but it is also able to show it at different times during its physical life. Materialization may occur where the spirit can be seen and sometimes touched by those present. This type of communication is very rare as the sitters are required to build up the energy in the room via attunement. The conditions have to be right and correctly controlled, creating a reassuring safeguarded environment. The cabinet used may be that which is described in the séance portion of the book, your own closet or a wooden structure of your choosing, providing it's safe.

For materializing to take place, the medium, which may very well be you, should be well educated on the subject, for safety measures. Once educated, and you wish to try your luck, be certain that you won't be disturbed in any way for at least an hour. Have an alarm clock, a fair distance away but not out of hearing range, to alarm at that time. Have a camera aimed at the cabinet door and a tape recorder recording any sounds. Once inside don't rush things along. Sit quietly, say your protection prayer, call on your spirit guides and welcome those of love and light from the spirit world. If at any time you feel a negative vibration send it away immediately and start over. Sit in quietness and attune. As you block out and clear your mind of all that you can, other than concentrating on spirit's, let your body relax and your mind become one with and at peace with God.

You may need soft background "new age," relaxation or meditation music as a beginner but total silence is more appropriate once you progress and have conquered the art of meditation.

In the past, materialization was very popular and happened frequently at séances. Some people are born with this gift, others are not, but one may train himself/herself with patience and diligent practice.

Take good care of yourself and be certain that you'll always be safe when you go within.

Week 23:

Table Tipping (psychokinetic (PK) is the manifestation of a human group energy that might be somehow augmented or influenced by discarnate spirits. Many feel this phenomenon is part of a Séance. Personally, I feel that all that Spiritualism practices, in ways of connecting with the spirit world, is a form of séance. Whether one personally respects this explanation or not, it should be respected; table tipping is a form of physical mediumship.

Table tipping or tilting was developed in home circles as a game, but those who practiced came to realize that the information coming through was genuine and authentic. Therefore, a number of participants began to believe that their attempts to communicate with the spirits were actually successful. We must take into consideration that in pioneer days there wasn't anything such as television, computers and the like, so friends got together to form some sort of entertainment. The home circle, which is best, is usually a small collection of like-minded people or family members and friends. Phenomena-determined people will frequently get together to attempt to contact the spirit world. This form of spirit contact will come easily, as all home owners have a table, and its use for spirit chatting will prove rewarding.

Table tipping has been considered to be entertaining and some believe that it's the collective work of the human minds involved. In addition, it has been noted that energy created by the gathered group of people, who were intent on a single purpose, could produce amazing results. Taking this into consideration, physical phenomena is the result of combined energy although some believe that the table is being moved by the participants themselves. Take the initiative and explore this amazing and wonderful past-time. You'll be surprised at what you'll learn and what you'll come to understand about yourself and others.

For table tipping you may chose four people to sit at a larger table with at least one, if not more, being an experienced medium. Balancing out the energy is important; for instance one experienced medium and a novice on each side. Two, one on each side, should sit at a smaller table. If you use a tall table where 2 have to stand then be certain that those using it know what they're doing. Don't assume that all will be well, because those who will be standing will need extra attention. Even though you may expect some form of communication; with a designator at all tables involved asking the questions and writing down the answers, prepare yourself for the unexpected. The designator should be knowledgeable as to how to care for the participants if something unexpected should happen that needed immediate attention.

The simple technique is quite basic. With each person resting his/her hands flat on the table say a prayer of protection; then have a moment of silence to go within and attune. While within have them telepathically call on their guides and welcome those of love and light to come forward and communicate. When all is in order and all have their eyes open, the questions may be asked. Don't become startled by other means of communication such as rapping or knocking noises that may vibrate the table before it eventually moves.

If you do this at home then the number of sittings will increase the power and the phenomena will also increase, with greater results. Make sure your group gatherings are always free from interruptions. Cell phones, television, and radio should be off, the dog and cat a distance away (in another part of the house) and the house phone unplugged or the ringer turned off. Do the necessary checks to prepare yourself for your evening of spirit contact, or whatever you wish to call it.

Exercise questions to start are important.

Answers are from past loved ones; don't settle for animal and pet communications via this means as pets can't speak, although other forms of animal communication are quite possible.

Once all has attuned, the designator with paper and pen in hand, will start the questions. Questions with 'Yes' and 'No' answers will be the simplest as using the alphabet is time consuming. Although time consuming it provides rewarding answers given through the 'Yes' and 'No' process.

Question 1 should be: What tip of the table is 'Yes'? If the table moves then you know what side is 'No.' As the table had moved we assume that there's an entity present. Always welcome the spirit. Then the designator speaks to the entity. With total focus on the table ask: "Who are you here for; are you here for (then mention each person at that table until you get a 'Yes' answer).

The next question should determine who the entity is: Ask if it's a man you're communicating with; if 'No' ask if it's a woman. One cannot expect that a small child would consider himself/herself a man or a woman. If you receive 'No' for both the man and woman, then ask if it's a boy. If 'No' then you may assume it's a girl, but ask anyway.

The next question could very well be finding the age at which they passed to spirit. Then the next question could be the year they had passed, and so on. If you ask them for a name you may have to go through the alphabet. Ask if the name begins with an A and so on down to the complete name. It's O.K. to jump around with the alphabet as one may be attracted to a certain name, and also know that certain letters are not followed by others.

Have fun and enjoy the experience, but have your questions partially prepared in advance.

Questions one could ask when 'Table-tipping'

1. What tip of the table is 'Yes'? If the table moves then you know what side is 'No'.

Welcome the spirit. Then the designator speaks to the entity via the table. With total focus on the table ask:

2. Who are you here for; are you here for, then mention each person at that table until you get a 'Yes' answer?

3. (a) Is it a man we're communicating with? If 'No' ask

(b) Is it a woman we're communicating with?

(c) Is it a boy we're communicating with? If 'No' ask if it's a girl anyway

(d) Is it a girl we're communicating with?

4. How old were you when you died?

5. What year did you die?

6. Will you tell us your name? If you ask for a name you may have to go through the alphabet. It's O.K. to jump around with the alphabet as one may be attuned with a certain name, and also know that certain letters are not followed by others.

7. Does your name begin with an 'A,' and so on down to the complete name?

*A reminder: the questions may go on as long as you have a connection with this particular entity and the sitters are not tired.

Once again, the designator is responsible in observing the sitters for any form of distress whatsoever.

A Ouija board is a tool used for scrying; meaning 'revealing.' The name Ouija means yes-yes. Oui means 'yes' in French and 'ja' means 'yes' in German. This is an ancient form of communicating with the spirit world, those whom we call the dead.

Although Ouija boards are usually sold in novelty and or the games section of a store, many people believe and swear that there is something occult about them and their use.

The layout of the board varies from country to country. Some planchettes, or the pointer-indicator, have a window and others do not. The original and best layout of a board appeared to have the 'Yes' at the top of the circle and the 'No' at the bottom. This is a matter of opinion as one adjusts to their surroundings.

Some people use the board as a play toy; some take it seriously as a way to communicate with their dearly departed. Some others take it 'very seriously' and is sacred to death of it as horror stories tend to be passed along about them. Although there are stories that Ouija boards are dangerous, these stories may have some truth and should not be totally ignored. Do not use it in the séance room as the human mind is capable of receiving quite the opposite of what you expect. Consider your first few practices as experiments and educate yourself as you would on any other interest. Don't always judge by rumours or speculation.

I take this seriously as many times accuracy was validated even when those using it didn't have a clue who was communicating. For instance, validation was given by an elder in the family, right down to the name and time of death. A word of caution here: any child, male or female, entering puberty should not delve into any activity that may hold supernatural powers until they've past this stage of life because, if one takes it seriously that one is very susceptible to evil or negative entity possession.

As a young adult I bought a board and used it with accuracy. My partner at the time didn't feel comfortable with it due to rumors heard about its evil intent. Although she participated she didn't like what was coming through and she felt that it wasn't right to have it in our home. Needless to say, I disposed of it, and to make her happy, I burned it. Looking back, it was the right thing to do. Appeasing her and her way of thinking reminded me in later years that the accuracy from the board was 'uncanny', or was it? Another 2 boards from different countries eventually ended up in my possession; one with a window and one without. I respect its use in the means of supernatural powers.

The Ouija board is not a part of Spiritualism although some tend to think so. Spiritualism does not practice the use of this board although many use it in the comfort of their homes, as do many different nationalities and religions.

If you decide to use this board, whether for play or seriousness to communicate to those passed on, then connect, ground and protect as one would do in prior meditations.

Requirements for its use are a minimum of two people to operate it. A one-person operator can manipulate to their satisfaction. A one person operator is not advisable. Two people should sit opposite each other and place the tip of the fingers on the planchette, a slide-able three-legged device. Some countries recommend only one fingertip per person. More profound results personally came from both hands gently applied with as many fingertips were able to be placed on it, in comfort. Each person should agree on how many fingers should be used before they start or the energy will be unbalanced.

Start out with the planchette located in the center of the board and be certain that you both have freedom of movement; the reasons being that in case you need to rise slightly from your chair to access all that the board has to offer is within your comfort zone.

Someone should start by asking a simple question. This question should be a confirmation of an entity present such as, is there a spirit present? Or, is there a spirit with us right now? If there's no response and the planchette doesn't move, don't give up. If one is new then a bonding may need to take place. Call on the spirit world and welcome those of love and light to come forward. Tell them that they are welcome in your presence to communicate through the board. Then the question should be asked again until some results are noted. If all are new, then getting together a few times may be needed for best results. Blending and balancing of energies are worth taking into consideration with any group participation. Positive group participation makes things run much smoother whether at this board or in any other situation.

Once the planchette eventually moves and answers your question it can be quite startling. One or the other will be accused of using human force. Be acceptable and open to the forces that lie beyond our material world. To prove that one is not manipulating the planchette, and that it's supernatural, ask a question that only you and the entity present would know.

It is helpful to write down the questions you wish to ask before you start. It is also helpful to have a person writing down the answers as you continue for future reference. Questions may take on a different route once communication begins. Be open to suggestions from those who attend but have only one person ask the questions. If there's no answer for a question asked, you may consider revising it, taking a different approach.

Once you become experienced you'll find that the pace of responses coming will increase as well as the speed of the planchette. In fact, sometimes it will speed across the board at such rates that it will challenge your ability to keep up. Furthermore, the responses you get will actually depend on your attitude and commitment. In addition, skeptics believe that those using the board either consciously or unconsciously select what is being given. Once again, you be the judge; *it all comes from the same source.*

Week 24:

Pendulum has been used in mystic rites for thousands of years. It, too is, one of the oldest as well as one of the simplest methods of obtaining intuitive information. Its phenomenon has been explained in several ways and its accuracy is questionable. One theory is that the pendulum is an instrument for tapping into the subconscious mind. Another is the use of supernatural powers directed to the user's hand through vibration.

You can get answers to anything you come up with or invent if you have faith in your invention. The pendulum is a tool that helps you to access the collective unconscious that's connected to your higher self as it's basically the amplifier of your curiosity. Everyone is capable of working with and succeeding in the use of a pendulum. All one has to do is to get acquainted with it by learning its movements and use. It may require a constant and considerable amount of practice and experimentation. To err is part of the learning process. The results you achieve will depend on patience and practice as it reflects on your stage of spiritual and mental development. When used for the wellbeing of others or yourself and not for egotistical reasons one is apt to succeed with clarity.

When selecting your pendulum follow your intuition and choose one that feels right for you. Having more than one gives choice for each individual you work with and for questions sought. It's easy to make your own. As a child I remember the adults using a needle hanging on about a 6 to 8 inch thread with a knot tied at the end for easy holding. This home invention was used to determine the sex of a baby about to come into our world. My younger brother tried this when his third child was conceived. When speaking to him about the wonderful news he said that the results were that it would be a boy. This was probably due to the fact that the whole family wanted a boy to carry on the family name. (When the child was born the results were inaccurate). There hadn't been a boy born to a son and this will probably be the last chance; this, too, was an inaccurate thought as with the next child we got our dream. We finally got our boy. Personally I feel that this particular experiment was mind over matter making the mind the powerful instrument that overruled all else to appease the family.

After you've determined what each pendulum movement means for you, anything you ask should be that which requires a Yes or No answer. As your pendulum swings you need to be totally undivided and focused on the presence of the moment.

Everything holds energy. Organisms in and throughout our universe is surrounded by all kinds of energy. Observe the flora and fauna in our world and you'll notice this to be true. Humans nonetheless, have something deep within that registers energy that communicates to the nervous system; known as intuition. As thought creates a physical reaction or a response, the effect creates motion in the pendulum to make it swing. This is similar to dousing for water, but with divining rods, which had been used with success over the years.

Pendulums have been used for many reasons. Let your use be that of good for someone else or betterment on your own outlook for health and well-being. If you gamble with the pendulum it may also gamble with you. Therefore, use it wisely because Spirit doesn't always supply us with a lot of material things. Spirit, God, provide for our needs and not always with an abundance of it.

To use the pendulum is easy. Choose a quiet place and relax. A light meditation may be needed to rid your mind of daily stresses and thoughts. As usual, one needs to connect with the God source and mother earth. Connect, ground and protect. You may sit or stand but stability is important; whatever your choice keep your feet flat on the floor.

If you have a design on paper, which you don't need, hold the pendulum 'center field' in the circle. To design such a map draw a circle with intersecting lines such as a + sign. One line should be labeled 'Yes;' the other 'No.' The back of your hand may also be used providing ink marks don't bother you. Many variations are possible as some receive a circular movement for Yes or No and swinging back and forth for the other. Test your pendulum prior to starting so as to be certain not to be confused about answers given.

Here's the key: hold your pendulum over the center of the map or hand, if used; look at it and feel a connection with it. Ask what motion is for 'Yes'; and with only the power of your mind make it move. Once you have the answer ask its direction for 'No'. It's important that you do not consciously intend any particular movement as mind will frequently override the source. You must have confidence. Hold your hand steady, and although you do not intentionally create the move, you should expect that it will. Simply watch and observe. As it moves in the appropriate direction, remind your subconscious that this means 'Yes' and this means 'No.' Better still, have a partner or a friend present to assist you when you need confirmation. Repeat this process as often as possible to familiarize yourself until the suggestions are accepted by your subconscious. Much practice brings many authentic results.

Week 25:

Tea Cup or Leaf Reading is considered to be foretelling. Patience, perseverance, and time are the keys to master the art. Although used by psychics anyone can learn it as it's a God-given talent. Having a recognized psychic ability enhances the outcome and increases knowledge to interpret what's right there in front of your eyes. If you mastered psychic symbolic messages then reading tea leaves comes easily.

Most people have their own technique in reading tea leaves and your own is what will work best for you. If some discrepancy comes between two readers both should realize that neither is right or wrong. What feels right and appears genuine in your reading is what is intended to be passed along to the sitter. Always consider your sitters' feelings and keep in mind that they are taking seriously what comes out of your mouth. Speak wise and uplifting words and not that which would cause worry or frighten anyone about future events.

In all methods of divination certain traditions must be followed; not his or hers but your own. Yes it's good to know of others techniques but techniques are as unique as the reader. Therefore, have your own uniqueness.

First of all you'll need a cup; Styrofoam will do if nothing else is available. Personally, I like an old-fashioned antique cup or something similar in size as it has a wide mouth and the sides escalate up in a V or U shape. The inside of the cup should be plain white without a pattern which allows the leaves to clearly form pictures.

The tea used should consist of larger leaves and not that of a dusty blend. As a beginner I could not find such tea so I broke open a Tetley tea bag. Bad idea, as the leaves remained soggy at the bottom of the cup making it almost impossible to detect anything. Personally after a little search and using different teas I now prefer Twinning's, Prince of Wales Tea. This tea comes in a perfectly sized tin with a cover for easy transportation.

One can only teach what they know, and I will teach you 'my way.' You'll learn something from 'my way' and eventually you'll have your own unique way.

Cup and saucer are ready. Tea is close by with a small spoon as well as milk and sugar for those who wish to have it. Kettle is ready and water is boiled. Have the sitter take a scoop of tea leaves and place it in his/her cup. It doesn't matter who pours the water as long as the sitter does the rest. Once water is in, the sitter stirs the tea and prepares it to taste. If tea is too hot and the reader or the sitter is anxious to get started, an ice cube or some cold water may be added once the tea leaves appear to be soaked sufficiently. Once most of the tea is gone, have the sitter sip out as much of the liquid as possible. I prefer that they turn the cup around with each sip so as to hold the leaves on the side of the cup. This makes for a better, longer and in-depth reading.

Next is a prayer to the God source and to those who may be observing and are trying to communicate from the other side. A prayer of protection will never go wrong. While in prayer I also call on my guides for support.

Once all the tea is gone the sitter is asked to turn the cup over on to the saucer. Then the sitter is told to make a wish while turning the cup around as often as he/she desires. Now this is a personal discrepancy. Your decision as to what direction the cup is turned is best for you. You should decide this before you start reading and stick with your decisions throughout your tealeaf reading years, if it should last that long.

Personally I let the sitter turn it in the direction he/she wishes and I'll use my intuitive thinking while watching the number of turns. In observing their facial features and the concentration of their thoughts I get a sense of connection with my spirit guides. Although guides are not considered a part of a traditional reading they're there nonetheless. All help from the world of spirits is appreciated and accepted and any uplifting message should also be passed on, along with the messages created from symbolic images that the tea leaves make. If a sitter turns the cup full circle with a wish and then stops, I tell the sitter that the wish will come true in one year. If the cup is turned half way around then in half a year the wish will be granted, and so on. (Personal choice made from observations). Then the cup and saucer are given to the reader.

When viewing the leaves and nothing seems to come to mind and all that appears are meaningless patterns, then turn the cup. Turn it slowly around, sideways and almost to an upside angle and you may see defined images and symbols. Consider what you're seeing and your interpretation of these images will have specific meanings. Use your intuitive mind and let your consciousness create from them. Those meanings are usually right as what you interpret is what should be given.

There's one more thing, however, that's a part of my uniqueness as a tea leaf reader.

At the end of a reading, whether it's twenty minutes or an hour, the sitter is permitted to ask a question; one question only. To find the answer I put the cup back on the saucer upside down. Then I ask the sitter to give the bottom of the cup a quick and forceful tap with his/her fingers. With success some tea leaves will fall to the saucer. In those tea leaves lies the answer to the question. Furthermore, going over the tea leaves inside the cup once more and what's in the saucer will add and extend the reading.

Be reminded as in pervious explanations; don't give anything to cause stress or fear in any way, even if you suspect that it's there. You gain nothing by causing someone to worry. In addition, it's not important to attempt to interpret all the signs and symbols but focus on the signs that pertain to the pleasure and well-being of the sitter. After all, it's only fun, isn't it?

Here's an additional input from one of my students who has been reading tea leaves for a number of years. I call her 'Queen of the tea-leaf readers.'

History of Tea Leaf Reading by Rev. Barbara Ann Hampson:

It has always been a universal desire for us to know what the future holds and tea leaf reading dates back to the time of Confucius. Biblical seers were seemingly aware of coming events. Egyptian priests considered it a high spiritual attribute to forecast the future. The cultured and refined Greeks consulted their sacred oracles and the mighty Romans believed the future could be known. And in our own era, persons with extra sensory perception (ESP) amaze us with their forecasts of the future.

Whether you give credence to tea leaf reading or not, it is fascinating to try to know the future. Tea offers you the possibility of experimenting with the tea leaf readings just for the fun of it during the happy sociability of enjoying a delightful cup of tea with family and friends. The success of reading fortunes in your cup of tea depends upon your desire to search for the exciting and fun-filled events forecast by the fascinating designs of the tea leaves. It's been fun for ages and now you, too, can read the future.

Method—When there is about a tablespoon of liquid left in the cup, slowly swish the cup counterclockwise three times to distribute the leaves. Next slowly turn the cup upside down over the saucer and leave it there until all liquid drains away. Place the palm of your hand on the bottom of the cup and make a very special wish.

Turn the cup back up, and gaze into the tea leaves. Some will cling to the sides of the cup and some will remain in the bottom. As you continue to search you'll notice that the leaf patterns will form lines, circles, small groups and figures; and so on. Be sure to use your imagination to identify the designs. This will become easier with practice.

Some readers always say that the cup is top to bottom (Jan. to Dec.) I say the top of the cup is the month we are in and runs through the year.

Some ways to practice or expend your intuitive nature are—studying pictures in the clouds—bubbles in the bath (interpreting their shapes) and listening to your inner voice for various interpretations. After some practice you will have lots of fun with your family and friends. End.

Week 26:

Channeling in Spiritualism is communication of information through a medium from a spirit/entity that's outside of the mind of the medium, through paranormal means. It's quite possible that you could channel a loved one as well as a spirit guide, or you may channel from, or of, your higher self. Rituals of many other religions such as shamanism, voodoo, umbanda and others include channeling in their way of life. Channelers enhance their psychic energy to tap into their higher self to achieve clairvoyance, clairaudience and clairsentience.

Conscious voice channeling and trance channeling differ greatly. Conscious voice usually comes from the mediums mind or higher self and the medium is fully aware of what's being said. The entity being channeled is questionable as much of the medium's 'self' may be part of what's being brought forward. This form of channeling is usually done with eyes open but closed makes for a better concentration and a higher level of thought. Moreover, conscious channeling is considered to be inspired messages through a light trance.

Trance channeling is when the medium calms his/her mind; goes deep within and connects to the source that's usually anxiously waiting; that source being a spirit-entity wishing to make contact. When given a spirit entity total control one could very well be considered as being temporarily in or diagnosed as 'Sleeping Prophet Syndrome'. This state can be induced, via guidance of the care person and/or the teacher, as that the body of the Medium, especially the facial area as it takes on the qualities of the entity being channeled; known as 'manifestation of personal characteristics'. The source being channeled uses the vocabulary and the knowledge of that of the medium. A trance channeler will remain in a calm state with eyes closed and is not always totally aware of what's being said. Sometimes, with much practice, the medium will totally step aside and let the entity being channeled do the talking. Furthermore, as the medium's consciousness leaves his/her body the source consciousness enters. As voice changes and speech differs, it will determine the depth of trance as some mediums choose to stay somewhat connected to their physical body.

If you wish to practice channeling you should have someone with you who you trust and that someone should know how to take care of you if the need arises, whether light or deep trance. When you have such a person, that person may very well be the one you're channeling for.

Now, when you do decide to channel you'll need to attune. Attunement is done by going within via a short meditation. Attuning to the spirit world is achieved by letting go of all thoughts previously going through your mind. Rid it of all that you possibly can and totally relax and calm your body. As you adjust you'll connect the resonance at a particular frequency, bringing harmony.

First of all you need to sense an entity. Feel the vibrations emitting from it and visualize the total body, especially the face. As you let you vibration and emotions blend together let your body contort to that of the entity. If the need be start to move the muscles around in your face and let it contract to appear like the face you clairvoyantly see. When you do sense a contact and make a connection, or feel that you have reached your higher self, keep your eyes closed. Once your posture and facial features have been transformed your voice will automatically flow using the words your channeled entity is passing on to you and through your voice box. Those words will most likely be of wisdom and of love. If your consciousness is slipping away you may feel a slight chill come over and within your body. You may also feel the sense of cobwebs on certain parts of your body, especially around your face and neck, depending on the depth you go. Remember, you need to have a trusted companion that is experienced in the field because when in trance loud noises and any abrupt distractions can easily disturb you to a harmful point. In addition, make sure your companion-protector knows to never touch you and to keep all others from doing so.

Once attunement is made you'll start to feel and channel universal life-force energy. This is a spiritual awakening and a time of transformation. This is when and where the two aspects of the greater person, the personal-self and the higher-self, come together as one. It's the blending of those two aspects into one expression of Infinite Spirit to gain entrance to the reality of spirit. With a peaceful frame of mind you'll be aware of the responsive changing trends. As you feel your soul grounding in your body the two will connect in an organic way.

As a beginner you should respect the self and not let yourself go to a deep trance. To channel in a light-trance state is more than enough. This source of channeling is similar to mental mediumship as your eyes may be open or closed with your senses wide open to the spirit-world. In addition, if you channel with your eyes open you're usually receiving what is of your own consciousness.

To practice conscious channeling, have two people sitting across from each other without touching. Each person, one at a time, will speak to the other person and say whatever comes to mind for up to 10 minutes and no less than 5. A designated timer is required; keep track of time for each other if not in a class setting. Once one is finished both may chat about the experience and validation may be made, or ideas will surface for the next attempt. Then the other person will speak for as long as agreed upon by both at the previous test.

To practice trance channeling, take a few moments and go within. Once within, feel and sense an entity. See this entity clairvoyantly and describe him/her to the person with you, or the one you're channeling for. Listen to what they have to say and speak as if it were speaking them selves. First of all say who you have and then as you channel always refer to them by saying, he/she is here to tell you or he/she wants you to know and so on. Always stick with the entity; if not, you'll find yourself speaking from your own mind by saying something like 'I feel' or 'I sense.' That's letting your trance state dissipate (go) and reverting back to conscious channeling.

A Poem

Make channels and may the grace of your mighty spirit bring millions within
Mourn amid God, my Father, for my heart was sad
Nay speak no ill
Nearer my God; Nearer my God with adoration
Make new every morning with new wonders of you.
No other creed
Where no power can die

A Meditation Affirmation

Spirit, flow through me; release my fears
Use me as your scepter to channel words of wisdom, love and peace
Fill me with your power to make me strong
I'm willing to be the receptor of your divine intelligence

As I become renewed I'll express perfection to the best of my ability
Fill me with your love, so that I may give love in return
Fill me with devotion as I live for thee.
I'll remain loyal to you
Thank you

Week 27:

Inspired and Automatic Writing: Inspired writing differs from that of automatic writing. Being inspired occurs when the controlling spirit uses its mind to transmit suggestions to the inner mind or brain of the writer. The entity engrains or prompts a word or a full sentence through the thought process to the consciousness of the medium.

The brain accommodates a vast network of intelligence and the knowledge accumulated in your memory banks is what's being used. Therefore, the more knowledgeable and educated you become the more educated the writings will be.

All the senses play a big part in receiving, and the entity that's programming your mind is able to make a positive impact on what you receive and write down.

Don't confuse inspired writing with automatic writing. Inspired writing is done through the movement of the writer's hand and not controlled by the entity. Moreover, the brain/mind of the medium is controlled by suggestion from the spirit controller. As it's impressed and inspired by the spirit, the medium writes it down. Oftentimes the flow is so rapid it may appear, to some, as being automatic.

The types of thoughts we are thinking and surprisingly enough, other people's actions definitely have an effect on the information being received. Maintaining and remaining in a peaceful frame of mind is the key to success with this phenomenon.

During the complete process the subconscious mind of the

medium is directly linked to the mind of the control by telepathic means. Furthermore, the vibrations of the spirit communicate ideas and thoughts that are then received in the brain of the medium. As this is in process the control continues to transmit to the subconscious mind which stimulates the brain to action. As the information is being sent it's collected, and the process of deciphering the correct message is then transmitted through the brain/mind, and the thoughts are then released through the writing. Everyone is capable of doing inspired writing, just listen to the thoughts you're receiving.

Automatic writing is done via the means of the spirit controlling the hand of the medium. This is called automatic because what the hand is writing is not what's coming from the mind or the thoughts. The hand is not being moved by the individual but by a spirit entity. So, therefore one doesn't have to concentrate on the hand holding the pen. As opposed to 'inspired writing,' automatic writing is not remembered by the medium once out of trance. Neither is anything known or remembered when the medium sits and does something else while an entity uses the hand. The writer's brain may be in a somewhat hypnotic state, as in trance, or could very well be at ease chatting away to a friend with pen in hand resting on paper. Furthermore, this can also be done with the medium sitting at the computer and both hands on the keyboard awaiting the control.

Sometimes it's a challenge, even to the writer, to distinguish whether or not the writings come from a spirit source, especially if it's not spiritual or highly educated material. However, if it contains knowledge or offers some sort of philosophical matter that rises beyond the understanding level of the medium, then it should be of acceptance as being genuine as that of a control. You, personally, should be the judge as to whether it's emanating from a spirit source or not.

Once again, as in inspired writing, the quality and development of the medium's own mind has a tremendous effect on the quality of the writing. One should also take into consideration that some spirit discarnate's passed to spirit with little education and may not have progressed beyond that intelligence. Therefore, spirit entities are at many levels of development such as those around us in the material world. However, during the association the personal characteristics of the communicator will be established, both in the nature of the writing and the method. In addition, there may be two discarnate's using your hand and a battle for control may be taking place. If that were the case, don't give up if the writing is somewhat confusing but continue until you feel that the control is coming from one source and not two.

I once taught this in a workshop and one attendee had two pens, one in each hand, and while she had her eyes closed 'in deep trance' both her hands were writing. It was an amazing piece of art, it looked like ancient Arabic.

Exercise to follow:

Have pen and paper nearby for both inspired and automatic writing. If sitting in a class, without a desk, a clipboard may be used. If sitting at a desk, which is recommended, pen in hand resting on paper is sufficient. A writing tablet or book should be considered, as one page may not be enough. Plus, keeping all your writings, dated, in one book are of value as you have the opportunity to review your progress.

As usual, with all that you do when connecting with the spirit world; connect, ground and protect. This goes for both inspired and automatic writing. If in class the leader/teacher will guide you. If at home, which is safe for inspired and relatively safe for automatic, a protection prayer is spoken and your guides are called upon for assistance. This is done to direct your doorkeeper, which most likely is a guide of some sort, to maintain and control those trying to enter your conscious or sub-conscious.

For inspired writing, go within and meditate, relax your total body and clear you mind, as well as you're able. If you're an avid meditator this comes easily; if new, you'll need to work on that aspect of it as it's most important. To begin inspired writing you may adopt a meditative posture, with both hands resting on your upper legs and palms facing up. Once you have attuned and feel connected with an entity, bring yourself back. With your mind in a receptive mode take the pen and place 'pen in hand' on the paper. If you have not received anything to write then close your eyes and reconnect. Once you receive inspirational words you may open your eyes to write it down, keeping the writing neat and tidy. You may then keep your mind telepathically connected with the discarnate with your eyes open and continue to write. If at anytime you feel the connection is weakening close your eyes again and reconnect.

For automatic writing, go within and meditate, relax your total body and clear you mind, as well as you are able. Have pen already in hand and resting on the paper on the table. With this in effect call on your higher self, your guides and most of all connect with your doorkeeper. Your doorkeeper is very valuable if you choose to do trance automatic-writing. Trance should not be taken lightly. Moreover, only those that have conquered the technique safely and have preformed in a trance state under direction, should consider this method. It's also wise to consider having someone with you, someone educated on the subject, as an extra protection. A protector is not necessarily needed if you won't be interrupted in any way, because if you do go into trance, your doorkeeper and highest guide will guard your safety, and provide a safe return from your hypnotic state.

For automatic writing at home in front of your computer, use the same scenario as above. Have the balls of both palms resting on the desk and all fingers ready for action. Once you've connected your fingers will be activated. If it's automatic you'll type like a professional and non-stop with eyes closed.

If you wish to try automatic writing while chatting with a friend or reading a book, be certain the friend knows what you're up to and is made aware that he should not pay too much attention when your hand begins to write. Like-minded people are best for situations like this when spiritual contact and growth are made. Have pen in hand on paper and when the control takes hold, your hand will begin to write. When this action starts your focus will be entirely on your hand, but you should continue your chatting or reading and let the hand continue to write. Furthermore, be oblivious as your focus may stop the writing unless you have great control over your brain.

Good luck and do take good care.

A guided meditation:

This meditation is also used for automatic writing with the changes made to suit the procedure.

Beginning Prayer:

Divine Holy Spirit

We ask for your protection

We ask that you surround us with your loving circle of light

Completely cover us and protect us as we commune with the spirit world

Send forth only those of 'love and light' and we ask that you remind our doorkeepers to keep all evil entities away

This is now guided by your care

Amen.

Ground, connect and protect.

Relaxation exercise:

Now, I want you to go to a safe place, whether it's a beach, a park, or in your own living room.

Be certain that you're alone and you won't be disturbed.

Feel the comfort within your environment and let it sink deep into your mind, your brain and your soul.

Feel the blissfulness.

Now, feel and sense the elation of a spiritual being.

Invite this spiritual entity into your place of refuge and feel the loving vibration emitting from it

This spiritual being is from God.

Feel comfortable, be relaxed and telepathically communicate with your contact.

If you cannot feel and sense a spiritual being with you, recognize and tell your higher self that there is one there.

If this being doesn't feel like it's from a loving source then bid it goodbye and start over.

Now, listen intently to what is being given to you.

This is being received through the thought process.

(IF INSPIRED WRITING; communicate, and once you have connected open your eyes and start to write what you receive.)

(IF AUTOMATIC WRITING; keep your eyes closed and give the entity permission to take control of your hand. Now let your hand be controlled and remain oblivious to its movement. Remain in your higher self state.)

Write at the speed you're comfortable with and write down whatever comes into your mind, as long as it's spiritual, educational, and loving.

Don't hesitate to ask for a name.

Also ask whom they are here for, if it's not one of your guides.

If you clairvoyantly see a discarnate, write down all that you see.

Ask them what they wish to pass on, through you.

Listen and write.

Ending prayer

Great source of love and light, we thank you, our guides and doorkeepers, for your assistance. We thank those that made contact and those who tried but couldn't. We ask that you leave now and return again when we're ready to commune with you.

Your divine presence was respected and greatly appreciated.

Amen.

Week 28:

Crystal Ball—Crystal-Gazing: By using a crystal, as in Ball, Ring or Stone, there is a connection with spirit through your higher self. Although telepathy is a possibility we need to believe that it comes through the spirit of a loved one or through our guides. Only the medium will know for sure and will recognize this through his or her senses. In cultivating your own clairvoyant faculty, you must remember that you have to rely solely on yourself and don't put a lot of emphasis on someone else's method—develop your own. Clairvoyance is sometimes referred to second sight or your sixth sense, and we all have a certain amount of this within us. Guides, as well as spirits of the sitter, will impress ideas on your brain; how else would they make this contact? Lack of success sometimes means lack of perseverance, but I must remind you to never accept what you regard as failure. No one fails in this; everyone progresses at their own speed with the help of guides and other circle development members.

An experienced crystal ball reader is very protective of the ball, respect this and don't touch it unless informed to. A personal set up is to have the ball covered at all times when not in use. When a reading is about to commence remove the cover and place it on its stand, on a piece of black velvet material, if not already there. Have 5 candles burning, in a horseshoe shape, around the outer portion of the ball between the sitter and yourself. If you use this method remind the sitter not to reach over the burning candles for any reason.

As you sit to give a crystal-ball reading you connect through psychic waves, as there is transference of energy, from the sitter infused in the crystal. In the classroom the sitter may hold the ball for at least 5 minutes and then place it on its stand for the other student to do the reading. (This is not a must or a rule as many crystal ball readers protect their ball from others' energy. This is a good method to learn in class as the sitter's energy, as well as that of spirit entities and guides, will be transferred to the ball. With this in motion, energy and information will be sent to the reader when he/she closes their hands around the ball without touching it). The reader should not touch the ball until the reading is complete. If this method is used the ball should be wiped clean with a dry piece of material to prepare for the next reading.

When the crystal has been held for the time recommended and is placed on its stand, the sitter and the reader should sit across the table from each other. Both should focus and gaze at and into the ball connecting combined energies via the crystal. This enhances vibrational waves from both of you, as it blends together in centre field, so to speak. Spirit will connect with the reader and he/she will read as they see, feel, sense and know, as in means of mental phenomena. As your energies collide 'centre-field' they are sent out into the universe and bounce back with a loved one from the spirit world. Hence, information is then given through the energy collected in the ball. After a moment of gazing, the sitter then stops and relaxes and the reader will proceed at his/her own pace with spirit. In time you'll perfect this technique. As the reader begins the reading he/she should visualize the loved one and describe this entity immediately before proceeding with any messages. Imagination, visualization and a creative mind is all that it takes. Your own method and definition is of the utmost importance, not that of someone else. Your perception and interpretation is the message meant to be given from the spirit world. As you, the reader, gaze at the ball, scyring is in effect. As this is basically a part of fortunetelling, look and search for future events relating to the sitter. Explain all that you see and the outcome, if any. No negative information should be given as in any other spiritual reading.

For those advanced in their mediumship, by all means use your ability to the fullest.

Crystal ball readers know that if someone comes for a reading he/she is totally focused on the ball. Therefore, as soon as the ball is uncovered the ball is gazed at, if not stared at, by the sitter. When the sitter does this they're sending all that they're searching for to the ball, as well as a lot of their knowledge and desires. A good reader will sense all of this and will give a good reading. When you start your reading hold the sitter's hands and say a prayer. You may wish to continue to hold hands for a while and pick up some psychometry as well as gaze into the ball for other messages.

For the medium wishing to do a reading for him or her self, the ball is at your disposal to do with as you wish, but I'd recommend that another reader do this for you, as you'll most likely see things that are not actually there. Remember, your mind has the ability to dominate.

Also remember never to doubt your instincts; give all the positive information you receive even if you personally feel it's not of value. Not of value to you may be very valuable to your sitter.

Crystal Rings and Stones:

The ring could be what is called a 'Mood-Ring' but there are many pure-crystal rings available at a reasonable cost. The stones, depending on the type of crystal you like, will vary in price. The mood ring, which holds some form of crystal, will probably be the most inexpensive of all.

Once the inventor noted the color changes by blending or infusing certain materials of the mood ring, the marketer or the owner of the design needed a means of making a profit from its invention. That's where the mood ring got its popularity quite sometime ago. Sex sells and it was noted and introduced for such as this. The ring lost its popularity over the years as it became known not to be as accurate as the color scheme represented by the guide, often given with its purchase. Color is frequently changed by vibrations, energy and most of all, body heat.

Putting history aside, this ring may have significance to your development; the color changes may or could be related to chakras and the aura field. Wear the ring and get a feeling of what the various colors mean to you. All colors don't mean the same for everyone. To enable yourself to verify the color scheme, as your own personal meaning, wear it for a period of time and take notice of the colors in the way you feel your energy level, state of well-being and environment. You may note them and be able to reflect back if your memory needs refreshing. If you already know what the colors signify to you then this won't be necessary.

If you're a novice (beginner) it sometimes helps to have an object to focus on when connecting with spirit. Sometimes we feel better about the messages sketched on our brain when we have another focus point; the same goes for crystal gazing. Visualize loved ones as you connect with the crystal surrounding the ring (or other crystals used) and the color the ring crystal has become once you've spiritually connected.

The stones which may be a pendant worn around the neck, and the ring which holds all the colours of the chakras plus darker colors, may be used as a consultant when a sitter asks a question or for psychometry means. If you feel stuck in connecting with spirit consult your ring or stone. Rub it gently and feel a connection and then telepathically communicate. You may also remove it and hold it in your hand, and perhaps fiddle with it to ease any tension you may experience. Turn it over in your fingers for comfort and a means of distracting other distractions. Remain focused on what you're doing, not what's about you.

Everything holds energy. A higher source connects your thoughts and blends it with the crystal. Wait until you've connected and then proceed to give what you feel from spirit. Keep holding and consulting your ring or stone, while giving your message. It's all clairvoyantly related.

Having gone through the process of explaining the theory of connecting with spirit through a crystal, none of this is actually needed. But it will give you a sense of connection and it is used as a "crutch" to help bring out your highest potential, which we all hold, and it makes for a more fun-filled event.

Listen and pay attention to your inner consciousness and your higher self. Be serious and confident but don't be afraid to create laughter; laughter creates a higher vibration and with that, tension is relaxed and spirit connection becomes easier.

Week 29:

Spirit photography is evidence of dead people or "ghosts" appearing on a photograph and is considered to be paranormal imagery. This sort of photography had an enormous appeal on the bereaved once it began in the nineteenth century after William Mumler made the first spirit photograph in 1862. During and after the Civil War, bereaved families sought some form of proof that their lost loved ones still continued on after physical death. Much proof was presented as many spirits imprinted their images on pictures alongside those that mourned them. Although some were faint or appeared as ghostly images floating beside them, their living earthlike appearance was nonetheless recognized.

Like most paranormal activity it attracted many critics. Critics felt that paranormal imagery-photographers were taking advantage of those stricken by grief. You have to be your own judge and not that based on other's opinions.

Oftentimes spirit needs to be invited in some form or another. This can be done unconsciously as if in denial of a death or a drawn-out mourning period to a point of nervous breakdown. Your loved ones are very aware of the prolonged grieving and in their attempts to console they often appear in ghostly form at a time such as this and there's never a camera close by as they appear most unexpectedly. Furthermore, a camera would be the last thing on your mind when one feels the pain of suffering caused by death.

Having explained this, the best results would be most likely to come from someone of that sort if you could get them to agree to have their picture taken for this phenomenon. Chances are they'll comply, simply for their own satisfaction, curiosity, and proof of death beyond the veil.

Any type of camera and film may be used but with today's modern technology the digital camera appears to have better results. Moreover, it's more cost effective as you're able to download your pictures onto your computer hard drive and reuse your memory chip.

As a beginner the results may be limited to orbs; if this should be the case it's verification that you have the ability to enhance this type of phenomena, so don't give up. Each time you experiment, the stronger the connection becomes with the world of spirits. You be the judge of your own experiments, outside assistance may be sought only after you have perfected it. If you wish to put it to the test then follow the instructions below.

Know your camera and its use, as well as you know the back of your hand. You need a candidate/subject or someone to take the pictures. You can't be both unless you have a camera with a remote, unless of course you're just taking pictures at random of different areas and locations. If there's any form of spiritual activity in that particular area you'll most likely see results of orbs. Strive to achieve your ultimate search; that is, passed loved ones indented on your picture.

Someone who just had a death in the family and feels at a loss and in need of comfort that person would be ideal. You, the photographer, should visit them as an entity is often attached to his/her place of residence where loved ones still dwell. A hospital, if you can get access to it, is another great place to take pictures. Empty rooms with empty beds are also an ideal location as many die in hospital beds and have a tendency to stick around in spirit form. The reason for this is denial of physical death and they may have spent a considerable amount of time in that particular room while in the material. In addition, nursing homes and long-term care facilities may also be of interest. The nursing staff and caregivers who have access to those areas have a perfect opportunity to encounter spirit photos. Working the night shift usually gives quiet time with little activity from the patients and residents; also, giving one freedom to be alone to shoot a few pictures without being noticed by other staff. If the staff is similar to that of many I worked with during my years in the medical field then most have witnessed some form of ghostly encounter. Furthermore, like minds make a good group to share with and to care for each other when intrusion from others about may create some danger when job security is threatened.

No way is the right or wrong way as many ghostly images are seen with all sorts of different backgrounds, different times of day, and in different shades of lighting. But if you're new at this and wish to better yourself then have the wall of the room you chose covered with a dark or black sheet. Consider that the images are in ghostly form, which is of a white substance, then dark backgrounds are recommended, especially for a weak entity that's not strong enough to make a deep or more visible impression.

Meditation may play a big part; when you meditate you're connecting with the spirit world through telepathy.

Have your subject sit in front of the wall but not directly by it. Have them in a chair or a recliner because comfort is subject to calmness; and calmness is the key to communicating with the entity wishing to make contact.

Dim the lights as close to being in the dark as possible; remember that you need to see to operate your camera. A red light may be used or you may use a small red glass candle-lantern placed out of danger of being upset. This lantern may be hung from the ceiling just above the subject.

Speak quietly to him/her and have them think only of the one being called upon to present him/her self for the picture. Don't be in a rush to take pictures. Focus on your subject and get them to telepathically call on their loved one, via meditation, for up to about five minutes. Once the five minutes are up, call your subject back from meditation but to remain in contact with their loved one. Tell them to remain where they are and inform them that you're going to start taking pictures. Take pictures from different angles, locations and distances.

If in a classroom with several students the same scene should be created with selected students to pose as the subject. Consider a recent passing in the family for those selected. The closer the connection with the sought loved one the better.

I currently have up to forty students in my closed development classes. Some say that seven is an ideal number to work with, with past experience I don't agree. Two subjects/students are chosen each a week prior to the event so that he/she will call forth their loved one throughout the week to attend the prearranged evening.

Once at the class it begins as usual with a full circle; the usual chant is said in unison and a prayer spoken to the God source for protection. Then the groups are broken into eight with one photographer behind the scene; meaning that he/she is outside the group of seven looking on and waiting to take the photos. Once again, this is a personal preference. Therefore as time advances develop your own.

The subjects are placed at each end of the room, which is about fifty feet long; near a dark wall sitting comfortably in a chair. Each subject is out of hearing range of the other. Both groups are set up and readily available to work. Six are sitting in chairs in a horseshoe shape, half circle, surrounding the subject. Quietness is important as attunement is crucial for attuning with those waiting to come through to oblige with their imprint on the photos.

Although I have one designated photographer per group of seven, others bring their cameras. Once the subject has attuned and pictures have been taken by the chosen photographer, others in the group (one at a time) may leave the group momentarily to also take pictures. This space or chair should be filled by the person previously taking the pictures to keep the energy at its peak. The chosen subjects/students are enhanced via the group's collective energy. This may go on until all have sufficient pictures. Then the subject is asked to go back within to thank the spirit entity for coming, whether seen or not on photos, and then brought back to full consciousness. If time permits, other methods may be used such as Spiritual and Reiki Healing. This too should be in front of the black background. With spiritual healing one is sitting; with Reiki one is lying down. The group focusing on the healing may sit until the healing is about half-way through or close to complete. The teacher/leader will say when to start and then those wishing to take pictures should stand, one at a time, to do so. With Reiki Healing one may need to stand on a chair but be careful not to fall.

When checking results and you see orbs, zoom in on them and look closely for faces. Good luck!

Week 30:

Dowsing: Scientifically known as radioesthesia, commonly known as wishing rods, dowsing is often used to find water and minerals. It has also been used to find lost objects and even people.

This is something of interest to a few as it involves interaction of the mind and the energy of the object, or the intended search. As it connects with the surrounding subtle energy field of objects, plants, animals and/or people it's bounced back to the dowsing rods or to the person holding them.

Dowsing rods are bent wires, which are pointed in the direction of the area of interest. Many years ago a wooden branch in the shape of a Y was used, and it was considerably effective. As one held the top of the Y in their hands one scanned the area for water. With the feeling of a gentle tug or pull towards the ground one often found it. Today's modern rods consist of two L shape rods which come in a box along with other forms of spirit communication. You may make your own, whether out of wood or wire coat hangers and plastic straws. When using them be sure that they are held horizontal to the ground.

Many have reported this method as being very accurate although scientists have not yet supported or refuted it. Some people use this as a form of 'making ends meet' to earn money. This as well as other things mentioned in this book does not pertain to Spiritualism; it's but another means of using the tremendous amount of energy that surrounds us and the spirit world, to assist us in our search for truth. Your use may be for fun and games but as your results increase you'll start to take it more seriously.

Week 31:

Sand, dust, lip, shoe, flower sentience and woodchip readings: Some means of doing readings, which one doesn't have to be a medium, such as 'Shoe Reading' 'Lip Reading' 'Sand Reading' 'Dust Readings and 'Flower sentience' can be done by any psychic. One doesn't need clairvoyant powers to do symbolic messages or look at a shoe and say what they feel and think; neither for lip, sand or wood-chip readings. Does this belong in Spiritualism? Yes and no may apply, as one craves somewhat of a change or variety along the path of their spiritual growth. These types of readings are never done in a Divine Service but as a fund raiser or at psychic fares. Shoe and lip reading lets your mind race to gather up some form of message but the message itself in usually very vague. Sand, dust and wood-chip readings are symbolic, somewhat like that of tea-leaf. Flower sentience may be just a little different as all are attracted to different kinds of flowers. The flower chosen may inform the reader somewhat of a personality and that of self-confidence and self-esteem, making it appear like the reader knows what he/she is talking about.

For sand, dust and wood-chip readings, which can be quite messy; have the elements available and the sitter will take a handful and either toss it on a large table top or let it fall gently out of their hand to form images. There's no wrong way to do this as long as the material used is spread out over a certain area with the intention of receiving a reading. Just remember that dust and fine sand residue will remain in the air and you'll breath it in your lungs, so don't be too vigorous in your toss. Wood-chips are fairly safe but I'd recommend fine chips like that left by a chain saw, not those chipped of with a knife or an axe. Psychic symbolic and your interpretation of the images is all that's required.

Week 32:

Trance is a form of Hypnosis, either done with the help of your spirit guides and teachers or guided by your development teacher. It's an altered state of consciousness and heightened responsiveness to suggestion. Trance could be induced in normal persons by a variety of methods and most frequently it may have been brought about through actions of a development teacher. Trance may be self-induced, which I had the privilege to witness other than myself by three different people, one being my development teacher, another being a spirit guide artist and the other a student in an advanced mediumship development class.

People are able to train themselves through relaxation and concentration on one's own breathing. It is also done by a variety of monotonous practices and rituals that are found in many mystical, philosophical, and religious systems. Trance results in a gradual assumption by the subject of a state of consciousness in which attention is withdrawn from the outside world and is concentrated on mental, sensory, and physiological experiences. When trance is induced, a close relationship or rapport develops between teacher, guide and the medium. The responses in trance and the phenomena manifested are the products of motivational set, which is in the behavior reflecting what is being sought. The depth of trance can vary extensively. Not knowing or remembering any trance events characterizes a deep trance. This state has the ability to respond automatically to posthypnotic suggestions providing that it doesn't provoke too much anxiety. The depth of trance is relatively a fixed characteristic depending on the emotional state of the medium. Trance control clairvoyance, partial and deep trance, direct and independent voice, transfiguration, and automatic writing are included in the mental and physical sense of it.

I have heard that there's approximately only 20 percent that are capable of entering somnambulistic states through the method of induction or guidance. Apparently this percentage is not significant since therapeutic effects occur even in a light trance. Moreover, many can be induced as in hypnosis, but this works only if the person consents and wishes it to happen. Furthermore, one has to believe.

In my first trance class I witnessed a few student mediums that produced a deeper contact with their emotional life. This resulted in lifting a repression and exposed buried fears and conflicts.

Mesmeric trance is of a deep interest offering a possibility of proof of the fact of clairvoyance to the skeptic. Some people might reasonably submit themselves to this type of trance but it's not something that one should experiment with except lightly, under careful guidance and very controlled conditions. That's why guided classes by a knowledgeable teacher are important.

A trance medium usually loses control of conscious or partly loses control and may not be aware of what is going on around him or her. Often in deep trance the medium's body is taken over, controlled or possessed by a spirit entity that may speak or act through the medium's physical body. Deep trance is not recommended for beginners and if you sense it happening, be wise, and don't permit it until further growth is accomplished. Deep trance in beginners can be frightening if the leader has little experience. One oftentimes acts in haste when they feel they had somewhat lost control. If this should happen to a student the leader should be assertive and aggressive towards the entity taking over the body. The leader must recognize that he/she is no longer speaking to the student but the control. **Remember**, no physical contact is permitted while in this state.

Making a spirit contact in a trance state is a form of channeling. A person who is able to channel is one who conveys thoughts or energy from a source believed to be outside the person's body or conscious mind, specifically one that speaks for non-physical beings or spirits. Channeling, as mentioned previously, is quite different from clairvoyance. Clairvoyance gives proof of survival of a personality after death and sometimes deals with related topics such as trance mediumship, haunting, apparitions, and sometimes out-of-body experiences and so on.

Recently I taught a workshop which consisted of almost a full day. I covered the basics of mental and physical phenomena and trance. With mental phenomena being the first on the list it went to overtime as there were many attendees. This was the most in-depth that some of them had in their spiritual development thus far. With the first teaching for some, one of them was a natural as spirit came through very readily and she was astounded by what she had experienced in the meditation. I encouraged her to join a development class so that she would enhance this wonderful gift she possesses.

Right after lunch, physical phenomena was on the agenda. In physical phenomena I taught how to move a small table via the use of ectoplasm, how to connect with spirit via table tipping and transfiguration. Moving the small table was done by more than one would think and for transfiguration I chose a gentleman who had attended every workshop I gave. For table tipping I chose four people to sit at the large table, with two being experienced student-mediums; one on each side with two novices. I chose two others to sit at a smaller table. And for the bigger table I chose two that would stand, one that was somewhat experienced with mediumship and another novice. With a designator at all three tables asking questions and writing down the answers, it was set in motion. Because I was the teacher I tried to keep an eye on the total action but the assigned designator was responsible for the workers. About twenty minutes into the session my attention was drawn to the novice standing at the tall table. As I approached, her body began to tremble. The other woman was very concerned and wanted to assist her. I casually told her not to touch her and let me deal with it. By this time she was not just trembling, her whole body began to shake. I spoke with her and knew that she was as close to being in deep trance as anyone will ever be. Because she was standing I refused to let her be taken over by her guide or by the entity trying to. I demanded that he leave her, but he was stubborn and reluctant to give up. I had to keep reminding the other woman not to touch her as they both had their hands on the table. I told her to keep them there for stability. The designator was asked to leave his chair so there'd be a chair close by for the time her spirit entity gave up control. I spent about three to four minutes with her, and three to four minutes feels like a long time to those watching a situation like this. My voice had gotten louder by the moment and more demanding by this time. I knew I was in control as she held her stance and position and did as I said. With all in the workshop at a standstill you could hear a pin drop between my commands. Finally, I called her by name and told her that I was going to shout very loudly at her guide. Having said that I shouted at the top of my lungs saying, *"Leave your medium now,"* and louder still in a more firm tone I added, *"right now."* With that, her head turned abruptly towards me and she stared into my eyes, and then I saw the entity depart. I told her that she was okay and that she could now go and sit down. She did; and then she began to cry, in great sobs, and gasped for breath. With Kleenex in hand she settled down and everyone wanted an explanation, which they got. Although I went over the procedure and explained it well, unfortunately, I didn't notice that she had kept her eyes closed during the questions asked at the table. Eyes should always remain open after infusing your energy with the table and the spirit connection made, unless you're advanced in your trance mediumship. Because her hair was long and her head bent down towards the table, we all thought her eyes were open, which were not. Lesson learned from this is to never assume anything, which we should always keep in mind no matter what we do in life.

Unfortunately due to the high volume of students and going over the time designated for this workshop she was pressed for time and could not stay for the next lesson. No, she was not afraid. She said she had an engagement in an hour and an hour would not cover what I had to cover next. And as for trance one should not get up and leave, as any interference will bring some sort of an impact on those waiting for their contact and especially for the one now speaking in trance. With this awareness she excused herself and left. I suspect that she will delve further into this as she now knows she can easily go in a trance-state through suggestion. All in all I think she was fascinated with the experience. It also taught the students to be certain that there's an experienced teacher in control when dealing with a situation like this.

Your first trance experience should consist of how to speak inspiringly through a light trance state.

Consent should be given for trance to take place like any other procedure.

Rules to follow when doing or teaching trance!

1. MAKE SURE ALL CELL PHONES ARE OFF; ALSO HOUSE PHONES.

2. MAKE SURE YOU WON'T BE DISTURBED IN ANY WAY.

3. BE CERTAIN THAT ALL OBJECTS ARE SECURE AND WON'T FALL TO THE FLOOR.

4. REMIND ALL TO **NEVER TOUCH ANOTHER** WHILE IN TRANCE.

5. IF SOMEONE HAS A DIFFICULT TIME COMING OUT OF TRANCE SPEAK TO THEM LIKE YOU WOULD A STUBBORN CHILD AND DEMAND THE SPIRIT TO LEAVE: LEAVE NOW, RIGHT NOW I DEMAND YOU. **LEAVE 'NOW'** AND CONTINUE TO RAISE YOUR VOICE AND BE PERSISTENT IN A FIRM DEMANDING WAY. CONTINUE TO DO THIS UNTIL THE SPIRIT LEAVES.

6. SOME WILL CRY, SO DON'T FORCE THEM TO CONTINUE IF THEY DO; BRING THEM BACK AS MANY BEGINNERS CRY WHEN EXPERIENCING FIRST TRANCE. FIRST FEELINGS OF THE SPIRIT WORLD CAN BE OVERWHELMING.

7. DON'T MOVE ON TO THE NEXT PERSON UNTIL EACH ONE IS BACK AND HAS THEIR EYES OPEN.

8. ALL STUDENTS SHOULD BE REMINDED TO **CLOSE ALL CHAKRAS AFTER** THEY HAVE FINISHED TRANCE, OR ANY OTHER TIME THEY ARE OPEN FOR OTHER PURPOSES.

Permission:

Doorkeeper/highest guide:

I give you permission to allow a spirit entity to speak through me.

I'm ready and willing to channel words of love and wisdom sent forth from the spirit world.

I ask that you continue to keep all negative forces away.

I feel protected and have no fear.

Thank you.

Trance meditation:

Protect—Ground and Connect. (Use your own way or that which is used above in other meditations)

Bring your attention to your feet. Relax.

Focus on your lower legs and knees. Relax.

Focus on your upper legs. Relax.

Focus on your hips, pelvis and buttocks. Relax.

Focus on your stomach and lower back.

Relax; let your intuition or gut feelings prepare for spirit contact. Ask your guide or doorkeeper to bring on this awareness. If you don't know them just telepathically ask your higher self and recognize that it has been granted.

Now bring your attention to your chest, upper back and shoulders. Relax.

Focus on your upper arms, lower arms, hands, and fingers. Relax.

Bring your attention to your throat, and neck. Relax.

Continue on; focus on your chin, mouth, and nose. Relax.

Focus on your eyes, ears, and forehead. Relax.

Focus on the crown of your head. Relax.

Now, bring your attention to your third eye located in the center forehead—between both eyes. Prepare your self for spirit contact.

Focus on Chakra # 1—the Base, end of the spine; open it gently.

Visualize the color RED and cover yourself with this color.

Chakra #2—the Sacral, over the genitals; open it gently.

Visualize the color ORANGE and cover yourself with this color.

Chakra #3—the Solar Plexus, over your abdomen; open it gently.

Visualize the color YELLOW and cover yourself with this color.

Chakra #4—the Heart, over your centre chest; open it gently.

Visualize the color GREEN and cover yourself with this color.

Chakra #5—the Throat, over the larynx; open it gently.

Visualize the color BLUE and cover yourself with this color.

Chakra #6—the Brow, center forehead, "the third eye" open it gently.

Visualize the color INDIGO and cover yourself with this color.

Chakra #7—the Crown, top of the head; open it gently.

Visualize the color BRIGHT WHITE. Cover yourself with this color and totally fill the room with BRIGHT WHITE.

NOW, SPEAK TO YOUR DOORKEEPER/GUIDE AND ASK HIM/HER TO KEEP YOU RELAXED AND IN A MEDITATIVE STATE UNTIL YOUR NAME IS CALLED.

I'll give you a moment and then I'll call your name and ask you to bring your spirit entity through. The rest of you—please wait your turn.

Don't forget to have all participating to close their chakras at the end of the exercise/class.

Week 33:

The Cabinet: If you believe in ghosts, haunted houses and cemeteries, then you believe that there's such a thing as the spirit world. Where do all those ghosts, deities and apparitions come from? When you believe in this, although you may be skeptic of past loved ones appearing to you, then you believe in what the religion Spiritualism is all about and what it represents.

The cabinet became very popular in the heyday of Spiritualism and is used occasionally today by some. From what I've gathered there is little activity from its use, if any, although I hear from some of the participants that they just feel and know something will happen soon. I heard nothing out of the ordinary happening from that source up to this point; if it had, it is not being made public.

Over the years of study I became aware of what a cabinet consists of and how to make my own. I can't be certain whether I acquired this knowledge through other peoples' views or the understanding given to me through my guides, higher self, or just plain old intuition.

From reading the Christian Holy Bible and the two books of *Encyclopedia of Biblical Spiritualism* by Moses Hull, I'm quite certain I came to understand what it consisted of back then. Why wouldn't it work as well today; natural law hasn't changed any?

Okay. A cabinet according to Webster's dictionary means*: a small room providing seclusion, a case or cupboard, a chamber.*

Personally, I feel a cabinet, in respect to a 'spiritualist-cabinet' for physical phenomena as in materialization, is an enclosed area without shelves and a door draped with linen, not wood. The inside should only consist of a seat or a comfortable chair for the occupant, the medium.

A cabinet is usually used in a ONE-MEDIUM séance for physical phenomena.

There are many ways one can make their own private cabinet. One way is to empty your walk-in closet or a small storage room, which has the door to the room you're holding the séance in.

Another way is that you may wish to have a carpenter build your personalized cabinet or build your own if you're that way inclined.

Another way, and the most convenient if you chose to have a specific cabinet for this purpose alone, is to go to a furniture store to purchase one, such as IKEA here in Toronto, Ontario, Canada, where they have a selection of large portable wooden pantries. They come in various sizes and chances are you'll find one large enough for any human to sit inside comfortably for trance purposes.

Now for the highlighter; to make certain the portable cabinet is at its peak for a spirit entity to use you and the cabinet for contact, be sure that it's put together firmly and all shelves are left out. There's usually a secure strap included and make sure it's secured to a wall or another area, so that it won't upset.

To give the spirit entity extra power to make that contact with the medium while inside the wooden cabinet, cover the roof and about a foot or two down the sides from the roof, with copper. Pennies will do if you have the patience to glue them all on. The pennies would give it a personal touch, and as it takes time to do this you'll put a lot of your own personal energy in there right from the start. One word of warning, and please pay attention, be certain that the copper will not come in contact with the medium inside when he or she stands. Copper is used to transport electricity and when the spirit world comes through, the copper holds the same; an electrical vibrating current. The medium may get an electrical shock if touched, as electrical currents are in effect through the means of spirit manifestation. If you use a cabinet such as this, do remind all present, to never touch the copper area when the séance is on or when the cabinet is in use for this phenomena. Copper may be used inside as well as outside, but one side is usually enough; it's your choice.

If it's a "ONE MEDIUM" séance, do not use the wooden doors (Doors may be left on for home use if one desires) leave them off so that they will not be closed accidentally; the medium needs oxygenated air. In its place put a curtain rod over the door and hang drapes, preferably dark material or some sort of linen that can be parted and entered through the centre or side. In class the teacher has to be able to see the students. So a see-through material should be used, such as curtain shears.

Another fact is, the higher the altitude the greater chance of materialization. Look at the many people who leave home to find that spiritual connection; for instance, the Tibetan Monks and many others who said they had to go off on their own to find themselves. Many go to the mountains. Take a look at where many of the monasteries are located and many of the castles were built, which have a history of some form of ghost or another. And again, those monasteries had limited space. The monks' quarters were only big enough for a small bed, making it the size of a cabinet that was used back in Leonora Pipers day. Do monks encounter spirit entities? My personal answer to this is, sure they do, as when they chant they're beckoning and welcoming the appearance and communication from the spirit world.

A substitute cabinet for travel, as in teaching workshops or for use in a development class, is a "Cabana Tent" known as a shower tent. This tent is tall and narrow and has the capacity to fit a chair comfortably for one student without touching the sides. I suggest that you tie the door back and cover the entrance with a see-through veil such as I use (a bed canopy).

One such story I fondly remember by reading her book is *Out on a Limb* by Shirley MacLaine. It felt like I was reliving some of my past events. This book tells of her experiences in the Himalayan Mountains. In such circumstances, most are guaranteed of some phenomena occurring. Moses and Jesus the Christ both transfigured on the mountains, according to scripture.

Once you've acquired as much knowledge as possible and know how to protect yourself then there's no reason why you can't safely use your cabinet at home. To acquaint yourself with the cabinet, your doorkeeper, guides, and the spirit world, use it for daily meditation. Be certain that this time will consist of total silence and you won't be disturbed. Familiarizing yourself to being in an enclosed small area may take some time. Using meditation or new-age-music to calm yourself is recommended until you do. Furthermore, start out with five minutes and the next time you do increase your allotted time, even if by one minute. Eventually meditate in your cabinet in total silence.

If at all possible, while using the cabinet at home, have a digital tape-recorder close by, (running in the Rec. mode) so that it will pick up anything being said; plus a video camera facing the cabinet to record if anything should happen out of the ordinary.

To be certain you don't spend too much time in trance or meditation have a timer set for a certain amount of time but place it a comfortable distance from you, perhaps across the room, so as not to be jolted back to reality.

If you have a partner that respects this then he/she would be perfect to keep an eye on you if you tend to go overtime. Moreover, he/she would need to be educated on how to safely approach you in your meditation if need be.

The cabinet introduction to my class was a success. Students are individuals and each student had their own individual experience. Each student remained in the cabinet for up to five minutes or more when trance had taken affect. The time may be increased in future classes. The first student had little contact with the spirit world but he enjoyed the feeling of extra energy accumulated while inside. The second student made a very good contact and channeled words from a spirit entity. She was somewhat overwhelmed with it all and upon being called back I noticed that she had tears in her eyes. The third student had a similar experience as the first but spoke a few words while in trance. The fourth student went into a slight trance and spoke words of love and some of the students said that his head was invisible for most of the time he was inside. It remained visible to me as I was sitting close by and always watching. The fifth student made a good contact and channeled entities. The sixth student made a remarkable contact with the spirit world, so much so that I could smell cigar smoke. This woman cried almost uncontrollably but was reminded to regain her self-control as she, the medium, must always be in control. Once she was brought back to reality I asked who smoked the cigars and who had affected her in such a way; she said it was her father. This made the seventh student nervous and she refused to enter. The eighth student made a very good contact and channeled words of love and peace. The ninth student entered; once she was brought to a trance state she laughed and laughed, which made the entire students laugh along with her. She laughed uncontrollably to a point where tears streamed down her face. She was gently reminded to compose herself and then she was brought back to reality. While leaving the cabinet she had to be assisted back to her chair as the uncontrolled laughter continued. I stated that she reminded me of someone high on drugs. She said that while she was inside all she could smell was marijuana, and, I assume that's what affected her behavior. The tenth student brought through another student's grandmother and channeled words of love. The seventh student was asked again whether she wished to experience it and she complied. Her experience was outstanding for her; she went into a slight trance, spoke a few words of love and the crying began. She was brought back to reality and was somewhat weak from her experience. She too had to be assisted back to her chair. The eleventh student did very well. The moment she sat in the chair I saw the face of a dark-skinned man superimpose himself over her. She was taken on a journey, but a journey in the dark. She was asked twice if she felt threatened or afraid and her response was "NO." She spoke of her journey, which was very nice, and her guide spoke words of love. Her spirit guide was told that he could leave after her time was up, but he would not as he wanted to remain by her side. That was good as we don't wish to send spirit guides away if they're not bothering us. The twelfth student chose not to enter. She has had a fair amount of training with trance in the past and due to a hearing impairment I used her to assist me in communicating with the others. The other four students were away that evening due to personal reasons.

Most people tend to speak quietly in trance until they become familiar with their guides and communicating with spirits. It's not unusual to cry while in trance, especially with first-trance connection with the spirit world. A first experience can be somewhat overpowering. The overpowering feeling affects the emotions, as what are coming through are entities expressing a tremendous amount of love. A feeling of tremendous love affects the heart chakra causing tears of joy to flow. Moreover, many experience their own loved ones, as their own departed remain closest to the heart.

If and when you decide to implement the use of a cabinet into your development, all students should give the spirit world and guides permission to use them when in the cabinet. This permission is similar to the one used in trance. If time is a factor, instead of passing it to each individual, they should repeat the words after the leader.

Cabinet Permission:

My name is ____________________ (Each person speaks his/her name).

Divine Spirit, cover me with your white light and protect me—always.

I call forth my guides, known and unknown to me.

I ask for only the highest and the best.

Loved ones and friends in the spirit world please come forward; I welcome you.

Doorkeeper and Guides, while I sit in the cabinet, and only when in the cabinet, I give you permission to use my body and energy for the purpose of mental and physical phenomena.

Thank you.

A General Relaxation Meditation is sufficient, with a few minutes in silence, for a personal request made to spirit that's trying to come through for each individual.

General relaxation meditation:

Sit comfortably in a meditative position and close your eyes.

Prayer:

Great Divine Spirit, protect us with your Infinite White Light. Guide us as we commune with the spirit world. Keep all evil entities away while we sit in silence and while we're sitting in the cabinet. Amen

Now: Visualize a white beam of light coming through the ceiling.

Don't let it travel further than my command.

It's descending upon you. It touches and covers your head; you feel a sense of peace and love from God.

It's slowly moving down around your shoulders.

It's now covering your upper arms, your chest and back, lower arms, stomach, hips and down over your hands.

It's moving down your upper legs, your knees, your lower legs and slowly moving down around your feet.

It's now covering your feet.

Now, visualize it going through the floor underneath you and going deep into mother earth.

You're now grounded and also connected to God.

Don't be afraid, relax, you're safe.

(Pause momentarily).

Bring your attention to your feet. Relax.

Focus on your lower legs and knees. Relax.

Focus on your upper legs. Relax.

Focus on your hips, pelvis and buttocks. Relax.

Focus on your stomach and lower back. Relax.

Let your intuition or gut feelings prepare for spirit contact. Ask your guide or doorkeeper to bring on this awareness. If you don't know them, just telepathically ask your higher self and recognize that it has been granted.

Now bring your attention to your chest, upper back, and shoulders. Relax.

Focus on your upper arms, lower arms, hands, and fingers. Relax.

Bring your attention to your throat and neck. Relax.

Continue on, focus on your chin, mouth and nose. Relax.

Focus on your eyes, ears, and forehead. Relax.

Focus on your head. Relax.

Now, take yourself to a beautiful quiet place, a place that holds fond memories for you. Make sure that no one is there but you, your guides, and those communing from the spirit world.

Prepare yourself and attune.

I'll call you back momentarily.

(Call them back in five minutes, five minutes is sufficient.)

After everyone is back call one person at a time to the cabinet.

The first time in cabinet should be guarded and five minutes should be enough. Therefore, you need a timer. That designated person should be sitting across from you (the leader) so that you can periodically glance at them to see the time remaining if the time is nearly up.

The timer should use fingers to let you know the minutes remaining. Please don't take your eyes off the person in the cabinet, if at all possible.

When they sit in the cabinet have them close their eyes and tell them to go back to that beautiful peaceful and serene place they were in while in their meditation.

When you feel they are there (which most are capable of reaching immediately) speak to them and say: attune to the spirit world: "go deep within, deeper within, go further and deeper; call forth those from the spirit world."

Give a moment and if they have not spoken, speak to them and ask: "is anyone with you?" If yes, ask who it is and continue to ask questions so that the medium will channel something, or speak for the entity with them.

If crying or laughing begins have them control themselves and bring them back. Assist them out of the cabinet and back to their chair if needed.

Closing prayer.

Divine Spirit, we thank you for being with us and for your light of protection. We also thank our guides and those that connected from the spirit world. As we go our separate ways I ask that you continue to protect us in our daily lives. Until we meet again we're under your care and guidance. Amen.

Chapter Six
Spiritual and Inspirational Lectures and Talks

Once you have finished reading this book and need a little more spiritual reading, read this chapter with an open mind and accept that which is of a personal opinion. I chose to share this with you, as I have with others in various churches.

The Seven Principles were handed down from spirit and so were the Ten Commandments of the Christian faith. As far as I know, the Christian faith did not change them. Why did some churches representing Spiritualism change the principles? If an explanation is given about each principle one will know its meaning and would understand the concept behind it. When one questions the principles, it has been noted that some of the churches had already added or deleted some of its words to suit their congregation. This would be acceptable if they stayed within certain boundaries to try and make their congregation happy. It's important to stay within the context frame of the meaning meant for that particular principle. If the Spiritualist churches stuck together as a complete team, which I feel is many light years away, maybe then there wouldn't be so much discrepancy.

Although Spiritualism has seven guidelines, they also follow all that is of love, such as the Ten Commandments and other 'Spiritual Laws' of love and peace. The Seven Principles were passed down through Emma Harding Brittan, by her guide. Since they were written on paper other churches decided to create their own, from it. By manipulating and rephrasing the words some congregational leaders created more than seven, calling them their own to appease their members, or themselves. Hasn't this not also been done with other spiritual words of wisdom from the past? Trying to appease everyone isn't always the answer as one can rearrange a set of words to suit their own interpretation, or a means of control. Nevertheless, no matter how many principles there may be in any given church you'll realize that they are of love, directed towards the human race.

You'll notice that I quote The Holy Bible frequently. I was raised a Christian with introductions, by my mother, to many other religions. I grew up with the idea that I should follow my heart when dealing with God and understanding others ways.

The highest service one can render to their fellow men and women is to follow The Golden Rule: "Do unto others as you would wish them do to you." The inequalities of modern society provide an incentive for love and service. In our daily lives we meet those who need material help, to whom a kind word or small act may work wonders. Man being a spirit, is immortal, and the brotherhood of man, or the sisterhood of women, (meaning the same) is extended into the spirit spheres. Spiritualism gives a new and higher meaning to mutual interdependence of shared love and kindness among our sisters and brothers.

In the lectures following those of "The Seven Principles" you may find some repetitive wording as some may be contained in chapter two.

Principle #1:

At one point in my life I didn't know what Spiritualism religion was; neither did I hear about it. I always believed in the supernatural: ghosts, spirits, etc. My personal past experiences had been very active when it came to seeing what lay beyond the veil. Communicating with such entities was a little unreal, so to speak, but I was aware that I was able to do that. Once I was introduced to a Medium, who has a couple of books published on the subject. I became fully aware where my life was going. I gained as much knowledge as I could from this Medium, and many others followed. As I look back I now realize that I spent a large amount of time on research, gaining as much knowledge as possible, which led me to a spiritualist church. Once I'd spent a considerable amount of time, in and about the church environment, I came to understand what it was all about. I felt like I had moved a little closer to my predestined home where my passed loved one's awaits me. The seven guidelines, known as the seven principles to a spiritualist, were given to a Medium by the name of Emma Hardinge Britten directly from spirit. They say that Emma is a pioneer of British Spiritualism and the philosophy of her channeled creed is most welcome among its followers.

I was taught the Christian faith in my childhood and the beautiful teachings of our brother Jesus. I found out that Spiritualism seeks to promote spirit communication and the development of spirituality because guidance and love surrounds us all by God, the Infinite Intelligence. This Infinite Intelligence is Spirit, and it guides us in every realm of our existence. Infinite or Divine Intelligence of Universal Laws is a sacred religion in the eyes of a spiritualist and is considered the only true one. There's a necessity for each individual to develop a higher understanding of God but, everyone has a right to the beliefs and methods that they choose, as they too become aware of their own higher understandings.

Working for and serving the Divine is very uplifting; respecting God brings attention to what exists in every person and transforms one's inner self. Those actions and attentions affect the people of the world through thought, sent out into the universe. Most spiritualists understand the power of thought and have taken on that responsibility.

Once you gain an understanding of the higher spheres it has a technique for expanding and transforming your mind and self change. Spirit helps us understand the universe and it also helps us develop the highest possible extent of communication. Continual eternal progress is open to us all so, therefore, take advantage of this opportunity whenever you can.

Erich von Daniken is an autodidact, which means he's self-taught. He had challenged many scientist and religions of the world on his theory about the beginnings of life on earth, which brings me to human creation and God as Father. The world needs minds such as his to open minds to other possibilities; and we're all entitled to our own opinions, aren't we? His opinions are not necessarily yours, or mine, but let's respect them just the same.

I'll read to you his quotes first, and then I'll have my say.

He wrote a book called *Gods from Outer Space*.

There's quite a bit that I have chosen to share with you. A lot you may not be ready to hear or accept, so please bear with me....

He says: "*I voiced the suspicion that homo sapiens became separated from the ape tribe by a deliberately planned mutation. Man is a creation of extraterrestrial gods. Regarding the prehistoric finds in the megalithic buildings in Peru in 1968, he says that this great complex was built by a method unknown to us, by beings unknown to us, at an unknown date. Traditional legends and existing stone drawings tell us that the gods met at Tiahuanaco before man was even created. In the language of our space age that means that unknown astronauts constructed their first base on the Bolivian plateau. They had a highly developed technology at their disposal, just as we today use laser beams, vibrating milling tools, and electric apparatus. The natives believe and had told the Spanish that Tiahuanaco was the place where the gods created men. That is why I hold the view that the gods of whom we speak must have been real figures who were so clever and so mighty that they made a deep impression on our ancestors, and dominated man's ideological and religious world for many centuries. Man is both the son of earth and the child of the gods. And since the gods program us men, we shall soon be masters of the same technological miracles. The small tribe of the Ainus, who lives on the Japanese Island of Hokkaideo claims, even today with complete conviction, that they are the direct descendants of gods who came from the cosmos, and they repeat this in their myths.*

He asks a question: How can an omniscient god make

mistakes? Can we really call a god almighty who, after creating man, says that his work is good, but a little later is full of repentance for what he has done? The same god who has created man decided to destroy His work. And he did it often. Why? Between yesterday and tomorrow lies the abyss that will be crossed. Most probably we shall only rediscover something that has already happened."

That's his food given for thought.

After I read this book and had started to reread what I had written for this lecture, I began to hear in my mind, Seven Guidelines, Seven Principles, and Seven Wonders of the World. How do they interact?

Below is an explanation of my personal understanding. You as a regular spiritualist of many years probably could add a lot more to my explanation, but I feel that I have covered the most important aspects on

The Fatherhood of God

Father is the most familiar term and perhaps the most theologically significant title for God.

What is the significance of God as Father? How does God exhibit Fatherhood? Is the image of God as Father outdated in Western society that is striving for an 'asexual' God?

Is God a man or should God be put as masculine when it takes both sexes to begin the creation of a human life, from birth? The questions could go on and on.

Fatherhood can be defined as one that establishes or is head of a household, an originator or patron and that he feeds his household, in a physical and spiritual sense. He loves and cares for them because it's his, but so do many of today's mothers.

Father, in the Greek language means the one that nourishes, the protector or upholder. Scripture presents father as (1) headship-generating and establishing a household; (2) feeding, nourishing or protecting his offspring; (3) maintenance, upholding that which he established.

God, Infinite Spirit, has shown His Fatherhood to us in a direct manner by creating all things and establishing man. God also shows His Fatherhood through an indirect or mediated manner, divine self within.

God mediates His Fatherhood and reflects this to the world through the mediated divine order of His creation. Therefore the order of beings created in God's image will be a constant witness to the world of the 'Fatherhood of God.' God, as a Father, upholds His relationship with His creation; Divine spark developing the Divine being, Man.

The apostles in the Holy Bible are called fathers. The Roman Catholic priests are called fathers.

From the many different religions there are many names for God but, to my understanding, it's the same God but known by different names and respected a little differently. All religious spiritual paths exist in harmony but have different avenues to the same goal, divine revelation.

Enlightenment, shifting the shadow world, creating the divine spark, which is the Divine Self, the human being, the divine has to move before any man is able to.

Is the Fatherhood of God an eternal, immutable attribute, or outdated in terms of human or personal characteristics? No, I think not. God as a divine entity, as we know him, is but that of a parent and head of a household as it has always been the case throughout history. Recently some people look at this in a different manner. God, portrayed as masculine, does not exclude the feminine mind; all human creation has both female and male characteristics engendered in their cellular memories. One could look at what people call the world, 'Mother Earth.' Mother Earth and Father Sky, God, work in harmony to feed and nourish the inhabitants within their encasement. The Fatherhood of God was originally mediated in His creation of the world and the human race. The image of God is fully represented in both genders.

Mankind is both male and female. Their offspring will be under their leadership. The father, mother and children are all equal heirs with God, yet they have an order of relation that reflects the Divine.

Since God is immutable, so is His chief agent, mankind, in mediating this divine order to the whole of creation. Men and women are equal heirs. This equality exists within the Divine's holy order. Just as the Father, the Son and the Holy Spirit are equal and yet have a different position and function so, too, does that of Mother Earth. Let them both work in unison, and accept the divine laws that rule.

The word Father does not mean that God is male (indeed that is heresy). It shows the relationship to the human race, his creation. In turn, it makes a relationship with God more intimate and possible through the power of prayer and meditation. When peace and fulfillment are found one is able to connect with their spiritual centre, at the core of their being, which gives them their own means of reaching that inner refuge, the source of light from the Divine Father.

In the Old Testament of the Holy Bible, God is often referred to in a metaphorical way as a father. It's important to note that most, if not all of the Old Testament's references, are metaphors. But, in the New Testament, the word God almost always refers to the Father. Our brother, Jesus Christ, refers to God as his Father. Most of us were taught "Our Father who art in Heaven." This progress of revelation of the Fatherhood of God has a substantial impact on how we view God and His helpers. God is no longer a father concept; He is father by direct address. This could have a direct impact on how we work for and address a divine. God, in the New Testament, is not "gender neutral." The push for gender neutral is a direct result of the broad loss of the sense that the God and Father are actually called Father by direct address, and not just by metaphoric allusions.

Should the image of God, as Father, need to be redefined as Mother-Father-God? I'll leave that thought with you. But remember, Mother Earth, Father Sky.

Masonry teaches that there's one God, and men of all religions worship that one God using a variety of different names. Belief in one God is required of every initiate, but having a conception of a Supreme Being is left to each individual's interpretation.

Once you believe in God the Father you'll notice how quickly your heart will desire to want to know Him better. Father means goodness. God is power, our Father, and is eternal. So let's believe and promise ourselves that everything from his divine laws is of natural causes and it's the law of the universe. That's why we hear of God the Father, as God almighty.

The central claim of the Jewish and Christian traditions is that at the very centre of creation, at the very centre of the void, out of which creation sprang, is a God who rejoices in Fatherhood. It's good to be a father. It's good to have a father. For those who didn't have a father or whose fathers were incompetent at fatherhood you now know that the Fatherhood of God loves you when you're in most need of love. So try to understand, within reason, that the world is a trustworthy and good place, not one that's cold and terrifying. God is the Father figure and the Divine Spirit of the universe. The word Father represents a true concept of a God of love who's perfect and knows no distinction of race, color or creed.

Silver Birch said, *"The Great Spirit is infinite and you are a part of the Great Spirit."*

That most of us truly believe. Thank you for listening. God bless you all. (Written July 2004).

Principle #2:

The Brotherhood of Man

Brotherhood of man—what happened to Sisterhood of Women? Just thought I'd stir your mind right from the beginning.

Spiritualist groups are fighting for the brotherhood of man, and the sisterhood of women. Spiritualism is teaching to educate the people to free themselves from the restraints of past teachings that don't apply to them as a person of Spiritualism faith. The principles teach that every man and woman is created free and equal, and has the rights to the products of his/her brain and brawn. Spiritualism is seeking to make the kind of society that one man equals another. This religion is seeking to rid the world of competition and to establish the brotherhood of man. Not only upon the world beyond our material, but right here, right now, while in the physical.

The golden rule symbolizes a wholehearted devotion to the service of humankind. The ethics of brotherhood had to compete with a concept of evolution. As it first became the centre stage of scientific thinking it came with the intention of unifying all the religions and all the people of the world. As civilization grew, the definition of brotherhood took on more of a spiritual meaning. Most people came to understand it as the basic principle applicable to all.

All men and women are brothers and sisters in the family of God and they formulate the essentials of the brotherhood of man. The phrase 'brotherhood of man' was used to include not exclude women; it's a universal principle.

The acceptance of this principle involves one in politics and/or economics, but it's not always considered by its leaders and not always pressed into force when they feel at a loss for themselves, or for their country. Choices made are often selfish ones without the concern for brotherhood. Although this is noted they have been known to follow this to perfection when disruption falls heavily on a certain aspect of life's misfortunes; such as world disasters and when wars begin and end. Spiritualism makes this meaningful by following the seven principles given from spirit. Implementing spiritual healing, and also by services rendered to all that are in need. It has no dogmas or creed (supposedly, as I sometimes question this when certain 'Ordained' ministers speak or try to control their congregation). Nevertheless, love is at the top of the list for all of mankind and for God's entire universe.

It's amazing just how many functions are performed by the combined concept of the Fatherhood of God and the brotherhood of man. This implies that those two are in unity, as they follow each other they defy the personality of God. The brotherhood of man is the social consequence of our relationship with God.

This is what a former USA President, Ronald Reagan, said in his speech that he gave at the Westminster College—Cold War memorial—in 1990.

He said, *"The truth of the matter is, if we take this crowd and if we could go through and ask the heritage, the background of every family represented here, we would probably come up with the names of every country on earth, every corner of the world, and every race. Here, is the one spot on earth where we have the brotherhood of man. And maybe as we continue with this proudly, this brotherhood of man made up from people representative of every corner of the earth, maybe one day boundaries all over the earth will disappear as people cross boundaries and find out that, yes, there is a brotherhood of man in every corner."*

There's a group called the 'Great White Brotherhood'; they consider themselves as a spiritual order of hierarchy. They say it's an organization of ascended masters, united for the highest purposes of God, in man, as set forth by Jesus the Christ, Gautama, Buddha, and other world teachers. The Great White Brotherhood also includes members of the heavenly host, the spiritual hierarchy directly concerned with the evolution of the world, and members from other planets that are interested in our welfare, as well as certain un-ascended chelas. The word "*white*" does not refer to the white race only, but to the aura or the halo of the White Light of the Divine that surrounds the saints and sages of all ages that have risen from every nation to be counted amongst the Immortals.

They say that it's a spiritual order from every culture and race: Western saints, Eastern adepts, and so on, who have reunited with the spirit of the living God and who comprise the heavenly hosts. They say that they have transcended the cycles of karma and rebirth. Ascended, as in accelerated, into that higher reality; this is the eternal abode of the soul. The ascended masters of the Great White Brotherhood, united for the highest purposes of the brotherhood of man under the Fatherhood of God, have risen in every age, culture and from every religion to inspire creative achievement in education, the arts and sciences, God-government, and the abundant life through the economies of the nations.

Quotes from their spiritual communications are:

"Gratitude for the many Blessings of Life would rise in wondrous Spirals of Attainment and God Consciousness if people were able to understand more, concerning the Spiritual Realities of themselves and less concerning the mask of mortal imperfection with which they disguise one another.

Men and women who have woven the strands of communion between worlds, it is unthinkable to deny Our Presence. Thus, it is sometimes exceedingly difficult for a spiritual teacher who has contacted the Divine to realize that there are men and women yet sitting in the shadows of disbelief. The qualities of mortals are all too frequently imputed to the immortals. It seems difficult for men and women to perceive that the ascended masters are completely free of any imperfect thoughts and feelings, having ascended into the perfection of the octaves of the universal Christ consciousness."

A very interesting group, don't you think?

In the Holy Bible, in the book of Romans chapter 12 verse 10 it says, *"But why does thou judge thy brother?"* And in Hebrews chapter 13 verse 1 it says, *"Let brotherly love continue."* Taken from, Authorized King James Version.

Brotherhood is also the term used for congregations in Islam that are partly set apart from the general community of Islam. We see the term, '*alikhwaan*,' used for religious-political groups stretching back in time to the Wahhabis of Arabia and is used today for groups of Islamists.

Quite often we recite the seven principles; most likely at about 99% of the services. Look at brotherhood and take in perspective how you interacted with your own family members, as a child, and as you grew into adulthood. Not all of one's past is fondly remembered with love and compassion. We all have some stored-up memory that just won't let go because we hadn't dealt with it, face to face, with those concerned. Easier said than done? Who needs to stir up past emotions and hurts anyway, right? Wrong. Up until now I still haven't dealt directly with mine but have been working towards it for some period of time. It will eventually be taken care of, when opportunity presents itself and when I feel the time is right. Actually, the time is right anytime, but the right opportunity may not present itself. One may need a few years to come to terms with it. Finally, after joining Spiritualism I refocused on my past hurt. Although I have dealt with it within my own consciousness I still have to approach those involved. That will come in time but approaching myself and trying to understand the reasons behind it all, was the hardest. At least one should recognize it, which is the first step. Eventually approaching the other person will be a piece of cake. One can say: I'm ready.

Here's a definition of someone's idea as:
The Brotherhood of Man
Side by side, they fought and died.
On the call of those who lied
Forward they fought marching united.
Forward they fought as death delighted.
Lies on lies, they fought for lies.
Today is the day—he dies.
Forward they fought on for each other.
Forward they fought for their brothers.
Death on Death yet on they go.
Death is the only truth they know.
Forward they fight, bravely, rather than…
Forward they fight, Brotherhood of man.
The author is Unknown to me.

The principle of Brotherhood means that it's directed at a universal brotherhood and that we should treat every thing, especially things with a soul, as brothers and sisters; for example, as a next-of-kin, but that depends on who it is, doesn't it?

As a spiritualist person, and one doesn't need to be of Spiritualism to be spiritual, should try to like and get along with everybody; putting aside all past negative teachings and malice feelings towards each other.

I was speaking to a friend about this lecture, and she said that the discrepancies of all the people of the world and even through our own religion is phenomenal in itself; maybe it's about time that we practice what we preach. Personally, I don't think she has started yet. Therefore, no name is mentioned.

The first Brotherhood that we encounter in life is our self, as the physical and the spiritual body are composed of many Brotherhoods. Man as a multi-dimensional spirit has the Brotherhood of man as his second principle to balance with the self. Establish a Brotherhood in yourself first before you try to attempt to solve other people's problems. It's the Higher Self that knows the exact nature of your constitutional imbalances as you strive to be aware of, and understand, your own dual nature. This means patience, love and an understanding of your fellow man, and woman, and for your own nature. This also means that the love you give to yourself should be extended in the very same measure, to others.

How do we establish a true Brotherhood? By serving the spirit of love, and not its opposite that is ever so eager to take advantage of everybody. I read that he who serves his neighbor serves God. Whoever said this doesn't know one of mine. Giving it some thought they probably think the same of me.

By service, spiritual progress is made, and in serving there are blessings from Infinite Spirit. Unselfishness enhances the soul, as spiritual qualities are recognized as a permanent treasure in life, here and hereafter.

Here's what Kahlil Gibran says in his book, 'The voice of the master:' "*I love you my brother, whoever you are, whether you worship in your church, kneel in your temple, or pray in your mosque. You and I are all children of one faith, for the dividers paths of religion and fingers of the loving hand of one Supreme Being, a hand extended to all, offering completeness of the spirit to all, eager to receive all.*" Another portion in his book that caught my attention is, "*A man's merit lies in his knowledge and in his deeds, not in his color, faith, race, or descent. Knowledge is your true patent of nobility, no matter who your father or what your race may be.*" Beautifully put.

We become more and more in harmony with the Infinite when we learn to love all of God's nature, and as we gain the knowledge of life we develop a higher stage of perfection. We should give if we hope to receive and this should be the motive of sharing, material and spiritual. If you want love, spread it, and then it'll be returned to you, tenfold. The greatest spiritual blessing of the universe is immortality. One that follows his heart and soul, as in the perfection that it was given, will experience this. The bonds of brotherhood, to the eternal spirit, indicate that we all belong to one great unity. Creating and maintaining a loving relationship with one another, in universal brotherhood, gives the true and higher meaning to this principle.

The great God, spoken of in the Holy Bible, and the one I perceive to be the one God of our universe said, *"Love thy neighbor as yourself.*" That means to love everyone; family, friends and neighbors alike, as difficult as it may be. In the Holy Bible in the book of Second Peter chapter 1, verse 7, it says*, "And to godliness brotherly kindness, and to brotherly kindness, charity."*

To attain knowledge of the Divine, it demands a willingness to try to sense beyond appearances, that light, which is the true light, that which dwells in every man and woman. Unfortunately to many it's the light that shines in darkness, and the darkness of a material sense, is not understood. Faith is the greatest spiritual agent to transport the soul into the realities of the octaves, of the Infinite Spirit; taking in consideration the love that's meant to be portrayed in principle number two, "The brotherhood of man." *Thank you for listening. God bless you all. (Written July 2004.)*

Principle #3:

The Communion of Spirits and the Ministry of Angels

This principle could be considered the main key of Spiritualism. We, of Spiritualism, bring out the basic difference between materialism and Spiritualism, and, between other religions, and Spiritualism as a religion.

Communication with departed spirits is essentially the backbone of Spiritualism. Mediums demonstrate 'survival of life after death,' which have transformed philosophy from theory into reality. Spiritualism and all other religions are concerned with the relationship we have with the supernatural realm. In the old world, as in traditional Israel, and also in many other areas, angels were assumed to have the form of human males, and consequently were sometimes mistaken for men. In the 1990s there was a phenomenal amount of popular interest in angels. This interest manifested itself into diverse phenomena. People were buying all they could on angelic awareness and wanted to get as much information as possible. Their eyes were finally opened to what some religions have always known about for years. Most of the world began to realize that there are spiritual beings assigned to watch over and guide us from birth.

Spirit messengers, those from a divine source, such as guides, guardians, and angels can function as protective guardians, heavenly warriors, and even as a cosmic power. They can be described as personified powers, mediating between the divine and you. I feel that personal guardians in the spirit world, our guardian angel and our spirit guides frequently work hand in hand. There's a great deal of activity from the unseen world, much more than we realize.

Take a look at the chief points of contrast between Materialism and Spiritualist philosophy. This serves to accentuate how much the spiritualist philosophy is so diametrically opposed to the materialist conception of life. All the great religions subscribe to some form of life after death in some spiritual heavenly existence. Some have failed to prove this to the satisfaction of modern realists and have lost their hold on their congregations as a whole. Spiritualism does prove this fact in no uncertain manner. In so doing they have profoundly revolutionized lives in that behaviour is not encompassed within the narrow limits of our earthly lives; it extends into eternity. Our way of living here will determine our spiritual status in the spirit world.

At times when we sit in meditation we often chat, so to speak, with spirit beings. We communicate through the thought process; we receive messages and answers to our questions. Not only do we communicate with our departed spirit friends, but to our guides, guardians and angels. In my opinion this principle, more or less, refers to all of the above.

Have you heard of the books, 'Conversations with God' by Neale Donald Walsch? Where do you think this information came from? When physical death occurs life continues without a break or interruption. It's none other than a move into another dimension that's much like our own. Although vibration levels differ our worlds go hand in hand. More smoothly for those who are aware of spirit presence; and believe it or not, it also goes hand in hand for those who are not. Past loved ones communicate proving their survival after death. They also spend a considerable amount of time helping and guiding in earthly problems. We're often guided by spirits; we too are essentially spirits and our subconscious is very sensitive to spirit influence. Those in spirit inspire mental impressions. We receive this by the subconscious and then it's filtered through to the conscious level. In various degrees it influences thoughts and actions, differentiating Spiritualism religion from a creed into practice with human nature and the spirit world.

In certain individuals, such as a Medium or a novice/student medium, there's a close relationship between the conscious and sub-conscious levels. It has to be in order to communicate. In a high quality medium this is to such an extent that they're more directly aware of a finer vibration, receiving the different frequency of spirit, thought, and form through the ESP faculty of their spirit body this makes it possible to communicate with the spirit world. Communication brings us precious and vital knowledge of eternal destiny. In our communications we learn that those who have passed have not changed, they remain the same. Realizing this helps to understand the continuation and evolutionary aspects of all life. It teaches to serve in harmony with God.

Spiritualism has left its trace on human life almost from the beginning of man's existence. Some have believed and many have disbelieved, like all religions. Spiritualists have introduced their literature and their proven 'life after death facts' to the world and what they claim is real. Spirits of departed family members and friends most definitely can be conversed with, seen, felt and so on. The spiritualists have communion with spirits, something that may need a bit of practice, but as you continue to believe in Spiritualism you'll realize that the spirit world is quite incredible. Some religions assume that because Spiritualism doesn't see Jesus as our savior that we consider him not of God. They couldn't be more wrong. We, as mortals, are all of God. Although Jesus was much different than most He was similar to other terrific messengers, teaching divine love, compassion and understanding. We have to realize that Jesus was mortal, born of a woman; and that he was divine as you and I are divine, and that he was highly gifted as many other prophets throughout history. Take a look at Moses and all that's written about him and many other biblical prophets. Not just the prophets of The Holy Bible but those of other religions as well.

In The Holy Bible, in the book of Acts chapter 27 verse 23, the apostle Paul said, *"There stood by me this night the angel of God, whose I am, and whom I serve.*" In the days of the Apostles, according to the bible, St. Peter was delivered from prison by an angel of God, who appeared to him as a man. The presence of these magnificent angelic beings is of the Divine. These angels have made simple, basic truths become alive and real, especially to those that are aware of them. Unfortunately some people's spiritual eyes don't always see or recognize them, but once encountered one cannot close the door to that overwhelming experience. Angelic visits are usually a subconscious awareness of God, His presence, and His reality at all times. These visitations reinforce that God and the spirit world is forever with us and hasn't forgotten us. A feeling of awe will surround you when this goodness is being brought to you via angelic beings. Recognize it when it happens and bathe in its blissfulness.

We, the human race, are spirit. Our subconscious mind is sensitive to spirit influence and we're quite often spirit guided. On saying that I've often heard in reference to mediumship, and had read, which I truly believe, *"we are spirit, receiving from spirit, giving to spirit,"* when we communicate, receive and relate from the spirit world.

Those that had passed from our material world did not change, when in spirit. This realization helps to understand the continuation of life and draws towards complete unity of body and spirit, the soul.

Angels are living spiritual beings that continue to minister in many ways. No two angels appear the same, other than a surrounding of light or an indication of space. We need to become aware of them when they communicate, and we should try to recognize their importance in our lives. Every person has a guardian angel; they minister wisdom and power by direct access from the God source. Although angelic presences are not always seen, one can most definitely feel and sense them. As I have said on many occasions, *"angelic forces are as near to those who do not see them as to those who actually do;"* it's similar to the curtain person in a theatre or those working behind the scenes for social gatherings; their ministry takes place behind the scenes.

Reverend Ferrier says, *"Just as truly are the angels real and never very far away from us, floating as it were in spiritual aqua. In their forms the angels are very much like ourselves. They have most delicate human bodies, very pure and capable of revealing through them the mystery of God. Their garments vary according to their order, for they have orders of service. They never wear black, for they love all the colors of the Rainbow and Spectrum. But all of them are most radiant, and their robes are of such fine spiritual fabric that they can become translucent and transparent. When they extend some of their planes they appear to have wings and they are giving a ministry of protection."* Spiritual and personal growth takes place when you welcome communication with angels and spirits of God. You'll progress spiritually in a smoother direct path, and calmness shall envelope you, if you permit it.

We're continually guided by highly evolved spiritual beings when they communicate. God's messengers are always watching and guiding to help make life easier. Therefore keep your awareness attuned and become one with that divine entity when your world intermingles on another level of consciousness, the spirit world. It speaks to you frequently; try to become aware of the messages sent. Think positively and you'll attract positiveness. Keep in mind that when you ask for something in prayer, you go through your angels and it is then brought to Divine Spirit. Angelic activity is always involved; they bring personally allocated messages from God. Oftentimes they require your authorization to put those thoughts in your mind. For instance, a friend of mine, who was not able to communicate with spirit guides, when I informed her as to how to make such a contact said, "*I have to learn to listen to that little voice I hear in my head.*" I said, *"Absolutely so."*

When you choose a spiritual path you develop emotionally. When you embark on a life of inner growth and learning you become more in tune with your material and spiritual worlds; you interact with your communicators. When you need help and advice, all you have to do is ask. I teach this to my students.

When a thought or a feeling of awe occurs instinctively, recognize it as if it had come from another source and not from your subconscious mind. The communication you receive is sketched on your brain but it often feels like it came from your own imagination. It pays to give that information special thought; it may be the answer that you're looking for. Be open to anything your imagination tells you; it's a valuable means of spirit communication. Spirit and angel friends work for your best interest and they'll never give up on you or give you bad advice. They won't interfere if you ignore their suggestions, but I personally feel that they'll make a stronger contact if it's a life-threatening situation.

There was once a lecturer who mentioned that the assistance of a medium would not be needed in the spiritualist churches in the future. The leader of that church was very annoyed at his words as he presented his thoughts to her congregation. Spirit communication! Isn't that what Spiritualism is all about and what the backbone of its teachings are based on? Needless to say I personally feel that this individual should re-evaluate his own understandings of what this religion, his chosen religion, represents. The communion of spirits and the ministry of angels, in the natural physical realm, are accomplished through the agency of passed loved ones and angels serving in harmony with Infinite Spirit, God, if you will. It expresses its relationship between our individual lives and a divine source.

Conclusion: As we live from day to day, we're not always aware of who's watching over us or silently standing by our side. Sometimes we feel there's something mystical happening when we're in trouble and need angelic assistance. But as its mystical, it's spiritual, and coming from someone angelic enough to be an angel, maybe a spirit guardian or a passed loved one who's with us every moment of our lives. God bless you all.

Principle #4:

Continuous Existence of the Human Soul

Many have questioned the continuity of life after physical death and many are raised to believe that it does continue. Many are less fortunate and grow with the idea that when they die it's the end of all. Others are sitting on the fence hoping that there is 'life after life.' Whatever your beliefs, give it some thought. What's the purpose of a physical life if at physical death all stops, even your soul. Take a look at the many books available today on near death experiences and out-of-body experiences. Years ago books like this were not published as many wouldn't write on the subject for fear of ridicule. With well-known educated individuals putting their findings on paper and releasing them to the world, one gathers a whole new outlook on the subject.

In being around death for a number of years I came to realize that the stories some patients spoke of, after cardiac arrest, were most definitely genuine. I listened intently to their stories. With compassionate understanding and all that was told to me I came to realize that there's something out there when we drop our material body. Dr. Raymond Moody was one of the first authors who held my total attention; I couldn't read enough about his findings. I shared those books with many patients that shared their experiences with me. When someone had borrowed them and I felt others needed them I went out and bought new ones. I wanted to share his wonderful work as my views were much like his. To me this was what I felt was for each and everyone, once life ended on earth.

Putting self-explanatory aside and looking at the reality of life one has to understand that earth-life experiences for each and everyone, directed at both the physical and spiritual levels of their being, stresses the necessity for separation between the physical and spiritual realities. The nature of the soul prior to its union with human beings determines the soul's earth-life experience.

The soul is pure spirit, individualized as it unites with a physical body completely imprinted with the goals of life on the earth plane. It possesses form, a consciousness and sensory capabilities of intellectual, spiritual, and creative results, capable of following its earth existence. It unites with its physical body when the biological development of the body has achieved the level of biological sophistication, as most of the soul's earth life experience is relevant to its spiritual existence. It needs the opportunity to experience the earth's natural environment. It needs to acquire the real sense of what the component of reality means. Only through an earth-life experience it's able to acquire the comprehension of the physical. The images required, visualizing and bringing into being, the environment of its spiritual world experiences creative capabilities from The Supreme.

When the soul enters its new spiritual life it finds that all physical needs are nonexistent. With its ethereal body and its special environment it will find that it no longer requires the instinctive patterns it acquired during its earth life. These aspects of earth life were not operable in the spiritual reality, but it will find that the experiences involving response patterns continue in its memory and its awareness of its material life.

Sir Oliver Lodge says in his book called *The Survival of Man*, Tenth edition page 83, "*The fact that such visions can also be produced through the agency of living people, even in health, was proved by the experiments conducted by Mr. S.H. B., as recorded in Human Personality, vol.1. p. 293. This gentleman willed himself or rather his phantom to appear to two ladies, without their knowing of the experiment; and he succeeded in his intention. They both saw him simultaneously, though he did not see them. Many ghostly appearances belong to living people, who are usually not aware that they are producing such effect. It is sufficient to indicate that a true hypothesis does not close the door to other and more extended theories.*"

I have permission to share this story given to me by a friend who had an 'Out Of Body Experience,' OBE, which she had never forgotten.

In the year 1997 I was diagnosed as having four clogged arteries around my heart. I was immediately booked for surgery and on October 27 of that year I had open-heart surgery. The surgery went well, so they said, but my body failed to cooperate and I remained in a coma for two weeks.

My children, who were now all adults, were called and were informed that my lungs, kidneys and heart had somewhat failed and that there was little chance of my survival. I was then taken to an intensive care unit (ICU) and hooked up to a respirator, which automatically gave oxygen to my lungs. My heart kept pumping although my lungs failed to work on their own, as well as my kidneys. My maintenance for continued physical life was now provided by machines.

Although I was as good-as-dead to the medical staff, doctors included, there was something spiritual, or some may call it paranormal, happening that they weren't aware of. My experience had left me with such awe that it remains as vivid as if it happened twenty minutes ago. For those who believe in continued life after physical death. You'll appreciate what I had experienced that which was not of this world; which I'll now share with you.

While in the ICU the doctor spoke to my family and said that tomorrow all treatment will cease because there was no chance of recovery. The following day I was disconnected from all life support and moved to the ward for my final hours. As this was taking place my spirit floated out of my body and went to a few floors above, where my body lay. Then suddenly I found myself in a world of wonderment. I was lifted to a place that felt of eternal bliss. Once there I found myself walking in a dark corridor that had a door at the end. As I approached the door it was guarded by an Apostle. His hair was a golden color; a color much different than that of the blond hair we're familiar with and much more energetic than the color of our gold. The whiteness that surrounded him was astounding, brighter than that of the sun but it didn't hurt my eyes to look at it. As I looked through the door I could see the Holy Family. Although I consider myself a Roman Catholic I respect all religions and their beliefs. Their faces were covered with white shields; a shield that one can imagine as that being from the light of God. As I stared in amazement my attention was focused on their feet as they were covered with "apostle shoes." Those shoes were made of soft comfortable leather with crisscross lacing up the front to just below the knees. I wanted to communicate with them but it wasn't my time; they started to walk away as if they had planned a family outing. I asked the apostle guard where they were going and was told that they were going to the market to buy something. I was not told what that was. I asked if they would be back and was given an affirmative answer. I said that I would wait for them. I watched until they went out of sight and heard a beautiful humming from the angels, but I couldn't see them.

My second daughter was very concerned about the doctor's and the family's decision. She phoned a very spiritual woman that's well known in a place called The Greensides Farm' in Marmora, Ontario, Canada; about three hours drive north of my home. She told her of my ordeal and requested her help and guidance. She came to my rescue immediately. When she arrived she was denied access to my room as family members were the only ones permitted. Eventually with enough encouragement and explanation as to why she had been requested, she was permitted entry. As she prayed over my lifeless body her spirit left her body and met my spirit-body in a world of peace. We chatted for a while and then she went back to her body, praying and awaiting my return.

I then found myself back in a big hallway and could see one of my sons. As I sat I looked down upon him. I spoke to him but he didn't acknowledge it although he was looking straight at me. Then it was brought to my attention why he couldn't; I was informed that I was in a much higher place than he. Nonetheless I called his name again and said "I'm here son, can you not see me?" I was told that he couldn't so I spoke to my other son also with no avail. I now began to feel distressed and was scared. At this thought I was presented with a replica of my oldest daughter. The angel which appeared very much like her assisted me, my spirit, to a wheelchair and brought me back to the ward, which was located on the tenth floor. Once there my spirit entered my body again and I could hear someone calling me. She was calling mother, mother. That someone was my eldest daughter. She continued to call me and once recognized that I was back in my body she said, "Open your eyes and let's pray the rosary." I responded, or I think I verbally said, that I could not open my eyes because I was too dizzy. Then I obviously spoke via the means of my mouth and said that she should speak the prayers and that I'd follow along with her.

All through these two weeks I was not aware of what was going on in the hospital or with my family. When I finally came out of the coma I was no longer resuscitated; my lungs worked normally.

Later that day, and during the prayer being said by the family, the doctor visited. He looked at me and said, "You're a miracle lady, I didn't expect to see you like this ever again." When he finally saw me walking independently he said, "I don't believe what I see."

Upon his departure, I verbally thanked the Holy Family, one at a time, for assisting me in my recovery and giving me a new lease on life.

Although I'm now in full renal failure and 75 years old I have thanked God on several occasions for his blessing. Furthermore, experiences such as this had not left me as I continue to encounter spirit beings. It's not unusual for me to wake and see my guardian angels standing beside me; either praying or giving me healing. **Mrs. E. M., Scarborough, ON, Canada.**

Her body was lifeless but her soul was very much alive. Her soul entered into its spiritual life totally unaware. It was only after the soul recognized the correlation between events that were occurring that she became fearful of what was actually happening. The possibility of extended confusion and disorder of environmental creativity in the spiritual was recognized through her fear of the unknown, although she felt at peace while seeing The Holy Family. Emotional stress and personal conflict with the free soul created emotional thoughts. In her further 'granted' material life she says that she had undergone significant beneficial changes in the way she approached life from that time on.

This lovely lady passed to spirit at 3 PM on August 27, 2007.

Souls, after completion of their physical lives, find their spiritual lives unfolding in distinct levels of spiritual reality. The range of activities in the spiritual reality is minor when compared with the complexities inherent in the physical world. There are many different possibilities open to the individual soul, which will be determined on the education learned while on earth. The more one has enhanced intellectually and creatively the memory data that's banked will inhibit its incredible resources. Furthermore, every soul has the capability of maintaining this information as it's carried across the veil with the soul. In addition, every soul has the same potential and will be granted the experience at the same level of opportunity, as all other souls.

If one expects to see the Holy Family, Mohammed, Buddha, Gandhi, Krishna and so on then they will encounter them as spiritual education remains with the soul. No matter what name you call God or who you go through to reach Him, He'll always be there for you. He doesn't mind having several names but He does mind when people kill in his name as he's not a revengeful god. He's a 'God of Love.'

Principle #5:

Personal Responsibility

What's taught to us by our parents as children has the biggest impact on our consciousness throughout our lives.

Through acceptance of our immortality through personal responses, acknowledges our responsibilities to others. As we assert our individuality, and we have to be in recognition of the effects created by everything, we are responsible for ourselves. Our actions, our words and even our unspoken thoughts are our responsibility. Although we sometimes think our thoughts are just thoughts, they're still our responsibility as thoughts are directed just the same, and hold energy directing to what's expressed inside.

Our spiritual progression is totally dependent upon ourselves. It's of the utmost importance that a full understanding of all implications regarding this principle is achieved.

Once you place responsibility for wrongful thoughts and deeds where it belongs, it is the acceptance of responsibility for every aspect of your life. Furthermore, the use of/or which you place your life depends entirely upon yourself. Some people think that it's not possible for any person, or outside influences, to interfere with spiritual development. I say that's incorrect. Although some people may remain ignorant to a lot of things regarding spiritual development, they are apt to follow the leader's guidance that wishes you to remain ignorant. But, one has a responsibility to realize that this won't continue unless one is willing to allow it. Those who take responsibility for themselves should hold the thought that they should have a similar responsibility for others. When one is unable to help themselves, such as the disabled, the young, and the senior citizen, or a stranded animal in need, we are responsible for our actions. Therefore, with respect, treat people and Gods creation lovingly and with dignity. We have a responsibility to be aware of this and act accordingly.

Other ways that people treat their fellow humans unfairly such as racism, sexism and so on, we have to allow for awareness of their circumstances and accept a personal responsibility towards them. A balance has or needs to be found to fulfill that role as a spiritual individual. Moreover, this makes for an act of high caliber consciousness, and an act of devotional love of God. The basis of the Christian religion rests on the belief that Jesus died on a cross to save us from our sins. This is strongly repudiated. Jesus' death was for political reasons. One does not have the right to go and sin as in "killing someone" if they believe this. Natural law says, and through the judges of the courts, that you pay for your own sins and do not depend on, or reply on, another soul in spirit to pay the price for you. Spiritualism asserts that no one can save us from our wrongdoing but ourselves. Man, through his consciousness, knows the difference between right and wrong and is given free-will to choose which road he will take. No one can escape the consequences of his own mistakes. God does not sit in judgment over you; you have to be your own judge. What we call sin is regarded as the violation of the divine natural laws made by God. Man alone has to atone for his sins and not disregard his responsibilities.

As one is aware in Spiritualism and other religions, nothing happens accidentally or by chance. There's no coincidences, or so it's taught, which I firmly believe. Everything is occurring and happening as it's meant to. You're where you are, and where you are is where you belong at this point in your life. We often hear 'I was at the right place at the right time.' Well, why do you think you were there? That's exactly where you were supposed to be. You took the responsibility to be there, as you are responsible for everything that happens in your life. Positive thoughts cause positive consequences, negative thoughts cause negative ones. Remain positive and strive to ignore the negative; eventually you'll find that your life will be more in the positive than previously. The world is a good place to live, some places better than others. Why for some and not another? Depends on where we are in our spiritual development or what level of learning is required for continued growth. Eventually everything works out for the best even if that may be the death of a material existence. Keep focused on the big picture and let all be responsible for their actions and deeds. Having said that, please don't let something harmful come to someone if you feel that your intervention can help in any way. It is your responsibility, if at all possible, to help those in need. It's by serving others that we serve ourselves.

We as individuals have 'freewill' and sometimes we ignore it; we often pay the price or suffer the consequences when we do. Although God gave it to us He also gave us total responsibility for our words, our actions, our deeds, and even our thoughts. No one died for our sins; we are responsible for our total being, here on earth and hear-after. We have the power to make changes and that is our responsibility, as well as everything else we do in life. We have this freedom of choice as it gives us the ability to make up our own minds and to do what we feel is the right thing to do. By using it we'll gain power to make right decisions, which gives direction to life. It's important because without it we may as well be an object. As it triggers a set of rules, rules set out by another using their 'freewill,' we come to terms with the responsibility behind it. Furthermore, an adequate system of beliefs maintains a freewill that explains a responsibility towards life.

Personal responsibility may be very difficult to remain accountable because it's not always easy to say, '*oh I was wrong* or *I'm the one to blame'* when you feel that you're not totally responsible but know deep down that you were the cause. We are responsible for anything created by us, from us, or through our behaviour. For example, if I said that I was going to meet you for lunch and chose to sit and chat with someone else, and knew that I was going to be late, I take that responsibility and don't put the blame on the person I chose to chat with. Responsibility for making a wrong decision teaches you how to make the right one if you're in similar circumstances again. You have the freedom to choose and if you choose wrongly you learn from it. Once one has taken responsibility, one realizes that the acceptance of it is fundamental to spiritual progress. Your positive spiritual influences will start to help you achieve harmony in your life.

No one can reverse wrongdoing except the offender. A student of mine said that she would like to give a spiritual talk on forgiveness, as the ones that hurt you are not actually hurting themselves. It's the offender that hurts, and forgiving the offender releases the hurt. Therefore, one is no longer thinking of the offence when one comes to terms with the offender and releases a forgiveness of the wrongdoing. In addition, I personally feel that the offender will finally begin to feel responsibility for the hurt caused by his/her actions and wrongdoings once forgiven. They have now given freewill to the offenders and have given them the ability to recognize what is right from wrong. In forgiving, one releases the hurt and pain, and that alerts the offenders which brings on awareness that they are totally, as well as personally, responsible for their past actions.

Principle #6:

Compensation and Retribution (Here and Hereafter) for all the Good and Evil Deeds Done Here on Earth

Natural law applies to this principle which indicates the Law of 'Cause and Effect'—you'll reap what you sow. This law begins with the first breath of life and continues from that point on. When in spirit or on earth, it should not be taken to mean reward and punishment by a divine power. Therefore, you cannot expect to be cruel towards anything that holds a soul and expect to receive love in return. It simply means to expect what you have given; nothing more, nothing less; but oftentimes what's returned is more than what's been given, especially if it's something given pertaining to love of another. In addition, what we make of ourselves in the physical is what we'll be introduced to, and what we'll receive, once we've crossed the veil.

Once a material life ends one finds himself/herself delivered to a spirit world. Life continues on but on a greater scale, spiritually proportioned at the base concerning the good and evil deeds done during an earthly existence. The cord severs that joins the two as one, and we find ourselves, 'soul,' in a world of spirit. When the body dies it transcends to a world that was made by 'self.'

Some believe in 'Karma,' specifically those who believe in reincarnation. There is no vindictive punishment handed down by a god in the spirit world. Retribution will be given by the higher aspect of the soul compensating for inevitable actions not already paid for while in the physical. Any and all good deeds concerning genuine motives bring grace and reward. This can very well start on earth, not when in spirit form.

Development of strong characteristics endorses that which is of the spiritual power. Although spirit grows brighter once a lesson has been learned, one should still thank God and express it by working towards the well-being of humanity. Moreover, right thoughts lead to right actions. Furthermore, as it dispels the clouds of illusion, the misuse of life's opportunities are thus rewarded through self-recognition that one holds responsibility, and has to be accountable for, oneself.

Spirit, God Himself, guardians and guides, continue to teach as they maintain a set of 'Natural' laws as they remain in motion and work in unison to cloud us from the spheres of darkness. One may say that someone has hurt them physically, or mentally, and may never forget it. One must realize that this form of hurt will only continue if one permits it. You may wonder if the one that did the hurt will receive their just reward, and so you should. Yes, most definitely they will, but you may never know of it as their retribution may only come into effect much later in life or in spirit. Don't be dismayed, put it behind you and let Natural Law, and God take care of such matters. One will not benefit from what causes another hurt or pain. Therefore, send love, although the hurt remains from another; the hurt will ease with the amount of love sent.

Conclusion: as one grows spiritually towards their spirit life and recognizes the self-set, so called sins, one should be expected to spread the knowledge that Spirit wishes them to share. Unhappy conditions become happy with this form of learning practiced here on earth, the lowest of the spiritual planes, which will evolve to the next once all lessons are learned. Simply put: one has to compensate for all positive and negative thoughts, words and/or actions. Therefore, do what's right, that which lies at the base of your heart: do for others, and all that's in your world, with love and compassion.

Principle #7:

Eternal Progress Open to Every Human Soul

There are two kinds of people: those that create their realities, and those who deny it. Which category do you put yourself in?

We are born with magnificent gifts: we hold the power to create peace, love in abundance and happiness in our personal lives, as well as for others. If one should see that this is the case, which it is, why is one constantly searching for it? Because, they somehow seem to recognize that there's eternal progress open to every soul, especially those who tread it by the path of eternal good. This is expressed in the revised principle of my designated spiritual home.

Eternal progress seems hard to understand when everything has an ending, but in the next world time is immaterial. Spiritualism points to eternal progress, but your own particular advancement will depend on your own desires. The day you're born is the day your soul started its progression.

There is a gentle, loving, peace-filled silence within, and now in this very moment you can sit back and realize that you have a say in what progression you'd like to reach, prior to your eternal home. It has always been this way and it's right there, within and all around you. Stillness, an apparent void, a seemingly nothingness out of which everything arises and exists and eventually returns to, dwells within and is reachable through your higher self. Each and every day progression of your soul is advanced a little more, whether you realize it or not. Sometimes you have to learn through trial, error and tribulations but your soul will progress nonetheless, sometimes for the better, especially when you learn your lessons the hard way. Then you look differently at others when they go through a similar situation. This knowingness is right there, in you, every single moment of your life. It's contained in the seat of the soul; it's your total being, so become aware of it. This allows the entire universe to be viewed as the mystery beyond mind, beyond what the human brain can fully comprehend, which reveals itself after the "earth school" is no longer required.

Like a beautiful diamond, one can only see a few facets at a time. This mystery is seemingly far beyond, making our ability to see beyond its capacity to understand and to know what lies beyond the veil. And yet, this is contained within the soul. Progression is totally your responsibility and it's by developing your individual spiritual qualities that you can progress towards enlightenment. Progression oftentimes demands sacrifice which enables the soul to obtain that which is necessary. This may not be an easy task but spiritual blessings will be in proportion to efforts made. Once the individual self stimulates spiritual qualities, the finer vibrations within the soul will rise to a higher spiritual development. Spiritual achievements are achieved through service given to your fellow man and to all of God's creation; the whole world and that which is in it, and its future.

It is said that we're born in perfection although the Christian faith say's that we are not: it says that we're born in sin. In perfection I do believe. As we continue on our spiritual earth-journey we find that we become somewhat imperfect on our way due to the choices we've made. We gain spiritual progression by correcting this and by rendering service to our fellow man regardless of race, color, or creed. One doesn't become perfect, but the soul's goal, which is to aim for perfection, thrives to accomplish this. There is but one perfect being, Divine Spirit, whichever name you may know Him by. Many reforms make headway as long as they compromise with error as the true man or woman becomes a brave soul. The brave soul departs with recognition from right thoughts, right speech and right actions with love being the top focus.

Eternal: How long is eternity? Think about it. It's way beyond this life existence, isn't it? Therefore, the further the soul progresses on earth the higher the plane, or level, is determined at the onset of death.

Let's start with the little things that will improve your soul. For example: stop daily negative chitchat about each other; learn to accept people as they are. If you can't do anything to help, then don't say or do anything to hurt. Your soul progresses with positive attitude put into action. Help a friend in need. Help a stranger. Help the poor. Offer your loving heart to those whom you feel needs a kind word or just a pat on the back, maybe something as simple as a smile. That's soul progression. Treat all human beings as equal, poor or wealthy alike; color or creed should never be an issue. God loves us all. The Christian Holy Bible says we're created in His image.

God gave all a soul and the soul will progress eternally whether you're similar or opposite to your neighbor. The greatest wonder of this is that you and I, above all other life forms on this planet, are consciously aware of this reality. Yes, you are aware of this, though perhaps you may not recognize it or believe it, but being of love and spiritual, one does.

One will be extremely busy in the next world pursuing continued paths, leading towards perfection. The soul has an eternity to do so and an opportunity to make spiritual progress, with no time limit. Transition does not alter your present make-up or character and doesn't stop your spiritual soul's progression. This awareness is yours. This consciousness of being is 'silence' itself.

Conclusion: go within, seek your soul and open it to a loving eternal progression. Once there you'll find a new door which will open a new existence that you already knew excited.

A Spiritual Quest

Many times in our lives we hear about the realities of one's life or the beginning of a new one. Some time ago Spiritualism wasn't heard of in certain parts of the world and believe it or not, it still isn't.

I feel reasons for this have to do with the promoting of it and the lack of integrity to do so, or lack of knowledge or means. Maybe one doesn't care if it gets to all parts of the globe as long as his or her congregation is up to par, with enough membership to keep the doors of their sanctuary open. Unfortunately, this is the outlook for certain individuals responsible for the promotion of this great religion that I found only nine short years ago.

Questions upon questions entered my mind about what it's all about and what it consists of and how to get a grip on the totality of it all. Many questions were asked and many were unanswered. The many that were unanswered were the ones of importance to me to enlighten the beginning of a new spiritual insight. Did I let this hinder my development or hinder the road to progress? Absolutely not; I reverted to books and the subjects of those books were about life after death and the supernatural, of which I had many encounters from childhood.

How does one fit into such a category when one is ignorant and remains so, due to lack of responses/education from those who were asked? Good question when put forth to those who wish to remain silent about a gift that one doesn't quite know how to control. This gift is what that individual possessed and chose not to elaborate on, for fear of giving a simple explanation to a brother or sister.

During a time of introduction to Spiritualism one has many questions, especially when one has experienced the supernatural and the phenomena of spiritual apparitions throughout life. As we all know, this can be a frightening experience when experienced later on in life for the first time. I was fortunate as I always believed in "Ghost" so to speak and had encountered a few in my early childhood. Moreover, making the adult experiences more acceptable when encountered after shutting out or turning off this ability we call a gift for many years due to the expectations of others and being told that one is crazy and/or *"You're ready for the mental hospital,."* where many were taken when they experienced it and related their experience with those who were trusted. After such brainwashing and being recognized as an illness, one doesn't wish to have this ability/gift, as now it scares them.

For two years I sat, practically in silence, in a Spiritualist Church, I should say I actually zigzagged between two, not knowing which one I'd gain the most spiritually or get more educated from. I approached the pastors and then some of the Mediums and asked questions. Often times my questions were diverted in a way that reason was expected to be understood from the answers given. Not good enough I thought; there has to be more. My point of view in retrospect to all of this is that while leaders, or church Pastors/ Reverends, continue to remain somewhat secretive about how to enhance this wonderful gift from spirit, a beginner lacks in knowledge and takes a longer time progressing spiritually towards development to a higher level of consciousness. This individual may just give up and not bother for some has been known to do so. That's why I chose to write books on the subject.

At this point I'd like to express my gratitude to those who reached out and offered their utmost best and also to those who took the time and effort to explain to a certain degree, enough to hold me within my spiritual frame of mind at the time, enough to encourage me to buy as many books on the subject as possible, and that wasn't an easy task. Books on what I was looking for were not easily accessible and I never heard of Lily Dale until much later, where there are books galore. Without those individuals I would not have developed or progressed to where I am today and without their guidance and help my spirit guides would still remain anonymous.

To those who are approached and questioned concerning spiritual development, please take the time to give your best; this promotes the spread of Spiritualism. Who knows what part of the world this message will be taken to next.

Conclusion: Spiritualism is a part of my life and chances are to those reading this. It plays a major part in it right now for without it I'd find myself lost in a material world without value or means. With it I find myself very rewarded and spiritually blessed as I have many friends of the same nature. Infinite Spirit works in many wonderful ways; make that way your way as you reach out to help those inquiring about their spiritual quest. Written, August 18, 2005.

Spiritually Minded

To be spiritually minded is to live life in harmony and peace. Peace is first to be found within or you won't find it at all. As you travel many different avenues in pursuit of it you may seek it through the channels directed by the God source, as it doesn't lie in the external world but within your very soul. To be one with God is to be at peace.

Once we come to recognize the spirit of infinite love, and once we come to recognize ourselves as one with it we're filled with love, then we see only the good in all. Once we realize that we're all as one with this Infinite Spirit we realize that, in a sense, we are all one with each other. When we finally realize the great fact of oneness of all life and that we all partake from one infinite source we recognize that the life of one individual is the same as in another. Prejudice and hatred will cease as love grows and reigns supreme. Once this is embedded within our souls we'll recognize God within our fellowman, as we'll always look for the good and find it. It's through our own soul that the voice of God speaks to us. This is the light of every one; this is the conscious, the intuition, the voice of the higher self, the voice of the soul, the voice of God. In the Christian Bible it says, "Enter into thine inner chamber and shut the door." This may be understood as going into the silence through meditation as you're guided by your own soul communicating with your higher self.

Buddha said to his disciples, *"All that we are, is the result of what we have thought: it is founded on our thoughts: it is made up of our thoughts."*

People in the old days expected to see angels and they did. There's no reason why we shouldn't see them today as well as back then; universal laws are still the same, they haven't changed. If we keep the doors closed to our angels, or we don't invite them they don't come to minister to us, unless of course we need them immediately and they hear our cries. When we open ourselves to the highest inspirations they never ignore or fail us. There is but one source of power in the universe, that of infinite power and it will continue to work and manifest through us. All we have to do is open ourselves, recognize it and follow its divine guidance. Those who realize this oneness, with this power, becomes a magnet that attracts a continual supply of His desires.

All the prophets, seers, sages, and saviors of the world became what they became and had the powers through a natural process. They recognized and came into the conscious realization of their oneness with the Infinite. Natural law indicates that God is no respecter of persons, races or nations. God didn't create those leaders as such; God creates men and women, as well as that of the rest of our world. Occasionally someone recognizes this true identity and the source from which he/she came, making that individual more recognizable in the crowd.

I received a document in the mail a while ago. I anxiously opened it only to be shocked by its contents. This document came from someone I respected and looked up to. After reading it I thought to myself, I don't deserve this, and no, I didn't. Maybe I read it differently than it was intended or maybe I was in a down frame of mind to begin with. Whatever the case I felt as if I was degraded and put down and was discouraged by someone I always felt was the most spiritualist person I had ever met. Ten years ago comments such as those would have left my mind like water off a duck's back. It wouldn't have bothered me in the least. Being in Spiritualism for about 10 years has changed me to a spiritual level that I have come to realize that some comments do hurt. Even though I'm a man, and sometimes people think that being a man one can take more abuse just because he is a man; well a spiritual man and woman are very sensitive to others' feelings and are in total awareness of their own especially when negativity comes from another 'supposedly' spiritual person.

You know, no matter what we do in life someone will complain, someone will criticize, someone will make a snide remark, someone will give you a look of disapproval and someone will be downright rude and verbally put you down continuously and intentionally. The world has many lessons, but, if we but realize it, we all reap what we sow.

A kind word, a good deed, a smile of appreciation, or a nod of recognition and approval is what makes one a spiritual person. From all the books I've read concerning Spiritualism, from our pioneers, and I have read many, it states over and over again to serve your fellow man and serve him and her with love and compassion. Basically it tells us to do what our brother Jesus taught to his disciples.

While I was having my down and discouraging time with the received document I had a strong desire to phone someone I love, respect and appreciate. She gave me the best advice one could give another when in a discouraged state such as I was in. I listened as she expressed her hurt and feelings regarding how I felt. She took a lot of my hurt and anguish on her own shoulders to relieve me of all that I was experiencing. It's wonderful to have a friend such as this; this lady has become a friend over time and is the leader of my chosen church, "Rev. Dr. Alva Folkes."

Infinite Spirit works in ways that we sometimes find hard to comprehend but one comes to realize its wonders and recognizes the amazing aspect of it the longer we remain in Spiritualism. By saying that, that very same day I received an email from a member of the Church, the treasurer of the Board at that time that contained something Infinite Spirit wanted to bring to my attention, or that's how I perceived it. I'm going to share this with you as I feel it brings a message to be shared.

It's called, 'Daily Guru,' taken from Elder's Meditation of the day.

It said: *"The ego wants to elevate itself in any way it can. It will happily set off on the spiritual path because it enjoys the feeling that is becoming more spiritual. It loves spiritual knowledge and power."* Immediately, I questioned myself, did my ego get in the way? Well—I didn't think so and I certainly hope not.

It went on to say, *"It will continue on the path as long as it continues to accumulate more spiritual knowledge or power. In other words, the ego is becoming spiritualized, which is most unhelpful for one who is truly committed to full awakening. The illusion that we need to awaken from is the world of the thinking mind, which includes all our spiritual knowledge and concepts. Even the spiritual path will ultimately prove to be an illusion. Just focus on what is here now. If you can see it, hear it, feel it, taste it or smell it, you can focus on it. This focus will bring you to the truth of life. All you have to do is bring yourself present with that which is present."* Lelia Fisher said, *"Wisdom comes only when you stop looking for it."*

There are many things that block us from wisdom such as: selfishness, secrets, hate, anger, jealousy, and judgments. Wishing implies doubt and trying implies control; we need to let go of these things. All permanent and lasting change starts on the inside and works its way out. No matter what's going on outside our selves, it is our projection that makes it so. When we are in alignment with the Divine we become very joyful and happy.

When I was about to stop writing for the day I received another email from the president of the church, Douglas Marshall. In it were a couple of short paragraphs that also brought me comfort.

It said: 1. *"We are here to ensure the movement into the "new earth" reality. We have had visions of living in complete harmony with nature, others and the earth consciousness itself. Now is the time to stand in the power of our own "knowing" and to trust the wisdom of our authentic self."* 2. *"The storm of fear which surrounds so many may get stronger; be the light, the beacon for others who are not yet awakened to themselves."*

I don't think they were informed or aware of my dilemma other than their intuition but Douglas also suggested that I should check out the Aramaic Lord's Prayer, the one he has a copy of. For those that haven't heard it, here it is:

Aramaic Lord's Prayer, translated by Neil Douglas-Klotz from Prayers of the Cosmos:

O, Birther of the Cosmos, focus your light within us—make it useful

Create your reign of unity now
Your one desire then acts with ours,
As in all light,
So in all forms,
Grant us what we need each day in bread and insight:
Loose the cords of mistakes binding us,
As we release the strands we hold of others' guilt.
Don't let surface things delude us,
But free us from what holds us back.
From you is born all ruling will,
The power and the life to do,
The song that beautifies all,
From age to age it renews.
I affirm this with my whole being.
Amen.

Three Universal Reference Points taken from A Cosmology of Oneness by Simeon C. Nartoomid are:

1. GOD-SPIRIT-SOURCE is ALL and in ALL.
2. The NATURE of GOD-SPIRIT-SOURCE is TOTAL AWARENESS, PURE LOVE, and ABSOLUTE ACCEPTANCE.
3. ALL THINGS and ALL BEINGS have a DIVINE PURPOSE.

Conclusion: to be spiritually minded, one needs to recognize that there is a divine intelligence, and ways to express it are through channeling words of love and light and share it with those who wish to hear. Written, September 13, 2005

Spirit Guides, Etheric Teachers and Guardians

How do you communicate with your spirit guides, teachers and guardians and also with the anxious spirit entities that are so willing to make that contact?

Many spirit guides have lived on the physical plane as well as other realms of existence. They, like ourselves, exist in a multi dimension reality. Spirit guides speak to us in many ways and sometimes they're more often than not the little voice we hear in our head and in our thoughts. They travel inter-dimensionally as they have no physical form such as when in astral travel. Oftentimes we are shown something symbolically and our guides expect us to decipher the meaning and give the message. With their help, upon questioning, they will assist but sometimes they prefer that we sort things out for ourselves as they wish us to remain as independent as possible.

From gathered research and past knowledge Native Indians have much in common with the way Spiritualism, as a religion, teaches in its services and class development. Example; within the order of things pertaining to the circle of life there's a belief that runs throughout the traditions of the Native Indians that all creation is interrelated. Many other religions also hold this belief, especially Judaism. They believe in spirit teachers but their spirit teachers are often referred to as a totem animal; a little different than that of Spiritualisms views. They believe that they all have helpers and teachers available that will guide them on the search for their own understanding and aid them in finding balance. They believe deeply in the spirit world and converse with spirits on a regular basis. It's noted that when one enters an altered state and deals with the spirit they soon learn that time in the physical sense is suspended; altered state meaning trance. They recognize physical differences and believe in freedom of choice that gives them their individuality. They also believe that no single teacher or teachers, physical or spirit, can teach all that will be needed to fulfill any individual. They believe that the Great Spirit is the one creator; the one Spiritualism refers to as Infinite Spirit, God. Native Indians are often a spirit guide to someone such as Silver Birch to Maurice Barbanell and most Spiritualisms' members are aware of who that is. They make one of the best guides due to the fact that right from the beginning of time they were aware of the Great Spirit, and had communicated with the spirit world. By being aware of this, and after having a human lifetime of practice, they were most definitely at a higher level than most in the spirit world upon physical death of the body.

Spirit Guides are entities who have chosen to aid others on the path to spiritual enlightenment. We all have at least one but they may vary in number. Each guide generally comes in for a specific purpose, initially to assist in a loving and caring way. They exist in a higher frequency and are beings of light that may sometimes physically appear in humanoid form so that the mind can conceptualize them better. They are also of a higher frequency. It's like when I put my hearing aid in, I hear much better due to the fact that the frequency is higher. Many use the phrase "*it's like turning on a television or radio, one need only to adjust the station to the matching frequency to connect.*" Connection is usually telepathic as in the thought process but there are many ways to communicate with spirit guides, for example, channeling.

Some consider spirit guides as a polar opposite as most spirit guides lived on the physical plane as well as other realms; they exist multidimensionality, somewhat like ourselves. They may remain with one medium for a lifetime or may come and go depending on the needs. Some say that they may also be viewed as extraterrestrial entities that connect you with another aspect of your soul, as in experiencing another reality in time and place. The Spirit guide's role is to facilitate the connection of love and light as it conveys essential clear information through the psychic that is helpful and which is of the highest and the best.

Spirit guides facilitate in many ways, oftentimes in meditation, dreams, altered states of consciousness and through the synchronistic things that occur in life. They travel inter-dimensionally and may exist multi-dimensionally as they have no physical form; similarly, they can be aspects of the self. Communicating with spirit means spending time in the silence of meditation; it is there that they'll be discovered. They are often unaware to the individual when communicating, but nonetheless, they are there all the time; one just needs to become more aware of the process. Spending quiet time focusing on intuition and the ability to use all the senses of perception one begins to align the frequencies within to recognize the internal communication. For this purpose, acknowledging guides on a daily basis, and in honoring the connection, brings spirit guides closer each time.

Aspects of Love

Whatever we do in life there's a purpose behind it, whether we're aware of it or not. We gain knowledge, we fulfill our life's missions.

As we grow and learn spiritually we come to understand that love is one of the best expressions we can give. It's one of the most sought in every human being, animal, and/or bird. Humans need validation and love is taken very seriously.

Love is the power of life. God loves us all equally, He has no favorites, we're loved just the way we are. His Divine love is what moves the universe. Love is the reason we're here and it's the most important thing in life. Someone you don't know can't hurt you like someone that you love or feel a close kindredship towards. A little sneer, an unkind word or something as simple as a look of disapproval, can alter an innerness of discontentment and sadness; that's intimidation. Just try some small acts of kindness for someone that you feel could use it and you'll be amazed what you'll receive in return. Show consideration, treat people with compassion, help, and care, understand, forgive and serve one another; the poor as well as the rich. Helping others should be our primary purpose in life with goals of important accomplishments in mind. Love reigns supreme.

We need not pretend perfection; the person sitting next to you isn't perfect either when it comes to actually being what the word means in our dictionaries. Don't search too hard for that perfect man or woman to be in your life, that special someone may not be found, but yet, it may very well be as close as to living next door or a working colleague. Perfection is a matter of what one perceives it to be. There are times when you find fault with yourself so chances are you'll definitely find fault with everyone else about you, given the right amount of time and circumstances. Whether you voice that opinion or not it's there nonetheless and oftentimes expressed through body language. Acceptance of another brings happiness and love. We're all born in perfection but we all become imperfect at some time or another. We may be perfect in our thoughts and actions but sometimes we falter badly with ourselves, and with others. Reality strikes when we realize we're not as perfect as we thought we were. We need not hide or bear shame. Let's take responsibility for our mistakes and then life becomes more realistic. Life's mission has a guiding principle to seek perfection in everyone. As I said prior to this, we're born in perfection, not in sin, although the Christian Bible differs with that of my opinion. Why would it be considered a sin when conception is usually an act of love? A friend happened to notice what I had written and said, *"That's not a Christian belief."* I said, *"I'm not Christian, I'm Spiritualism."*

Being in love changes an outlook from charcoal to gold when a new love appears in your life; you feel the gift of God all around you. Fall out of love or be rejected by a lover and the world loses its luster. Heavenly dimensions are filled with love.

Your heart is a muscle, love radiates from it. Did you ever hear the loud sound of drums and/or the bass vibrations beating in the music of today's teenagers? I guess we all have, especially when we're driving by a car with it unbearably high and all you hear is thump, thump, thump. May I suggest to you to put your ear on someone's chest, preferably someone that you feel comfortable with or have affection for. The sound of the heartbeat is exactly the same—thump, thump, thump. If you don't have someone who you're comfortable doing this with then fill your bathtub with water, lie down on your back and let your ears submerge. Listen to the sound of your own heart beating. Oh, you can hear it. It's thump, thump, thump. The thumping of the drums represents 'heartbeats' to our teenagers and young adults searching for love. They may not even realize that this sound is equal to a heartbeat but it attracts them to turn the music higher to get a fuller effect of the sound, hoping that someone's heart is beating with love and admiration for them. A beating heart is the sign of life, the sign of affection, the sign of admiration, the sign of acceptance and, once again, the sign of love.

How do we show love? How do we know it comes with love? How can we be certain that it's genuine? Whether showing, giving, receiving and/or feeling, it's all in the approach and the perception of it. So, do it with tenderness and a caring attitude. We often hear that someone needs a little TLC. Well, we all do, stronger at times than others but it should be included in our daily lives. Show kindness. Here's a poem I wrote quite some time ago. Brother mentioned, is also referred to as a sister and is also referred to as the man across the street, or the woman on the other side of the planet.

Kindness

Show some kindness—do your best
Kind words put aching hearts to rest
Enlighten a soul, do a kind deed
Care for a brother when he's in need
Don't wait for tomorrow, do it now
Don't borrow a promised future vow
Words spoken of peace, nighttimes shall rest
Stars brightly shine on God's people blessed
Fulfill your vow my dear brother
No time to dream, help another...

What's so difficult about giving someone a smile or a glance of recognition? What's so difficult about loving and accepting another person of a different skin colour, religion and or creed? It depends on who it is, doesn't it. We, as loving human beings amidst our own race, or, our own kind of people, as I have heard some people say, have no problem doing this. We're all the same really, some people look and appear a little different but the structure of the body is like that of ourselves and they say, we, the human race, are made in

God's image. They'll bleed if their skin is cut; they grieve and also have to be of acceptance when a loved one has passed. They hurt, they're sad and they cry when a companion has left them for another. Therefore, let's promote our soul and recognize how to love and respect all the people of our world. We have to try to accept the unchangeable past and leave the past where it belongs—behind us.

Let's practice how to love and respect others, putting aside all that we have read, taught to us by other adults and the bad feelings that we may have had once felt for some individual or another. Let's express the love that we know is in our hearts, through the expression of ourselves. Some people may find this a difficult thing to do, but why should it be?

Accept past faults and move forward, living in harmony with the rest of God's people whom you're associated with, and living with, in the same world.

While I was waiting for my mother to finish her appointment one day, I was inspired to write this poem.

Vespers message

Welcome each new day with grace
Togetherness as one need be your base
A soul's enlightenment, like grains of sand
Principle number two—brotherhood or sisterhood of man
For what do we mean?
Such a statement as this
It's a message—a loving dream
Carries forth a heavenly bliss
As you arise from sleep each day
Remember this principle on your way
Live up to those words
Greet people with love
Don't think it absurd
Cause it's granted from above…

We all need love in our daily lives. We need to feel it and we should express it. Sometimes we tend to forget about those closest to us as we spend more time together. Sometimes we take another person for granted and assume they know that our love and affection continues without any expression of it for them. This is unacceptable and needs to be taken into consideration at all times. Take a look at the smile on someone's face when you give a compliment of appraisal and approval. Loved ones at home would also like to hear this on a regular basis, as you would like to hear it from them or someone else who's important in your life. For instance, people in a management situation have the best composed staff if he or she compliments them on their successes and their job performances. Words of praise in a caring and loving way gets a better assurance and a better feedback out of anyone who's concerned, especially those you're intimate with, such as a partner of your choice.

From the time I understood what Spiritualism was all about, I felt that I was a spiritualist and belonged in Spiritualism more so than any other religion I've been in contact with. Since my greater understanding I'm not so sure that we always practise what we preach. We're all different and we're all unique. God didn't make two people the same; DNA testing has proven that.

There are numerous love songs out there and they sell well, because we all yearn to be loved; but love comes to those who give. I read in the Christian Bible, *"Give and ye shall receive,"* that also pertains to love.

John Lennon composed a song called 'Imagine.' I was quite young the first time I heard it and was alone in my room preparing for bed. I sat down and listened to the words. The impact of the meaning that he was sending out into the world with his musical lyrics, had touched a teenager's heart. Here are some of the words:

Imagine there's no heaven
It's easy if you try
No hell below us

Above us only sky
Imagine all the people
Living for today…
Imagine there's no countries
It isn't hard to do
Imagine all the people
Living life in peace…
You may say I'm a dreamer
But I'm not the only one
I hope some day you'll join us
And the world will live as one…

I still remember it so well; I was alone with tears in my eyes.

I needed some unconditional love in my life about seven years ago. So, I got myself a little puppy. I never knew that I could love something so much. It's a different kind of love than that of my child but it's a wonderful feeling none the less. All those who have such a pet experience a relationship that's shared between human and animal, as it too is love unconditional.

Why, sometimes does the bad overrule the good in first reactions or impressions? Is it because evil will show itself in threatening felt circumstances, or is it a form of self-defense?

Nevertheless, it has to be ridden so that one is able to recognize the good and loving aspect of it.

When we're young we seem to go through many relationships, one after the other, but some of us get burned and hurt along the way. We have to realize that we've met this person for some reason or another, whether we stay friends for a long or short period of time. We meet people and usually learn from those experiences, sometimes it's a hard lesson learned but learned nonetheless. We move on with a little gained knowingness and awareness, a little wiser with a greater knowledge from past sorrows and hurts. Being young, and being adventurous, one can cope a lot better with a hard lesson but as we grow older we tend to blame ourselves when something goes sour. We're not to blame personally, nobody is.

Fate, destiny, natural law or harassment, whatever we wish to call it, it was meant to make us wiser for when we're in similar circumstances. When we move on with a loving heart we're much wiser once we grasp the knowledge or the lesson that was meant for us.

It bothers me when one is trying very hard to advance spiritually but continues to hear gossip and lies by those that are supposed to be spiritual people with an advanced knowledge of Spiritualism. We reap what we sow but knowing this doesn't lighten the heart of hurt, pain and betrayal when done by someone that's respected and thought to be a friend. Infidelity doesn't belong in Spiritualism. One may ask, where is Spirit in all of this, where is the love and where is the light?

Some may think that controlling is a form of love but it isn't, it's none other than what it is, 'control.' To control is selfish, love is not controlled, it's letting another be whom they really are. Self-love is of the greatest importance to every human being; never forget to love your self, always, but don't overdo it or you'll spend your time looking in the mirror. Without love there'd be nothing that could stand in the universe. We must realize that love is supreme and we need to show consideration for all things. As we fulfill life's missions and grow spiritually we come to recognize and show love through humanity; it's usually the answer to many things.

Freddie Mercury composed a song entitled; "One year of love is better then a lifetime alone." Sometimes we ask ourselves was it all worth it? Most definitely!

Conclusion: all life has meaning and a purpose. Love is something that was placed in our hearts and souls by none other than Infinite Spirit. Once we bring that forward we start to recognize the Wondrous Being that had placed it there.

What is Spiritualism? Put in to practice the theme of what you just read, because what you just read is a major part of what Spiritualism represents. God bless you all, Thank you for listening. Written March 2004: Revised, December 2005.

Death and Dying

Death; is it the final stage? Is it the end? I think not. It's but a transition from our material life into the spirit world.

Could one look directly at the sun with the naked eye for any period of time? No and neither at the reality of one's own death. Yet throughout history both have been the enduring themes of myth and religion, science and magic, curiosity and fear. From the late twentieth century vantage point we find that as the sun is understood as being the source of life in the natural order; death is becoming recognized as the central dynamic that underlines life, vitality and structure of the social order. Which reminds me of John Edwards's book called, *'What if God were the sun.'*

Death is an unremarkable event in nature. To die of "natural causes" as in modern human society, is not to typically die young but to expire peacefully in old age. We seldom hear that any animal found dead in the wild has ever been found to die of natural causes. Natural death, according to the scientific perspective, is mostly a random event, an event without meaning. Death is a part of our life's goal, although it's one we never look forward to reaching, or even recognizing that we'll ever come to terms with it while we're still healthy. We, in a sense, look forward to that time but we do this only in terms of having a very old age in mind when it happens.

I was speaking with a friend about death and she said, "*There's a lot of people who are afraid of death and many won't even talk about it."* That's so true. But we all have to face it at some point and why not talk about it as we're all heading towards it anyway, some faster than others but they're not aware of it, and maybe that's a good thing. If we dwell on dying we wouldn't continue living as we normally do because of fear of accidentally killing ourselves and/or dying long before our time, so to speak. Death is a part of life. It's the final stepping stone from our material world into the spirit world. Life, as we know it, stops but we continue to live on, in spirit, as soon as we make that transition.

I have permission to share this story with you.

A friend called and said, *"Today was a horrible day."* I asked why and he said that a lady friend of his, who was only 25 years old, had just died from leukemia. He continued as I listened, and said, "*The story is so tragic I've been in tears since I got home. I got a call at work from her cousin who was beside himself with grief. It's just so painful I have never felt so sorry and distraught for anyone and his family like this before. This young woman was supporting her family financially as they had hit hard times. Early this year she was diagnosed and the whole family was in a state of shock. This was all happening at the time my dad was receiving chemotherapy for some form of cancer. I could console them and provide some form of hope as I've been in the midst of something similar. She just never got better and today she died. My God! What does this life mean? She was always so nice to me. I'm very upset about all of this.*" Expressions of emotional grief need no encouragement when someone this young has been called back to spirit. The advice I gave him was to be as supportive and caring as he'd always been.

Sometimes God calls young people home… Sometimes he calls the earth-like angels first and leaves others here for a longer learning period. Who knows why He does this, it's His reasoning. God gave them warning that she would be called home at an early stage in her life. God didn't take her tragically and quickly. She could say farewell to those she loved and those who loved her. She was a life-like angel here on earth. She'll be fondly and lovingly remembered for all of her beautiful qualities and support she'd given to her family and to others.

The meaning of this is that we learn to live and love, accept and also to accept death within reason. Prior knowledge to someone being called home early gives people the opportunity to give of themselves. It also gives the one being called home the opportunity to do the things that he or she always wanted to do, or say. Don't wait for tomorrow to do, say, or give what you wanted to do yesterday. Do it now; do it today.

I also told him. This is not to make you more open to things that you're not ready for, but to touch that special place within your loving heart to bring on the awareness that we, as mortals, don't live forever in a physical sense, but as immortal and of God **do**, although in spirit.

Elisabeth Kubler-Ross wrote a book with David Kessler called, Life Lessons. In this book she said, *"We eventually lose everything we have; yet what ultimately matters can never be lost. Our houses, cars, jobs, money, our youth, and even our loved ones are just on loan to us. Like everything else our loved ones are not ours to keep. But realizing this truth does not have to sadden us. To the contrary, it can give us a greater appreciation for the many wonderful experiences and things we have during our time here."* I heard many times over the years in my medical profession the five stages that describe the way we respond to our losses, are: Denial, Anger, Bargaining, Depression, and finally Acceptance. Not always in the same manner but one goes through all of them before finally accepting. We have to be who we are and hold no regrets for past faults because we usually benefit from those experiences.

I also have permission to share this next story with you.

A particular person had touched a certain part of my inner soul like no other had during my medical years. I grew very fond of him, his gentlemanly ways, his mature disposition, and his adult expressions of love for others. I began to respect him as I would my father. He often called me "son" and gave me a hug when he entered the procedure room; we respected each other and became friends. This gentleman had relied on a machine for survival for a number of years and eventually his wife came down with the same illness. I was introduced to her when she started to come to the hospital for in-house clinic visits. I heard so much about her and when we met it felt as if I had known her for years. I had actually, but through her husband.

I grew very fond of her as I had him and was invited to their home for coffee and a chat, which ended up as being a beautifully prepared lunch. We chatted and had many laughs. The illness they both had and the medical aspect of it were not spoken of. This energetic and beautiful woman didn't particularly like depending on a machine to live. The long hours that it took to be effective was taking its toll on her. She decided to have her treatments at home. Her husband was taught how to do this, which he did when he got home from **his** treatment and most of the time he was exhausted. She didn't do well at home and returned to the hospital. As time went by that treatment didn't do well for her either and she went back to doing it at home again, with her husband's help. This was hard on him and she knew it, which also made it hard on her to continually accept the responsibility she now feels that she had placed on him, involuntarily. They struggled from day to day with both of them having a common interest in survival and relying on a man-made device that seemed to work better for him than it did for her. She deteriorated very quickly; she didn't respond well to this treatment. She eventually made a decision that was finally agreed on, by both of them, after the many times she suggested it before; to discontinue treatment so that she may pass to spirit: to die. It didn't take long for her to go. She passed to spirit a couple of days later. This gentleman is now without his life companion.

A couple of weeks after his wife had passed; he needed a document to send away for insurance purposes and government protocols. He searched all over his home. He couldn't find it anywhere and it became very frustrating for him. He told me that he did what he felt I he had to do and the only thing he actually could do at that time, after searching for hours. He said, *"I went into the living room and sat down, I closed my eyes and said to God, please ask* ***my wife*** (he called her by name) *where this document is."* He said, *"The very moment I spoke those words I was shown, in my mind, where to find it."* He then said, *"I got up out of the chair and went to a drawer that was shown to me and there it was, underneath some other papers where I had looked before."*

On a couple of occasions when all three of us sat and chatted, they both had confided in me that they had an out-of-body experience where they met a loving spirit being that they felt was from God. The gentleman expressed his while chatting during his treatment. Then with my first visit to their home his wife voluntarily told me about hers. She started by saying that she was not afraid of death because she had been to the other side and back and she loved it. She said, *"I'm not afraid to die and I'm ready anytime God calls me."*

Neither one of them feared death. He felt that when his wife passed he would go shortly after. He thought he was being kept here to help care for her, which he did willingly and lovingly. This gentleman passed to spirit on February 16th 2004, just eleven months after his beloved wife. At his memorial they sang a song called: Make me a channel of your peace. I spoke to his daughter and said how appropriate it was because he so truly believed.

Lyrics are:
Make me a channel of Your peace
Where there is hatred let me bring Your love
Where there is injury, Your pardon Lord
And where there is doubt true faith in You
Where there is despair in life let me bring hope
Where there is darkness only light
And where there's sadness ever joy
Oh Master, grant that I may never seek
So much to be consoled as to console
To be understood as to understand
To be loved as to love with all my soul
It is in pardoning that we are pardoned
It is in giving to all man that we receive
And in dying that we are born to eternal life...

When I heard those words I knew I had heard them before, but couldn't remember where. In September 2004 I attended a church service and the chairperson's opening prayer was 'The Prayer of Saint Francis of Assisi.' That prayer and this song is one and the same. We can take solace in knowing that they're now together once again.

Each new day, while here on earth, offers new challenges, new opportunities, and new ways to enrich our soul's development and inner growth. Think love and we're surrounded by love; think hate and the world is a loathsome place. Growth of spirit as well as the development of a soul is essential whether in a material or a spiritual body. The things we do in life to enhance our spirituality, no matter how small or how big it is, is progression of the soul. And progression of the soul is the key to advancement upon entrance to the spirit world.

Don't look at a loved one that has died as losing someone; look at it as they're going home from their time of learning in our school world. When we, as an individual are faced with this, it's easier said than done, isn't it? Some believe that when the physical body dies, you wait in some form or another until God calls you forth on what is called Judgment. There's no judgment by a powerful being sitting on a throne, **we** will be the judges of our own selves. Religious beliefs vary greatly but most religions believe in some form of life after death. Spiritualism says that life after death is a fact, proven by mediumship.

No matter what conclusions we may come up with about losing a loved one, we have to accept natural law and what God has done. We all have to go to spirit eventually. Even if a death is traumatic the transition will be filled with love and guidance directed by past love ones who'll help us cross over.

In the late 1800s many people felt that they had experienced proof of life after death. Spiritualism was at its peak and mediumship was providing answers to questions about this. Evidence revealed that love, like life, is stronger than death. To achieve spirit communication it's love that proves to be the compelling force that's striving to break down the barriers between this world and the next. The home that awaits us in the spirit world depends upon the life we have led on earth. If we have lived as a spiritualist person then we need not have any fear of death. We're automatically transformed to a better and happier life as we are reunited with our loved ones, friends and pets. When we die the cord that links our Spiritual body to our physical body is severed. The material body returns to the earth and the spiritual body becomes the vehicle of our spirit, our soul. We are spirit, right here and now which means we don't have to wait until death to become spirit. When the spirit body awakens, conditions seem much the same as before death. Material possessions are no longer needed. The character and individuality remains the same, with the same faults and virtues. **But that can be a bit scary can't it?** Have no fear; we, those who believe, will be O.K. upon physical death because we already have this awareness gives us the opportunity to work on our spiritual growth while still on the earth plane. Don't wait 'til crossing, do it now.

The world we inhabit after death is not far away; it's around and about us, interpenetrating the world in which we now live; therefore, those we have loved and lost are very often close by our side, striving to help, guide and still love us just as they always had. Silver Birch says, *"The spirit is immortal, it cannot die. Death is its second birth. Once you leave your world you have a richness awaiting that's almost impossible to describe."*

Seven years ago, my best friend died. He was in his forties but his death was expected. He died on May 1. I felt such a loss that I made a tape of spiritual music in his honor and faithfully listened to it each year on this day. One of the songs was '*The first of May*' by The Bee Gees. On the first of May in the third or fourth year, he came to me, in spirit, and said, *"You have to let me go, stop remembering me in this way every year."* The next day I took this tape to work and gave it to a female patient who was very spiritual; she accepted it with gratitude.

Preparing for physical death with a chronic illness is quite different than that of a sudden illness. It's great when end-of-life choices can be made by the ill person; like CPR cardiopulmonary resuscitation or DNR, Do Not Resuscitate. It's a personal choice and it gives them personal responsibility until their physical end, and one that's usually respected by the family.

Conclusion: Death is a part of life; it's the end of a cycle. Live life like there's no tomorrow and protect yourself along the way. Life is to enjoy to the fullest. Who knows when it will be our turn to face it and cross through the veil? Once across the veil, one will realize that each lifetime in duration is but a little more than a flash of lightning.

But remember: there's no death. Upon entrance to the spirit world, don't be afraid, love awaits us all. Thank you for listening. God bless you all. Written November 2003, Revised March 2006.

In Search of God

Since spiritual reality is perception and not proof as such, we all stand in our own different place when it comes to being as one with God.

There's a God-conscious inside all our hearts. Although people are supposedly substantially the same there's often an occasional hunger for spiritual truth. God, whom I call Infinite Spirit, is the first fundamental of our universe; when prayers are offered for spiritual guidance nobody is turned away. You may not get exactly what you asked for or wanted but you'll receive what you need for your own personal spiritual growth.

Webster's Dictionary defines God as "*the supreme or ultimate reality: The being perfect in power, wisdom, and goodness, the one worshiped as creator and ruler of the universe. The Incorporeal-Divine-Principle ruling over all as Eternal Spirit. Infinite Mind. A being or object believed to have more than natural attributes and powers and to require human worship. One controlling a particular aspect or part of reality. A person or thing of supreme value and a powerful ruler.*"

I refer to the Christian Bible again as well as the Holy Koran, as I have read both. In their religious teachings God wishes us to have compassion and forgive, over and over again. But that's very hard to do for some of us. We figure once is enough, and most often that's what they get, if that. A divine intelligence is always nearby; we're never alone. God never stops loving; He loves and forgives and won't ever give up on you. He'll love you even when you don't love yourself. Reassure yourself of this wonderful divine love because you're loved in your aspiring as well as in your stumbling.

God's existence is a subject that has occupied schools of philosophy and theology for thousands of years. The atheist has always believed that there was no beginning. The idea is that matter has always existed in the form of either matter or energy; and all that has happened is that matter has been changed from one form to another, but it has always been. The Humanist Manifesto says, *"Matter is self-existing and not created."* That is a concise statement of the atheist's belief. Scientists said in A practical man's proof of God: *"The atheist's assertion that matter/energy is eternal is scientifically wrong. The biblical assertion that there was a beginning is scientifically correct."* Why worry over something you cannot change? Make your own assumption and feel what is right for you.

Theologians refer to God as Omniscience, which means, He knows everything. God is eternal, He's not subject to time, decay or corruption. He's Infinite, the most pure and yet the simplest. He's the source of all things, the highest purpose of life; He's perfection and unconditional love. You'll only realize this when you get to know him personally. If you would like a better understanding you'd learn a lot if you read about the teachings of Jesus. You're not looked down on because of the color of your skin or that you may be connected with a certain creed, or your place of origin. He doesn't put one or the other on a pedestal. God sees only one race here on the earth and that's the one He created, the human race.

Most mediumship demonstrations are usually God's message to mortals. I say most because some are fraudulent and only there for a material and personal gain. With false prophecy and one totally believing in the message, or reading, is subject to manipulation. In so doing one is apt to fall for tricksters and lose a lot of money unwisely. Believe in the fact that there is no death and that all who have passed on, still live; the spark of divinity dwells in us all.

The Theo-Quest learning centre says. *"Your desire to learn more about God is evidence that you've already found him. The desire to find God is proof that he has found you but you don't know him well enough to recognize him. The desire to know God is evidence that the true spirit of God lives within your heart. If more people knew about the goodness and the love of God then they could be led to live a new, deeper and richer life. All good things come to us from the Father of light, He does not change or shift, He's steady in his affection for all his children. We come to know God through our own personal experiences. God is beautiful, loving, merciful, positive, and personal. Most importantly, He's your spiritual Father and you are his child. Begin a relationship with this marvelous God and begin your eternal life."*

Albert Einstein said, *"Science without religion is lame; religion without science is blind."*

How many times have we heard or said, *"God, give me a sign?"* Often the reply is vague and ambiguous. Maybe the phone rings or you hear an inner voice and think it's of your own mind. Something may fall from out of the blue such as a book from a shelf that catches your attention. You may see something that reminds you of the pass or had hoped for in your future. We all want to know if God exists; recognize and appreciate any reliable method that comes to you to let you know that's He's with you.

In The Holy Bible in the book of Psalms chapter 19, verse 1 it says, *"The heavens declare the glory of God; the skies proclaim the work of his hands."* God was worshiped by His followers, his Divine name from ancient times is known as YAHWEH in Hebrew. I read that YHWH has both male and female energies. From research I found that the name was regarded as sacred, so sacred that it was ineffable and it was not to be pronounced so, therefore Adonai, "Lord" or "Elohim," "God" was used. This was widely accepted and practiced throughout ancient history. In the Jewish tradition God's name is seldom ever mentioned but is often referred to as "Hashem," meaning, the Name. God has many names from various religions.

We've all heard stories about the beginning of time and how it's referred to as what's said in The Holy Bible, in the book of Genesis. The first week of God's creation is of most importance and mentioned throughout history and it's preached about and discussed time and time again. The first chapter of Genesis tells you what God created each day of the week and how He rested on the seventh day. The first day consisted of the making of light and darkness, dividing it into day and night; notice that the earth wasn't first to be made. The second day, Heaven was made; dividing the waters that existed within the void. The third day earth 'appeared' and the creation of many grasses, herbs, and trees were brought forth. The fourth day the sun and moon were 'created' making day and night. Take notice that God made light and darkness in the first day but made the sun and moon on the fourth. Where did the light come from the first three days? It came from God, the Divine source because God is the source of all light and you have this ability to sense, feel, and witness this light first-hand through deep meditation. Notice that it says on the third day earth appeared. From whence did it come? The fifth day God 'created' the living things in the waters as well as those which crawl the earth and all that fly. On the sixth day God 'wanted to' create man. It appears that in the book of Genesis, Chapter one verse 26, that he didn't make this decision all on his very own, it says, *"And God said, let us make man in 'our' image, after 'our' likeness: and let them have dominion over…etc."* Then the following verse 27 says, *"So God 'created' man in 'His' own image."* Further on it tells how He did that. He created man from the dust of the ground and breathed into his nostrils the breath of life and man became a living 'soul.' Just look at that. If you believe the scriptures, right from the beginning we're informed that man is a living soul. Believe it and open your heart to a better understanding that you did come from a divine source.

Who was God referring to, who was he speaking with when he said let us make man in our image after our likeness? I'm not trying to be facetious here but whom was he addressing, a committee? Was he speaking to other Gods? Was he speaking to his God or his father? Who is he referring to as us? Who is our? Are there other

Gods that govern other worlds? Do they all congregate together for comparison or group together to make suggestions to better their domain? The questions could go on and on.

Why is so much emphasis based on the Bible? It was written by man, supposedly received from a divine source. Who questions this but those who are able to receive spiritual contact themselves, knowing in their hearts and souls that it's an interpretation of what was shown and telepathically received; such as a medium with clairvoyant powers.

Buddhism doesn't believe in a God. Judaism follows the Old Testament of the Bible as well as Christians do. Islamic religion accepts Mohammed, Moses, Jesus and others as prophets but they have their own bible-book like many other organized religions. I've read scripture books of various religions and they consist of harsh words directed at the human race. Sometimes I ask myself, why this and why that when God is so loving and merciful.

Mormons have a long tradition of carefully documenting deathbed visions for over a hundred years. They've gotten a wonderful view of first-hand knowledge of God and the afterlife. Dr. David Frawley said, *"As a universal formulation Hinduism accepts all formulations of Truth. According to the universal view there is only One Reality, but it cannot be limited to a particular name or form. Though Truth is one it is also universal, not an exclusive formulation. It is an inclusive, not an exclusive oneness—a spiritual reality of being—consciousness—bliss, which could be called God but which transcends all names. The different Gods and Goddesses of Hinduism represent various functions of this One Supreme Divinity, and are not separate Gods. Without recognizing the feminine aspect of Divinity one cannot claim to know God. To recognize the feminine aspect is necessary to restore wholeness, completeness and universality."*

What is the meaning of life? I have often heard the saying 'Live and learn' and have said it a few times myself; each day we do learn something.

What is the meaning of death? We all have our own ideas on this, such as knowledge taken from others' teachings and knowledge that we found stored in the depth of our own memory banks. As I have often heard in my spiritual travels from various people who were publicly speaking "there's no such thing as death." That I truly believe. The Bible in the book of Matthew, Chapter 5, verse 14 says, *"Ye are the light of the world."*

Sometimes I like a non-Spiritualism friend's point of view, on certain things. I asked one how he sees God and what part God plays in his life and his beliefs in the afterlife. This is what he said: *"That's a tough question but God has always been around me in my life. In my upbringing, Sunday school, plus Sunday church service, seeing my mom my grandma with their bibles, my aunt watching her Evangelical TV shows to seeing my Muslim friend praying five times a day, every day. Then it's how I personally see God. It's been a personal quest all my life in trying to figure God out. Mostly when I feel vulnerable and don't know what's happening to me or where I'm heading, I talk to Him. When I'm scared, I pray. Sometimes, when things are good, I thank Him. I see him as an entity that I can't visualize. I see death as entering a state of knowing everything, things we can't fathom here while alive. I believe it all could become clear then, and then I have my doubts as my scientific schooling feeds that. Sometimes I'm down about the possibility of death being the end and then I say, but it makes no sense. I could go on at length but it comes straight from the heart for that's just the eternal quest for finding out what it's all about."* Everything in life has a purpose. Satan is the evil force, which also plays a role in our lives, for without the bad we wouldn't have such a great respect for the good.

I refer to the Bible once again in the book of Isaiah chapter 45 verses 6 & 7 it says, *"I am the Lord, and there is none beside me. I form the light, and create darkness, I make peace and create evil: I the Lord do all these things."* That's interesting enough in itself.

Sri Yukteswar says, *"It's the Spirit of God that actively sustains every Form and Force in the universe; yet He is transcendental and aloof in the blissful uncreated void beyond the worlds of vibrations."* Jesus, Krishna, St. John, Gandhi, Pantanjali, St. Paul, Kabir, Mohammed and other prophets are all past Masters. A lot of us have learned a great deal by recognizing that the loving messages received and the teachings of unconditional love are of a divine source. An infinite intelligence pervades and controls the universe. It's without shape or form; it's impersonal, omnipresent and omnipotent, which is God, the light giver. The Light of God removes darkness immediately; we're very fortunate to be in that all pervading everlasting light whether it's at night or during the day; light (knowledge, spiritual awareness and insight) is with you always. You need only to accept this as fact that it's there and recognize it. You often accomplish this through meditation.

I asked another friend about God and the afterlife. He said, *"God is our creator and we have to respect him in our own way; He gave us life. The Bible says God created us in his own likeness, to love and to respect each other. Sometimes I think what a troubled world we're in when I see the terrible crimes, devastation, and destruction on this earth done by those who are people in the likeness of God."* Unfortunately, at times this appears to be gaining the upper hand but look at all the love from humanity when disaster or devastation takes place through natural law; many people are there to assist with unconditional love. To accomplish a high quality mediumship through psychic awareness you need to open your heart and meet God in your daily life.

I was drawn to a little book that was thrown among other things on a table at a yard sale. One word on the cover caught my eye. The title is: I was afraid I'd lose my soul to chocolate malt, written by Mike Tighe. The word soul stood out and I picked it up and bought it. He states in this little book that the perfect prayer is the Lord's Prayer. Mr. Tighe has done some research because he goes on to say that Jesus Christ did not compose it. Further on he says, *"does it matter who composed the Our Father when what is more important is living its message?"* Below is a poem that gives you a sense of direction about what it means to send a prayer out into the universe.

God's Listening

In earnest prayer the holy stream flows
Where warm devotions dwell the theme sweetly glows
Blessings desired grasp upward gaze
Celestial love eloquence of praise
God's heart rejoiced then dried bitter tears
Spirit ascends utterance from out there
Voices of sweetness heard by our ears
God lovingly accepts the comprehended prayer...

God is perfect and all-powerful, He is Spirit. One need not picture God as a human being; this imposes limitations, He was not once a human spirit. He's not an old man that sits on a throne in heaven waiting to judge you. He's the creative universal Spirit. Wherever there is life, there is Spirit; and wherever there is spirit there is life. We exist because a spark of divinity is within; this divine relationship, (in which God is recognized as Father and/or Mother, or both), confirms that we're all the creator's children.

Conclusion: we have freewill to reject and ignore that which we feel is of value, or not, in our lives. Sometimes you'll fail to progress, as you should, by denying yourself what life has to offer. Be alert and try always to make wise decisions. Who will hurt the most by deciding unwisely? God bless.

Infinite Spirit and World Prayer

Don't take to heart and don't believe everything you read, hear, or what has been taught to you in the past. Deal with the here and now; concentrate on who you are and what you have become because of it. After all, the opinion of others is merely that of an individual or a group of individuals agreeing on the same subject, sometimes with you being the subject. Let it pass and pay no attention to such trivial gossip. Take a look at the interpretation of the Bibles of different religions of the world. Read, listen, but take from it what you feel is important and what pertains to you. You're also an individual with a mind and soul all your very own. Value your own opinion as well as that of others and especially value what you receive from intuition, psychic awareness and from God. The God I know and worship is a loving, merciful, and forgiving God. It also says this in The Holy Bible as well as in The Holy Quran/The Koran. Yet then again it also contradicts itself several times by saying that God is revengeful and will punish severely for different reasons mentioned. Human beings did the interpretations of the Bibles. Human beings do make mistakes and falter even in language translation at times. Some things get lost along the way, as from passages that I'd read I realize that there's a lot left out and/or added because organized religions wanted control. I believe that yours and my God will not punish us in any way.

When we pass to spirit God will bring on awareness and let us be the judge of our own faults and sins, giving us the opportunity of decision-making to sentence and punish ourselves. Judging ourselves beyond the veil takes on a totally different aspect. The outlook on us will be judged severely by no other than, our own selves.

As a spiritual being we become more aware of the saying, *"we reap what we sow"* therefore giving each individual soul the ability to sentence oneself accordingly. Granting the ability that provides us with our own punishment, taking into account past errors, mistakes and/or blunders, to give ourselves the most effective punishment for lessons that need to be learned towards spiritual growth. Stillness, quietness and inner peace are received through meditation. Once there listen to the God within, ask questions through the thought process, listen for the answers. Answers will be sketched in your mind on your inner slate: images and scenes will be presented on your inner television screen. Seek the God within and once there you'll most likely find the correct answers through awareness. You don't need mans interruption of anything as long as you listen to God's voice within, with love, and compassion.

When we were children most of us had spiritual inner peace. As we approach adolescence some of us tend to lose it and lean towards an indispensable thinking. Some feel indestructible by harm, causing a number of deaths at an early age through accidents and self-neglect. Many are more fortunate in adolescence, getting through it with minor cuts and bruises. Some young people experience little difficulty because they have never lost the awareness that was given to them at birth or lost that contact with the God source throughout life. Once through the difficult adolescent stage we tend to change as we mature and take a closer look at our spiritual selves as we again start our search for God.

We remember our childhood and the peacefulness we once had that stayed buried deep within the subconscious mind. When we recognize it, it will resurface, as we're now ready to accept, focus, and press onward to meet that spiritual individual that has always been there.

We all know the same prayer said by many, whether together as a group or as many individuals, have a major effect. The power of thought put together as a prayer and then sent out into the universe as thought energy can create a balance where needed, getting attention from God, our Divine Intelligence. It may take a while to receive for an answer or to get a desired effect but it will eventually get the recognition and attention that's required, or desired, if love and peace are involved, but it may happen in a totally different way that has been expected.

This time in our world there are many disasters, new viruses to contend with and incurable illnesses popping up from who knows where. Also there's a war in the UAE between Iraq, USA and the UK. Below is a prayer that I created and had sent out into the world through cyber, via internet-email. I sent this prayer out to everyone in my address book before the war in Iraq began. I sent it out again when the war had started and having witnessed, via TV, the loss of human life. Please say this prayer with me, a prayer for all innocent people that may be affected in our world.

Great Divine Spirit, Lord Jesus Christ, Blessed Mother Mary, Buddha, Krishna, Allah and all other names referred to as God.

Dear Heavenly Spirit, hold planet earth and all innocent people in your loving hands.

Protect them all.

Bless those that commit selfish acts, acts they feel they have to commit to protect our world.

Guide them safely with as little harm as possible.

Grant peace within and between the countries of our planet.

Let there be a quick solution to created human problems.

Make our world a safe and happy place to live in.

Omit all hatred and wars.

Watch over all of your many wonderful different colored people of the universe. I ask this in your name. Amen.

Thank you for listening and God bless.

The Afterlife

What do we know about it? We know many things from research and medium-ship demonstrations. I did my research on this so that I could share with you what I have learned.

To describe afterlife it would be an impossible task because my understanding is it's a mystical place, seemingly full of ghosts, angels, spirits, and other apparitions. Some people say it's a world of dreams but who's responsible for all the unexplainable phenomena? A place without substance, where Infinite Spirit dwells, does exist. In theory, the spirit world, the afterlife, is beyond the capacity of almost every human to make sense of. It's so beyond our comprehension that it's often dismissed as mere fantasy. It defies all logic and can't be rationally explained but we, the spiritualists, know it's there.

Webster's dictionary says that the meaning of afterlife is: *an existence after death and a later period in one's life.* A later period in one's life, meaning life continues after what we call death? Albert Einstein said, *"If it's beautiful, it must be true."*

There are probably a number of people who are able to

understand the spirit world but find it hard to explain. People don't seem to like to talk about it because it's death that's being discussed. Also, declarations are based on faith and not first-hand knowledge. There are many who we call sitting on the fence, who'd like to believe it exists and hoping that it does.

Deathbed experiences have been examined and recorded over the years by many doctors, certain religious groups and others. People who have witnessed this have passed this information on for documentation to those who had an interest in knowing.

I've read many books on near death experiences long before I knew Spiritualism existed. Near death experiences and out-of-body experiences are similar but also different. I was absolutely amazed at all the wonderful things I've read and what I believe to be actual fact. Those factual events were recorded and published by highly educated men and women. Doctor Raymond Moody studied deathbed experiences and approached patients after they had a cardiac arrest or another reason why their heart stop beating, making a person clinically dead. Dr. Moody wrote a book with Doctor Melvin Morse and Paul Perry called "*Closer to the light.*" I think that was his fourth. In this book, a man who had a near death experience said, *"I learned that life is precious and death is nothing to be feared. We're all born with the knowledge we need to solve life's problems. The answers are all inside if we can just climb over our egos."* Further on he writes about a nurse that had worked with children. She said, after her own experience with the light and listening to the children speak about their happenings that *"Many children and adults have said that their near death experience made them more sensitive to people around them. The message given to these children of the light are not new or controversial. They are as old as mankind itself and have served as the primary fuel of our great religions. These messages are: "Love your neighbor and cherish life. Clean up your own mess. Contribute to society. Be the best that you can be. Be nice, kind, and loving. Do unto others as you would have them do unto you...Those messages were given to them at the brink of death so they must be important."*

In his study he says, *"God is in each and every one of us and the ability to perceive God is located in the right temporal lobe, within the Sylvian fissure*, which is the deepest and most prominent of the cortical fissures, extending from the anterior perforated substance first laterally at the deep notch between the frontal and temporal lobes of the brain". Did you get all that?

In his book called *Reunion* I found a piece of information that said, *"Studies suggest that as many as 66% of widows experience apparitions of their departed husbands."* I also read that somewhere else. I know for a fact that my younger sister has had such an experience. Her husband passed at a very young age and she grieved deeply, almost to a point of breakdown. His spirit came to comfort her more than once. She was somewhat shocked but gained comfort in his concern beyond the grave.

Dr. Moody goes on to tell of a woman who was visited by her grandmother. She said, *"My grandmother appeared to me but was much younger than when she died. I felt so much love, empathy, compassion and she was transformed in a very positive way. I'd recognize her anywhere. Telepathic communication had started, but spoken words were also a part of the togetherness. She appeared no different then any other person other than that she was surrounded by light, or an indication of space. I was left with an abiding certainty that what we call death is not the end of life."*

Let's take a look at science. I read that scientists can't explain electricity yet and have no idea what the spark of life is. Scientists have been able to explain the physical world and more often than not, brushed the unexplainable aside. I may be wrong in saying that but I feel that I'm not. They don't want to look at anything that doesn't make sense; it's embarrassing not to have answers. Most scientists don't look beyond their established premises or outside of their circle for answers.

In Brad Steiger's book called *'Shadow World'* he says:

"Accounts of ghostly manifestations, regardless of how frightening they may be, demonstrate that life exists in more than one dimension of reality."

The main understanding from all of the recorded near death experiences is that most of those involved were moving up or down a dark tunnel and seeing brightness at the end. Why would so many people have the same experience if there wasn't any truth in it? Energy can't be destroyed and at the brink of death psychic energy separates itself from the material body to begin a new existence in a higher spiritual dimension. Therefore while we're still on the earth plane the more we use our psychic sense the more it will grow, it's like any other gift. We sometimes hear *he or she is a mean drunk*, that's because with alcohol intoxication they lose control of their bodies and minds and they mistakenly open themselves to chaotic entities. These evil entities remain closest to the earth plane and are always ready to take advantage of any opportunity.

Gathered from my own personal experience, which I call an out of body experience, is a departing of the spiritual body from the physical. While this is happening one is able to observe himself/herself and their surroundings from outside of the material body. This sort of happening has always been quite common and people are beginning to talk about their experiences. It's not a hushed situation anymore, it's a part of ourselves, experiencing the spirit world, the afterlife, and getting a glimpse into our next realm of existence. There are many ways that people have experienced this: through drugs, anesthetics, car accidents causing trauma, or just having a mild attack of dizziness and vertigo such as I had. I didn't find myself going up or down a tunnel; I literally floated up towards the ceiling and didn't look back. I felt so at peace and protected. I didn't have the need to observe my body below. I knew very well where I was and went along for the experience of a lifetime. My astral travel has opened a new door to my consciousness, one I'll never forget.

Don't always feel the choice is yours to leave your material body and stay in spirit. I wasn't given one. I was told that I had to go back; I wasn't asked if I'd like to stay.

After this experience I found myself more open and able to talk willingly about death. My acceptance of death and dying and the afterlife has opened a new door for me. I'm more willing to help, give guidance and consoling to anyone who needs it. I've become more loving, kinder, and more understanding and am more aware of what happens after we leave our world of learning behind.

In your moments of solitude, listen. You'll become aware, and when you feel the truth in your hearts, you'll believe that we're here to learn and to share love with each other.

Thank you for listening. God bless you all.

The Human Soul

Throughout the ages man has been intrigued by the question, what becomes of the soul after death? This question still arises today because it's connected with our nature. This had led to a lot of research. The famous scientist, Dr. J. B. Rhine had expressed himself in belief of soul continuation after the body dies. Some people that dearly love life don't want to die. Those that don't appreciate life and have no respect for other life forms don't want to die either. Both have a fear of what lies ahead in the unknown. One has been conditioned to expect judgment for any so called sins they've committed, but what is sin in the eyes of some may not be in the eyes of others, or in the eyes of God. Only you know what sin is for you. Those that have a loving heart and gave of themselves unconditionally have no fear of the beyond. They feel and know within their very soul that they'll be greeted with love and acceptance. Your soul is in the right place when it's in harmony with everything and everyone, and when it has a peaceful relationship with them. Once you have respect for all nature, peaceful feelings envelop your total being and you'll feel an amazing balance between the conscious and subconscious mind, body and soul.

The animating and vital principle in humans, credited with the faculties of thought, action, and emotion are often conceived as an immaterial entity. The spiritual immortal nature of the human body separates from the material existence at death as the soul progresses to the next realm. Alec Guinness says, *"An actor is... often a soul which wishes to reveal itself to the world but dares not."* Where are the souls of the evil people, who have died, that were once among us? That's right, they're also in spirit, so be alert and practice awareness, not only in your meditations but also in your daily thoughts. In the Holy Bible in the book of Isaiah chapter 26 verse 19 it says, *"The dead shall live."*

We're all unique. We respond to Infinite Spirit's initiative differently and we develop a relationship with Him that's all our very own. Our creation in his image, as most of us believe, forms the basis of our relationship with others, hopefully mirroring that person as ourselves. We have a responsibility for one another and how we exercise that responsibility is through personal choice of intelligence and free will. Dignity and human uniqueness sets us apart from all the rest of God's creation. However, human beings are not always faithful and don't always exercise their intelligence and free will; but there's always hope.

A material, human body, is a person and the soul is the transcendent dimension of a person, which emphasizes unity of body and soul. The soul is associated with the Holy Spirit that dwells within us. A spirit being only lives in a body when there's an availability of energy, and regular heartbeats creating a blood flow that provides life. The human Souls characteristics are an exact replica, or duplication, of the entire human itself. Intelligence, personality, emotions, body structure, memory and so on, continue after what we call death. The soul is very much alive; it has intelligence, a conscience and keeps the same identity. But our two worlds differ; material and spiritual are separated in terms of vibration levels, making the physical world at the lower vibration rate.

Most religions believe that the Human Soul does not become extinct when it dies but follows an infinite path as to be rescued to a holy place and to be transformed into a higher realm. The Dalai Lama say's, *"I feel that the essence of all spiritual life is your emotion, your attitude toward others. Once you have pure and sincere motivation, all the rest follows. You can develop this right attitude toward others on the basis of kindness, love, and respect, and on the clear realization of the oneness of all human beings. This is important because others benefit by this motivation as much as anything we do. Then, with a pure heart you can carry on any work."*

There are many types of spirit-beings in the Universe, the human spirit entity is that of a white light and sometimes we can't see a shape or form other than that of light. The soul is deep inside; it has much kindness, generosity and has true intentions. As I said prior to this, we all have free will. Some chose to ignore the goodness of the soul although free will gives them the choice of good over evil. Your soul is your true self. You are your soul and your soul is you, it never changes throughout life or death, it continues its existence. Listen to your soul and choose the goodness that it holds within.

Socrates argues, *"Justice is the principal virtue of the human soul. A good human soul is a just soul, a well-ordered and virtuous soul, and only such a soul is a beautiful soul. Our only choice is whether or not to have a well-ordered soul."* There's freedom of choice again.

Nothing in God's creation holds more value and is more beautiful and wonderful than a human being; it has within it the most precious divinity, the soul of light. We as humans are in a position to experience the source of endless treasures, the source of eternal life, unending peace, joy, beauty and perfection with the Divine upon the release of our physical body and our material world. The capacity of the soul holds within all that which there is in the creator, Infinite Spirit. We're all endowed with spiritual capacities and we're able to experience God, right here in life, and there after death. Death is the casting off of a material body. At the death of the body the soul can consciously experience its oneness with the Divine. The body, the shell, has now been left behind and the soul has been released from its holding. Recognize your inner identity, right now while in human form. In the Holy Bible in the book of Genesis, chapter 2, verse 7, it says, *"And the Lord formed man and breathed into his nostrils the breath of life; and man became a living soul."* It also says in Genesis that we're created in God's image. But our body is not one with God, neither is our mind and heart at times, but the depth of our soul is identical in all circumstances. Get in tune with the Divine and stay above the limitations of your mind. Reach for a higher plane of evolution and try to place your soul in a position where you'll consciously experience a Supreme Being. You can build your life and enhance your soul's awareness on a central foundation of this reality of boundless Intelligence.

Our soul perceives oneness with God. It's all knowing. As it witnesses everything, it reacts and is able to protect through your guides, and enlighten you to the perfection with all nature. Infinite Spirit is always at your service and knows the soul's potential in the highest sense. He has that inner connection to assist and recognize the divine qualities and cosmic feelings that it holds in its ageless, space and time. That which is ageless and timeless does not die. The soul has no bounds; it's absolute in perfection even though we may feel that we had marred it somewhere along the way. So, use the rest of this life, wisely by having a positive attitude and disposition. Constantly progress in your mystic perception and experience the reality of the God within.

In July 2004 I was invited to go to hear a Reverend, who is a great speaker and clairvoyant from the USA at a church outside the Toronto area. In her lecture she told a story about a young woman banging on her door at four in the morning. She said she opened the door and let her in. She then said that as she looked into her eyes she could see that she was lost and that she had no soul or spirit. She also said that there was no hope for her. I went to her after the service to shake her hand. I held her hand in mine and brought up about her experience with this young woman. I politely mentioned that her opinion differs from that of mine as I feel that the presence of human life is an indication that there's a soul and spirit within; although the soul and spirit may be somewhat lost there's always hope. She thanked me.

A soul in a good devoted person yearns for supreme truth. One should strive and reach for such a treasure. As the divine principle unfolds great wisdom it discloses a greater power as it lets you focus on faith and the purity of heart. By holding such devotion and purity in our hearts one takes wisdom and instructions from the soul and puts it into practice. Man is one among many animals. We, as human souls, belong to the animal kingdom but we are in fact the children of the light of God, revealing infinite dignity in man. Our immortal being contains the light of wisdom. When a soul progresses towards the light, it awakens to an inseparable true eternal relationship with God as the soul progresses past the stage of a mortal body discovering omnipotent consciousness. Human existence as we know it becomes one with God, God becomes one with soul and human life with all its limitations is now transformed. All darkness vanishes and no one is more blessed, more beautiful and contented once merged with the God-consciousness. The boundless soul becomes light once it dwells in the heart of eternal life. Intelligence is filled with dimensions of infinite truth and sees the world much differently as you're now one with the Divine source. This wonderful experience can be present right here and now, it's just waiting for you to take possession. From this standpoint see yourself as a light of God; see others, as lights of God and you'll receive boundless courage and power of endurance. As love becomes unending, cosmic selflessness grows inwardly and becomes unlimited. Experience the Divine, enjoy, express and fulfill your soul, in the 'here and now,' why wait?

All life is ruled by a powerful awareness, that which is born dies, but the human soul has a single central motive and that is to attract the Infinite because the Infinite attracts us in many ways. The law of cause and effect governs life and death, this law governs everything and the whole world runs under this supreme law. All other laws come under this. Many times we hear "you reap what you sow." Does this mean Karma? If so reincarnation is most likely to be a possibility. Reincarnation made its appearance in the early Christian Church when it stated that Elijah was reborn as John the

Baptist. Our brother Jesus also believed in reincarnation when he said: *"Before Abraham was I."* The ancient Egyptians believed in it and the doctrine of reincarnation is the foundation of Hinduism and Buddhism. I find this funny because Buddhism doesn't believe in a Supreme Being. Where man believes in reincarnation, he or she becomes somewhat afraid of death because past experiences of pain remain in the subconscious mind. For example, the whole tree lies within a little seed, in a potential form. According to Hinduism, life is one continuous never-ending process and it's based on two fundamental doctrines (the law of Karma and the law of transmigration). The Sage has no fear of dying because he identifies himself with the all-pervading, immortal soul; words that all of us could take some comfort from.

The individual soul is an image or a reflection of the Supreme soul. Your soul is spirit and it's immaterial, endowed with a subtle astral body as it proceeds toward the Divine Light of God. Merging itself with the Supreme is actually the soul's goal in life. Life flows to achieve its conquest of the universe and it continues to flow until it merges into eternal. Be good and do well in this human life, believe in a good conscience and respect the worthiness of an individual and the ethics of life.

Philosophy says that the Charvakas, which was found in some ancient Hindu and Buddhist Scriptures, are atheists who deny the existence of the soul after death of the physical body.

They also believe that the body only, is the soul and the soul does not exist outside of the body and it dies when the body dies. They believe in nothing that cannot be known or understood by the senses. They obviously didn't have any good Mediums in their environment.

According to the spiritualistic school of thought, the other world to which we go after death consists of a number of spheres, representing various shades of luminosity and happiness for which our spiritual conditions have fitted us. In these spheres the scenery and conditions of this world were closely reproduced, and so also was the general framework of society. Death is made easy by the presence of celestial beings that lead the newcomer into his existence. The soul takes all of its desires with it and it creates the objects of environment by mere thinking. Death is not the end of life; death is only the casting off of the physical. There's birth and death for the body but the soul continues indefinitely. What dies belongs to this world. The body may disintegrate but the immortal fragrance of the soul remains to make life continuous but in a different world much like our own, back to where once it came. Some say life begins after death of the material body; we'll all eventually experience it when we come to the end of our physical journey.

An impure mind binds, but a pure mind liberates as it merges into Immortal Essence where perfection is attained in the presence of supreme peace. The body is dead, only when the soul is absent. The Maya says, *"He who is born begins to die. He who dies begins to live. Birth and death are merely doors of entry and exist on the stage of this world."* Isn't that an eye-opener?

In my conclusion: as our soul separates from the physical body the starting point of a new and better life begins. Personality and self-consciousness continue as death opens a new door and promotes a gateway to a higher and fuller form of life. Once you realize that the soul is eternal, you'll free yourself from the fear of death. Remember: eternal bliss lies within. Thank you for listening.

Expressing Oneself to the Creator

Affirming is a way to speak to God confirming your awareness, confidence, and the ability to remain in control of your future, recognizing the God within as well as the God outside that you believe in.

All words spoken never go unheard by God. Believe in your spoken affirmations and prayers. As you speak also listen to your own words carefully and recognize God doing the same with you. God and you work together as a team and will work on what you ask, seek and require. Keep in mind that God gives what He feels you need, not the material things that you'd like to have or want. When your wants become your needs then don't expect to get them without some sort of sacrifice, but when your wants are actually your needs then there's no other obligation but that of God granting you your request, within reason and how he feels that you will benefit from it the most. I once said that one always has to pay the price for something gained. One does not receive without some form of payment, whatever that may be. Speak this example below, out loud in a normal voice with vigour and eloquence; say it with meaning and from the heart.

Infinite Spirit Shadow Me

I am a descendant of your first creation
I shall follow your rules and laws
Your love is sweet as life and it's a beautiful gift
I will love you as you truly love me, unconditionally
I will continue to strive for your blessings
You will continue to give them where they are needed
My life is where it has always been, in your loving hands
You will guide me always until I return to you.
I am who I am.
I'll continue to be that what I am
You God, gave me this gift of life
I'll strive to be happy
I will succeed.
Amen.

There are three inner feeling that rise to the surface when people like you and me reach out with affirmations. They are, the people that remain skeptic; the people that wonder about it, and the people like me, and hopefully you, who believe. For the skeptic I suggest that you give it a try when you're badly in need of something; something that you feel is within reason for the wellbeing of others or yourself, especially when it pertains to your health and emotional stability. Now I don't think asking to win a lottery would apply, or be a reasonable request at all, although, if it should happen, it would be magnificent.

For the wonderer, if you didn't wonder about this and give it some extra thought you wouldn't be reading this in the first place. I would also suggest you give it a try, your best shot, so they say, because wondering about it will tend to lead you in a direction that will enable you to eventually believe. Some of you may probably feel that something of this nature had occurred somewhere in your past. Give yourself the needed time and have the confidence that this will work for you.

For the believer, continue believing, that has gotten you where you are right now. It will continue to give you blessings and it will continue to give you peace and happiness while the wonderful light of God shines upon you. You believe, therefore you are already blessed. A believer's affirmation goes as follows.

I believe in the God source
I believe in the powers that be
I believe in natural law
I believe that God loves me
I believe I'm being cared for by a divine presence
I believe in myself; so therefore I shall do my part for thee.
Amen.

Let's look at a few affirmations that may be spoken aloud by you, confirming within yourself, through God, that you do have this power, a power that will enable His divine intervention so that He will assist and guide you. Take for instance that you're unemployed for some reason and desperately in need of a job. We all need a job to make money in order to provide for family and for a healthy survival; and as the old saying goes, "To make ends meet." First of all consider the job you're qualified for and begin your search. A job you know that you'll do well and one you feel will eventually be yours.

A couple of days prior to an interview send loving thoughts towards the person you feel will be interviewing you. You don't need to know who that person may be. You just need to find a quiet place, sit in silence and visualize yourself sitting across from your potential interviewer. Sit in reverence holding respect for him or her as well as holding a respectful feeling for yourself. Once you have imagined all of this, with your eyes closed and actually seeing yourself there in that office, open your eyes and speak out loud and truly believe what you are about to say. Feel strongly that what you are seeking is already yours.

God has surrounded me with His white light of energy, protection and love
I will be guided towards a better life by His divine source
I am a good person
I have confidence
I am worthy
I qualify for this job
My resume will be accepted and valued
I will get this job
This job is mine
I will be honourable

We're all students of life. We continue to learn on a daily basis even though we're sometimes not aware of it. Begin to take notice of the new things you learn and also take notice of how many times you hear or actually say to your self: "I've learned something new today." Everyday of our lives we learn something new, sometimes unaware to us because we learned an added extra to something that we had already been aware of. When it's something totally new that we appreciated knowing then we immediately become aware of it. That's when you recognize the lesson learned for that particular time or day. Students, whether grade school, high school, college or university want to better themselves and become mature adults with a good educational background. Doing this is providing them with the ability to accomplish a set goal and a purpose in life. They struggle for advancement trying to move forward towards a goal and facing a battle that we're all very familiar with, exams. If you're like me you have an awareness that what you read in textbooks, goes in, and immediately out the back door of your brain. It's difficult to concentrate on study when your mind is so preoccupied with girlfriends/boyfriends, dating and enjoying life's wonders and pleasures of love and emotions. Look at what the brain has to contend with as well as studying for an exam.

You, as a student, know when there's going to be an exam. You're usually given advance notice. Set a time limit and a time frame for study. Keep telling yourself that this time is set-aside for you and nothing else. Condition your mind and let nothing else interfere in your decision, nothing that you can't control. Give yourself the time you're entitled to for the betterment of yourself through your education and career choice. Repeat this affirmation once a day prior to your study. This will affirm between you and God. Don't break your promise of affirming to yourself once you agreed to it, you'll be going against your own moral ethics and self values if you do.

God loves who I am
I'm well liked by others
I love the person that I am
I will study for my exam
I will do well with my studies
I'll absorb the knowledge in order to pass
My designated time is *Say your set time here*
I will pass my exam;
This I truly believe and will benefit from it

Assure yourself of all your capabilities and put forth nothing but your best for those you're connected with, those that you love, and those that you don't love so much. Never hate; tame that aspect of your mind and brain towards a way of forgiveness, no matter how difficult it may seem to you. Continue to work on that little dark side that we all have within us. God is well aware of that little dark patch, He's been aware of it since His creation of human beings. It says in The Holy Bible in the book of Genesis chapter 8, verse 21, *"for the imagination of man's heart is evil from his youth."* I ask you not to believe this but to believe that you're as beautiful as that of the most sacred of all living creatures, and that you'll make a difference to the world in a most loving and positive way.

Life's Journey and Those Who Reach Out

It's not easy being alone and feeling unwanted. When we're younger we can't wait to grow into adulthood and we think all things wonderful will happen. We grow in size from year to year, but our minds are always way ahead, by a long shot.

Remember when we thought we knew it all?

Looking at our children and reflecting back to when we were their ages, we begin to take another look at ourselves and realize that we were right there once; and then we begin to think about what we were actually like, at that time in our lives. We may have experienced a recognized similar circumstance at the same age. It frightens you when you know that you were doing similar things at the same age as your teenage child. You begin to think; my God, did I put my parents through this when I was a child? Probably yes; and if so, you need to take your children into consideration and guide them the way you feel that your parents should have reacted to your concerns and hard-set ways. We take notice that young girls are having babies, as early as 13 and 14 years of age. We have to try and understand the reasoning behind it. Sometimes it's very difficult for the parents to come to terms with this and may actually lose touch with them because they couldn't accept what they had done. Take in mind 'dear parents' that you may have been a little luckier than your children and that unfortunately your child wasn't as lucky as you were. But then again, you need to give their concerns some extra thought, especially when it concerns nature's little/big mistakes, because there's a reason for everything and there's definitely a reason why this little soul is coming into the world. We as parents love our children, we also have to live along side of them, learn from them as they do from us, and we also need to grow along with them. We've been there and we should lovingly guide them as best we can. Never forget the love that's in your very soul, the love for a child that God has granted. Maybe that child is a child exactly like you when you were in your teens. Remember, we as parents are role models. If we smoke, cuss and swear then what can we expect from our children? It may be a little late to recognize and try to correct matters once they start doing this around the home because they have already been doing it outside with their friends and peers.

I know a couple of people who had experienced nothing but hardship and heartaches throughout their lives because they never got the opportunity to experience what it feels like to be wanted and loved by another. I send my prayers and healing energy out to them because there's nothing worse than feeling alone and unwanted. Life is hard enough as it is but facing it alone is sometimes terrifying. Oftentimes they rely on friends but never seem to keep them for any period of time. Because of the state they are in they feel that they're too dependent on another and don't keep in touch as often because of feeling that they are only reaching out to them when they're in need. Be that as it may, a true friend will always be there no matter what.

I recently met a gentleman who said he's always sad because he's always alone and no one cares for him. I feel he's mostly to blame. He's a well educated and caring man with a great disposition. His entire problem is that he's lacking self-confidence. This is probably due to the fact that when he looks in the mirror the reflection is not that of a handsome man. Personally, I see nothing wrong with his looks. He may have been teased, often, as a child and has carried it into his adulthood and it remains ingrained in his conscious mind. Chances are, he feels that what he had heard hundreds of times over and over, is actually fact which, of course, it isn't. Each time I correspond with him, usually via phone or e-mail, I try to give him some form of upliftment. I feel it has had some effect and all he needs to hear is that he has a friend who sees him for the wonderful soul that's inside the brilliant mind, behind the not-so-handsome face.

I sat and meditated, as I usually do when focusing on another's hurt; and once I have done so, I begin to write what spirit gave. The affirmation poem below is a reminder that we don't have to be alone because there's someone out there for all of us. One just needs the confidence within themselves to go out and look for that 'special someone.' Here's an affirmation for those who need affirming regarding this.

Sadness Reversed

All alone and oh so sad
Reaching out for peace
I feel a hint of upliftment now
And it will never cease
I will meet a new friend
One who takes my name
Once together, two as one
It'll ease away the pain
We will take the necessary steps
To understand each other
Now a pair a perfect match
We'll cherish one another
God provides the things we need
In our material abode
What's given with love will remain with love
As the two of us grow old...

Life as a human can be funny at times. We find pleasures in the silliest little things. As I have heard many people say," Little things mean a lot." When someone slips and falls they usually get back up and laugh while doing so. Why is that; embarrassment? Of course, if they were hurt they'd show it by their facial expressions wouldn't they? Not necessarily so. I used to do the same but I finally realized that when I did something like that everyone else laughed. Not any more. Now if I happen to slip and fall I'd make some comment to an unknown spirit not seen by anyone else but me. I may sputter a little to myself and then get on with what I was doing but my embarrassment is concealed and my hurt expressed, not sure if I'm embarrassed anymore either. With hurt expressed, those of love immediately feel your pain and with this reaction they're sending healing, whether they're aware of it or not, to help you recover. Drop something sometime, there's someone who will laugh, no matter what. You, yourself, may laugh after the anger and frustration has subsided. Watch a small child run and play. She'll often end up on her little bottom with a plump. We laugh or have an inner chuckle even when she cries because we know it's natural for them to fall on their backside and not get hurt. The plump is usually cushioned by a padding of some sort, besides, it's the seat and it comes cushioned. Another example: when we have a little pet, like a puppy or a kitten, we laugh at its excitement and its playful ways. We enjoy the little things in life. The things that touch a special place in our hearts are what make the little things very special and unforgettable. Someone may compliment you in some way after you have had a hard day; or you receive a kiss from a loved one when you arrive home to show you "just how special you are" and that you're still loved. A flower brought to you by your spouse of 10 years when you thought he or she didn't care anymore and you thought they took you for granted. Someone to hold you and call you baby even though you're 50 years of age; now that should make you feel good about yourself. In the Holy Bible in 1 Peter chapter 5 verse 14 it says, *"Greet ye one another with a kiss of charity."* We will learn a lot about ourselves if we communicate more. Don't speak words that you don't feel in your heart. Trust in those you love. The world can have its uncertainties so make life safe within your own environment. Trust is one of the most important virtues that you should strive to obtain, for God desires our trust and our revenant spirit. Therefore, trust your children after you teach them right from wrong. Truth comes from the heart where the feeling of God is felt the most, so be honest with yourself. Trust that your children will follow your leadership. Be upfront and honest as one lie leads to another, then another to cover up the first one, and so on. Express love as love unheard is not the way love is meant to be. Expressing makes a big difference in everyone's life. Believe me, there will be a tremendous difference, especially in how it's reflected back to you or passed on to another who also needs to hear it. Love unspoken is love unexpressed. Love unexpressed is love unfelt. Love unfelt is no love at all. No love at all is unwanted. Here's an 'unblocking' affirmation.

Divine Father

Feelings of love are sometimes hard to express
You will show me and guide me as to how to do this
Awareness of a spouse over a period of time is sometimes taken for granted
You will bring this to my attention and also guide me to be more aware
Trust is difficult to have when one has been hurt too many times
You will remove all of my past hurts so that I will trust once again
Telling the truth is sometimes hard when it involves hurt in some way
You will open my heart and enlighten my soul so that I will always be honest in all my spoken words
Little things mean a lot
You will continue making 'special' little things happen as they are important in my life.
Amen.

God will provide you with what you need, not what you want, or would like to have. When darkness leaves the soul, one begins to see the light. With this set in motion one begins to see a brother and/or sister in any man or woman they come in contact with. Having a positive attitude towards a better understanding of failures and successes will begin to bring importance towards appearances you have not noticed before.

Here's a story I wish to share with you.

Taxi drivers drive to make a living as you and I may have a more stationary job. Not all like taxi drivers because it appears that they think they own the city roads. It's only that they have driven for such a long time that they know it well and feel comfortable on it. But yet again they're likely the ones having and causing the most automobile accidents.

Back in December 11, 1995, I was standing at a bus stop in the freezing cold at 5:30 in the morning. The buses usually run every half hour at that time and more often on major streets. I'm not sure how long I was standing waiting, but because of the weather conditions the bus had been delayed. A driver of 'Beck's Taxi' with the cab license number 2130 pulled up to the bus stop. He rolled down the window and said, *"It's too cold to be standing there, get in."* I told him I didn't need a taxi because I was waiting for the bus with a metro pass but he said, *"Get in, it's a free ride, I'm going that way."* I got in and he drove me a distance where I could catch the streetcar on the main street, which arrived at the time he dropped me off. This is so unusual for a 'city taxi driver' but I still remember that morning when a man I had never met went out of his way to show kindness towards another human being. Although my skin color differs from that of his, it had no effect on what his kind gesture offered. I was grateful and thanked him and he wished me a good day with a friendly, 'you're welcome brother.' I'm sure that in his childhood he had been taught by loving parents.

The love of a brother, whether born of the same parents or not, reflects a loving God. The past is past and unchangeable and we cannot can we change the way people will act in certain set ways. God blesses those that bless another.

Thank you 'Beck's' taxi driver. God bless.

Extended and Eternal Love

Everybody and everything craves, wishes for, wants and needs love; without it life is a sad and depressed affair of loneliness that has no meaning. Why do you think that Harlequin romance novels sell so well? People associate themselves with one of the characters and it's usually the one that's receiving all the attention and affections of love. Those people, young and old alike, still yearn for the utmost and remain open for such as this happening to them. Love has to be a matter of feelings and not only action directed by a consciously willed choice for the other one's benefit. Everyone loves a love song that pertains to togetherness and mutual happiness like we find in fairy tales but occasionally in the lives of a devoted pair, but rarely found today in this generation. Some birds and animals mate and stay together for life until one dies or is killed in some way. They may choose another partner, yet may not, but continue to search for one until they themselves die. Why are humans so different and remain promiscuous even after taking solemn vows and oaths? We're only human, aren't we? Yet, certain wildlife has no problem doing this. Reason, because man is able to think beyond the moment and plan for future events. Man does not go by seasons, and scents given of, when it's time to mate. Wildlife knows by this means and follows the pattern for propagation where man is always aware of this knowledge and 'knows' that he knows this. Man is readily available year in and year out with a continued sexual urge to fulfill. Man expresses love and also seeks and gains personal pleasure from it. The lowest of the low, which we as humans consider here on earth, seeks and needs affection and attention. Did you know that a worm is a hermaphrodite, self sufficient and able to reproduce all on its very own? Yet it comes to the surface of the ground in search of another for contact, to mate, because it also likes to be loved, feel love and give love in return. This affection is not only subjective to humans but to all walks of life, animals, birds and mammals alike etc. to carry on the existence of its species. As we get older in years and some of us alone, we search for something to love that gives us a feeling of joy. This is often from a pet of our choice. Most of us choose a cat or a dog but others have a more exotic taste and choose something a little more unusual and messier, but unconditional love is in acceptance. When it comes to two humans sharing love and togetherness, do have respect for each other and show it on an ongoing basis. Love can be mysterious and challenging. So, whether you have broken your vows to each other or not, remain caring and loving. Remember the vows said and taken during a wedding ceremony: 'Honour and obey, till death do us part?' something similar in any case. What an expectation to be expected of any given person. 'Honour and obey' should be a decided agreement between the two. 'Till death do us part' should be for a wedded pair that has lived up to all other agreements of understanding, otherwise why should this be? In some cases a person feels used and abused throughout their lifetime just because she or he had taken those words literally and made a truce with themselves and God, to stick by them no matter what. Now-a-days you don't often find this except in an abusive relationship. Prevent this from happening by noticing from the beginning any changes in attitude and the 'taken for granted stuff.' Address the situation immediately and put a stop to it before it escalates and gets out of control. Thus, not making you feel owned like a part of the furniture or an old workhorse, what you feel the other is probably considering you as. At this point, one or the other has a fear of leaving due to an expected happening that had been told to them or of what would occur if they did. Love each other as you did when you first began, why should that change? Don't take each other for granted, as sometimes we tend to do over a period of time.

A friend is someone you can trust, lean on, and able to turn to, in your bad times as well as in your good. In times of distress we need a shoulder to cry on and someone who we feel comfortable enough with to express our concerns. The time when we need to express, and badly need to do so, is the time we seldom ever turn to them. Why? Because they are a friend and we don't want to burden them with our problems. True friends accept and understand. They'll be more upset if you don't confide in them and seek their help and assistance than if you try to conceal your anguish and hurt, and don't reach out to them for help.

Friendship starts to develop at introduction, whether by someone else or by yourselves to one another. You'll feel the connection and a bond will begin to grow just as if you had known each other for a long time. You will both know at once whether a friendship will evolve from it, and I'm not just speaking of male female relationships. I'm also speaking of female-female and male-male, young and old alike. My best friend here in Toronto is a woman 20 years my senior. She and I have a bond like I have with no other person and we spend many hours in each other's company. Age has no boundaries when a friendship evolves and another who feels that bond loves one as a friend. Once a friendship materializes one has to be aware of the other in all due respect in an acceptable knowing agreed relationship. For some reason I don't have a strong friendship with a male since my best 'male' friend passed away some time ago. I have male acquaintances who I consider myself friendly with, but, I'm not sure what will evolve with them in the future. My close friends are female. There are times when it would be nice to have a male friend to sort of talk male things with. A female friend I have had a friendship with for about twenty-nine years is a fair distance away but our friendship has lasted. We visit each other; chat on the phone and also via Internet email. She gets to hear what I would discuss with a male friend and she's also the one I feel closest to regarding sharing my past. It's amazing what we both have in common and what we found out about each other through sharing. We are very similar in all respects of the word except for the difference in gender. So, needless to say we're very good for each other and we know that we can turn to each other whenever either one is in need.

Divine Spirit

You have your reasons for doing the things you do
Time waiting on my part seems very long until it's in the past
Anxiety and restlessness makes it so
Lessons learned, although the hurdles are rough at times
You guide and provide as I encounter each meaningful task
The impact will be less with each occurrence
As I travel on life's journey you'll offer roads
Destined to new spiritual beginnings… Amen.

Another kind of love, the most sacrificial of it all is total love of God. Those are the men and women who give up everything, such as you and I take for granted, for the soul purpose of serving God's creation and a chosen religion. I stress and speak about the Roman Catholic religion for that is what I feel has the strictest laws regarding celibacy. Once perpetual vows are made they commit their lives to suffering. In their deepest suffering, and in their decisions, they are alone with God. Although their friends and family may reach out to help they still have to face it alone. Celibacy is neutral in and of itself to most of those who have chosen to serve. They view sexuality as a reserved kind of attachment with a need to discover a deeper sense of meaning of reality to their lives. Yet again, once involved in their vows the suppressed remains at the break of the subconscious mind with still a questionable desire to explore the unexplored. Taken vows 'under oath' for God, Jesus Christ or The Blessed Mother if you will, cause a person to examine their chosen path when craving and desiring love, companionship, and sexual intimacy. This appears to make a person totally dependent on others for a sense of self worth, belonging and maybe even a justification for living. It can teach them about delusion and how this sense of autonomous being can be, making it a positive and a very powerful lesson. The earmark of positive celibacy is to seek and find a deeper sense of self-worthiness, preliminary enlightenment for themselves and others without any conditions. A celibate life style must not be regarded as superior or inferior to any others. It says in the Holy Bible in 1st. John chapter 4 verses 7, 18 and 21, *"Beloved, let us love one another: for love is of God; and everyone that loveth is born of God, and knoweth God. There is no fear in love; but perfect love casteth out fear: because fear hath torment. He that feareth is not made perfect in love. That he who loveth God love his brother also."*

We should have respect for all and accept any personal choice made by others for what do we know of their reasons. All intentions are good when it concerns love no matter where it's directed. Isn't love our major goal and isn't it what life is all about? The book of 1st.

Timothy chapter 5 verse 1 says, *"Rebuke not an elder, but entreat him as a father; and the younger men as brethren, the elder women as mothers; the younger as sisters, with all purity."* Other words to pay attention to are those in 1st. Corinthians chapter 15 verse 33 says, *"Be not deceived: evil communications corrupt good manners."* Because, in 1st. Corinthians chapter 15 verse 44 it says, *"there is a natural body and there is a spiritual body."* We're all here for a reason and once passed through the veil of death we're back to where we came from; body to ashes and souls guided through the tunnel towards the light, back to the Divine.

Love is love, love yourself and love others, within reasons of protection concerning your welfare.

A Created Abode

Heaven versus Hell. God versus Satan. What is there to differentiate? Heaven deals with God. Hell deals with the devil—Satan.

The summer land, Nirvana or what you personally know as Heaven, is the most beautiful sacred place that one is ever capable of entering. To enter Heaven you must die. You must leave your body behind and then your spirit will soar towards the beautiful light that you'll see in the distance. Don't miss it and be at a loss. Be aware and look for it when you feel yourself in total darkness, at the onset of death, as you pass through the veil. If you're a little scared and frightened Jesus the Christ and Blessed Mother Mary, Mohammed or any other spiritual being don't mind if you call on them for assistance; neither Allah, Buddha nor Krishna for that matter. Here or hereafter. All you have to do is look at the light, which is usually above you in the distance, and you'll be guided safely on your way. If you see yourself falling feet first into a dark musky tunnel, don't look down, look up and visualize the light, it will appear because God will hear your inner cry for help. Heaven represents contentment; happiness, peace, love and blissfulness among passed loved ones in a beautiful chosen environment where there is a supreme being that has unconditional love for you. You have a right to choose a place of residence to make it all your very own or share it at will with others and your once loved pets that had passed on before you.

Hell is the worst place ever imaginable. To enter Hell you also have to die but would have had chosen the dark side while here on the earth plane. Satan deals with Hellfire and Brimstone, literally. If your life on earth has always been on the negative side of God then what would you expect when you die or pass to spirit? Satan represents hatred and evil. The dark side consists of the opposite of what God represents. Satan was once an Angel, so they say, known as Lucifer. He had chosen the dark side creating Hell and is always in search of followers. Satan is also a spirit but of an evil source. Eve's serpent in the Garden of Eden was Satan himself, so Satan has been around for a long time. If you die, pass through the veil, and find yourself around miserable and unhappy occupants then you know you've chosen the wrong path. Call on God, or any other holy person you're aware of and you'll be rescued. God and Heaven are real and so is Hell and Satan, if you believe they exist. God, Great Divine Intelligence, is always waiting for you to turn to him. He's always there for you. When called upon for assistance he'll help guide and release you if you find that you're in the clutches of evil—Satan. The essence of Heaven comes and deals with love; all else leads us away from the Divine towards a dark void we all know as Hell.

Never invite an unknown negative force to be close to you, send it away with your loving thoughts or reach out to God in prayer. It's possible to experience Heaven or Hell right here on earth. It's what you make of your life and the choices that you make. Heaven is light and love, happiness, contentment, peace, love and blissfulness. Hell is an empty void of darkness, misery, suffering, evil and hatred.

God makes no demands on you other than ask you to live by His loving guidance the best you possibly can. All good souls go to the light of Heaven. All evil souls are not looked on as being pure and will immediately go to the darkness.

Happiness versus misery. Wellness versus suffering. Light versus darkness. Hate versus evil. God versus Satan. What do you choose?

Here is an email that I received from a friend. I have permission to share it with you. I asked, *"Do you believe in heaven and hell?"* The answer was, "*I'm not sure it's that simple. Don't think God is that judgmental as they make out, but then there are some really horrible people out there committing horrible acts. I just wonder about how it all works and what it's all about. I know that there is a lot of controlling that goes on through organized religion and that turned me off it. I was always spiritual but never really knew what was true. There's a U2 song which sums up my quest, "Still haven't found what I'm looking for." The first time I heard it I cried. It was my song. Every time I hear it I still feel it profoundly. I would like to read more on everything you have and write on that is spiritual."*

Satan has great power and evil darkens the earth. You have a choice of where your soul will end up; choose your own private hell here and the noise will be wailing within waiting for you to cross over from physical life where it will continue on a louder scale. This imprisonment has a way out, Divine intervention is your escape. Think about the awful reality of Hell and the beautiful contentment in the glory of Heaven. If you have to fight for your soul, fight, no matter how sweet Satan will appear to you and bargain for it. Don't reject the means of God and don't bring condemnation upon yourself.

I have broken a couple of the commandments throughout my lifetime like everybody else: but the ones I broke there is forgiveness for. If I have to pay a certain price when I go to the light for what I have done in this material world, even after my own downright self-punishment for it here on earth, so be it. I feel that 'the judge' for my wrong doings will not be a judge at all but it will be decided between God and me. There won't be a committee such as a judge and a jury. Why would a supreme being of the universe need a judge and jury? Personally I feel that there is no such place as hell but a dark side that's evil, full of passed evil spirits that have died. When I pass through the veil I'm going straight towards that beautiful light of peace, love and blissfulness, and nowhere else. Love wins over hate at all times. What direction will you follow?

Those that Satan has a hold on will most likely try to commit suicide. Satan can't wait to have possession of a soul and he'll entice you to leave your body long before your time. Those that are lucky enough to be found or caught in the act of self-destruction are still loved by God. The great source of love and light will never forsake you and your terrible act of self-abuse can be forgiven, just ask. Never feel that you are at a loss. All you have to do is realize that what had happened was not an act of your inner soul but an act controlled by the evil source, Satan, which you once let inside of you. Realize that what has taken place in your attempt to take your own life is a problem that you have to face and solve right here on earth. Once you manage to kill yourself chances are Satan will have governorship of what had once belonged to God. That's Satan's sole purpose. In The Holy Quran/Koran, in the book of Surah 4 AnNisa', The Women, section 11 verse 79 it says, "*Whatever good, (O man) happens to thee, is from Allah/God; but whatever evil happens to thee, is from thy (own) soul.*"

If you feel that the dark side has a hold on somebody, or there is an evil within someone you know and that you had witnessed first hand, don't be afraid to pass the Bible, or a spiritual book they believe in, to show that someone cares. Be tactful with a caring approach and encourage them to read a portion of it.

In the revised English Bible with the Apocrypha planned and directed by representatives of several churches in the UK it says in Tobit chapter 6 verses 7, 16 and 17*: "You can use the heart and liver as a fumigation for any man or woman attacked by a demon or evil spirit; the attack will cease, and it will give no further trouble,' 'take some of the fishes' liver and their hearts, and put them on the burning incense. The smell will spread, and when it reaches the demon he will make off, never to be seen near him/her anymore."*

Recognition of Hope
I know you're always there God
As I worship through the one
Jesus Christ was taught to me
As a savior and your son
I know it's well with you God
If I go through a loving spirit
For when it comes to you God
Any worship would be a merit
God bless, and thank you.

Natural Laws

Natural laws of the universe play an important part of our daily lives. Where attitudes and concerns are a big factor we need to concentrate on who we are, what we have in life and what desires we harbour. What is it that we're all searching for, have or haven't found and what do we need to do to change things for the betterment of ourselves?

A natural law worth considering is the positive and negative energy that's constantly about us each and every moment we live. Each one of us is like a magnet; we attract that which is within us, accomplished through a natural resource, 'cause and effect.'

It's difficult to be in a positive mood all the time when negative situations get in the way. Those of you who do not wish to have this negativity about you, move onward to a better location within yourself, or physically grasp an opportunity to be within those that you feel most comfortable with. Those about you lacking positive qualities are in the negative but still have that magnetism within and able to change even though you may feel that a positive magnetizing force is far beyond reach. With some constructive treatment for hostility, withdrawal or pessimism, just to name a few, will begin a new development that'll extend and generate in a direction opposite to an arbitrarily chosen 'regular direction' or "position," if that were the case.

You being concerned, and having taken on such a difficult task, just remember the old saying, like attracts like, as it remains true. Once you begin to show love and give off positive energy you'll notice that the current emitting from you, which flows externally, will affirm the connection you have as you continue to strive for the betterment of that person you're dealing with. There has to be an attraction to help a fellow man or to help an individual such as this.

Positive and negative consists of light and dark parts in approximately inverse order and lies within all. One cannot always be positive but one can recognize when the negative tries to sneak in and one is able to keep it at bay as he/she wishes. Deal with the anger immediately and get it out of the way so you may once again be more balanced positively. Affirmations act upon the subconscious mind and can be used as a tool without interfering with the logical mind. Choose what you create because we affirm with every word and thought.

HUMAN RACE DECLINING

MAY BE EXTINCT IN A FEW SHORT YEARS:

Will this be a news headline to come in the future? Imagine this being on the front page when you pick up your daily newspaper. My goodness, what is happening in our world? Where are the different strains of viruses coming from? With the AIDS epidemic I thought that this had to be the worst ever and that it would stop at that. I actually didn't think we would ever have another virus that there wasn't a cure for, or that a cure couldn't be found in a relatively short period of time, considering our modern technology. I was wrong. There's still no cure for AIDS after the drawn out, ten-year plus period that was predicted at its start. Although there are wonderful drugs available today that mask the illness and the ongoing symptoms so well that the viral load decreases enough that the virus can go undetected in a blood test, yet the virus continues to kill.

It's a sad affair when one has to be concerned about a mosquito bite. Once bitten, or I should say stabbed, one often wonders if this pesky little insect will be a calling to the other side or they'll just sit back and wait to see if they had been infected with the West Nile Virus, possibly leading to death. I've been doing my part around my property to help control their population but there are still hundreds of them around. There was an outcry from certain individuals from certain places in the world for years about the crow population. They even have crow-shooting season when hundreds of crows would group together at a certain time of the year and they were shot for pleasure. People don't eat crows and it's nothing but a sport for some hunters. If over-population has occurred and they have become a pest then most people would agree with a mass slaughter for pleasure. So be it. Let's say, for instance, what would happen if a few were caught and experimented on in laboratories and then set free with the intent of infecting other crows and reducing the population in this manner. God forbid. If this were the case then man isn't thinking properly with the brain God gave him. He's not taking the big picture in perspective or considering the transference to other birds, animals and humans. Every year there had been a nest of crows in the tall evergreen tree behind my property. This year there's no sign of them at all. In fact I seldom see one anywhere and when I do it's usually alone and it looks out of place. I miss the crows behind my property because they reminded me that I live in a somewhat rural area away from the hustle and bustle of the city.

Needless to say, I don't spend as much time outside in mosquito season as I had in the past, and I'm being extra cautious with my household pets.

Then we're faced with the SARS virus from China, so they say. A friend sent me an email; she's clairvoyant and a very good Medium working with polarity. Her recent study is psychic surgery. She's also precognitive and is often shown future events and happenings. She said in her email that the SARS virus is but the tip of the iceberg for what lies in our human future. She also said that there are many more viruses to come and one has to work on the immune system through self-healing, through God. Three weeks later I heard of another new virus, Monkey-Pox. I thought, what the heck is that? Where is this all coming from and why so many new ones? Is it possible that it may be related to scientists in laboratories, experimenting, searching for clues, looking for cures and using animals for such purposes? Who's to say? Do animals go missing or are some released back to the wild after use, carrying new strains of viruses that don't affect that particular animal but will affect others? Will they eventually get into the human body and humans become the guinea pigs? God forbid again, but who's to say. And let's not forget mad-cow which isn't totally deleted from our midst either, although we don't hear a lot about it these days. Where did that come from and why are so many cows in so many different parts of the globe infected without any known reason? Overuse of certain antibiotics tend to strengthen certain viruses especially if the dosage is stopped before the body is cleared, making the immune system weaker as a self-defence mechanism.

Whatever your outlook on the above, I wanted to shared it with you, which I now have. But you must realize that this is my personal point of view in speculating the 'how come' of it all.

When dealing with our world of nature we have to examine what's in it and the reason why some nature attracts hardships and misfortunes.

Here's another story, which wasn't included in the lecture above, that has affected me more then I had ever thought.

I'm a lover of nature. I have nest boxes about my property for birds to have housing for their young. I feed them as well as provide them a home. Most people don't like Rock Doves or Pigeons in the city but since I started to feed the smaller birds they were attracted to the feeder.

OK, they have to eat to survive too. They quickly became very friendly with me. I began to look for certain birds to arrive at feeding time and I got attached to certain ones.

One day I went to the Stoffville Flee Market and saw that they had several colored pigeons for sale. I bought some white, rust, cream and silver colored ones over the years.

I brought them home and set them free to mix with the wild ones. I watched them fly away and looked for their return for food, which a lot of them did.

A year later I started seeing different colors arriving, not just grey birds anymore. The colored ones mated with the wild grey birds and gave off very unusual colored offspring's. They brought their young to the feeder.

The fall of 2003 I counted up to 12 unusual mixed colored birds at the feeder at a time and was happy with the results.

Each day at feeding time I'd watch for them and waited to see if any new arrivals would appear. One day there was one that had impressed me more than the others. It was the most speckled bird of different colors I had ever seen in a pigeon. It had a mix of white, red, cream, silver, grey, black and brown. It was as if it was a total poke-a-dot.

"What a beautiful bird," I would say each day as I watch it fly in and land a couple of feet away to feed. I looked for this unusual and unique bird daily.

Eventually the amounts of unusual colorful birds were not showing up anymore. I wondered why. One day in the fall when I was in the back garden wrapping a few shrubs for winter protection all the birds flew away at once making a loud flutter of wings. I looked up only to see that a hawk had descended down upon them searching for food and wanted one for a meal. This hawk moved swiftly and was upon them in no time. I watched in horror as it grabbed a bird in flight and both fell to the ground. I ran to the front garden and both birds were under a low shrub. Once the hawk saw me it flew away leaving the pigeon behind. I walked over to it and it walked out of the bush. It appeared unhurt. I picked it up and started to caress its head to comfort it. I noticed it was bleeding. I thought for a moment that I had saved its life and that I'd care for it until it was fit to fly again. Within seconds that little bird died in my hands. The sadness hit me with an impact that I would never have expected.

I know it's an act of nature and survival but the impact was hard because it was the little poke-a-dot bird I had been so proud of just a moment ago.

I begrudged the hawk that bird for its meal but I reluctantly and sadly put it back down on the ground for it would only come back to kill another.

The Summary

Summary, as mentioned in Webster's dictionary means, *covering the main points briefly.*

A book published in 1999 and written by Lyn G. De Swart called *Thorsons Principles of Spiritualism* is a great read. It states on its cover that it's *"The only introduction you'll ever need."* This book only contained 109 pages.

I reviewed this book and prepared the lecture you're about to hear although I knew and read most of this information somewhere else. I also heard most of it spoken by ministers of various churches or by a presentation of a lecture by some of the mediums I had the privilege of hearing. The reason I quote the name and author of this book is because it is so well compacted with what one needs to know about Spiritualism and what it all entails.

Our psychic being is our intuitive self. We're all psychic, some more aware of it than others.

In 1848 in a cottage in Hydesville, New York State, there was a family called Fox. On March 31 the two teenage daughters heard loud banging and noises that they couldn't ignore. Once they learned how to communicate with this noisy spirit they were able to find out all about him and what had happened to him. A traveling salesman called Charles B. Rosna was a guest in this same house when it was owned by a family named Bell many years before. He was murdered and buried in the cellar. He wasn't happy and needed to have rest in the spirit world and the only way he could rest was to have his body found and his identity known. The body was eventually found. They also found what he said was in his unwanted grave with him. We thank Mr. Rosna for kicking up such a ruckus because that was the beginning of this wonderful religion and what was the first recorded proof of survival after death. The soul lives on once we leave this material world.

The American dream and its Bill of Rights allowed for freedom of worship and churches began to appear that gave a regular and safe venue for the exponents of mediumship.

In 1852 a medium named Mrs. Hayden took Spiritualism to Britain. One year later a church was built in Keighley, Yorkshire, and it was called the Mother of all Spiritualist churches in Great Britain. To this day the church still stands with the same name.

Mr. Robert Owen, a friend of Emma Harding Britten, had passed to spirit. He passed down the seven principles to her and was later adopted by the Spiritualist National Union.

Some other churches came up with their own interpretations, some of which are very strange. Some other churches wrote their own but, as history has it, a spirit handed down the seven that we follow. Some churches have nine, others more.

Arthur J. Findlay, not a medium himself, studied every aspect of Spiritualism including mediumship and comparative religion. In his book called *The Rock of Truth* he elaborates on the fifth principle, Personal Responsibility. *"Each one of us is responsible for his own actions and thoughts. We create our own heaven and our own hell. Our minds condition our surroundings here to a certain extent, but to a much greater degree in the etheric world. Kings and Queens here are looked upon and honoured but their characters only determine their positions. We think, so we are. Evil-doers congregate together. Birds of a feather flock together."* He gave one of his beloved country homes to the Spiritualist National Union now known as The Arthur Findlay College.

Policy in the Spiritualist churches welcomes all cultures and faiths. They ask no one to put aside their own religion to come to the church for a service. Spiritualists believe that the mainstay of their way of life is the philosophy of unconditional love.

Part of being spiritually inclined is to search out and visit a few churches to find out where you're most comfortable attending. My suggestion to you is don't judge a church by one service. Leave yourself open to being one of the congregation when the Reverend is chairing, lecturing and/or the medium for that service. I'd suggest that you attend when the Reverend does all three and chances are all three won't be in the same given service. That's a lot of hard work to accomplish, so do attend again before making your final decision.

When I heard the name Maurice Barbanell I said to myself, *"now who would that be."* I found out and now for those of you who still don't know, he was an accomplished writer and erudite speaker, *erudite* meaning learning or scholarly, the same as Mr. Arthur Findlay. Maurice Barbanell was a Jewish man living in Britain. He became a medium once he was discovered by a medium by the name of Mrs. Bauerstein, another Jewish person. He was the mouthpiece for the highly-evolved being in spirit, none other than Silver Birch. Mr. Barbarnell passed to spirit in 1981 at the age of 79 leaving behind much written wisdom from his guide, Silver Birch, which many books have him as the author. A recommended read if you ever get the opportunity. A few phrases that got my attention are: Silver Birch said: "*The spirit that breathed life into us has given us a common link, because throughout the whole world all the children of the Great Spirit are fundamentally connected. Realize that you are the Great Spirit and you realize that the kingdom of heaven is within you. It cannot fail. Spirit is not subjected to the limitations of matter. And, it is through simplicity that you learn."*

Another Pioneer Spiritualist medium was Ursula Roberts, she communicated with the spirit being known as Ramadahn. She was a great teaching medium who didn't mind utilizing her wonderful gifts to help those just beginning to explore and develop their psychic potential. She would allow novice students to have access to Ramadahn through her. She too had written about her experiences. Books are still available but, more likely than not, found only in second-hand book stores.

Spiritualist churches are known for their mediumship demonstrations. Albert Batten said in his book called, *Love and progress*: "The spiritualist churches have become adult churches, where are the children?" Spiritualism is a new religion, so to speak, based on old truths that still stand.

Someone sent me an email, it said: *"At a simple and informal level, the notion of a subconscious mind would seem a straightforward way of accounting for aspects of the mind of which we are not directly conscious or aware. Upon deeper examination, however, the topic reveals extraordinary complexity. At this stage, there are fundamental disagreements within psychology about what the nature of the subconscious mind might be whereas outside formal psychology a whole world of pop-psychological speculation has come to attention. The subconscious mind is held to have any number of properties and abilities from the animalistic and infantile through the innocence of the medium. Creative ideas that do not appear to come from conscious thinking are ideas that come from the subconsciousness. All memory is unconscious and when a medium is in a subconscious state validation is immediate as the act of remembering something means bringing the information stored outside the conscious mind into awareness."* Author unknown to me...

Thank you. God has blessed you all.

CPSIA information can be obtained at www.ICGtesting.com
Printed in the USA
BVOW010559240812

298675BV00002B/59/P

9 781605 636573